W9-BUN-410

The Men Who Made Baseball History . . .

Babe Ruth: "Shucks, I coulda hit a .400 lifetime average easy. But I woulda had to hit them singles. The people were payin' to see me hit them home runs."

Lou Gehrig: "I'm not a headline guy, and we might as well face it. I'm just a guy who's in there every day. The fellow who follows the Babe in the batting order."

Joe DiMaggio: "The games were the easiest part. It was the constant calls from fans and well-meaning friends and newspapermen . . ."

Casey Stengel: "I was such a dangerous hitter I even got intentional walks in batting practice."

Mickey Mantle: "They'll boo the ass off anybody sometimes. I used to get it . . . and in Yankee Stadium besides."

Reggie Jackson: "I don't want to be a hero. I don't want to be a star. It just works out that way."

I'd Rather Be a Yankee

". . . displays a fresh and unique approach to the history of the New York Yankees, as told by the men who made that history. Full of stories—both tall and true, delightful and exciting—the real story behind the greatest dynasty in baseball history is finally told. *I'd Rather Be a Yankee* is a must for baseball fans of all stripes."

—Donald Honig, author of *Baseball America*

"Exceptional. . . . All baseball fans, whether pro- or anti-Yankee, will enjoy this."

—*Publishers Weekly*

I'D RATHER BE A YANKEE

FOR THE FIRST TIME, THE MEN BEHIND THE LEGEND TELL THE COMPLETE STORY OF BASEBALL'S GREATEST TEAM IN THEIR OWN WORDS

JOHN TULLIUS

JOVE BOOKS, NEW YORK

Grateful acknowledgment to the National Baseball Library
for permission to use all the photographs included in this
book, except those of Don Larson, and Billy Martin and
George Steinbrenner, which are included with
permission courtesy of United Press International.

This Jove book contains the complete
text of the original hardcover edition.
It has been completely reset in a typeface
designed for easy reading and was printed
from new film.

I'D RATHER BE A YANKEE

A Jove Book / published by arrangement with
Macmillan Publishing Company

PRINTING HISTORY
Macmillan Publishing Company edition published 1986
Jove edition / August 1987

All rights reserved.
Copyright © 1986 by John Tullius.
This book may not be reproduced in whole or in part,
by mimeograph or any other means, without permission.
For information address: Macmillan Publishing Company,
866 Third Avenue, New York, New York 10022.

ISBN: 0-515-09073-5

Jove Books are published by The Berkley Publishing Group,
200 Madison Avenue, New York, New York 10016.
The name "JOVE" and the "J" logo
are trademarks belonging to Jove Publications, Inc.

PRINTED IN THE UNITED STATES OF AMERICA

10 9 8 7 6 5 4 3 2 1

For Shannon and Somerset

I'd rather be the Yankees' catcher
than the president.

—YOGI BERRA

Contents

Acknowledgments

First of all, I wish to thank my editor, Arlene Friedman, who had the original idea for this project and whose persistence and professionalism made this the best book it could possibly be. Also, thanks to her assistants, Ed Novak and Randi De Jong, who wove together the million details that unravel a writer's mind.

A warm thank you to my agent, Wendy Lipkind, whose faith and skill have brought me most of my success.

A lot of the credit for the quality of this book must go to my brother and my lifelong closest friend, Fred, a fine writer himself, whose untiring research fills these pages. A book of this type requires a fanatical desire to dig up every last quote from the most forgotten sources and his relentless hunts unearthed most of the real gems in this book.

Thanks to Mary Ann Rovai, H. B. Laski, Toni Fish, and Berry White for their painstaking work of cutting, pasting, and typing that goes into turning a pile of scrap notes into a finished manuscript.

A special thanks to Tom Heitz, the librarian at the Baseball Hall of Fame Library in Cooperstown, New York, and to all his staff whose warm hospitality and helpfulness were a welcome aid to a writer a long way from home. Tom, a very busy man, always had time to help with information and suggestions and even fixed up a room so I could work without distraction.

I want to make a special mention and thank you to

Lawrence Ritter, Donald Honig, and Peter Golenbock who generously permitted me to use selections from their published works. Ritter (*The Glory of Their Times*) is the father and Honig (*The Man in the Dugout, Baseball Between the Lines*, etc., etc.) is the master of the baseball oral history. Golenbock's *Dynasty* will be around as long as people care about baseball. Their work inspired me.

And, of course, I want to thank all those Yankees, past and present, living and dead, whose words grace these pages. It was their story and they told it well.

Finally, I want to express my gratitude and my love to my wife Shannon who while I incubated this project was pregnant with our first child, Somerset Marie. The baby and the manuscript were delivered almost simultaneously. It was a hectic and a wonderful time—the best moment of my life. Thank you my beautiful girls.

Preface

When Waite Hoyt, the great Yankee pitcher, was inducted into the Hall of Fame, he closed his speech by saying, "I was at the dinner last night with the Hall of Famers from the past and all those great players sat around all night telling baseball stories. Man, was it great! I can't wait to come back next year so I can tell some lies."

You will find many exaggerations, inconsistencies, stretched truths, and, yes, downright lies in this book. Such is human memory. Facts stream into our memory banks, and when we try to make a withdrawal some years later, we often find ourselves shortchanged. But something is gained from this loss of memory, for along with these transmogrified facts comes a deeper knowledge, a cured, metamorphosed truth, more accurate than fact, more revealing than the damn score. What you get when an old-timer drags and dredges and then hauls up some heirloom of the deep past is the thing all great writers have tried to conjure since Chaucer—the human spirit. What you get is the ghosts of Babe and Lou and Casey and Hug. The breath of these men is on these pages.

Most important of all, their legend is here. Before they were written down, all the great legends were oral. King Arthur, Robin Hood, the Headless Horseman. They were passed from man to man about the campfire, over a heady brew on a summer evening. The legends grew until they became the spirit of a whole civilization.

Baseball legend is no different. Did Ruth point to center? Did Casey really have a bird underneath his cap? Did Gehrig play on through seventeen broken fingers? Did Lancelot bring Sir Dineden back from the dead? Who cares if they're true or not? I believe it all because I can feel the woe and the tragedy and the laughter they felt when it all happened.

I first began to truly understand the spirit of this book when I met Mickey Mantle. I caught up with Mickey, appropriately, in Cooperstown, New York. And what I remember most of that meeting was not Mantle at all but something that happened afterward. A retired professor of chemistry at UCLA now in his seventies stood next to me in the living room of the guest house where we had all stayed—Mantle and the professor and myself—and he kept saying over and over and over, "Imagine Mickey Mantle, *Mickey Mantle*, stood right here!" And he pointed down at the rug below his feet. "Imagine. Mickey Mantle."

The moment stayed with me. It wasn't so much Mantle the man that impressed me, but that his past deeds could produce such a sensation of reverence, that he could bring this distinguished man of learning to speak in such hushed tones about him. Mickey Mantle is a legend. And that's when it struck me that I was writing more than a baseball book. I was writing about legend and the spirit of that legend that breathes in all Americans. For the Babe and DiMag and the Mick *are* America. I was gathering the words of legendary heroes to put into a book so that people could feel and imagine and then reimagine Mickey Mantle. *Mickey Mantle!*

I once traced my genealogy, and after I had constructed the entire family tree, I realized I actually knew very little about my family. It was only after I began to talk to the old folks and they told me of the family legends, of the rascals and saints, that I began to understand the Tullius family.

I came to know the Yankee family the same way. When you view Yankee history—the many talented players, the sheer weight of all those victories year after year, decade

after decade—the mind reacts as a simple taxpayer does
when told that the national debt is two trillion dollars.
Truly impressive but inevitably incomprehensible. The
magnitude of the Yankee achievement ultimately boggles
even the fanatic's mind.

Until you hear it firsthand, that is. Then, suddenly,
meaning is breathed into those three-quarters of a century
of excellence. The staggering statistics are more than a
stack of numbers, more than some long-ago name calling his shot or hitting in fifty-six straight or pitching a
Series perfecto. Suddenly they have a full day's growth
on their mugs and a way a talkin that puts you in the
bleachers on the day they smacked that apple into the
seats.

After I'd gone through all the rosters and pennants and
statistics, I still knew very little about the Yankees. It was
only when the old Yanks began to lie to me that I felt the
history of the Yankees come to life.

There are hundreds of important games and incidents
and heroes in the pantheon of Yankee history, and when I
first began to interview players I tried to steer the conversation toward those momentous occasions, those great
heroes. But I quickly discovered that I couldn't just get a
player to answer my specific questions. Each player had
within him something he burned to tell, something that
he'd chewed on or fondled or slept with, something that
had gnawed at him or kept him warm for years, and finally
I realized I just had to let them say what they were going
to say. If there were holes in the history, I'd just have to
putty them in as best I could. And then get the hell out of
the way so the *real* players could do the talking.

Getting them to talk was another matter, of course. The
interviewing process itself is a lesson in human behavior
and personality. Some men you simply have more rapport
with than others. And they're not all of a type, either.
Perhaps the two men I got on best with were Moose
Skowron and Eddie Lopat. Lopat is an articulate, very
intelligent, and knowledgeable fellow who can speak
eloquently about many things besides baseball. He's a

sweet man, too—accommodating and gentlemanly. It's not hard to get on with Lopat.

But Skowron is another package altogether. A gruff man with green, twinkling eyes, Moose is a baseball man who doesn't have much use for the modern ballplayer. "Horseshit" is his usual tag for most of the rich kids prancing around the diamond these days. He knows only one thing, talks about only one thing—baseball.

When I approached Moose with my tape recorder at an Old Timers' Game, he shooed me away like a bad-smelling goat. So I didn't press him. But I didn't run too far, either. I'd seen Moose's act before. He'd tell kids he couldn't sign their autographs. "Later, later," he'd bark and you'd feel bad for the kids. But then you'd see Moose off in the corner somewhere feeling bad, too, and then he'd march on over to the kids, say some nice things, and sign everything in sight. I knew I just had to wait awhile and Moose would talk.

He came over to me about half an hour later. He had turned me down flat before, saying, "No way I'm talking into that thing," and pushing me and my tape recorder away. Now he said, "You wanna do it now?" like we'd made an appointment and he was ten minutes early. Skowron is a lovely man, underneath the Skowron scowl.

When I started this book I thought I would interview all the Yankees I could and then have an oral history of the team. But I soon found that many of the players simply were not available. The history of the Yankees is a long one, stretching back over eighty years to 1903. The men who played on that first Yankee team have long since died, and so have most of the Yankee players right up through the forties. And sadly, what I often found was that a more recent player whose picture I had before me, a big rippling-muscled guy launching some long drive, had died years before. Sometimes his widow would break the news to me, sometimes his children or grandchildren.

But I was determined to write a true oral history of the Yankees, not just interview the survivors. That meant a tedious, painstaking search through old baseball books,

magazines, and newspaper clippings. That alone took
three fanatics over a year of unrelenting labor. Then the
search led me to the National Baseball Hall of Fame
Library in Cooperstown, where I struck the mother
lode—a dusty, uncatalogued, lost-in-the-archives library
of hundreds of hours of old tapes. From this pile of
deteriorating recordings I was able to salvage some of the
real gems of this book.

Finally, after thousands of hours of interviewing and
reading and clipping and gluing and sorting, I had what I
wanted—the real oral history of the Yankees. I've gathered not just my own interviews but the interviews of
others, the history-making quotes, the famous quips and
the momentous speeches of the Yankees. Here are the
farewell addresses of Gehrig and Ruth and DiMaggio and
Mantle. And here are many of baseball's immortal one-
liners, from Ping Bodie's "I don't room with the Babe, I
room with his suitcase," to Yogi's "It ain't over till it's
over."

So pull up a chair, all you Yankee fans out there. The
Babe just put down his beer and I think he's going to tell
another whopper. "Casey Stengel was one of the daffiest
guys I ever met. . . ."

I'D RATHER BE A YANKEE

PART I

The Highlanders

1

The Birth of the Yankees

BAN JOHNSON AND THE BATTLE FOR NEW YORK

The greatest team in the history of American sport, a team that has won half the American League pennants and one-third of all the World Championships in the last sixty-five years, started like many other legends, from very humble beginnings.

The Yankees were born amid a plethora of political shenanigans and backroom double-dealing when they joined the newly formed American League in 1903. Ban Johnson had created the American League two years earlier, raiding the National League to stock his own teams with players. Johnson, who became known as the "Czar of Baseball," was president of the Western League, the strongest of all the minor leagues, with most of its franchises in the Midwest. He had planned for years to challenge the National League's dominance of baseball, and in 1900 he simply renamed it the American League and brashly declared it a major league. He then set up franchises in three National League cities: Boston, Chicago, and Philadelphia, and, within two years, in

St. Louis and New York. And the battle was on! The owners of the National League, in existence since 1876, did not take kindly to Johnson's pirating tactics and started a bitter and costly bidding war. The salaries of the star players skyrocketed from four or five thousand dollars a year to ten and even twelve thousand dollars! Those were considered dizzy figures in those days, and the owners who paid that much for a mere baseball player were thought to be foolhardy at best.

Stars like Cy Young, Iron Man McGinnity, Nap Lajoie, Jimmy Collins, and John McGraw were eagerly jumping to Ban Johnson's renegade league and gave it immediate legitimacy and appeal for even the most die-hard baseball fan. Even the optimistic Johnson was surprised when his new league nearly matched the senior circuit's attendance in its first year. The following year the Americans actually outdrew the Nationals, finishing with an attendance mark of 2,206,457 compared to 1,683,012—a devastating drop for the older league of a quarter of a million fans in one year.

Encouraged by his unexpected success, Johnson prepared his final assault on the National League. His plan was to move the Baltimore franchise into New York and thus invade the stronghold of major league baseball.

New York, however, is where the National League owners drew their battle lines, led by an underhanded character named John T. Brush. Brush, who owned the New York Giants, had strong ties with Tammany Hall, the New York political machine without whose say-so nothing got done in the Big Apple.

Every time Johnson tried to secure a site to build a stadium for his team, Brush, backed by his political cronies, was there to stop him. "No matter where you go, the city will decide to run a streetcar over second base," he bragged to Johnson.

Johnson was not about to take three strikes and call it a day. When he went shopping for someone to buy the new franchise, he found a couple of characters with a little New York political muscle of their own—Big Bill Devery and Frank Farrel.

Devery was a former police commissioner, known as the most corrupt ever (a genuine feat in those days), who, like Farrel, had started out as a bartender. Having accumulated a considerable rake-off as New York's top cop, he was now retired, heavily invested in real estate, and, at the time, running for the leadership of the Democratic machine in the North District.

Farrel, known as New York's pool room king, was a professional gambler. He owned racehorses and, at the time that he and Johnson were putting together the deal that would bring the faltering Baltimore franchise to New York, was in the process of opening a gambling house "the splendor and extent of which will not be exceeded by any similar establishment in the world."

Like Devery, Farrel had money. Perhaps not the cleanest money around, but Johnson needed someone with a bankroll to battle Brush in his all-out effort to shut the American League out of the city. When Farrel and Devery handed over $18,000 to Johnson—the full purchase price for the new franchise—the New York Yankees were born.

Farrel soon found a spot in rural Washington Heights to construct a new stadium for the club. Although Brush tried to circulate a petition stating that the ballpark would attract undesirable elements to the neighborhood, Farrel and Devery succeeded where Johnson had failed. The site was swiftly approved, six weeks before the season was due to start.

A wooden grandstand and bleachers seating fifteen thousand, as well as a wooden clubhouse and fence, were thrown up in record time. The modest little park was formally named the New York American League Ball Park, but everybody just called it Hilltop Park.

Now the club needed a name. Since Farrel and Devery had picked Joseph Gordon, a respectable enough looking front man, to be their president, and since the club's new park was built on a tract of land atop Manhattan's highest point, and since one of the most famous regiments in the British Army was known as Gordon's Highlanders, somebody decided that the team should be named the Highlanders.

Just about everybody objected to the new name, from the sports columnists who couldn't fit the long moniker into a one-column headline to the anti-British Irishmen who filled the boroughs of New York. In a matter of weeks most fans were calling them by the patriotic name that would eventually become baseball legend—the Yankees. Although the two names were used interchangeably for a decade, by World War I the team was known exclusively and officially as the Yankees.

THE FIRST YANKEE TEAM

Opening day, May 1, 1903, was hot and sunny, and an overflow crowd of 16,243 fans jammed the new stadium. All was in readiness—except for the huge ravine in right field that the workmen had not had time to fill. A rope was stretched across that part of the field and any ball that found its way past this makeshift barrier was ruled a double.

A band marched across the field playing "Columbia, the Gem of the Ocean," "Yankee Doodle Dandy," and finally, "The Star-Spangled Banner." Meanwhile the fans waved the little American flags they had each been handed as they passed through the turnstiles, stretching and pushing to see the new team dressed in white uniforms, white flannel hats with black insignias, and fancy maroon jackets with mother-of-pearl buttons.

The uniforms were designed by the club's new manager, Clark Griffith, and were described as "the swellest thing in the business" by some and "louder than Bowery hose" by others. Most of his players claimed that "Griff was drugged at the time."

Dan Daniel: "The Highlanders or Yankees or whatever the hell you want to call them. I was a boy in knickerbockers and I went with my cousin, a semipro pitcher of some consequence, and, that first day, we sat in the bleachers. It rained, and due to goddamned inexperience, the front office hadn't provided for rain checks and made an announcement that anyone present could get in free the next day.

"Well, the next day my cousin and I, elevated by the rainout from the bleachers to the grandstand, sat in a box on the third-base side of the old ballpark, which was at Broadway and 162nd Street. Of course, hearing about the previous day's announcement, everyone in New York turned up, claiming they'd been there when it rained, and there was a riot. Inexperience in the front office."[1]

The chaos that occurred when thirty thousand fans showed up and tried to get into the tiny stadium was inevitable. The crowd broke down one of the fences and overran the field. It took police an hour to clear the diamond so play could begin.

The Highlanders were more than respectable their first year. With a bevy of great players, they made a run at the pennant. Manager Clark Griffith, a crafty left-hander known as the Old Fox, did some pitching for his new club, but his playing days were about over. Griffith's ace on the mound was Jack Chesbro, who had pitched Pittsburgh to the pennant in 1902. John Ganul, still one of the game's best fielders, was at first base; Johnny Williams covered second; Herman Long, for many years one of "Boston's Big Four," was at shortstop; Wid Conroy was at third; and Jack O'Connor, in the twilight of a long, steady career, was behind the plate. The outfield consisted of George Davis in left, Dave Fultz in center, and in right was one of the greatest hitters of all time, Wee Willie Keeler.

William Henry Keeler was the son of a Brooklyn trolley car motorman who first came up to the big leagues as a left-handed third baseman with the Giants and then went to the Dodgers. When Keeler, who stood five feet four inches tall and weighed 135 pounds, was traded to Baltimore in 1894, he went out to right field and developed into a great outfielder.

The Baltimore teams were a rough-and-tumble bunch. "They ate gunpowder and warm blood for breakfast," said one umpire. Keeler, the smallest man on the team, may also have been the toughest.

Wid Conroy: "Willie, small as he was, wasn't afraid of nothing. I guess that was the way he had to be though. Once in Washington I saw him go back for a ball that was out of the park sure, but Willie leaped up and over this rusty old barbed wire fence they had out there. He kind of laid there on top of it for a second with his arm poking through the barbed wire. When he threw the ball back into the infield it was dripping with blood."

Keeler was a certified character. He just loved to play baseball. His teammates would see him out in right field laughing uproariously for no apparent reason. Once when he came back to the dugout the players asked him what the joke was all about. "I'm laughing about those suckers, the club owners. Paying me for playing ball. Why, I would pay my way into their parks if that was the only way."

Keeler was the greatest place hitter the game has ever seen. In 1897 he hit in forty-four straight games, a record that stood for forty-four years until a fellow named DiMaggio came along. Keeler's bat control was phenomenal. He could drive pitchers batty by simply fouling off pitches, dozens at a time, until the pitcher made a mistake and either walked Willie or grooved one.

Keeler also invented and perfected "The Baltimore Chop." He would deliberately chop the ball down into Baltimore's notoriously hard infield, and while the opposing infielders waited for the ball to come down, he'd leg it out. Keeler could motor, too. He stole seventy-three bases in 1896.

Sam Crawford: "Wee Willie Keeler. That little guy couldn't have been over five feet four, and he only weighed about 140 pounds. But he played in the big leagues for twenty years and had a lifetime batting average of close to .350. Think of that! Just a little tiny guy.

"'Hit em where they ain't,' he used to say. And could he ever! He choked up on the bat so far he only used about half of it, and then he'd just peck at the ball. Just a little snap swing, and he'd punch the ball over the infield. You couldn't strike him out. He'd always hit the ball somewhere. And could he fly down to first! Willie was really fast. A real nice little guy, too, very friendly, always laughing and kidding."[2]

Kid Nichols: "Beyond any question of doubt, Keeler was the smartest hitter I ever faced. He could do everything with the bat. I never will forget a game we played in Baltimore when Big Dan Brouthers of the Orioles, a powerful slugger, hit a home run over the center field fence for the first time. They put a flag on top of the fence to mark the spot where the ball disappeared from view. But the next week little Keeler duplicated Big Dan's homer, and the flag was taken down."

THE ALMOST PENNANT

The team finished fourth in its first season, with Chesbro and Griffith combining to win thirty-five games and Keeler hitting .313. And the next year, 1904, the Highlanders made a serious run at the pennant.

Griffith, not one to stick with a losing team, made some vital trades, picking up catcher Red Kleinow and beefing up the pitching staff. Keeler had another big year at the plate, hitting .343. But the big story was Jack Chesbro. "Happy Jack," who stared down from the mound with a deathlike grimace, started an astounding 51 games in 1904, completed 48, and won 41! A feat no one has come close to matching in over eighty years. Chesbro also struck out 239 batters, a club mark that was to last for seventy-four years until Ron Guidry struck out 248 in 1978.

The Highlanders were in first place by half a game on October 7. But three days later the Boston Pilgrims had overtaken them and stood in first place by one and a half games, with one day left in the season. As luck would have it, Boston and New York were scheduled to play a doubleheader in New York on the last day of the season. If the Highlanders could take both games they would be the champions of the American League.

Chesbro took the mound that day in his fifty-first start. The opposing pitcher, Bill Dineen, hero of the 1903 Series, had had another good year, notching twenty-one victories. But next to Chesbro with his forty-one wins, Dineen looked overmatched.

It was a great duel for eight innings. Then, with the score tied 2–2 in the top of the ninth inning, Pilgrim catcher Lou Criger singled, moved to second on a sacrifice, and took third on an infield out.

John Anderson: " 'Happy Jack,' they called him. He was no fresh loaf, you know. He'd been around plenty. Came over from Pittsburgh. But he still had something left. Threw that spitter 'bout as good as anyone, I guess. That's how we finally lost the pennant that year too. Jack had 'em stymied until the ninth. Louie Criger got on on a bloop and ended up on third with two men out.

"Then with two strikes on the last batter Jack loaded up his spitter and that was probably the best spitter anyone ever threw. Probably broke four feet. Red Kleinow was behind the plate—best catcher in the league at the time. He never had a chance. The ball went back to the screen and Criger, slow as he was, just walked on in from third. And that was that. After that the Yankees never came close to winning a pennant until Ruth came along."

THE ODOR OF HAL CHASE

In 1905 the Yankees acquired the enormously gifted first baseman Hal Chase from Los Angeles of the Pacific Coast League. Chase was a magician with the glove and is still considered by many the greatest fielding first baseman in history. He literally revolutionized the way the position was played. Agile, quick, and graceful, Chase played away from the bag on every pitch, a rare practice in those days. He also charged bunts and was uncanny at throwing out runners at second or third. In an age when the bunt was a frequent and powerful offensive weapon, Chase's skill around the infield made him a superstar.

But Chase was also an unscrupulous character. Witty, charming, and intelligent, the team's star attraction on and off the field, Chase was a very popular man in New York for a while. But he socialized with gamblers and eventually was suspected of betting against his own team and throwing games. Chase was also later suspected of being the go-between for gamblers and several Chicago White Sox players in the infamous Black Sox scandal during the 1919 World Series.

Babe Ruth: "Others will feel that I should pick Lou Gehrig over Chase. Or George Sisler over both of them. But I pick Chase. I saw him first in spring training before the start of the First World War. I felt the sting of his tremendous ability in that angry Red Sox—Giants exhibition tour in 1919. Hal had been in the big show for fifteen years then, but he was so much better than anybody I ever saw on first base that—to me—it was no contest, and I still feel that way.

"We've got some nice first basemen in the game today, and maybe once a year you'll see one of them charge a would-be sacrifice—with a man on second, heading for third—and throw out the runner at third. Hal would do it dozens of times a year. He even did it on the third-base side of the pitcher.

"I believe he was just about the quickest thinker I ever saw in baseball. He was always one thought ahead of the runner. His trouble—if he had one—was he was too smart. He had to wait for the reflexes of his fellow infielders to function, which were often too slow.

"Chase left baseball under a cloud. Maybe if he had been tossed out when [Judge] Landis was in charge of the game he would have been as looked down on today as the worst of the Black Sox. I don't know. All I know is that he was—for my dough—the greatest first baseman who ever lived. That he was thrown out of the game is a tragedy, but that doesn't lower his ability in my eyes, any more than the banishment of Shoeless Joe Jackson will ever make me doubt that he was the most natural and graceful hitter who ever lived."[3]

Roger Peckinpaugh: "Hal Chase was the first baseman when I joined the Yankees. Prince Hal. He later was suspected of betting on games. I was just a kid breaking in, and Hal Chase had the reputation of being the greatest fielding first baseman of all time. I remember a few times I threw a ball over to first base [from shortstop], and it went by him to the stands and a couple of runs scored. It really surprised me. I'd stand there looking, sighting the flight of the ball in my mind, and I'd think, 'Geez, that throw wasn't that bad.' Then I'd tell myself that he was the greatest there was, so maybe the throw was bad. Then later on when he got the smelly reputation, it came back to me and I said, 'Oh-oh.' What he was doing, you see, was tangling up his feet and then making a fancy dive after the ball, making it look like it was a wild throw. I don't know if anybody suspected anything at the time, but I do know they got rid of him later in the season."[4]

After 1904 the Yankees went downhill. They finished sixth in 1905, a very distant second—fourteen games out—in 1906, fifth in 1907, and, finally, dead last in 1908.

When the Yanks hit bottom, Farrel and Devery had had enough and they fired Griffith as manager and replaced him with the team's shortstop, Norman Elberfeld. Elberfeld, known as the Tabasco Kid, made Griffith look like a genius, bringing the team in with a woeful 27–71 record, a winning percentage of .276—the worst in Yankee history.

Elberfeld got the boot, and Farrel brought in George Stallings, who later engineered one of the greatest comebacks in sports history when he brought his 1914 Boston Braves from dead last in July to a pennant and then a four-game sweep of the powerful Philadelphia A's in the World Series. Stallings was a proud man who knew his baseball, and he took no slack play from his men. He immediately brought the Yankees back to respectability.

But even though Stallings had the Yanks on the right track, there was trouble brewing in the form of Devery and Farrel. The owners had fired general manager Joe Gordon in 1907 and taken over the running of the front office themselves. They also liked to tell their manager, whoever he happened to be that year, how to run things on the field, which, along with the dismal showing of the team, accounted for the rapid turnover of managers. None of the managers liked the on-field meddling from the owners, who they felt were simply two old blowhards who knew nothing about baseball.

Stallings was no exception. The crisis came when Stallings and Hal Chase butted horns. One day at the end of the season Chase quit the team after a run-in with Stallings and stormed into Farrel's office and delivered an ultimatum: Either Stallings goes or I go!

Jimmy Austin: "Late in the season we had just finished a series in Cleveland and were on the boat going over to play Detroit. Nobody could find Hal Chase. Well, he'd just disappeared. The next day we found out what had happened. When we had gotten on the boat to Detroit, he had taken the train to New York. He'd gone to Mr. Farrel, the president of the club, and complained about Stallings and a lot of other things. Mr. Farrel supported Chase, so Stallings quit, and Chase was made the new manager. God, what a way to run a ball club!

"Well, you know how good a manager Hal Chase was: so good that he took over a club that finished second in 1910 and took them straight to sixth place in 1911. And the year after that they wound up last. And you know what Stallings did a few years later with the Boston Braves: he managed them from last place on the fourth of July to win the pennant, and then beat the Athletics in the World Series. . . .

"I remember in 1910 we had a utility infielder on the Highlanders by the name of Jack Knight. Somebody gave Jack a new bat, and it just suited him. Boy, he hit like a fool with it. Hal Chase had a thousand bats himself, but he always wanted the other guy's, especially if it was somebody's who was hitting good. So Hal says, 'You don't mind if I use your bat, do you, Jack?'

"'I'd rather you didn't,' Jack said, 'because it's the only one I've got.'

"Well, by gosh, Chase got so mad that he took Jack's bat and slammed it up against the dugout wall as hard as he could. That's the kind of guy he was. So they made him manager!"[5]

Devery and Farrel finally came to their senses about Chase and brought in the colorful Harry Wolverton to manage in 1912. Wolverton, who had never managed a single game in the big leagues before he took over the Yankees, liked to stand in the dugout with a sombrero on his head and a cigar the size of a cucumber in his mouth. He declared that he would take the Yankees directly to the top. Instead they finished dead last, a woeful 55 games out of first place. Exit Harry Wolverton.

Enter Frank Chance of Tinkers-to-Evers-to-Chance, one of the most famous managers in baseball. Chance was a tough bird from the old flock. He once broke his finger when Wild Bill Donovan hit him with a pitch. Chance spit tobacco juice on the finger and finished the game. He was also known for crowding the plate. He'd been beaned so many times, in fact, that he was deaf in his left ear. But Chance, as tough as he was, couldn't get the Yanks going either. They finished seventh in 1913 and 1914 under his leadership, and he was replaced for the last seventeen games of the 1914 season by young shortstop Roger Peckinpaugh, the team's best player.

Roger Peckinpaugh: "I managed the Yankees the last few weeks of the season in 1914. I was only twenty-three years old then, so I guess I'm the youngest man ever to manage a big league club. Sometimes I look at some of these twenty-three-year-olds today, and I have to laugh and think to myself, 'Gee, when I was that age, I was managing the New York Yankees.'

"Of course, the Yankees at that time were what we used to call a joy club. Lots of joy and lots of losing. Nobody thought we could win and most of the time we didn't. But it didn't seem to bother the boys too much. They would start singing songs in the infield right in the middle of a game. There wasn't much managing to do outside of selecting the starting pitcher and hoping we didn't get beat too badly."[6]

2

The Two Colonels

The Yankees were a dismal team, and no matter what Farrel and Devery tried, the club remained only a slim cut above awful. But what really bothered the two owners was that they were losing money faster than they were losing games. By late 1914, through some bad business and a lot of bad gambling, Farrel had gone broke. The rakish owners of the Yankees began to look for someone to buy the club.

At the time two wealthy men, Colonel Jacob Ruppert, a proper New York socialite and former congressman who had inherited his wealth from his family's brewery, and Captain Tillinghast L'Hommedieu Huston, a big cheerful man who had made a fortune in construction in Cuba following the Spanish-American War, were pestering John McGraw to let them buy their favorite team—the Giants.

The Giants were the most popular team in baseball. They had a winning record, a huge following, a healthy profit margin, and were definitely not for sale. McGraw, however, knew of a team that Ruppert and Huston could get—and they could get it cheap. McGraw approached Farrel and Devery with the idea of Ruppert and Huston buying the

Yankees, and a deal was quickly struck.

In January, 1915, after receiving assurances from Ban
Johnson that the American League would do all in its power
to help them rebuild the team, Ruppert and Huston paid
Farrel and Devery $460,000 for the New York Yankees.
Devery and Farrel had plunked down a mere $18,000 for
the franchise only a decade before. But even for nearly half
a million dollars, the Yankees were considered a bargain.
The huge appreciation in the value of such a mediocre franchise graphically displayed just how popular the game had
become and how much it had grown since the turn of the
century.

The new owners were as different as God ever made two
men. Referred to as the two colonels, Ruppert and Huston
were an odd couple. "When Ruppert and Huston agreed to
buy the Yankees," Ed Barrow said, "it must have been the
only time they ever did agree, because they never agreed on
anything in my presence, [and] were continually, and violent-
ly, opposed."

Colonel Jacob Ruppert wasn't really a colonel at all. His
rank was an honorary one given to him by New York's
Governor David Bennett Hill when Ruppert was just twenty-
two. He clung to the title for fifty years until his death,
however. Ruppert, who was to emerge as the real leader of
the franchise, was a man of substantial wealth. His fortune
when he bought the Yankees was estimated at about $75
million, an enormous sum in those days when a dime bought
a decent meal and a nickel rolling across the floor attracted
some real attention.

Cool and reserved, Ruppert came from an elite social
strata. He had a valet who dressed him and saw to his
personal habits, and every article of his clothing was custom
made. He had a fifteen-room apartment on Fifth Avenue, an
estate on the Hudson, and he belonged to the finest clubs in
the east. The Jockey Club, the New York Yacht Club, and
the New York Athletic Club were just three of dozens with
which he was affiliated. He also collected jade, first
editions, racehorses, St. Bernard dogs, peacocks, and rare
monkeys.

And he was a baseball fanatic.

Waite Hoyt: "Ruppert was a meticulous fellow who insisted that everything he possess in the entire world be clean and well groomed. He was the first owner to buy four sets of home uniforms and four sets of road uniforms and insisted that they be dry-cleaned every day so his team would look like champions.

"He was an owner who looked at the game through the eyes of a fan. He could not tolerate those 3–2 and 2–1 games. They made him too nervous. Ruppert would sneak into the clubhouse during close games because he couldn't bear to watch the game. You could hear the crowd cheer and Ruppert would yell, 'What's going on, what's going on?' He was a highly nervous guy. Ruppert wanted to win every game 100–1.

"In 1922 a lot of us were invited to go to Japan. Well, as it boiled down only [Herb] Pennock, myself, Freddy Hoffman, and Bullet Joe Bush went. But we had to secure Ruppert's permission to go. But the team wasn't doing very well so we waited until the middle of August when we were doing better before we approached him.

"Well, we played a doubleheader that day against Detroit and Bush pitched the first game and beat them 13–2 and then I beat them 2–1—two noble victories.

"So me and Bush went up to Ruppert's office and Bush said, 'Colonel, I came up to the office to ask you if I couldn't go to Japan and China with that All-Star team. I'd like your permission.'

"Well, the Colonel didn't even bother to hear Bush through. He said, 'Joe, I'm very glad to have my boys go to Japan. I think it'll be a wonderful trip. Go over there and see the entire world if you can. Oh, and by the way, great pitching out there today, Bush. That's the way to win them—13–2!'

"I thought to myself, well, I pitched a 2–1 game. I'm a cinch. So I stepped up and said, 'Colonel, I guess if Joe's going, it's okay if I go too, huh?'

"He said, 'You, Hoyts, get away from me, get away.'

"'Why?'

"'You make me so nervous. That lousy 2–1. Why the heck don't you pitch them 13–2 like Bush!'"

Despite his fancy clothes, easy life-style, and dislike of close games, Ruppert was not a pushover. In business matters he was shrewd and passionless.

Waite Hoyt: "Ruppert used to hold forth in his inner sanctum in his offices. Jacob and I had quite a few set-tos about money and I guess all the Yankees did at that time.

"This particular day I had to go to Ruppert's offices at the brewery. The idea was that you'd go talk to the business manager at the Yankee downtown offices, who happened to be Ed Barrow. Barrow would tell you in very strong words, 'Oh, you didn't lead the league and you didn't do this. And you can't have any more money.'

"Well, you'd argue and argue until in a very disgusted tone Barrow would say to you, 'Well, go on up to see Ruppert. He's got all the money anyway.'

"To get from the downtown offices to Ruppert's offices in the brewery took twenty minutes, which gave Ed Barrow time to call Ruppert at the brewery to tell him not to pay you the dough.

"So uptown I went to the brewery and walked in Ruppert's office—oh, it was a beautiful thing right out of Metro-Goldwyn-Mayer, wood paneling, a big, beautiful desk—and there's the Colonel. As soon as he spots me he yells, 'Well, Hoyts, what's the matter with the contract?'

"'Well, Colonel, there was a slight discrepancy between the figures I saw on the contract and those I mentioned in my letter.'

"'Well, Hoyts, we're not going to pay that kind of money to ballplayers anymore. All the ballplayers are getting rich off Ruppert.'

"So we went around and around and finally he says, 'I'll tell you what, I'll give you the extra money in the form of a bonus. If you win twenty-two games next year, I'll give you the extra money.'

"I said, 'No thanks, Colonel. If some of the guys get hurt, my chances of winning twenty-two games are slim.'

"So Ruppert got mad and he told me to go off to this anteroom to cool off like a bad kid in class. So anyway in the room are pictures of real estate all around the room. All these were his holdings and I was engrossed in these pictures when in came Ruppert.

"'Those are all my properties. That one over there is the Ruppert Building—4.5 million [dollars] I paid. That one is an apartment building on the West Side—10.5 million. You see that one there, that's a little factory I picked up out in Long Island—2.2 million dollars. That's my home in Tarrytown—1.1 million I pay for that on a foreclosure. It's a nice estate, don't you think?'

"He went on and on this way for about twenty minutes and finally he says, 'Shall we talk about the contract now?'

"'Yes, Colonel, let's talk about the contract.'

"So he put his arm around me very affectionately. 'You know, Hoyts,' he said, 'I love all you fellows. I don't like to get mad at you. But sometimes you ballplayers make me so mad. There's that Babe Ruth, he's got a bad stomach and he wants $85,000. Joe Dugan wants $25,000. You want $25,000. What the heck do you fellows think I am, a millionaire?'

"I looked at him, looked at the pictures, and said, 'Give me the contract, Colonel.'

"I should have stayed downtown with Barrow."

Unlike Ruppert, Cap Huston (who really was a military colonel) cared nothing for social standing and even less for how he looked. A big, gregarious, friendly man, Huston liked the company of ballplayers and sportswriters. He often wore the same suit for a week, and his pants were off the shelf and baggy. He also wore the same derby hat every day, and the players began to call him the Man in the Iron Hat. Not to his face, however.

Huston, like his partner, was wealthy and just as shrewd. "There is no point in haggling with a player," he said. "Listen to his demand, give him your top figure, and impress upon him that there is to be no further bargaining. Protracted contract fights invariably wind up with the player or the club, or both, being dissatisfied. If you can't come to terms, trade him."

Perhaps the only thing the two colonels truly had in common besides wealth was a burning desire to win, and they didn't mind backing it up with their money. From the beginning they spent a lot and often to purchase the talent they hoped would bring the franchise a winner.

In 1915 the Yankees acquired a young, slick-fielding first baseman named Wally Pipp from Detroit, who could also hit the long ball. He led the league in home runs in 1916 with twelve and in 1917 with nine. Big numbers in those days. The Yanks also picked up Bob Shawkey from Philadelphia, who turned out to be their best pitcher since Happy Jack Chesbro.

But the nucleus of the club was still the same for the 1915 season—a mediocre bunch including Paddy Baumann at second, Fritz Maisel at third, and Roy Hartzel, Birdie Cree, and Hughie High (whom the two colonels had also purchased from Detroit) in the outfield. The best player on the club was still Peckinpaugh at short, but he had been replaced as manager by Wild Bill Donovan.

Donovan, now thirty-nine, had had a great career as a pitcher with Detroit. Recently retired, he took over as manager of Providence in the International League in 1914 and brought them to an immediate pennant.

The optimism was high as the Yankees started the 1915 season. There was new blood on the team, and with Donovan at the helm and Ruppert and Huston willing to spend their money for good players, there was sure to be an American League pennant in New York before long.

Despite the optimism the team finished a distant fifth in 1915. At the party celebrating the one-year anniversary of their purchase of the club, Huston and Ruppert looked into each other's eyes and simultaneously yelled "Sucker!"

But the two colonels didn't quit. A few weeks later they reached deep into their pockets and bought the biggest name in baseball—J. Franklin "Home Run" Baker. Baker had gotten his name from his long ball feats in the 1911 and 1913 World Series against McGraw's Giants.

Home Run Baker: "I believe I hit nine one year, eight another and eleven another year. And they called me Home Run.

"Well, you know we had a dead ball to hit. We didn't have that live ball like you have today. And we didn't have the white ball to hit either. We had a black ball. First of all, it's a whole lot different hitting that black ball on a dark evening than hitting a white ball. And we had a spit ball to go up against. And the emory ball such as Russell Ford used to use. And a number of other pitches that are not allowed today."

Baker was an immediate sensation with the fans in New York. He was the Yankees' first real star and biggest drawing card since Hal Chase.

Baker, a bullnecked man with massive forearms, used a 52-ounce bat—an untapered hunk of wood that looked more like a fence post than a bat. Once Hugh Gowdy borrowed one of Baker's bats when the team played Philadelphia. Gowdy went hitless for a week and then gave it back to Baker. "Here, take your damn tree back," Gowdy shouted at Baker. "I've hit all the wind out of Shibe Park with it."

With a great infield of Baker, Peckinpaugh, Pipp, and the newly acquired Joe Gordon, and a solid pitching staff headed by Urban Shocker and Bob Shawkey, the 1916 Yanks looked like a good bet to be in the race to the end.

But it wasn't to be. Baker hit ten homers in a hundred games, but one day, chasing a foul ball, he fell headlong into the stands, injuring himself. He was lost for the last fifty games of the season. The outfield, never a strong point anyway, fell apart and the pitching was a disappointment.

The Yankees finished fourth.

THE HIRING OF MILLER HUGGINS

The team dropped to sixth in 1917, and Ruppert and Huston decided, like just about all owners before and since, that the problem with the team was the fault of the manager. Donovan was sacked and they started looking for a replacement.

Huston wanted to hire his friend Wilbert Robinson, the rotund, blasphemous Dodger skipper. Cap Huston and "Uncle Robbie" drank and hunted together in Georgia in the off-season and Robinson was very popular with the Brooklyn fans, having led the team to a pennant the previous year.

Ruppert had other ideas. He asked Ban Johnson for advice about who he thought could pull the Yankees out of mediocrity, and the "Czar of Baseball" immediately suggested that Miller Huggins, the diminutive Cardinals manager, would fill the bill. Curiously, even though Huggins's record was far from spectacular with the Redbirds (he finished last, third, sixth, last, and third in his five years at the helm), Johnson was adamant in his praise of Huggins. If the Cardinals owners had backed Huggins, he'd have led them to the top, Johnson insisted.

Ruppert was sold. All he had to do now was hoodwink Huston. But fate intervened. Huston enlisted as a colonel in the Eighteenth Engineers, a construction battalion, and was called away to France in 1917 when World War I broke out. While he was over there, Ruppert hired Huggins.

When Huston heard of the move he exploded. He fired off several cables threatening Ruppert with lawsuits and accusing him of doublecross and even treason against a soldier of the Republic. But with an entire ocean between Huston and his team, Ruppert did as he liked. Huggins was to remain the Yankee manager.

Huston and Ruppert were never close to begin with. Huston saw Ruppert as a spoiled dilettante, and Ruppert considered Huston to be a crude lout at best. But the two colonels had always reined in their distaste for each other for the good of the team. After the Huggins incident, however, they were openly hostile to each other and a terrible rift developed between them. Poor Huggins was caught in the middle.

After the war, when he was again involved in the operation of the ball club, Huston never warmed to Huggins and often criticized him loudly and publicly. But Ruppert, convinced he had made the right choice, stood behind his manager all the way.

Miller Huggins was thirty-nine when he took control of the Yankees. He broke in with Cincinnati in 1905 and was a scrappy, aggressive second baseman nicknamed Mr. Everywhere. In 1910 he was traded to St. Louis, eventually taking over the managerial post in 1913.

At five feet four inches and 135 pounds he was not an intimidating presence. "Me and McGraw," Huggins once said, "could enter a crowded room at the same time and be introduced and in two minutes the crowd would be all around McGraw and nobody would even remember I was there."

Most of his players towered over him. But Huggins was a highly intelligent man and he displayed a strength of character and dignity that made even the great, arrogant, unmanageable Babe Ruth respect and admire him.

Grantland Rice: "Huggins was content to go his way in the wake and shadow of the mighty Yankees that he had put together. The crowd swirled about Babe Ruth, Lou Gehrig, Tony Lazzeri, Bob Meusel, Herb Pennock, and the rest of that glamorous crew—and never noticed the little guy tagging along behind them. He was a lonely figure . . . yet Huggins was one of the greatest managers baseball ever has known."

George Pipgras: "Miller Huggins was my favorite manager because I came in under him. He had a lot of temperamental guys on that Yankee club, but he handled them. He was a little bitty guy, but he had an iron fist. He had plenty of intestinal fortitude, that fellow.

"I saw Huggins go on the ball field once. He went after [umpire] Bill Guthrie, the big guy who used those 'dems' and 'dose.' One day Whitey Witt was on first base. Somebody hit a line drive to the shortstop, who threw the ball into the stands, trying to double Whitey off first. Guthrie motioned Whitey to go on to second base. Whitey said, 'No. I get two bases. I'm entitled to go to third.' Guthrie said, 'I *am* giving you two bases. One dis away (pointing toward first) and one dat away (pointing toward second).' Well, they had a big rhubarb about it. Huggins went out and said, 'Bill, you are wrong. He goes to third base.' Finally Guthrie put Whitey out of the ball game. Then he said, 'Mr. Witt, take da batboy wid ya.' Oh, that made Huggins mad. Guthrie was gone the next year."[1]

Huggins went immediately to work beefing up the team with wholesale trading, sending Urban Shocker and four other utility players to the Browns for second baseman Derrill Pratt. The team finished fourth in 1918, up two notches from 1917. Then they finished third the following year behind the mighty White Sox and a very strong Cleveland team. The Yankees were not a great team yet by any measure, but Huggins had them moving in the right direction.

TWO SCANDALS THAT ALMOST KILLED BASEBALL

There was optimism in New York in 1919. The Yankees finally had a manager who knew how to win *and* get along with the players. Although the full genius of Huggins had not yet emerged, the Yankees were on their way up for the first time since they were formed in 1903.

But that year an incident occurred that extinguished most of the optimism of the Yankee fans and nearly destroyed baseball itself. Eight members of the Chicago White Sox, forever after known as the infamous Black Sox—Eddie Cicotte, Joe Jackson, Lefty Williams, Swede Risberg, Chick Gandil, Happy Felsch, Fred McMullin, and Buck Weaver— were accused of throwing the 1919 World Series to the Cincinnati Redlegs.

Even though all the players were eventually acquitted by a jury, Judge Kenesaw Mountain Landis, the cantankerous, fierce, and honest new commissioner of baseball, banned all eight players for life from professional baseball.

"Regardless of the verdict of juries," said Landis, "no player that throws a ball game, no player that entertains proposals of promises to throw a game, no player that sits in a conference with a bunch of crooked players and gamblers where the ways and means of throwing games are discussed, and does not promptly tell his club about it, will ever again play professional baseball."

On the heels of the Black Sox scandal came another incident the next year that once again shook the foundations of the game. On August 18, 1920, Cleveland shortstop Ray Chapman was hit on the head by a pitch from Yankee Carl Mays. Chapman, a scrappy perennial .300 hitter, was a dazzling fielder and a daring, fleetfooted base runner. He was also the most popular Cleveland player, both among his teammates and with the fans.

Mays threw a high and tight fastball and it struck Chapman in the head. The sound as it hit his left temple was clearly audible in the stands. Though he was eventually helped to his feet and led off the field by his teammates, Chapman collapsed on the outfield grass and had to be carried the rest of the way. He died the next morning at the hospital.

Roger Peckinpaugh: "I was at shortstop for the Yankees when Ray got hit in the head with a pitched ball and was killed. . . . I'd say that pitch was almost a strike. Chapman crowded the plate more than anybody in the league; in fact he hit with his head practically in the strike zone. What happened was at the last second he turned his head and got hit right in back of the ear. The ball hit so solidly that it went out toward third base in fair ground, and Mays fielded it and threw it to first base—he couldn't tell from the sound whether it had hit the bat or not. That's how hard Chapman got smacked."[2]

Carl Mays: "It was a fast ball. I knew it would be high and tight and I expected that he would drop as the others [do] when pitchers swing them in close to drive batters away from the plate. Instead he ducked and the ball hit him."

Ray Chapman: "I'm all right. Tell Mays not to worry."

Bob Shawkey: "Chapman died soon after—only big leaguer ever to die after being hit. He had changed his batting style that year; he was leaning over the plate more. That didn't make any difference to Mays, of course—he'd knock a man down anytime if he thought it would do some good. Was he throwing at Chapman that day? I wouldn't like to say. I don't know. It never seemed to bother him afterward, though. Nothing bothered him. He wasn't too popular with the boys. Down south in the spring the next year none of the regular players would mix with him. He corralled some of the younger players and told them, 'If you got to knock somebody down to win a ball game, do it. It's your bread and butter.' He says this after killing a man! That's the type he was.

"He was a stinker. One winter I worked for an insurance company in Philadelphia, and I insured his automobile. He went out and hired a guy to steal it in order to collect on the insurance. He promised the guy a certain amount of money to do it and then never paid him. That's how I happened to find out about it—the fellow called me up and told me what Mays had done. Of course, we didn't pay Mays anything. Then he went to Cincinnati and did the same thing with somebody else. That's the way he was. A stinker."[3]

The Black Sox scandal and the Chapman beaning rocked the baseball world. Thousands of fans quit the game in disgust over the crooked sham and the obvious brutality of the game. The fans who loved baseball were now as bitter and wounded as a jilted lover.

Judge Landis, however, did a lot to restore the credibility of the game by his quick and severe handling of the players. It was obvious that baseball was making a real effort to clean up the game and prevent any further underhanded dealings from creeping into the game.

But the man who restored the luster to baseball even more than Landis was the most glamorous and colorful figure the game has ever seen—George Herman "Babe" Ruth. He not only saved baseball by overshadowing the memory of those scandals with his herculean feats, but his great talents triggered the dynasty that was to dominate baseball from then on. Once the Yankees acquired Ruth from the Boston Red Sox, they started a reign of winning that has never been equaled.

The Yankee legend was about to be written.

PART II

When Ruth
Was King

3

Babe

When the Boston Red Sox traded George Herman "Babe" Ruth to the New York Yankees, the greatest dynasty in sports history was born. With his prodigious power he changed the game of baseball overnight from punch and slap to *boom! boom! boom!*

The Babe was a living legend in those more innocent days, Paul Bunyan in pinstripes. He was a rollicking, carefree character with astounding brawn who performed unbelievable feats. In the three years from 1919 to 1921 in which he hit 142 home runs, no one else hit more than 40!

He also led a legendary off-the-field life-style that made headlines and gave the Yankee management headaches. His roommate, Ping Bodie, was once asked what it was like rooming with the great Ruth. "I don't room with the Babe," he said. "I room with his suitcase."

Ruth was the son of a Baltimore saloon keeper and, from the beginning, a hell-raiser.

Babe Ruth: "I spent most of the first seven years of my life living over my father's saloon in Baltimore. When I wasn't living over it I was living in it, studying the rough talk of the longshoremen, merchant sailors, roustabouts, and waterfront bums. When I wasn't living in it I was living in the neighborhood streets. I had a rotten start, and it took me a long time to get my bearings. . . .

"I was listed as incorrigible, and I guess I was. Looking back on my early boyhood, I honestly don't remember being aware of the difference between right and wrong. If my parents had something that I wanted very badly, I took it. I chewed tobacco when I was seven, not that I enjoyed it especially, but, from my observations around the saloon, it seemed the normal thing to do."[1]

By the time George was seven, his father couldn't handle him anymore and sent him off to a so-called industrial school for boys named St. Mary's, run by the Xaverian Brothers. At St. Mary's, Ruth's skills with a baseball were discovered and nurtured by his lifelong confidant and counselor, Brother Matthias. But it was Brother Gilbert who got Ruth signed to a professional contract in the spring of 1914.

Brother Gilbert: "I was coaching Mt. St. Joseph's College team, and we had a great kid pitcher named Ford Meadows, and scouts from five major league clubs were on his trail that spring. Then Jack Dunn sent Fritz Maisel down to look him over for the Baltimore club and I was so afraid Dunnie would sign the boy—because I knew Fritz would recommend him—that I said to Dunn:

" 'Jack, if you let this fellow alone, I'll give you the best young left-hander I ever saw.'

"Now the truth is that I never had seen this young left-hander pitch. But I had seen him play ball and, while I do not profess to be one of those who can look down the years and see greatness in line for any individual, I had reason to believe that with proper handling, this boy would become a great pitcher someday. His name was George Herman Ruth.

"I was at St. Mary's Industrial School one day, and I had seen this boy who, so far as I was concerned, was just a big kid in blue overalls in the beginning. He was catching for one of the teams in a league they had at St. Mary's, and if you ever wanted to see a bone out of joint or one of nature's misfits, you should have seen him, a left-handed catcher, squatting behind the plate. All he had was a mask and a glove, which he wore on his left hand. When he had to make a throw to second base he would take off the glove and tuck it under his right arm before he made the throw. And how he could throw! The ball was three feet off the ground when it got to second base.

"I knew that with an arm like that he could be made into a pitcher. And then I saw him go to bat. The pitcher for the other side was a tall, lean boy by the name of Tom Paget. As he wound up, he turned his back to the hitter before he let the ball go. I looked at him winding up and then I looked at Ruth. There he stood, just as you saw him standing at the plate when he was at the very peak of his career. There was determination in his attitude—he had the will to do. Paget pitched the ball and Babe hit it over the right-field fence. The next time up, he hit it over the center-field fence. The third time he hit it over the left-field fence. Ah, but the fourth time he delightfully, deliciously, delectably—struck out. And he looked better striking out than he did hitting home runs."[2]

Jack Dunn signed nineteen-year-old Ruth to his first professional contract at twenty-five dollars a week. He was a wide-eyed, overgrown kid with a shotgun arm, but at the time Baltimore, still a minor league franchise, had a bumper crop of strong-armed youngsters. So, in 1914, Ruth was sold along with pitcher Ernie Shore from Baltimore to Boston for $22,500. The Red Sox sent him down to Providence in the International League for more grooming, but by mid-season he was up to the big leagues, where he would dominate baseball with his mighty feats and his bigger-than-life personality for the next twenty years. But all this fame and fortune was going to take a little getting used to.

Mrs. Claire Ruth: "One day he was in that jail [St. Mary's], the next day he boarded a train for the first time, and rode to Fayetteville, North Carolina, a professional ball player reporting to the Baltimore Orioles, a team just a notch below the major leagues. He had only five dollars in his pocket. And that was more money than he had ever had in his possession before.

"Then the world exploded for him. Up to then it had been

failure, poverty, humiliation. In something akin to overnight, life became success, riches and fame beyond the dreams of any bum of the waterfront."[3]

Babe Ruth: "We went to our hotel for breakfast and while I was studying the menu I heard a player near me say, 'Order anything you want, kid. The club pays our feed bills during spring training.'

"I looked at him, unable to believe it.

"'You mean I can eat anything I want, and it won't cost me anything?' I asked him.

"'Sure. Anything.'

"I was on my third stack of wheatcakes and third order of ham, and hadn't even come up for air, when I realized that some of the other fellows were watching me. I looked at them silently, and kept chewing.

"'I wouldn't have believed it if I hadn't seen it,' Rodger Pippen, one of the Orioles, said.

"I grinned at him. "'A guy's got to be strong to play ball,' I said.

"Dunn dropped by my table and took a look at the ruins. He smiled at me and put his hand on my shoulder.

"'We've got twenty-seven other fellows on this club, George,' he said. 'Leave them a little food, will you?'

"It had gotten to be a joke the way I walked around wide-eyed all the time. I used to get up at five in the morning and walk down to the station to see the trains go through, but I always got back to the hotel in time to be first in line for the opening of the dining room.

"The hotel elevator was just about the greatest piece of mechanism I had ever seen up to that point in my life. I'd ride up and down on it by the hours, just for the ride and to watch how the Negro operator worked it and how close he'd come to getting the thing on a level with the floor stops. Finally, one day, I couldn't keep my hands off the control another minute. I gave the operator most of the money I had left from what Dunnie had given me and bribed him to let me handle it myself.

"My playing life, in fact my life, nearly ended a few minutes later. I left a door open on the third floor and was rubbernecking up and down the corridor while I made the elevator go up another flight. Suddenly a player screamed at me to pull my fool head inside, and I did—just in time to keep it from being crushed.

"Dunnie bawled me out until the stuffings ran out of me, and what he didn't say to me the older players said for him. But finally one of them took pity on me, shook his head and said:

"'You're just a babe in the woods.'

"After that they called me Babe."[4]

Harry Hooper: "Babe Ruth joined us in the middle of 1914, a nineteen-year-old kid. He was a left-handed pitcher then, and a good one. He had never been anywhere, didn't know anything about manners or how to behave among people—just a big overgrown green pea. You probably remember him with that big belly he got later on. But that wasn't there in 1914. George was six foot two and weighed 198 pounds, all of it muscle. He had a slim waist, huge biceps, no self-discipline, and not much education—not so very different from a lot of other nineteen-year-old would-be ball players. Except for two things: he could eat more than anyone else, and he could hit a baseball further.

"Lord, he ate too much. He'd stop along the road when we were traveling and order half a dozen hot dogs and as many bottles of soda pop, stuff them in, one after the other, give a few big belches, and then roar, 'Okay, boys, let's go.' That would hold Babe for a couple of hours, and then he'd be at it again. A nineteen-year-old youngster, mind you!

"He was such a rube that he got more than his share of teasing, some of it not too pleasant. 'The Big Baboon' some of them used to call him behind his back, and then a few got up enough nerve to ridicule him to his face. This started to get under his skin, and when they didn't let up he finally challenged the whole ball club. Nobody was so dumb as to take him up on it, so that put an end to that.

"You know, I saw it all happen, from beginning to end. But sometimes I still can't believe what I saw: this nineteen-year-old kid, crude, poorly educated, only lightly brushed by the social veneer we call civilization, gradually transformed into the idol of American youth and the symbol of baseball the world over—a man loved by more people and with an intensity of feeling that perhaps has never been equaled before or since. I saw a man transformed from a human being into something pretty close to a god. If somebody had predicted that back on the Boston Red Sox in 1914, he would have been thrown into a lunatic asylum."[5]

Ruth became an immediate sensation as a pitcher in the big leagues. In 1915 he won 18 games. In 1916 he won 23 and led the league with a 1.75 ERA. The following year he was 24-13 with a 2.01 ERA. Along the way Boston won three World Championships and Ruth set a record for pitching 29⅔ consecutive scoreless innings in World Series play that stood for more than forty years, until Whitey Ford broke it in 1961.

Ruth won only thirteen games in 1918, but it wasn't ineffectiveness as a hurler that made his victory total fall off. He was just too potent a hitter to waste on the mound. As a part-time outfielder, Ruth was playing almost every day, pitching less and hitting more. He led the league in homers with 11 and batted .300, and the baseball world knew that the Babe was no ordinary sticker.

In 1919 Ed Barrow, then the Red Sox manager, made one of the wisest decisions in baseball history when he moved Babe Ruth permanently to the outfield. The great pitcher was now about to become the greatest slugger of all time.

Ed Barrow: "Babe was a tall, slim fellow in those days. His face was moony but his body hadn't started to fill out. You must remember he was only twenty-three. At first I thought —and tried it, too, in the exhibition games—of having the Babe pitch every fourth day and play the outfield on other days.

"Ruth complained of being tired, and I went right back at him and told him if he stayed home nights he wouldn't be tired. I realized, however, there was some justice to his complaint. Finally, I asked him if he would be willing to give up pitching and concentrate on the outfield. I told him he had a chance to become one of the greatest left-handers of all time, maybe the greatest, which was true. The Babe agreed to play the outfield principally, I think, because it got him in the game daily."[6]

Harry Hooper: "I still remember when the Babe was switched from pitching to become an outfielder. I finally convinced Ed Barrow to play him out there to get his bat in the lineup every day. That was in 1919, and I was the team captain by then. Barrow technically was the manager, but I ran the team on the field, and I finally talked Ed into converting Ruth from a pitcher into an outfielder. Well, Ruth might have been a natural as a pitcher and as a hitter, but he sure wasn't a born outfielder.

"I was playing center field myself, so I put the Babe in right field. On the other side of me was a fellow named Braggo Roth, another wild man. Sakes alive, I'd be playing out there in the middle between those two fellows, and I began to fear for my life. Both of them were galloping around that outfield without regard for life or limb, hollering all the time, running like maniacs after every ball! A week of that was enough for me. I shifted the Babe to center and I moved to right, so I could keep clear of those two.

"Sheer self-preservation on my part, pure and simple. I'm still amazed that playing side by side, those two never plowed into each other with the impact of two runaway freight trains. If they had, the crash would have shaken the Boston Commons."[7]

Benny Bengough: "He never got the credit he should have got as an outfielder because he was a good one. He had a great arm. Of course, he was a great pitcher. He was very accurate, too, and I never saw him throw to a wrong base. His ball was easy to handle from the outfield—beautiful throws. He'd throw that ball in and it was soft. It would hit and come in to you nice."

In 1919, without the pressure of pitching every fourth day, Ruth batted .322 and clouted a record-breaking 29 homers— a mighty total for that day of the dead ball. That mark nearly doubled the American League record of 16, set back in 1902 by Socks Seybold of the Athletics. In fact, as Ruth neared Gavvy Gravath's major-league record of 24 home runs, a baseball historian dug up the *real* major league record of 27 logged way back in 1884 by Ed Williamson. Williamson's total, however, was suspect, since he played that year in a park where the right field fence was only 215 feet from home plate. But the Babe blasted that figure into memory.

THE YANKEE TRADER

Colonel Ruppert's motto was, If you're buying, buy the best! And from 1912 to 1918 the Boston Red Sox were the best. Luckily for Ruppert and for Yankee fans for decades to come, Harry Frazee, who owned the Red Sox, wasn't averse to selling off his talent—if the price was right. Frazee, a theatrical producer, was hocked to his haunches in Broadway plays that had flopped. (Some years later, though, he was to produce the smash hit *No, No, Nanette!* and get it all back.) He was strapped, and when Ruppert came up with $100,000 in cash (double the amount ever paid for a player) and a $300,000 "loan" for the Babe's services, Frazee couldn't sign the papers fast enough.

Colonel Ruppert: "In October, 1919, I asked Miller [Huggins] what we could do to win. Miller said, 'Get this man Ruth from Boston. Frazee needs money. Ruth hit 29 home runs last season. Bring him into the Polo Grounds and he will make 35, at least.'

"I told Huggins to see Frazee, and a week later Miller brought me word that Frazee would begin talking business if I recognized $100,000 as a fair price for Ruth.

"I told Huggins, 'You are crazy and this man Frazee is even crazier. Who ever heard of a ball player being worth $100,000 in cash? I could have bought both Eddie Collins and Tris Speaker for that!'

"Huggins laughed and said, 'Buy Ruth. Frazee's crazy, all right; he's crazy to let you have Babe for so little.'"

Frazee came under immediate fire in Boston for selling Ruth, arguably the best player in the game even then and undoubtedly the biggest gate attraction. But Frazee nonchalantly dismissed the deal as "necessary" and tried to put the blame on Ruth for Boston's sixth-place finish in 1919.

Harry Frazee: "It would be impossible to start next season with Ruth and have a smooth-working machine. Ruth had become simply impossible, and the Boston club could no longer put up with his eccentricities. I think the Yankees are taking a gamble. While Ruth is undoubtedly the greatest hitter the game has ever seen, he is likewise one of the most selfish and inconsiderate men ever to put on a baseball uniform."

The sale of Ruth opened a floodgate of talent from Boston to New York. Frazee even let Ed Barrow, his brilliant manager, get away. Barrow, who had brought the Sox a World Championship in his first season as manager, was signed in October, 1920, to head the Yankee front office as general manager. From there he supplied Huggins with the raw material needed to produce a winning team.

Barrow certainly knew right where to go for the players he needed—Boston. Every time Frazee needed more money, he sold another player to Barrow. By 1922 Frazee had reduced the mighty Red Sox to a perennial loser. Starting in 1922, the Sox came in last place nine out of the next eleven years. Meanwhile Barrow had transformed the struggling Yankees into a winning juggernaut of unparalleled talent.

4

The Legend of Ruth

In 1920 Babe Ruth took New York by storm. He hit an unbelievable 54 home runs in his first year in the Big Apple, to shatter his record of 29 hit the previous year. That was 35 more than the second-best total that year of 19, by the great George Sisler. Everyone else's hitting looked puny next to the colossal clouts of the Babe.

Slowed by an injury early in the season, he didn't hit his first homer as a Yankee until May 1. But then the ball began to jump off his bat. He hit 12 homers in May, 12 in June, and 13 in July, breaking his old record at mid-season. By the end of July he had 37. If he had kept up that breathtaking pace, he would have finished with well over 60. But with no number to shoot for but the stars, he simply slowed down and ended the season with 54. No other team hit as many that year. In fact, the Red Sox, from whom the Babe had been kidnapped, managed only 22 all season.

His statistics that year were simply awesome. To go along with his 54 homers, he hit .376, with 9 triples, 36 doubles, 137 RBIs, and 158 runs scored. He even stole 14 bases, and his slugging percentage was a staggering .847, still a major league record.

38

Ruth's phenomenal success in 1920 carried over to his teammates. Shawkey and Mays both had twenty-win seasons, and the team challenged for the pennant down to the final week, finishing third, only three scant games behind the Indians.

Beyond Ruth's astounding athletic achievements, he became an American phenomenon. He brought people to the game who had never seen or cared about baseball before. They wanted to see Babe Ruth, to watch him hit one of his tremendous blasts, and when he did, a new fan was born.

The Yanks of 1920 smashed the all-time attendance record of the 1908 New York Giants of 910,000 by attracting 1.3 million paid customers. No other team drew as many as 700,000 fans that year. The Babe doubled the gate by himself.

Roger Peckinpaugh: "Ball players weren't the celebrities then that they came to be later on, with a few exceptions, of course, like Cobb and Walter Johnson. But the Babe changed that. He changed everything, that guy. So many, many people became interested in baseball because of him. They would be drawing 1,500 a game in St. Louis. We'd go in there with the Babe and they'd be all over the ballpark; there would be mounted policemen riding the crowd back. Thousands and thousands of people coming out to see that one guy. Whatever the owners paid him, it wasn't enough—it couldn't be enough."[1]

Waite Hoyt: "Don't tell me about Ruth; I've seen what he did to people. I've seen them, fans, driving miles in open wagons through the prairies of Oklahoma to see him in exhibition games as we headed north in the spring. I've seen them: kids, men, women, worshippers all, hoping to get his name on a torn, dirty piece of paper, or hoping for a grunt of recognition when they said, 'Hi ya, Babe.' He never let them down; not once. He was the greatest crowd pleaser of them all.

"There used to be an expression back in those days that there were two real champions—Ruth and Dempsey. They didn't mean their abilities. They meant their personalities.

They could meet people and create a magnetism and a warmth.

"Ruth was a carefree guy, took life as he found it, but his basic personality was one of utmost indulgence and warmth to people, kids, and the underprivileged. That's why he was what he was."

Joe Sewell: "Anytime that fellow was involved in anything, good, bad, or indifferent, everybody paid attention. You could love him, hate him, or be neutral, but you couldn't ignore him. There never was such a personality on a ball field. Talking about him can never do him justice. You had to be there, you had to see for yourself."

Tommy Holmes: "Some twenty years ago, I stopped talking about the Babe for the simple reason that I realized that those who had never seen him didn't believe me."

Joe Dugan: "To understand him you had to understand this: he wasn't human. No human could have done the things he did and lived the way he lived and been a ball player. Cobb? Could he pitch? Speaker? The rest? I saw them. I was there. There was never anybody close. When you figure the things he did and the way he lived and the way he played, you got to figure he was more than animal even. There was never anyone like him. He was a god.

"Born? Hell, Babe Ruth wasn't born. The son of a bitch fell from a tree."

Rube Bressler: "There was only one Babe Ruth. He went on the ball field like he was playing in a cow pasture, with cows for an audience. He never knew what fear or nervousness was. He played by instinct, sheer instinct. He wasn't smart, he didn't have any education, but he never made a wrong move on a baseball field.

"One of the greatest pitchers of all time, and then he became a great judge of a fly ball, never threw to the wrong base when he was playing the outfield, terrific arm, good base runner, could hit the ball twice as far as any other human being. He was like a damn animal. He had that instinct. They know when it's going to rain, things like that."[2]

Mel Allen: "He dominated the game with his outsized personality as much as with his home-run bat. He was a national hero in the grand manner. It made sense that years after Ruth had retired from the game, a Japanese infantryman, eager to shout an insult at the Americans facing him across a malarial field on Guadalcanal in the early days of World War II, screamed furiously, 'To hell with Babe Ruth!' "[3]

Connie Mack: "One of the thrills in my career was when I was delegated to go with the American [All-Star] baseball team to Japan. . . . The Japanese were literally crazy about baseball and walked miles to see the American athletes. Every game was sold out at least three weeks in advance. Ruth was their idol.

"The Japanese even began to get up before daylight to play at sunrise. One day when we went out about twenty miles from the city to practice in a place where there were no houses, about twenty thousand came to watch us."[4]

Charlie Gehringer: "Yeah, I was on that trip to Japan. Quite an experience. I liked the Japanese: They were real fans—knew us all from reading their sports pages, I guess. I remember going through the streets of Tokyo in a motorcade and having trouble getting the cars through, there were so many people. It was almost as bad as Detroit after the '35 Series. And they jammed into the ballparks too. It seemed like every day was sold out, and that stadium in Tokyo held sixty thousand people. That place would be filled by the time we were halfway through batting practice. Ruth was the headliner on that tour, and they really loved the big guy. He'd hit these long home runs during batting practice, and the whole place would go 'O-o-oh.' He loved it. He liked to clown around a little bit during the games too. He used to play first base sometimes, and when one of their little guys would get on, Ruth would stand up on the bag to emphasize the difference in heights. That never failed to get a big laugh from the crowd. So there was a lot of goodwill."[5]

THE LEGEND AT BAT

The legend of Babe Ruth was built on his incredible feats on the baseball diamond. He averaged more than forty home runs a year for seventeen straight seasons, and from 1926 to 1931 he averaged more than fifty a year! When he hit his seven hundredth homer in 1934 it was more than twice as many as any other player had ever hit.

He retired with a .342 batting average, bested only by Wee Willie Keeler, Ty Cobb, Rogers Hornsby, Tris Speaker, Ed Delahanty, and Shoeless Joe Jackson. But all six of these greats *combined* didn't hit as many home runs as the Sultan of Swat. And only the immortal Cobb scored as many runs.

Babe Ruth: "Shucks, I coulda hit a .400 lifetime average easy. But I woulda had to hit them singles. The people were payin' to see me hit them home runs."

Sad Sam Jones: "Babe Ruth could hit a ball so hard, and so far, that it was sometimes impossible to believe your eyes. We used to absolutely marvel at his hits. Tremendous wallops. You can't imagine the balls he hit. . . . It was hard to believe the natural ability that man had.

"Well, to give you an example: in 1920 he hit over fifty home runs all by himself, and everybody else in the whole rest of the league added together hit only about three hundred homers. That's a fact. Look it up if you don't believe it. About one out of every seven home runs hit in the American League that year was hit by Babe Ruth.

"My God, if he was playing today! Nowadays they hit about fifteen hundred home runs a season in the American League. If Babe was as good relative to everybody else today, like he used to be, he'd hit over *two hundred* homers a season. That'll give you an idea of how the big fellow dominated baseball back then. Take Mantle, Mays, Kille-brew, and anybody else you want to name, and *add them all up,* and they still won't match Ruth's home runs relative to the rest of the league!"[6]

Miller Huggins: "Ruth was the most destructive force in

baseball. I don't mean the force of Ruth's homers alone. The mere presence of the Babe created a disastrous psychological problem for the other team. We won the 1922 pennant because of that factor. The last month of 1922, Ruth didn't hit at all, but the opposing pitchers kept walking Ruth to get at Wally Pipp, and Pipp was hitting .400 at the time."

Paul Gallico: "It was impossible to watch him at bat without experiencing an emotion. I have seen hundreds of ball players at the plate, and none of them managed to convey the message of impending doom to a pitcher that Babe Ruth did with the cock of his head, the position of his legs, and the little gentle waving of the bat, a feather in his two big paws."

Waite Hoyt: "I always remember the one he hit off me back on Labor Day when I was with the Philadelphia Athletics. We were playing in Shibe Park in Philadelphia. There was the great Babe coming up and naturally I want to beat my old teammate.

"Well, you never saw the Babe but he leaned in toward the plate and they always said the place to pitch the Babe was high outside. But I saw him leaning in so I said, 'Well, he's been leaning in so much if I can get a pitch in over his hands, he'll pop it up.' So I got him to hit two foul balls and it's 2 and 0.

"Now I'll have to digress a little. In Philadelphia in those days, back of the right-field wall there was a street, then a line of those houses that are all the same with those marble steps, then back of that another line of houses.

"Well, now, Babe had the fastest set of reflexes I've ever known on a batter. So I put one in over his hands and the Babe hit the ball and did he hit it! I'm standing there on the mound watching the ball, forgetting all about the ball game and the fact that the home run was being hit off me. I was just amazed at the tremendous distance that the ball was carrying and I thought, 'By George, that's the longest home run I ever seen.'

"And here I am in complete amazement, sheer astonishment, standing on the mound and there goes the ball out over the right field wall, over the first row of houses, out over the second row of houses and lit in the second street beyond.

"Then all of a sudden, I remembered that the ball was hit off me and, by George, was I mad."

Casey Stengel: "He'd hit a pop-up so high that everyone on the field thought he had a chance to get it. They'd all try to get under it to make the catch, and it looked like a union meetin'."

Babe Ruth: "A delegation of cricket players called on me while I was there [London, England] and in the course of chewing the rag with them one of them said, 'Of course, old chap, you're not accustomed to a very fast ball. No wonder you've hit well.'

"I asked him to repeat it, to make sure I'd heard him correctly. I guess I should have told him about Walter Johnson, Lefty Grove, and a few others I had done pretty well against, but he wouldn't have understood.

"Then we got around to talking about the difference in the bats used in baseball and cricket, and the same fellow said that if I could use a cricket bat in baseball I'd never have to worry about replacing it—for no one had ever broken one, as far as he remembered.

"I got a sudden itch to play cricket immediately. They took me out to Lords, or some place like that, and got the best bowler they could find to throw me a couple.

"As you probably know, in cricket the bowler gives it to the batter on the first bounce, which automatically turns the pitch into what we'd call a slow ball. I hit the first pitch farther, they said, than they had ever seen a cricket ball hit.

"And on the guy's second pitch I swung and broke the bat right in two."[7]

RUTH, THE MAN

The Babe electrified New York with his larger-than-life personality and his superhuman feats. Everybody wanted to see the Babe, to hear about him, to touch him, to buy him a beer. And the Babe obliged nearly all of them.

Off the field the Babe drank, ate, chased women, and got

into trouble with an abandon that left even the most worldly
spectator in utter disbelief. Ruth led such a raucous nightlife
it was a wonder he could even show up at the ballpark, much
less play. Once he got to town, whatever the town, he started
on a round of nonstop partying and carousing.

Lee Allen: "Ruth was a large man in a camel's hair coat and
camel's hair cap, standing in front of a hotel, his broad
nostrils sniffing at the promise of the night."

Jimmy Breslin: "The only sports legend I ever saw who
completely lived up to advance billing was Babe Ruth.

"It was a hot summer afternoon, and the Babe, sweat
dripping from his jowls and his shirt stuck to him, came off
the eighteenth green at the old Bayside Golf Club in the
borough of Queens and stormed into the huge barroom of
the club.

"'Gimme one of them heavens to Betsy drinks you always
make for me,' the Babe said in a gravelly voice.

"The bartender put a couple of fistfuls of ice chunks into a
big, thick mixing glass and then proceeded to make a Tom
Collins that had so much gin in it that other people at the bar
started to laugh. He served the drink to the Babe just as it
was made, right in the mixing glass.

"Ruth said something about how heavens to Betsy hot he
was, and then he picked up the glass and opened his mouth,
and there went everything. In one shot, he swallowed the
drink, the orange slice and the rest of the garbage, and the ice
chunks. He stopped for nothing. There is not a single man I
have ever seen in a saloon who does not bring his teeth
together a little bit and stop those ice chunks from going in.
A man has to have a pipe the size of a trombone to take ice in
one shot. But I saw Ruth do it, and whenever somebody tells
me how the Babe used to drink and eat when he was playing
ball, I believe every word of it."

Ty Cobb: "I've seen him at midnight, propped up in bed,
order six club sandwiches, a platter of pigs' knuckles, and a
pitcher of beer. He'd down all that while smoking a big black
cigar. Next day, if he hit a homer, he'd trot around the bases
complaining about gas pains and a bellyache. . . . How that

man could eat! If he'd ever been sawed in half on any given day, I think three-fourths of Stevens's concessions would have been found inside him."

Joe Dugan: "He was an animal. He ate a hat once. He did. A straw hat. Took a bite out of it and ate it."

Benny Bengough: "Babe did things the other fellows couldn't possibly do and still play because he was a superhuman man in a way. His constitution was terrific. I never saw the man sick. Only the time he had the operation in '25 when he had to have his glands cut in his groin.

"But I never heard Babe ail. He'd say, 'I got a little indigestion.' And he'd belch or something. But never seriously sick in his life. Oh, he'd never lay out with injuries. He'd play."

Sam Jones: "You'd see Ruth at the ballpark and the next time you'd see him would be at the ballpark. You never saw him around the hotel. Huggins had a rule for Ruth that he had to be in by one o'clock. But he never said whether it was one A.M. or one P.M."

Mrs. Claire Ruth: "The presence of the Babe in any town gave a lot of odd females telephonitis. We could arrive anywhere and no sooner was the newspaper on the street with his picture in it than the telephone began to ring. And the fact that my picture was often printed, too, and my role in the Babe's life clearly defined, seemed to make no difference.

"The Babe brought out the beast in a lot of ladies the world over. . . ."[8]

Ford Frick: "Ruth recognized the difference between right and wrong. What he did not recognize, or could not accept, was the right of society to tell him what he should do, or not do. He drank a great deal and he was a ladies' man, but he never led a young ball player astray and he never took advantage of an innocent girl."

Ruth owned a succession of expensive cars and he drove them full-throttle around Manhattan, ignoring speed limits and traffic lights. Stopped frequently by police, Ruth usually dodged any citation. The cops were all fans.

One day in June, 1921, however, he ran into a cop who was not a fan and Ruth soon found himself in front of a magistrate who fined him $100. Ruth peeled a C note off a bulging roll that he pulled out of his pocket. But the judge had another surprise. He sentenced Ruth to one day in jail, which meant until 4 P.M. that same afternoon.

The Yankees had a game that day at 3:15, so he could at least play part of the game. He phoned the ballpark and had someone hustle his uniform down to the jail. He dressed in his cell, and as he left in a great hurry, bidding good-bye to cellmates and jailers alike, he yelled, 'I'm going to go like hell to get to the game. Keeping you late like this makes you into a speeder.'"

Waite Hoyt: "Babe had a red Marmet automobile. One of the longest automobiles you ever saw in your life. We used to call it the Ghost of Riverside Drive. He used to drive it around and we'd find it at sundry places around New York and we'd bring it up to the stadium so it wouldn't get lost. He'd forget it here and there. We'd drive it up to the stadium and leave it there and Ruth would recover it there. Well, he wore it out in a year. In a year's time, it had no radiator cap and the rusty water used to spout out of it like a Roman candle.

"He finally had to get rid of it and bought a Packard. Oh, he was very proud of this job and it was another giant thing—it looked like a Pullman car. So one time on the way to Miami, he stopped in Palm Beach for gas.

"Well, you couldn't miss Babe. He was recognizable anywhere you saw him. He had sort of flaring nostrils—big wide things. Joe Bush, one of our pitchers, said, 'If Babe ever slept in the rain, he'd drown.' So Babe was unmistakable when you saw him.

"Just then in pulled a Ro-o-o-o-o-lls Royce at the adjacent pump—a chauffeur-driven Rolls with one of Palm Beach's 400 sitting in the back very sedately.

"The chauffeur got out and recognized Babe Ruth and he got all excited and he ran back and said, 'Madam! Madam! That's the great Babe Ruth!'

"Well, she got curious, and as she was giving him the once over lightly through the lorgnette, Babe looked up and caught her peeking. She got kind of flustered but she had to say something, so with great dignity she says, 'You are Mr. Babe Ruth, are you not?'

"And Babe says, 'Ya, that's me.'

"'Mr. Ruth, imagine meeting you. Mr. Ruth, I've been admiring your motor.'

"'Ya, some boat, hey kid.'

"'Mr. Ruth, my husband is in the automobile business. That's one of those new cars with four-wheel brakes, isn't it?'

"'That's right. Some boat.'

"'Are those hydraulic or mechanical brakes?'

"And Ruth looked her right in the eye and said, 'Madam, I haven't the slightest consumption.'"

Predictably, all this excess inevitably brought the Babe trouble. But the big man must have had the Almighty in his corner, for even the most dangerous, hair-raising experience seemed to turn into just another good belly laugh.

Babe Ruth: "One day a loud-mouthed fan got on me and called me every kind of bum he could think of. I just wasn't in a mood to take it, after an hour or so. I jumped over the bleacher fence and climbed up the stands after him. He was a little squirt but he didn't run. Instead, he pulled a knife on me. It looked about a foot long. I paused for a moment, but before I had a chance to tackle him, Colonel Huston jumped in between us. He had seen me go into the bleachers and had run across the field and jumped the bleacher rail to act as a peace officer. He didn't have much trouble keeping me from tangling with that knife."[9]

Perhaps Ruth's most dangerous altercation came at a roadhouse outside New York where Ruth used to drink bootleg liquor and listen to jazz. One night Ruth got into an argument with a man, and the two squared off to fight. But teammates separated the two, things calmed down, and the man left.

Soon after, Ruth decided he'd had enough for one evening, jumped in his car, and sped away. Luckily for Ruth, teammate Harry Harper was watching from a window. As Ruth drove away, a second car pulled out and followed.

"Come on," Harper said, "there's going to be trouble."

A carload of Yankees took off in Harper's car. About a mile up the road they came upon the two cars parked at the side of the road. Ruth was standing near his car with his hands in the air, looking down the barrel of a pistol.

Harper gunned the car and headed straight for the man who had the drop on Ruth. When he leapt out of the way to avoid the onrushing vehicle, Ruth grabbed him, and Harper, jumping out of his car, wrestled the gun away.

Afraid of what Huggins would say if he found out about this latest fiasco, they let the man go with just a few idle threats, minus his gun.

Outside of these occasional run-ins, Ruth was a well-liked and friendly man and certainly one of the most unpretentious superstars ever. He was a spoiled prima donna to be sure, but he was a likable one.

Jimmy Austin: "What a warmhearted, generous soul he was. Always friendly, always time for a laugh or a wisecrack. The Babe always had a twinkle in his eye, and when he'd hit a homer against us he'd never trot past third without giving me a wink.

"The Babe would give you the shirt off his back. All you had to do was ask him. The big fellow wasn't perfect. Everybody knows that. But that guy had a heart. He really did. A heart as big as a watermelon, and made out of pure gold."[10]

Jack Redding: "When I was a boy, I caddied for Ruth out at Wheatley Hills in Long Island. He'd give us a two-dollar tip if he won, a dollar and a half if he lost. The usual tip was a quarter, or at best a half dollar. And on the thirteenth hole, where the refreshment stand was, that's where you tested your man. Some golfers would buy you a soft drink, some wouldn't buy you anything. Ruth always said, 'Get whatever you want.'"[11]

Waite Hoyt: "Names never did mean much to the Babe, especially important ones. Herb Pennock, the great Yankee pitcher, once asked Ruth who he'd been out to dinner with the night before.

"'Oh, some movie people,' Ruth answered.

"'What movie people?'

"'Oh, you know, what the hell are their names?'

"It turned out the Babe had been at a veddy fashionable dinner party with the two biggest stars of the day—Mary Pickford and Douglas Fairbanks. But that didn't mean anything to Ruth.

"Ruth was so busy from early morning until late at night that he didn't have much time to read the newspapers and so prominent people, well, he just didn't know who they were. Back in the early twenties there was an influx of dignitaries from abroad. They'd be given a great ticker-tape parade and then if it was summer they'd bring them over to Yankee Stadium, principally because Ruppert was a very great friend and compatriot of the Tammany Hall group. He'd kick in with a lot of dough to the campaign funds. As a consequence, Colonel Jacob Ruppert and the Yankees were recipients of a lot of political favors. Among them was the escorting of these different dignitaries to the local ballpark. Of course, we met the President and English Channel swimmers and foreign celebrities. And this time it happened to be Marshal Foch. This was way back when.

"Anyway, here he was being greeted in the United States with fanfare according the celebrity that he was—the marshal of all the allied forces of World War I. So he was greeted down at City Hall. The motorcade brought him through New York—with 46,000 people waiting for him at the ballpark. There were two bands in the grandstand—one to play the French tunes and one to play the American tunes.

"Sure enough, at three o'clock the gates swing open and in comes the motorcade and the bands start playing and the cars come to a halt in front of Colonel Ruppert's private box. There was Marshal Foch in a powder blue uniform, battle ribbons across his chest, medallions and all.

"Then, the players lined up to march by and shake hands with Marshal Foch. Babe, at the end of the line, is going to make a speech for all the players. And Foch was clicking his heels, giving each of us a generous salute.

"Finally, he reaches Ruth and Ruth looked at those

medallions and battle ribbons, leaned on the box seat railing, looked Foch right in the eye and said, 'Hey, Gen, they tell me you were in the war.' "

One group of people Ruth never forgot and always had time for was children. Ruth remembered his own childhood, shunted off to St. Mary's, and he never forgot to treat the kids special. He adored them and always went out of his way to say hello or pat one on the head.

Branch Rickey: "He has had probably more direct influence on the youth of this country than any other player during my time. He has created an expectation of hero worship on the part of the youth of this country and it was a most fortunate thing that Ruth kept faith with the boyhood of America because they loved him."

Mrs. Claire Ruth: "Babe Ruth and kids went together. They loved each other, and that is the only word to describe the relationship. Kids understood Babe. Babe understood kids. Babe was bluff and blunt but he could reduce the shyest of kids to the status of a bosom companion in three minutes or less. It was a job he loved doing. . . .

"When Babe hit his five hundredth homer in Cleveland a few months after we were married in 1929, he arrived at the hotel with two baseballs. He dropped them on a table and said, 'There is the ball I hit for my five hundredth big league homer.'

"I asked him how he could hit one home run with two balls.

"He explained. 'A couple of kids showed up in the clubhouse after the game. They each said, "I got the Babe's five hundredth homer ball." So I gave each of the kids twenty bucks for a ball.'

"I pointed out, 'You've wasted forty dollars because now you'll never know which is the real souvenir you wanted.' Babe laughed and said, 'Yeah, I know. But what's the difference? Neither of the kids looked like he'd had a square meal in months.' Then he picked up the cleaner of the two balls and said, 'This must be the real one, if either is. That other ball is too dirty to be used in a game. Could be a batting practice ball.' "[12]

Babe Ruth: "During the spring of 1928 a man came up to me in a Knoxville hotel lobby. He had been crying. He begged me to drive out with him to his cabin—somewhere out in the hills—where he had a sick son. I told him I was awful sorry but I had to play ball that day and take a train along with the rest of the Yankee team as soon as the ball game was over.

"It was hard to look at his face when I told him. But then I heard something. It was the sound of rain. I looked out and, to my complete surprise, it had started to rain. It came down in buckets, and I told the man to wait.

"Finally, we got the word. The game had been called off. I looked at the man and said, 'Come on, show me the way.'

"It took all day to get to the cabin and back to town. But the look in that kid's pale face was enough of a reward for me."[13]

5

The First Yankee Dynasty

THE FIRST PENNANT

In 1921 Ruth had another believe-it-or-not season. The muscular boy had become a man with a big belly and skinny legs who "looked like a cone stuffed with too much ice cream." The Babe broke his own record of 54 home runs when he air-mailed 59 long ones that year. Ruth was walked so much he reached base more than half the time he came to the plate. He also chalked up 170 RBIs, while hitting .378, and his slugging percentage of .846 was only a point below his record.

Right fielder Bob Meusel had one of his best seasons, driving in 135 runs and hitting 24 homers, more than any other player in the major leagues—except Ruth, of course.

Meusel, the powerfully built rifle-armed right fielder, was one of the greatest but least-known players ever to wear pinstripes. He hit over .300 seven different times, and the power and accuracy of his arm were legendary.

George Pipgras: "Bob Meusel was the most underrated ball player I know. He was a real good hitter and an outstanding fielder. And he had the strongest arm I ever saw. One time Ty Cobb was on third base with one out. Somebody hit a fly ball to Meusel out in left. Meusel caught the ball and held on to it, daring Cobb to go. Wally Schang, our catcher, yelled down to Cobb, 'Come on, Ty. Come in.' Ordinarily Cobb would have tagged up and scored on a fly like that. But he just stood there, glaring. Nobody was foolish enough to challenge Bob Meusel's arm."

Casey Stengel: "Bob Meusel was a big tall man but amazingly nimble. One of the best base runners if he decided to run. He was a fellow that if he could put it all out he had it some days better than anybody. He was the most amazing thrower I ever saw in my life. He could stand flat-footed in the outfield and throw to home plate. That's the kind of arm he had.

"In the 1923 World Series I hit a ball right near the bull pen, and as I was circling the bases Whitey Witt picked up the ball and flipped it to Meusel. With that tremendous arm of his he cut the ball loose and it came clear into home plate and it was just four inches off or I'da been out at home plate. It was one of the most tremendous throws ever made.

"It was nothing for him to throw the ball in and if the third baseman or the catcher didn't protect himself the ball would hit the ground and, shoot! It took on English and when it hit instead of slowing up it took off and it was hard to catch, believe me."

Despite his prowess at the plate and in the field, Meusel was never a popular Yankee. He was a taciturn man who never warmed to the press, had few friends on the team, and appeared totally indifferent to the fans' reaction. Meusel was an enigma. Boo him or cheer him, his expression and demeanor never changed.

The Yankees, led by Ruth and Meusel, played the best ball in the team's history. Mays, Hoyt, and Shawkey had sixty-four wins between them, and the Yanks took home their first American League pennant.

Waite Hoyt: "In 1921 the Yankees had a crucial series with the Cleveland Indians at the end of the season. It was in the

Polo Grounds when the Yankees were still playing there. We had to play them four straight. In those days the position of Miller Huggins as the Yankee manager was not as solid and strong as it was a few years later.

"I pitched the first game of that series [the winner of three out of five would be champion] and beat Cleveland 4–2. We won the second 19–4 and lost the third. So in the fourth game, Huggins called a meeting of the pitchers and he left it up to us who would pitch—Old Jack Quinn or bring me back for the second time in the series. They voted to start Quinn and if he ran into trouble, they'd put me in.

"So Cleveland jumped on Quinn in the first inning for three runs before Quinn got anybody out. Before I knew what was happening I was in there. So I got them out and the game seesawed back and forth.

"Remember, this game was for everything. If the Yankees won, it would be the first time the Yankees won a pennant in the history of baseball. Also, it meant the first 'City Series' in New York [against the Giants]. The first time two New York clubs would play. So we were very anxious to win this game.

"I can remember I was twenty-one years old at the time and all my emotions were right at the top with the effervescence of youth and I sat there between innings saying to myself, 'Bear down! Bear down! Put everything you've got in every pitch.'

"So that's what I did. I tried to keep it outside so they couldn't hit it into the seats. Just rear back and throw the ball as hard as I could. Letting fly with everything I had, just as hard as I could throw the ball.

"And the game seesawed back and forth. We tied, then went ahead. Cleveland tied the score. Then Ruth hit a home run and we went ahead again. And we got down to the eighth inning and the score was 7–6 in favor of Cleveland and Ruth belted another home run and put us ahead 8–7.

"I was so tired and so worn out—not only from throwing the ball as hard as I could but from my own emotion and anxiety—that I was blowing goose in the eighth inning. So they took me out and put Carl Mays in. Mays got out of the inning.

"Now remember in those days games used to start at 3:30 in the afternoon and now it's 5:15 and it was early October and the night shadows were falling. The Polo Grounds was always sort of a dark ballpark anyway. And the shadows were deepening—lowering and lowering. There was a sort of haze over the field and it was a very dramatic setting.

"In the ninth Mays loaded the bases and with two outs a good .300-hitting catcher, Steve O'Neill, was at the plate for the Indians. And Colonel Ruppert was in the bull pen with us in the deep shadows and Ruppert was walking up and down in front of the players yelling frantically, 'I give you the brewery! I give you the brewery! Win the pennant and I give you the brewery!'

"And finally Mays, with 2 and 2 on O'Neill, wound up with that underhand pitch of his and we saw O'Neill swing. Then we saw Elvin Miller, the center fielder, start back and we thought O'Neill had hit one deep. But we couldn't tell because it was so dark. We all held our breath and then bedlam broke loose.

"See, what had happened was O'Neill had actually struck out and Miller was heading for the clubhouse, which was in center field at the time. And, by George, we had won the pennant.

"Two or three people died in the grandstand that afternoon from heart attacks. That's really the truth. It was one of the most exciting occasions I can ever recall. Now *that* was a ball game!"

In the World Series the high-flying Yankees ran up against the Giants, led by the indomitable John McGraw. In a best-five-out-of-nine-games World Series (played that time for the third consecutive—and last—year), the Yankees, with two straight shutout games pitched by Mays and Hoyt, led the Series 2–0.

Babe Ruth: "Up until the time I came to New York it was pretty much of a National League town. The Giants had been the pennant winners, and the Yankees, known as the Highlanders in their early days, were always the poor relations. But the home-run hitting of the Yankees changed all that and we easily outdrew them in 1920 and 1921.

"John McGraw didn't like that for a cent. He was proud of the past records and prestige of the Giants and his own position as the top man of New York baseball. It was evident then that the 1921 World Series would be for blood. As I say, we had outdrawn the Giants, and if we could defeat them in the Series we'd have McGraw playing second fiddle."[1]

No team had ever come back from a two-games-to-zero start in the Series. What was worse for the Giants, the Yanks got quickly out on top in game three when the Babe drove in two runs, and the Yankees went up 4–0 in the third inning.

But the momentum turned dramatically and swiftly. Led by Frankie Frisch, the "Fordham Flash," the Giants scored four times in their half of the third inning and never looked back. They scored eight more runs that day and won the game 13–5. Then they won game four to even the Series, dropped game five, and then swept the next three games for the World Championship.

The big story of the 1921 World Series, however, was an injured Ruth. In the fourth inning of the fifth game, Babe uncharacteristically laid down a perfect bunt along the first-base line and beat it out for a single. Then Meusel socked a double to deep left, and Ruth scored all the way from first. But the Babe was suffering from a bruised knee and an infected right elbow. He collapsed on the bench, and the game was stopped while the Babe was attended to. The crowd gave him a wild standing ovation when he returned to left field in the Giants' home half of the inning. But the Babe was too hurt to play the next day and, except for a pinch-hit appearance in the last game, Ruth sat out the final three games of the Series, all of which the Yankees lost.

Babe Ruth: "It still burns me up, for I accidentally played a part in the loss. I developed an abscess on my left elbow a few days before the Series. I played in the first five games under difficulties, and even though I hit .313, knocked out my first World Series home run, and batted in four runs, I should have done more. I had to sit on the bench for the sixth, seventh, and eighth games, though I made one pinch-hitting appearance in the last contest.

"Anybody who knows how I loved to play baseball and

liked to hit can imagine how I felt, sitting out those games when my bat was needed so badly in the Yankee lineup."[2]

But a *New York Sun* columnist had another version:

Joe Vila: "Ruth possibly enjoyed the trick he played on the fans by going into the game after the report had been spread that he had been forced out of the series by an operation on his 'infected elbow.' On numerous occasions during the pennant race the public was informed that Ruth had been disabled and couldn't play, yet the Home Run King invariably bobbed up to battle for the Yankees. According to official information on Saturday, the Babe had been seriously injured and the Hugmen would have to worry along without him. But Ruth, with a bandage around his elbow, surprised everybody in the stands by taking his place in left field and by hammering the ball for a single and a four-bagger. Further reports of the Bambino's indispositions will be taken with plenty of salt."

Babe Ruth: "I blew my top and decided to show him my arm. The lancing job on it had left some of the bone exposed. I went after him.

"Joe was a big man, but considerable older than I. I found him in the front row of the press stand. The screen was between us but as I approached him with fire in my eyes he picked up his typewriter to defend himself as though he expected me to punch my way right through the screen. I called him something and added, 'You're accusing me of not having any guts. Now, if *you* have any, print a picture of my arm with this hole in it and let your readers see my side of it.' "[3]

Vila did not print the picture as Ruth had suggested, but he did have something to say about the incident in his column the next day.

Joe Vila: "Peeved over something that had appeared in print, Ruth tried to pick a fight with a newspaper writer. . . . Ruth, it seems, is no different from other baseball stars who consider praise and flattery belonging to them as a matter of

course but are unable to stand criticism without showing their
true colors.''

THE BATTLING BOMBERS TAKE
ANOTHER FLAG

When the Yankees took the field for the 1922 season, Ruth
was not with them. In a test of personal power, Ruth had
tangled with Judge Landis, the commissioner of baseball, and
the Babe had lost.

Immediately after the 1921 Series, Ruth, along with teammates Mays, Schang, and Meusel, prepared to leave on a
barnstorming tour, as he had in 1919 and 1920. These tours
were usually huge financial successes, often earning the Babe
as much as $100,000 for a few weeks of exhibitions. But in
order not to dilute the importance of the World Series, there
was a rule that members of World Series teams were not
allowed to participate in postseason exhibitions.

To make matters worse, people were asking how Ruth
could play exhibitions when he was not well enough to play
the last three games of the Series. "I heal quickly," Ruth
tersely but inadequately explained.

Ruth ignored the rule. But Judge Landis wasn't about to
let any player, even Ruth, ignore a baseball by-law, and he
summoned Babe into his office. When Ruth blithely ignored
Landis's summons, the judge let the Babe know who was
boss but good.

He suspended Ruth and Meusel until May 20, 1922, which
meant they would miss the first thirty-nine days of the season.
He also withheld their World Series shares. Even though he
was roundly criticized for suspending America's greatest
hero, Landis stuck to his decision.

"This is tough on me," said Landis. "I walk down Michi-
gan Boulevard and I hear the tough little kids saying, 'There
goes that white-haired old bastard who's keeping the Babe
out of baseball.' And that's just what they are saying all over
the American-speaking world. But I'm not going to ease up
on that big ape. I promise you that."

That year the Yanks fought a down-to-the-last-day battle
for the American League pennant with the St. Louis Browns.
In fact, it was a battling season all around for the team.

Al DeVormer, a reserve catcher, had a brawl with Carl Mays, and the next day he took on "Bootnose" Hofmann, another catcher. Then Meusel and Schang fought each other on the bench during a Browns game, and later in the same game Wally Pipp and Ruth went at it. Even little Miller Huggins got into it—once on the streets of Manhattan with Mays (who fell into disfavor with Huggins after that and was sold to the Reds the following year), and another time during a game with Waite Hoyt.

The Pipp-Ruth fisticuffs happened because Pipp had been having an off-year and Ruth was riding him. During a game with the Browns, Ruth goaded him, and Pipp exploded. With no warning Pipp sucker-punched Ruth in the nose, knocking Ruth on his rear. Ruth picked himself up and jumped at Pipp, but by then their teammates had them both in tow. Pipp, with order restored, was next up to bat and he socked a vicious home run. The next batter, Ruth, ripped the following pitch a little farther.

That season the Yanks fought and then they generally took their anger out on the opposing team. In only 110 games Babe hit 35 homers, and Meusel and Schang each hit .319, while Pipp was at .329. Huggins also had a superb pitching staff to go along with his power hitting. With the acquisition of Bullet Joe Bush and Sad Sam Jones, the Yankees had a starting rotation of five right-handers who started 151 games and won 90 of the team's 94 victories.

In fact, the Yankees of 1922 were stronger in almost every position than the '21 team. Aaron Ward was moved over from third to second when Home Run Baker returned from a brief retirement in 1920 to play third and general manager Ed Barrow obtained the swift-footed Whitey Witt to fill the hole in center.

Joe Dugan: "One day there was a long hit between Whitey and Ruth. 'Go grab it, Whitey!' Next one goes between Whitey and Meusel. 'Go get it, Whitey!' Next one's hit right over Whitey's head. He comes in, puffin', and Huggins calls him over. 'Whitey,' he says, 'I'm watchin' those two big stiffs. Keep chasin' 'em and I'll see that Colonel Ruppert gets you a bonus.'

" 'To hell with the bonus,' says Whitey. 'Tell him to buy me a bicycle!' "

The Browns made a fight of it, though. With the mighty George Sisler hitting a fabulous .420, including a forty-one-game hitting streak, St. Louis pushed the Yankees to the last day of the season.

Waite Hoyt: "I can remember that series with the Browns in which they had brown-and-white barrels on the streetcorners of St. Louis, so the fans could contribute to the celebration if the Browns won the pennant.

"Those were the days of George Sisler, 'Horseface' Ken Williams, 'Baby Doll' Jacobson, Marty McManus, Urban Shocker, and Johnny Tobin. They had a real good ball club.

"The ushers at the St. Louis ballpark were standing up behind the Yankee bench yelling out imprecations at the Yankee ball club, and Joe Bush, one of our pitchers who used to box with Lou Fendler, the great lightweight of his day, climbed into the stands and beat up on a couple of ushers. The fans were gonna run the Yankees out of the park. Ruth had to climb out a window to avoid a mob. It was very precarious around the park to even enter or leave.

"The Yankees managed to beat the Browns two out of three. Whitey Witt was hit with a pop bottle in the first game and he was laid low so he couldn't play in the second game. But in the third game against Urban Shocker they brought him in to pinch-hit in the eighth and Witt singled into center field to beat the Browns and we won the pennant."

A WOEFUL SERIES

The Yankees again met their Polo Grounds landlords, the Giants, in the Series, and again they were defeated by McGraw's men. This time, however, they were humiliated in a four-game Giant sweep.

As Ruth goes, so goes the Yankees, was a popular dictum in those days, and it was never truer than in the '22 Series. Ruth got only two scruffy hits and batted a pathetic .118.

McGraw was credited with masterminding the undermining of Ruth. When Rosy Ryan took the mound in relief of

Art Nehf in the first game, McGraw issued the following instructions to catcher Hank Gowdy:

"You tell Ryan to throw the slowest ball he's got. And don't let him get it anywhere near the plate. The big baboon will swing at anything. If Rosy gets it even close, I'll fine him a thousand dollars."

John McGraw: "I signaled for every ball that was pitched to Ruth. We pitched but nine curves and three fastballs to him throughout the Series. All the rest were slow balls. Of those twelve, eleven set the big fellow on his ear. He got just one foul off those twelve strikes. And usually we crossed him with the curve when there were men on bases."

To add to the humiliation, the Giants bragged about having stolen the Yankees' signals.

Heinie Groh: "I had the Yankees' signs in that 1922 World Series. Not their pitching signs, their hitting signs. I knew when they were going to bunt and when they were going to hit away. Which is something it's very nice for a third baseman to know. I figured them out in the very first game from what Miller Huggins was doing, and had them the whole Series. That was also the Series where Babe Ruth crashed into me at third base and almost started a real donnybrook. Whew! The Babe wasn't doing very well—I think he only got two hits in the whole Series—and the Yankees were getting beat and I was hitting like nobody's business. So in the third game the Babe got on base, and when the next man up singled, Babe came tearing around into third and as he came in he gave me the shoulder and sent me flying. I didn't complain. That's baseball. But the fans really got on him and gave him a terrific going-over.

"When I finally got on my feet the Babe said to me, 'Kid, you know we're both entitled to part of that base path.'

" 'Okay,' I said, 'you take your side and I'll take mine. And if I ever find you on my side, you better watch out!'

"Hell, I couldn't have budged that big guy if I'd have hit him with a locomotive, and he knew it, too. But you got to let them know who's boss, right?"[4]

WORLD CHAMPIONS

The year 1923 was a historic one for the Yankees. In 1920 the owner of the Giants, Charles Stoneham, after constant badgering from his field manager John McGraw, told Ruppert and Huston to find another home for their club "as quickly as possible." That year the Yankees had outdrawn their Polo Grounds landlords, the Giants, for the first time, becoming the first team ever to surpass the million mark in attendance. In 1921 and 1922 the Yankees continued to kill the Giants at the gate even though the Giants were the World Champions.

McGraw reportedly warned Stoneham that "the Yankees are getting too powerful. We can't afford to let them play in the Polo Grounds any longer. If we kick them out, they won't be able to find another location on Manhattan Island. They'll have to move to the Bronx or Long Island. The fans will forget about them and they'll be through."

McGraw could not have been more wrong.

With Huston's experience in handling large-scale construction projects, the building of the Yankees' new stadium progressed swiftly. After looking over several sites, the two colonels chose a spot in the Bronx directly across the Harlem River from the Polo Grounds. Construction began in February, 1922, and after a year of feverish work, the grand structure was completed in time for Opening Day, April 18, 1923.

Over 74,000 fans jammed the stadium that day, and police had to turn back another 25,000, easily the largest crowd that had ever seen a game. Always primed for the drama of an important moment, the Babe christened "the House that Ruth built" by hitting a three-run homer to win the game for the Yankees, 4–1.

Soon after the magnificent opening of Yankee Stadium, Cap Huston sold out his interest in the ball club to Ruppert for $1.5 million, six times more than he had paid for it only eight years before.

Although they seldom saw eye to eye on any matter, it was Ruppert and Huston's ongoing argument over Huggins that ultimately triggered the split. After the last game of the 1922 Series, Huston declared he'd had enough of Huggins. With the support of Ed Barrow, Ruppert pressured Huston to sell him his half of the Yankees. It didn't take much persuading. The following May (Huston had stuck around to see the completion of the stadium) the deal was completed, and Ruppert sent this simple but firm telegram to the Yankees, who were playing in Chicago:

"I am the sole owner of the Yankees. Miller Huggins is my manager."

The 1923 season was the greatest season in the franchise's history. The Yanks won their third straight pennant and, after two successive drubbings in the Series by the Giants, they took home their first World Championship.

The Babe, of course, led the league in homers with 41, and hit .393, his career high. He shared the RBI title with Tris Speaker at 130. He also had 45 doubles, 13 triples, and a career high of 205 hits and was named the American League's Greatest All-round Player—the MVP. It was the Great Bambino's first and only Most Valuable Player award.

The pitching sensation that year was Sad Sam Jones, who tossed a no-hitter.

Sad Sam Jones: "I guess in all those years of pitching my biggest thrill came when I pitched a no-hitter for the Yankees on September 4, 1923. It was against the Philadelphia Athletics. I realized it as I was going along. Round about the fourth or fifth inning you begin to realize that nobody's got a hit yet, and then you start to get a little tense. But when I'd come back to the bench between innings no one would say a word to me about a no-hitter, or anything like that. The scoreboards then, they only gave the score. They didn't have things like hits and errors on the scoreboards in those days.

"Along near the end of the game I started to get real tired, way more than usual. Chick Galloway, the A's shortstop, was the last man up in the bottom of the ninth. 'I'm gonna break it up if I can,' he yelled at me, and he bunted down the third-base line. I fielded it and threw him out and there it was: a no-hitter.

"It was a terrific thrill as soon as it was over, the fans and all the players flocking down on the field to congratulate me. But I think the biggest kick of all came the next day, when I got telegrams from all over the country, from people all over the whole country who'd taken the time to send me a wire. . . .

"I guess I liked playing with the Yankees best of all. I was there for five years, 1922 through '26. It was a good club to play for. They always had plenty of money, paid real well, and drew good crowds. And three of the five years I was there we won the pennant. What more could you ask for? The Yankees always did things in a big way. Why, when the season was over they'd even give each player three brand new baseballs. Just *give* them to us. No other club ever did that.

"People forget that the Yankees in the twenties were more than a great offensive club. They were the best *defensive* team in both leagues, as well. That outfield, terrific pitching, a great infield. It was a well-balanced ball club in every way. Everybody played in the shadow of George Herman Ruth, of course, so a lot of people don't even remember who else was on that team."[5]

In the World Series the Yankees took revenge by crushing the Giants four games to two. Both Giant victories were by the slimmest of margins and both were won by a wiry thirty-three-year-old outfielder whose name, ironically, has become synonymous with the Yankees—Casey Stengel.

In the ninth inning of the first game, with the score tied 4–4, Casey lined a ball between Whitey Witt and Bob Meusel that rolled to the fence. Casey, who had a bruised heel, staggered like a drunken man around the bases and finally stumbled across home plate for an inside-the-park home run and a 5–4 victory for the Giants.

The Yanks took the second game 4–2, but in the third game Art Nehf shut out "Ruppert's Rifles" 1–0 and Casey's home run again proved the game winner.

Babe Ruth: "Casey Stengel, one of the daffiest guys I ever met. . . . We had a lot of fun with Casey all through the Series. There never was anything abusive about him. We rode him just to hear his clownish comebacks. I know I kidded him plenty. And when he won the 1 to 0 game he ran around the bases with his thumb to his nose and his hand pointed toward the Yankee bench. I think it was meant for me in particular as he tried to show me he, too, knew how to hit home runs. Ruppert didn't like it and later said it was undignified. But we didn't mind Casey having fun."[6]

Casey Stengel: "I made like a bee or fly was bothering me, so I kept rubbing the end of my nose, with my fingers pointing toward the Yankee dugout.

"I heard about that in a hurry. Commissioner Landis called me over and said he didn't like that kind of exhibition before sixty thousand people, and he told me, 'If you do that again, I promise you one thing: You won't receive a dollar of your World Series share.'"

Judge Landis: "When a man hits a home run in a World Series game he should be permitted some exuberance—particularly when his name is Casey Stengel. Casey Stengel just can't help being Casey Stengel."

Stengel finished the Series batting .407 with two homers. If not for Stengel, the Yankees instead of taking the Series four games to two would have swept the Giants. Despite Casey's heroics, a few weeks later McGraw, in gratitude, sold Casey to the cellar-dwelling Braves.

Casey Stengel: "Well, maybe I'm lucky. If I'd hit three homers, McGraw might have sent me out of the country. We were in two World Series while I was with the Giants and they gave us watches, rings, fobs, cufflinks, and necktie pins. If we win another, the only thing left to give us is earrings and old Casey would look great walking around with earrings bobbing out of those big sails of his, wouldn't he?"

After twenty long years the Yankees had finally reached the top of the baseball world. At the victory celebration in the Yankee clubhouse after the sixth and final game, Ruppert got up on a chair and said it all.

"Well, in 1921 we won the pennant but we couldn't win the World Series. In 1922 we won the pennant but we couldn't win the World Series. But this year we won the pennant and the World Series. I have the greatest park, the greatest players, and the greatest team. Witt is a great player; Meusel is a great player; Dugan is a great player; and Ruth is the greatest player in baseball. But most of the credit goes to Miller Huggins. He is the greatest manager."

THE BELLYACHE HEARD ROUND THE WORLD

After three straight pennants the Yankees tailed off in 1924, finishing second. But it wasn't the fault of the Bambino. Ruth won his first batting crown with a .348 average and, as usual, led the league with forty-six homers. He just missed winning the triple crown when he relinquished the lead in RBIs in the last few weeks of the season.

In fact, though Ruth came close five times, he never did win a triple crown. He led the league six times in RBIs and home runs and finished in the top three in batting average six times, but he never was able to put all three titles together in one year. Someone in one category or another edged him out, often in the last week of the season.

Despite his flashy statistics that year, Ruth could not pull the rest of the injury-riddled team to the top. They were edged out by those perennial cabooses the Washington Senators, who had a great year behind the pitching of thirty-six-year-old Walter Johnson, who went 23–7.

The gargantuan appetites of the mighty Babe finally caught up with him, though. In the spring of 1925, during the team's annual exhibition tour with the Dodgers, Ruth was stricken with acute indigestion and collapsed at a train station in Asheville, North Carolina. In a wee-hours binge, Ruth had reportedly wolfed a dozen fully dressed hot dogs and washed the entire mess down with a gallon of soda pop. It was known as the Bellyache Heard Round the World. The press had a field day. RUTH GRAVELY ILL, screamed the headlines. Several European newspapers reported that the great Bambino had, in fact, died.

The truth was that the Babe was a very sick man. His late-night carousing and his rampaging appetite for anything at all, at all hours, would have long since killed a less hearty man. Paul Kirchell, a Yankee scout at the time, was given the assignment of getting Ruth back to New York in one piece. It was to prove a weighty task.

Paul Kirchell: "Babe staggered off the train in Asheville with Steve O'Neill and a big kid named Levi holding him up. Then he collapsed. Levi and O'Neill had to catch him before he hit the ground, and a couple other players ran over and they dragged Babe back on the train. He had had a hell of a winter. Weighed something like 275, 280. So it was some job.

"They took him on over to the hospital for a couple of days, then I took the train back to New York with him. Sick as he was, the Babe never did learn though. First thing he did was dig into a breakfast a horse couldn't eat—coffee, toast, eggs, and a plate of fried potatoes.

"A little while later Babe started throwing up and collapsed in the toilet. Cracked his head up real good on the basin falling down, and he was out cold. The conductor had to haul him by his feet back to his berth.

"When we got to New York the ambulance attendants—must of been ten of them—passed him like a slab of beef through the windows onto a stretcher. He was still unconscious when they put him in the ambulance but then he suddenly woke up delirious and started kicking and screaming. That's the last I saw of him until he came out of the hospital."

Ruth seemed to make a quick recovery, however, and after several days it looked like he'd be ready for the season opener on April 14. But Ruth's troubles were more than a mere bellyache. Suddenly, even though he was on a strict diet, Ruth's temperature shot up again. On April 17 Ruth was operated on for an intestinal abscess, and he would not play until June.

Ruth and the team struggled through the summer of 1925. Babe's average was below .250, and the team wallowed in dead last most of the season. More than one person thought the Babe, now thirty-one, was through as a ball player.

Frank Lieb (in his sports column in 1925): "It is doubtful that Ruth again will be the superstar he was from 1919 through 1924. Next year Ruth will be 32 and at 32 the Babe will be older than Eddie Collins, Walter Johnson, and Ty Cobb at that age. Babe has lived a much more strenuous life. Nevertheless, we see no reason why Ruth should not be a good dependable hitter for several more years, a .325 hitter with some 30-odd home runs. Still, he may surprise the baseball world next year with one of his better seasons."

Despite the dire predictions, Ruth continued to live life the way he pleased, staying out all night and eating and drinking to Ruthian excess. Huggins was fed up with Ruth and he constantly made remarks in the locker room that some of the players were out of shape and pulling the club down. Everyone, including Babe, knew who he meant. The great slugger and the great manager were headed for a showdown. Huggins stood in the way of Ruth's undisciplined appetites, and Ruth didn't like it. He called Huggins the flea and he began to criticize the manager, openly politicking for his dismissal.

Babe Ruth: "People have been asking me all year what the trouble with the team is. I haven't wanted to say it before, but I will now. The trouble with the team is Huggins. Last year we lost the pennant to Washington when we should have won by fifteen games. That was Huggins's fault. He didn't get the most out of his players. I think we have the best team in the league this year and look where we are. The truth is Huggins is incompetent."

Bob Shawkey: "The ball club was out on the field loosening up, and I was in the clubhouse with Hug. Just the two of us. I was about to go out on the field and he said, 'Wait a minute.' He was sitting on the bench with his eye on the door. I sat down next to him. We talked for a while, not about anything in particular, and all the time Hug kept watching that door. "Then the door opened and in walked Babe, in his street clothes. I was surprised to see him. I thought for sure he was out on the field with the rest of the boys. He took off his jacket and hung it up in his locker. But then Hug said, 'Babe, you don't have to dress today. You're fined and suspended. The secretary has your fare back to New York.' "Babe took his jacket out of the locker, put it on, and started to leave. Then he turned around and called Huggins every name under the sun. Hug got up and walked over to him—he was about half Babe's size—and said, 'Babe, someday you're going to thank me for what I'm doing now. You're never going to play another ball game for the New York Yankees until your straighten yourself out.'

"The fine was a whopper—$5,000. I don't know if a manager could fine a man that much money today, what with the Players Association and agents and lawyers. It's different today. But of course you don't have a Babe Ruth today.'"[7]

Ruth slammed his way out of the clubhouse, and that night he spent an orgiastic evening in a famous St. Louis bordello that catered to the high rollers like Ruth. On his way back to New York, a cocky Ruth blasted Huggins in front of the press.

Babe Ruth: "I come in an hour and a half late and he fines me $5,000. I was with friends until midnight, and then we took an auto ride because it was so hot. I was back at the hotel by two-thirty, and we were supposed to be back by one. If Huggins says I was drinking, he's a damn liar and you can make that as strong as you like. I never trained so hard in my life as I did this year. I'm in condition to play. Huggins only suspended me because he wants the publicity. It's a grandstand play for the public, so he can shift the blame on me for the team being in seventh. I'll never play for the Yankees again as long as Huggins is the manager. He's trying to alibi himself at my expense, and I'm not going to let him get away with it. It's either me or him. If Jake still wants him to run his club, he can get somebody else to play right field."

When he laid his demands before Ruppert, Ruth was sure the colonel would back his great slugger. Ruppert knew who put the fannies in the seats in "the House that Ruth Built." But Ruth had a rude awakening coming. Back in New York, Ruppert, hearing of Ruth's ultimatum, had news for Mr. Ruth.

"I'm behind Huggins to the limit," Ruppert stated. "There will be no remission of the fine, and the suspension will last as long as Huggins wants it to last. I understand Ruth says he

will not play for the Yankees as long as Huggins is manager.
Well, the situation is this: Huggins will be manager as long as
he wants to be manager. So you can see where we stand and
where Ruth stands."

Ruth got wind of Ruppert's statement, and by the time he
got back to New York, the bombastic Babe had softened. He
offered to make peace with Huggins, but Miller would have
to meet him halfway—at least.

Babe Ruth: "I know I said in Chicago I wouldn't play for
Huggins again. I guess I was a little too rash. What I really
meant was that I couldn't do my best playing for him until we
straightened things out between us. I don't want to be traded.
New York is my city.

"I think Huggins realizes now that he didn't treat me
exactly right. Imagine fining a baseball player $5,000! If they
slapped a fine like that on some of the boys, they'd be
working all season for nothing. Hell, people murder people
and get away with it, and I get fined $5,000 for staying out
until two in the morning.

"If I had kept on hitting, this never would have happened.
When I was going strong, Hug never bothered me about
where I'd been or what I was doing. He never complained
that staying out late was interfering with my hitting. But now
that I'm down a little and the club is seventh, it's a different
story.

"Aagh, maybe we're both wrong. I know I came back to
the team in June with an incision in my belly six inches long. I
was a damn fool. It didn't heal until this last trip. I should
have taken more time, but I wanted to get back in the game.
In all sincerity, I wanted to help Hug and the club."

In the end a thoroughly contrite Ruth was brought to his
knees. When he came out of his meeting with the Yankee
owner, Ruppert addressed the assembled media that jammed
his offices.

"The fine and the suspension stand," said the colonel. "I
told Ruth, as I tell you now in front of him, that he went too
far. I told him Miller Huggins is in absolute command of the
ball club, and that I stand behind Huggins to the very limit. I
told him it is up to him to see Huggins, admit his errors and

apologize for his hot-headedness. It is up to him to reinstate himself."

Ruth was now eager to apologize to Huggins, but Huggins gave him the cold shoulder, letting Ruth stew for a week before he'd even talk to him. Said Ed Barrow, "You can call it the turning point in the history of the New York Yankees. Thereafter the so-called bad boys realized that we meant business."

Ruth was finally reinstated in September. He played well, raising his average 40 points in six weeks to finish at .290. But it was too late for the Yankees, who ended the season in seventh place. They were not to finish in the second division again for over thirty years.

6

The Iron Horse

THE CROWN PRINCE

In 1925, when the Yankees had sunk into seventh place, a rookie first baseman named Lou Gehrig joined the team, and his brute physical power and gentle soul would lift the Yankees out of their doldrums. Gehrig bolstered the struggling Yankee attack, and by 1926 they were once again a potent championship team. He looked like he was made of iron and, apparently, he was. He played in 2,130 consecutive games and never asked to be replaced, though he had broken his fingers on seventeen separate occasions. Once when he was hit by a pitch and suffered a concussion that would have put any other man in bed for a week, Gehrig suited up and played the next day as usual and never even took an aspirin.

Gehrig didn't have great talent, he had great strength. He was a mammoth tree trunk of a man with huge hands that enveloped another man's when they shook. He had a back as wide as a refrigerator, legs you could build a bank on, and a physique like Steve Garvey, if Garvey were four inches taller, weighed another fifty pounds, and had a chest that expanded

73

to fifty-two inches! He hit the ball harder than any man who has ever played big-league baseball, even Ruth.

The way Gehrig swung a bat can only be described as savage. He didn't just hit a ball, he clubbed it. He hit shots at opposing infielders that literally tore the gloves right off their hands.

When Lou Gehrig retired he held twenty-five different major league records, including most career grand slams with 23. He led the league four times in runs scored and RBIs, and his 184 RBIs in 1931 is still an American League record.

If Ruth was the king, then Gehrig was the crown prince.

Mrs. Claire Ruth: "From the beginning he was simply a gorgeous hitter. My husband's long drives were much like his swing—gracefully arching balls that seemed to flow from a bat that, in turn, was flowing effortlessly, propelled by a gracefully twisting body.

"Lou hit that ball like a Mack truck running into a stone wall at 100 miles an hour. You could see mighty muscles tensing and exploding under his taut uniform. He personified power, and his line drives literally screeched as they headed for the outfield or the bleachers.

"No opposing infielder liked to see either the Babe or Lou at bat. But they were physically far more afraid of Lou's bulletlike smashes. . . ."[1]

Bill Dickey: "He was a streak hitter. He'd go for days hitting line drive after line drive. Then suddenly he would stop, for no reason. He worried a lot about his hitting. He always had to be reassured. He could probably hit a ball harder in every direction than any man who ever played. Lou could hit hard line drives past an outfielder the way I hit hard line drives past an infielder. . . .

"Lou drove in 150 runs five different times. You know I never drove in 150 runs in my life."

Joe DiMaggio: "Gehrig was the type of ball player to command respect, even if you weren't his teammate. To see his broad back and muscular arms as he spread himself at the plate was to give the impression of power as no other ball player I ever saw gave it.

"I not only admired Lou but I was amazed by him. . . . I used to marvel that the other Yankees didn't jump up and yell every time they saw Lou hit one, even in practice, but the rest of the club took him for granted, too. I never saw such power, but as Lazzeri had remarked that first day I joined the club, 'Kid, you should have seen him when!' "[2]

GEHRIG, THE MAN

Born into a strict German family with an authoritative, doting mother and a humorless father, Gehrig was a shy, extremely quiet man of great character. But there was an underlying strain of insecurity that, coupled with his shyness, left many puzzled.

Benny Bengough: "He was a fine boy—his actions, his mannerisms. Everything he did. He was very congenial to everyone. You never heard him pop off or get mad or anything. He was wonderful to his folks—very devoted to his mother and dad. Just a good-living kid.

"He was shy for a while until he became a star. When he was in the shadow of Ruth, of course, he was young. He used to ask Ruth different things, have his advice. But as he got older, he became a little more outspoken, took over a little more than he did before. But he was a very modest guy. He was well met. Everyone liked the guy. He wasn't fresh. Just a nice guy, a nice boy.

"Lou liked fun, he'd go out and have fun with you. He'd go to banquets and make speeches. He wasn't a great orator but he could get up and talk. He eventually became a fellow who could do things on his feet if he wanted to. He wasn't a comedian or anything like that. He'd just talk baseball.

"And he used to treat the kids wonderful. When he was first with the Yankees he'd go down after a ball game and play stickball with 'em in the park near his house—Morningside Park."

Ben Chapman: "We used to have a regular card game on the train and Dusty Cooke and the Babe and Gehrig and I would play hearts. Of course, Babe was the extrovert and Lou was a little subdued. He wasn't what you'd call a real

introvert. He was just a regular good man. Just a good man.
If you can say that about anybody, you've covered the
waterfront."

Mrs. Claire Ruth: "Babe wanted to go on the town when
he could. Lou wanted to build a home for his folks in the
suburbs and get home to them just as soon as the ball game
was over. Babe hated authority. Lou accepted it as just and
right. Babe loved people. Lou was a loner, his early shyness
replaced by suspicion that came with success.

"Who knows who was right? Surely Babe was ridiculous
when he left a ten-dollar tip where fifty cents would have
been generous. But Lou's dimes were just as silly."[3]

Mrs. Eleanor Gehrig: "On the sports field, Lou was as
good as anybody and better than most. Off the field, he was
terribly shy and insecure. He was afraid of his father, he
loved his mother. His father's word, backed up by a Teutonic
fist, was law. So Lou and his mother became allies in a kind
of resistance. Not much money, not much joy. . . .

"He wasn't simply the strong, silent type; he was vulnerable, easily hurt, quickly cut. So much so that when he
thought he had treated me brusquely, he'd go around the
house and refuse to talk to me for what seemed like hours. By
then, I was thoroughly rattled and wondering what I had
done to *him*. I am not the silent type, and I would soon be
begging for his forgiveness for whatever I might have done,
real or imagined. But then, it would turn out that he really
had been suffering through a little spell of self-rebuke, exiling
himself and not me, sulking at his own moodiness.

"What he needed badly was confidence, building up; he
was absolutely anemic for kindness and warmth. He had
never known the closeness of close love before, and when he
found it, he grew frightened to death that he might lose it. So
he needed constant reassurance, and I'd prop him up again
and again, until his next sinking spell. . . .

"I still hadn't come into close contact with the people or
problems *outside* that household, out there where I'd be
spending the rest of our life together.

"My first clue to *that* side of things came one day when it
rained, the Yankees got the day off and Lou came over to

[Lou's sister] Blanche's house early. That's when she came up with the perfect rainy-day idea: Why not spend the day in some place like Macy's basement getting together some of the things we were going to need when we got down to the really practical, bread-and-butter chores of keeping our own house—like kitchen utensils? We had not yet come down to earth long enough to think about little items like knives and forks. So the three of us drove into town, parked the car and headed into Macy's basement.

"I got my wish, all right. We had just about entered the place when we were surrounded by bodies, dozens of them drawing a bead on the one and only Lou Gehrig as he walked the aisles of the store hunting bargains in spoons. It turned into a mob scene . . . until Lou did what any red-blooded American boy would do under those pressing circumstances: He turned and got the hell out of there. Straight into the men's room. So Blanche and I pulled ourselves together while the mob dispersed, got our hair patted down, and started buying things left and right while Mr. Hero languished in the john. We finally rescued him and drove him home."[4]

Frank O'Rourke: "Gehrig had walked and Tony Lazzeri hit to short. I went over to the bag to pivot on the play and I thought a truck hit me. The interference was so obvious that Billy Evans, who was umpiring, allowed the double play at once. When I picked myself up, Gehrig was trotting to the Yankee bench, which was on the third base side of the park in those days.

"I yelled some names at him—strong names, too, which was customary in that era—and Gehrig stopped and started back to me. I figured this was the end but Harry Heilmann came in from right field and shouldered Gehrig away from me. I never was so glad to see a guy in my life as I was to see Harry. The next day I was at second base in the pregame infield practice for the Tigers and I happened to look up and there's Lou standing behind first base with his arms folded. He was looking straight at me as though he was going to bore a hole through me. Our bench was on the first base side and I would have to pass Gehrig to get to it.

"I fielded grounders as long as I could but realized I

couldn't stand out there all day, so I finally tossed my glove aside and started for our bench. Gehrig took a few steps to meet me, put out his right hand and said, 'Frank, I'm sorry I went into you so hard yesterday. I shouldn't have done it.'

"I shook his hand as warmly as if he had been the President and said, 'Forget about those names I called you, young fellow.' We were firm friends forever after."[5]

On the field Gehrig was a team man. Everything he did he did in order to help the Yankees win. He was a Yankee in the grand tradition, representing an organization of dignity with a quiet confidence and a raging will to win.

Stanley Frank: "Lou was not the best player the Yankees ever had. Ruth was number one by any yardstick, DiMaggio a more accomplished performer. Yet Lou was the most valuable player the Yankees ever had because he was a prime source of their greatest asset—an implied confidence in themselves and in every man on the club. Lou's pride as a big leaguer rubbed off on everyone who played with him."

Paul Gallico: "There is no greater inspiration to any American boy than Lou Gehrig. For if this awkward, inept, and downright clumsy player that I knew in the beginning could through sheer drive and determination turn himself into the finest first-base-covering machine in all baseball, then nothing is impossible to any man or boy in the country."

Bob Shawkey: "The year I had the ball club, we were rebuilding. We had some new faces, especially in the infield. Connie [Mack] had put together another great team in Philadelphia, with Foxx, Grove, Simmons, Cochrane, and those fellows, and we had to make some changes if we were going to keep up with them. That caused a little problem for Gehrig. He was so used to all those good boys throwing strikes to first base that he'd got into the habit of taking his foot off of the bag too quickly. Because he knew the ball was going to be there, you see. Well, with some of the new boys the pegs weren't always so good, and he was getting off the bag to catch them and then not getting back on.

"'Lou,' I told him one time, 'someday you're going to cost

us a close ball game doing that. You'd better keep that foot on the bag as long as you can.'

" 'These boys don't throw that ball as accurate as some of the other ones did,' he said.

" 'I know that,' I said. 'But that doesn't make any difference. You've got to keep that foot on the bag because one of these days they're going to call it against you.'

"Well, one day in Chicago we lost a 1–0 ball game because of that. When we got into the clubhouse, all I said to him was, 'There's that game I told you about, Lou.' He sat down on the bench and cried like a baby. He was that type. Very sensitive boy. Later on, after he'd had his dinner, he came up to my room and apologized, promised it would never happen again. And it didn't. He stuck to it after that."[6]

IN THE SHADOW OF THE BABE

Lou Gehrig played and lived in Babe Ruth's abundant shadow. Ruth was not just the most famous baseball player in the 1920s but probably the most famous human being on earth. Everyone knew him in Europe, Japan, and certainly in every burg in America. Gehrig was famous, all right, but his flame was obscured by the tremendous wattage of Ruth's spotlight.

Arthur Daley: "To me a part of the tragedy of his career was that he never escaped from the shadow of Babe Ruth. It was his fate to remain under that shade. If there had been no Bambino, the Iron Horse might never have been challenged as one of the brightest of all stars. He had a lifetime average of .340. But Ruth's was .342. See what I mean?

"In 1931 the home run champion should have been Gehrig with 47 to Ruth's 46. So what happened? With Lynn Lary on base larrupin' Lou larruped one into the stands. Lary inexplicably let the notion creep into his head that the fielder had caught the ball. Since there were two out at the time, he rounded third base and headed for the dugout. Gehrig modestly jogged with downcast eyes around the paths and never looked up until he'd crossed the plate. That made him out for passing a base runner and his home run disappeared from the books. So all he could do was tie the Babe for the home run championship. That's the way it always seemed to go."

Benny Bengough: "See, Babe got most of the publicity. Lazzeri hit a couple of home runs one day and Babe hit one and it came out in the papers, BABE RUTH HITS HOME RUN. But nothing was said about Lazzeri—except down in the little print. And they used to kid about it. They'd say, 'Geez, I hit two home runs, I get nothing. He gets one, he gets all the headlines.'

"Of course that's what Babe was getting paid for. You were under a shadow when you had a fellow like that because he was the one they were paying the money to. He was the one drawing the crowds. Even Gehrig when he was going great, he never got the publicity Babe did. See, Babe was such a colorful figure. Not just the homers but the things he did. He was always in a jam. He was always good copy."

Lou Gehrig: "I'm not a headline guy, and we might as well face it. I'm just a guy who's in there every day. The fellow who follows the Babe in the batting order. When Babe's turn at bat is over, whether he strikes out or belts a home run, the fans are still talking about him when I come up. If I stood on my head at the plate, nobody'd pay any attention."

Despite the difference in personalities and the fact that Gehrig never got the credit he surely deserved, lost amid the pile of Ruth's press clippings, the two titans of baseball in the 1920s were good friends.

Mrs. Eleanor Gehrig: "Lou admired Babe as a ball player. You had to, he was superb. Lou liked him as a man, too, and got a kick out of his shenanigans—even though he didn't want to copy them, and couldn't. I think Babe liked Lou as much as he liked anybody. For a time, they were even roommates. Before that, Babe's roommates had been selected by the team in the hope that they might exert some good influence on him; instead, he exerted some of his own rousing influence on them. No curfew and no set of training rules was invented that could hold Babe down."[7]

Eventually the Ruth-Gehrig friendship cooled and then turned bitter. Perhaps it was inevitable when two idols collided, especially when one of them got all the headlines. Bill Dickey, however, though circumspect because of his love for Gehrig, hinted that something else was at the heart of the quarrel between the two men. Gehrig, it seemed, had been courting a very beautiful woman and Ruth met her and with his charisma just swept her away, right out of Gehrig's arms. The sensitive, insecure Gehrig apparently never forgave Ruth.

Bill Dickey: "I really don't like to talk about the relationship between Ruth and Gehrig. It just is unpleasant to think about even now. When I went up there they were good friends and they kidded each other a lot and they got along fine. Then something happened. I don't want to tell you about it. They were never friends again. You know that famous picture of Babe hugging Lou when Lou had that retirement ceremony at the stadium in 1939? Well, Babe put his arms around Lou and hugged him but, if you look close, Lou never put his arm around the Babe. Lou just never forgave him."[8]

7

Prelude to Greatness

After two miserable seasons the 1926 Yankees were not expected to contend for the pennant. But their pitching staff was solid, and they had Ruth and Meusel in the outfield and the veteran Dugan at third. Gehrig, who was still unproven, was starting his first full season at first; Tony Lazzeri, a rookie, was at second; Koenig, a second-year man, was at short; and Combs, another sophomore, was in center. None of the experts gave the Yanks much of a chance to rebuild in one short year. Huggins knew he had to take some chances after the slump of '24 and the debacle of '25.

Every one of those unproven starters turned in championship performances, and the Yanks, who had barely escaped the cellar in 1925, went all the way to the top in 1926, winning their fourth pennant and the first of three in a row. The 1926 team, though no one knew it then, was the prelude to the greatest teams baseball had ever seen—the 1927 and 1928 Yankees.

Waite Hoyt: "I'll never forget 1925. We'd had four great seasons without a replacement, and in that fifth season—1925 —we were tired. A team can get tired just as an individual gets tired. We were tired of the pressure of being on top; tired of the pressure of having everyone try so hard against us.

"It was still a good ball club, but we seemed to lose our desire. We had bickering and fights. We thought we should have won our fourth straight pennant in 1924 and thought it was an accident that we didn't. Nobody bothered to make any changes; nobody realized the team was falling apart.

"But in 1926 Lou Gehrig started at first base, then came Earl Combs and Mark Koenig and Tony Lazzeri.

"It sure was great to be young and to be a Yankee."[1]

The Yankees didn't run away with the pennant in 1926. They weren't the greatest team yet. They were up by ten games in mid-June, but Cleveland, led by Tris Speaker, slowly closed the gap. By mid-September the Yankees led the Indians by four games, with a six-game series scheduled in Cleveland. When the Yanks lost four out of the first five games, the young players seemed to panic. Waite Hoyt, sensing the sinking-ship mentality of his raw teammates, quipped, "I would offer to buy their World Series shares cheap, but I'm afraid some of them might take me up on it."

Mike Gazella, a tough veteran utility infielder, let them have it at a dinner after the Yanks had lost their fourth game in a rout to the Indians.

"You fellows have been kidding me about the old college spirit ever since I have been on this ball club. If you gutless son of a bitches had a little of it, you wouldn't have quit as you did out there this afternoon."

That seemed to spark the team. They won the next day, to up their lead to two games, and held off Cleveland in the stretch to eke out the pennant.

Gehrig batted .313 and rookie Lazzeri drove in 114 runs. Babe Ruth, who had gone on a training regimen in the off-season and came to spring training in the best shape of his career, batted .372 with 47 homers (the runner-up to Ruth had but 19) and 155 RBIs.

Despite all this power, it was probably the Yankees' first-rate pitching staff that got them to the Series. Waite Hoyt, a nine-year veteran at only twenty-seven years old, won sixteen games. Urban Shocker, who pitched with a broken finger, won nineteen. "The broken finger may not be pretty to look at," Shocker said, "but it has been useful to me. It hooks over a baseball just right, so I can get a fine break on my slow ball, and that's one of the best balls I throw."

The ace of the staff, however, was Hall of Famer Herb Pennock, who won twenty-three games that season. Pennock was easily the greatest left-hander in baseball at the time. Once a scatter-armed thrower, Pennock had become a pitcher whose control was lengendary. He had a graceful, easy motion that belied the speed of his fastball. His arm flowed gracefully toward the batter, and suddenly his screamer would shoot past the batter.

Babe Ruth: "He was a left-handed Mathewson. Though weighing little more than 165 pounds, he had one of the easiest, most graceful deliveries of any pitcher I have ever known. Certainly Rube Waddell and Lefty Grove had more smoke, but they didn't have Pennock's class. He was a real artist on the mound, doing with his artistry what Waddell and Grove did with their superior speed."[2]

Miller Huggins: "If you were to cut that bird's head open, the weakness of every batter in the league would fall out."

Ben Chapman: "[Lefty] Gomez came up when I did. He couldn't hit the grandstand the first two games he pitched in St. Pete. Wild as a March hare, and he was a skinny kid about 150 pounds. But he learned how to pitch. I give Herb Pennock credit for that. Of course, I gave Pennock credit for a lot of things.

"You know Pennock had five different pitches—slow, slower, slower, slower, and slowest. He never threw the same speed to the hitter on consecutive pitches. In my opinion Herb was the smartest baseball man I ever knew. For instance, when we got Robin Roberts over in Chicago I was the manager then. Pennock went to work on that boy and showed him change of speeds, mixing pitches, how to keep the hitter off-balance. He made Roberts.

"Herb was also one of the best friends I ever had. There's his picture up there on the wall. He was one of the best men I ever knew. Of course, I'd have to say that—he hired me to manage his club."

Herb Pennock: "The first commandment is observation. Look around, notice the little quirks in the batter, and notice your own quirks. Your doctor never stops learning. The great pitcher imitates him."

ALEX THE GREAT AND THE 1926 WORLD SERIES

Even though the Yankees hadn't exactly stormed the opposition on their way to the pennant, they were heavily favored over the St. Louis Cardinals in the 1926 World Series. The Cards, led by Rogers Hornsby, had won their first National League flag ever, despite having the lowest winning percentage for a pennant winner in baseball history, stumbling home at .578. Lucky to get to the Series, they were given little chance of taking home the big prize. But behind the amazing pitching of the great Grover Cleveland Alexander, the Cards took the Yankees to seven games. Then, leading the final game 3–2 in the seventh inning, the Cards called on forty-year-old Alexander for the third time.

Les Bell: "With two out they loaded the bases against Haines, and Tony Lazzeri was up. Haines was a knuckleball pitcher. He held that thing with his knuckles and he threw it hard and he threw it just about all the time. Well, his fingers had started to bleed from all the wear and tear, so he called a halt. Rog and the rest of us walked over to the mound.

" 'Can you throw it anymore?' Rog asked him.

" 'No,' Jess said. 'I can throw the fastball but not the knuckler.'

" 'Well,' Hornsby said, 'we don't want any fastballs to this guy.'

"You see, we had been throwing Lazzeri nothing but breaking balls away and had been having pretty good luck with him.

"So Rog said, 'Okay, I'm going to bring in Pete,' which is what we sometimes called Alexander."[3]

When Alexander, the tired old veteran, shuffled in from the pen to face Lazzeri, the rookie sensation, one of the most dramatic moments in baseball history was about to take place.

Tony Lazzeri was a soft-spoken San Francisco Italian known as the quiet man of the Yankees. "Interviewing that guy," said one writer, "is like trying to mine coal with a nail file and a pair of scissors."

Though he was tall and slight, Lazzeri was very strong. For years he had worked as a hot riveter in his father's boiler shop, and he had the forearms of a blacksmith. In 1925 in the Pacific Coast League, Lazzeri hit 60 homers and drove in an eye-popping 222 runs! In 1926, his rookie season with the Yanks, he smashed 18 homers and had 114 RBIs. Most experts credit Lazzeri with pulling the Yankees together that year.

Sad Sam Jones: "Tony was an epileptic, you know. They say that's how he died: had a seizure and fell down the cellar steps. He had one of those spells most every spring on the trip back north. But never during a game. Tony was a very witty guy, full of fun. Quiet, but always up to something. A real nice guy. And a great second baseman, too. . . . He was an awful strong fellow. He had real big muscles on him. He could hit a ball as far in right field as he could in left.

"How they can keep leaving him out of the Hall of Fame is beyond me."[4]

Lazzeri performed best in the clutch. When you needed him most, "Poosh 'em up" Tony could really push those base runners up the bases with timely hits. And what the Yankees needed now as Alexander came strolling in from the pen was a clutch hit.

Grover Cleveland Alexander: "Well, I was sitting around in the bull pen, not doing anything, when someone said, 'He wants you in there, Pete.' I didn't find out what had happened until after the game. The bull pen in Yankee Stadium is under the bleachers, and when you're down there you can't see what's going on out on the field. All you know is what you learn from the yells of the fans overhead.

"So when I came out from under the bleachers, I see the bases filled, and Lazzeri's standing in the box. Tony is up there all alone with everyone in that Sunday crowd watching him. I say to myself, 'Take your time. Lazzeri isn't feeling any too good up there. Let him stew.' "

Les Bell: "We were all standing on the mound waiting for him—me and Rogers Hornsby and Tommy Thevenow and Jim Bottomley and Bob O'Farrell. When Alec reached the mound, Rog handed him the ball and said, 'There's two out and they're drunk'—meaning the bases were loaded—'and Lazzeri's the hitter.'

" 'Okay,' Alec said. 'I'll tell you what I'm gonna do. I'm gonna throw the first one inside to him. Fast.'

" 'No, no,' Rog said. 'You can't do that.'

"Alec nodded his head very patiently and said, 'Yes I can. Because if I do and he swings at it he'll most likely hit it on the handle, or if he does hit it good it'll go foul. Then I'm going to come outside with my breaking pitch.'

"Rog looked him over for a moment, then gave Alec a slow smile and said, 'Who am I to tell *you* how to pitch?'

"Then, to show you what kind of pitcher Alec was and what kind of thinking he did out there, he said, 'I've got to get Lazzeri out. Then in the eighth inning I've got to get Dugan, I've got to get Collins, and I've got to get Pennock or whoever hits for him, one, two, three. Then in the ninth I've got to get Combs and I've got to get Koenig, one, two, so when that big son of a bitch comes up there'—meaning Ruth, of course—'the best he can do is tie the ball game.' He had it figured out that Ruth was going to be the last hitter in the ninth inning. . . .

"There are so many legends associated with that game. For instance, they say Alec was drunk, or hung over, when he came in. And they say that Hornsby walked out to left field to meet him, to look in his eyes and make sure they were clear. And so on. All a lot of bunk. It's too bad they say these things. Now in the first place, if you stop to think about it, no man could have done what Alec did if he was drunk or even a little soggy. Not the way his mind was working and not the way he pitched. It's true that he was a drinker and that he had a problem with it. Everybody knows that. But he was not

drunk when he walked into the ball game that day. No way.
No way at all, for heaven's sake. And as far as Hornsby
walking out to meet him, that's for the birds too. Rog met
him at the mound, same as all the rest of us.

"So after the conference on the mound we all went back to
our positions and Alec got set to work. Sure enough, the first
pitch to Lazzeri is the fastball in tight, not a strike. Well, Tony
jumped at it and hit the hell out of it, a hard drive down the
left field line. Now, for fifty years that ball has been traveling.
It has been foul anywhere from an inch to twenty feet,
depending on who you're listening to or what you're reading.
But I was standing on third base and I'll tell you—it was foul
all the way. All the way."[5]

Benny Bengough: "I was in the bull pen down in the left
field corner. We all thought it was a home run. But it went
around the pole foul by, oh, I'd say, probably a foot. Not
over a foot.

"He was a terrific drinker. Everybody knew that. He'd
drink while he was pitching. I can't recommend that to kids. I
don't know what Alex would have been if he didn't drink. A
lot of the fellows in those days if they didn't drink it would
have made a difference with them because when they drank it
made 'em loosen up. You can relax when you have a few
drinks. But you still have to get the ball over the plate.

"Alex could see the plate because he could hit the eye of a
needle with the ball. Most of the games he pitched he was
under the influence."

Grover Cleveland Alexander: "There was a crack and I
knew the ball was hit hard, but the drive had a tail-end fade
and landed foul by eight-ten feet. . . .

"There have been all kinds of stories that I celebrated the
night before and had a hangover when Rog called me from
the bull pen to pitch to Lazzeri; that isn't the truth. After I
had beaten the Yankees the day before, Rog came over to me
in the clubhouse and said, 'Alex, if you want to celebrate
tonight, I wouldn't blame you. But go easy; I may need you
tomorrow.'

"I said, 'Okay, Rog, I'll tell you what I'll do. I'll ride back
to the hotel with you and I'll meet you tomorrow and ride out

to the park with you.' Hell, I wanted to get that big end of the Series money as much as anyone. I had a few drinks at the hotel on Saturday night, but I was cold sober when I faced Lazzeri."[6]

Bob O'Farrell: "I don't believe Alex was much of a drinker before he went into the army. After he got back from the war, though, he had a real problem. When he struck out Lazzeri he'd been out on a drunk the night before and was still feeling the effects. See, Alex had pitched for us the day before and won. He had beaten the Yankees in the second game of the World Series, and *again* in the sixth game, pitching the complete game both times. He was thirty-nine years old then, and naturally wasn't expecting to see any more action.

"Alex didn't really intend to take a drink that night. But some of his *friends* got hold of him and thought they were doing him a favor by buying him a drink. Well, you weren't doing Alex any favor by buying him a drink, because he just couldn't stop.

"So in the seventh inning of the seventh game, Alex is tight asleep in the bull pen, sleeping off the night before, when trouble comes. . . .

"Well, the first pitch is a perfect low curve for strike one. But the second one comes in high, and Tony smacks a vicious line drive that lands in the left-field stands but just foul. Oh, it's foul by maybe ten feet. Actually, from home plate I can see it's going to be foul all the way, because it's curving from the time it got halfway out there. Of course, I'm giving it plenty of body english too, just to make sure.

"The next pitch was a low outside curve and Tony Lazzeri stuck out. Fanned him with three pitches.

"Most people seem to remember that as happening in the ninth inning and ending the ball game. It didn't. It was only the seventh inning and we had two innings still to go. In the eighth Alex set down the Yankees in order, and the first two men in the ninth. But then, with two out in the bottom of the ninth, he walked Babe Ruth. Bob Meusel was next up, but on the first pitch to him the Babe took off for second. Alex pitched, and I fired the ball to Hornsby and caught Babe stealing, and *that* was the last out of the game and the Series.

"You know, I wondered why Ruth tried to steal second then. A year or two later I went on a barnstorming trip with the Babe and I asked him. Ruth said he thought Alex had forgotten he was there. Also that the way Alex was pitching they'd never get two hits in a row off him, so he better get in position to score if they got one. Well, maybe that was good thinking and maybe not. In any case, I had him out a mile at second."[7]

Waite Hoyt: "To make matters worse after that ball game we all came up to the Yankee Stadium the next day after losing the Series to get our effects and we started asking each other, 'Did you lose any money yesterday?'

"Somebody had gotten in the clubhouse and picked all the pockets. Sixty to ninety bucks apiece!"

Grover Cleveland Alexander: "There must be a hundred versions of what happened in the Yankee Stadium that dark, chilly afternoon. It used to be that everywhere I went, I'd hear a new one, and some were pretty farfetched. So much so that two or three years ago I ran across Lazzeri in San Francisco and said: 'Tony, I'm getting tired of fanning you.' And Tony answered: 'Maybe you think I'm not?' "[8]

Miller Huggins: "Here was the man who really made the 1926 club, and all people ever said about him was that Alexander struck him out. He was a tower of strength to Gehrig and Koenig when they were unsure of themselves. Everybody forgets that Tony's second strike against Alex was a foul ball down the left-field line which would have been a grand-slammer if it had stayed fair. Anybody can strike out, but ball players like Lazzeri come along once in a generation."

8

The Greatest of Them All

The 1927 Yankees have been picked by most experts as the greatest team of all time. By any yardstick there are some very persuasive arguments to back that claim. They were the only team in the first century of baseball who went wire to wire in first place to win the pennant. (Only the 1984 Detroit Tigers have matched that feat.) The Yankees won 110 games, a record at that time, to finish a whopping 19 games ahead of second-place Cleveland, another record. They had already clinched the pennant by Labor Day, when they led by 24 games with 23 to play, also a record.

The Yankees, of course, had Gehrig and Ruth, without doubt the two greatest players at their positions in history, each enjoying one of the best years of their careers while batting back-to-back in the lineup. Ruth set the home-run mark, whacking the famous and fabulous total of 60 round-trippers. He also managed to hit .356 even though he obviously was swinging for the fences. Gehrig grew to superstardom that year, batting .373 with 175 RBIs. He also ripped 47 home runs, more than any other man had ever hit besides Ruth. But then, whoever said Ruth was merely a man.

91

The rest of the players in the Yankee lineup, almost without exception, had their best years. Lazzeri hit .309 with 102 RBIs and 18 homers (third in the league behind Gehrig and Ruth). Combs, the greatest lead-off man in Yankee history and one of the greatest defensive center fielders ever, hit a hefty .356. Muscleman Meusel hit .337 and knocked in 103 runs.

In all, the '27 Yanks hit 158 home runs, a new record. Philadelphia had the next highest total that year with 56! So Ruth alone hit more than any other *team* in 1927. The Yankees also led the league in hits, triples, RBIs, walks, batting average, and slugging percentage.

The pitching staff was like a machine, rolling through opponents with businesslike efficiency. The mainstays of Huggins's mound corps—Herb Pennock, Waite Hoyt, and Urban Shocker—had brilliant years. Hoyt went 22–7, Pennock was 19–8, and Shocker was 18–6. Dutch Ruether, acquired from Washington in mid-season, went 13–6, and George Pipgras, called up from the minors, had a fine rookie season, finishing 10–3.

But by far the biggest pitching story of the year was Wilcy Moore. Moore, a relief pitcher whom Barrow plucked from the Carolina League, had one very great year in the major leagues—1927. He went 19–7 and saved game after game for the World Champions.

Moore was an Oklahoma farm boy who pitched for six years in obscurity until, while recovering from a broken wrist, he developed a deadly sinker. In 1926, at the age of thirty, he won thirty games in the South Atlantic League, and that's when Ed Barrow took notice of the lanky, balding sidearmer. Barrow figured any pitcher who could win thirty games in the tough Sally League could do all right in the Bigs.

Babe Ruth: "I don't know where Moore was when all the scouts were gumshoeing around those parts, because he was just about the best pitcher in our league in 1927. Hug used him mostly as a relief man, but he was just as good as a starter, winning nineteen games and coming up with the best earned-run average in the league.

"Wilcy was a farmer who had some cotton acres in Oklahoma. He was a big, easygoing, good-natured guy and the lousiest hitter in baseball history. I took a look at him the first day he worked for us and laid him $300 to $100 he wouldn't get three hits all season. It looked like a cinch, but the double-crosser bore down through the last half of the season and finished with five hits.

"Wilcy took the $300 and bought a pair of mules. He named one Babe and the other Ruth, which probably surprised both of them."[1]

Only the 1954 Cleveland Indians, with their overpowering pitching staff of Bob Feller, Bob Lemon, Al Lopez, and Mike Garcia, won more games in a season (111), but that team cannot be seriously considered alongside the '27 Yanks because they did not win the World Championship that year. While the Yankees crushed the Pirates in four straight in the 1927 World Series, in 1954 the Indians met the New York Giants and the catch-everything Willie Mays and got embarrassed in a four-game sweep.

In 1927 the Yankees did all the embarrassing.

Babe Ruth: "Those Yankees were the best team. Figure it out. After we got going we won twelve straight World Series games—twelve in a row. It was murder. The Yankees had the greatest punch baseball ever knew. We never even worried five or six runs behind. Ruth-Gehrig-Lazzeri-Combs-Dickey —wham, wham, and wham!—no matter who was pitching."

Joe Dugan: "It's always the same. Combs walks. Koenig singles. Ruth hits one out of the park. Gehrig doubles. Lazzeri triples. Then Dugan goes in the dirt on his can."

Paul Gallico: "I used to sit in the press box with my heart in my throat, my palms sweaty, my mouth all dry and cottony, and my nerves prickly and on edge, watching the Yankees play. It was like when I was a kid and there used to be a lot of blasting going on down on Park Avenue where they were digging out the cut for the New York Central tracks. There would be a laborer with a box with a plunger handle, and they would spread the mats and get ready to dynamite. There would be a nerve-racking suspense and what seemed like an interminable wait. But then there would be one hell of a big *boom* and chunks of Park Avenue would go flying through the air. Well, it was just like that with the 1927 Yankees. You never knew when that batting order was going to push the handle down. But when it went, you could hear the explosion all the way to South Albany, and when the smoke cleared away, the poor old opposing pitcher wouldn't be there anymore. And Yankees would be legging it over the plate with runs, sometimes in single file but more often in bunches of twos and threes as home runs cleared the bases and they could get together and chat comfortably on the way in."

Waite Hoyt: "You must understand that Huggins developed as a manager in the same way that ball players develop as ball players. He handled each player differently, and by 1927 one of the things that inadvertently meshed was the personalities of the fellows playing on that club. We all got along. We had inordinate pride in ourselves as a unit. We believed in ourselves as a unit. . . .

"The '27 Yankees were an exceptional team because they met every demand. There wasn't any requirement that was necessary at any particular moment that they weren't up to. . . .

"It was a team that didn't often beat itself. Most baseball is a play on errors. In other words, the pitcher looks for the deficiency in a batter. And he works on that, he tries to capitalize on the weakness of his opponent. So many times you beat yourself. Once in a while, you take a walloping, but the 1927 Yankees probably beat themselves less than any ball club that ever lived.

"When we were challenged, when we had to win, we stuck together and played with a fury and determination that could only come from team spirit. We had a pride in our performance that was very real. It took on the form of snobbery. We felt we were superior people, and I do believe we left a heritage that became a Yankee tradition."[2]

Mark Koenig: "Just putting on a Yankee uniform gave me a little confidence, I think. That club could carry you. You were better than you actually were. If I'd been with a tail-end club the year I went up, I don't think I'd have been around for 1927."

THE BAMBINO HITS SIXTY

The real drama that year was not for the pennant. It was between the two Sultans of Swat, Gehrig and Ruth, to see who could break the Bambino's own fantastic total of fifty-nine home runs in one season, set back in 1921.

Gehrig was in his prime by now, and he matched the Bambino home run for home run right through the middle of August. On August 10 Lou, in fact, led Babe 38 to 35. But then the Babe picked up the pace, as only the Babe could. While Gehrig hit only 9 the rest of the way, Ruth knocked out 25 in the last forty-two games. At that pace Ruth would have hit nearly 100 homers over a full season.

On September 30, 1927, in the next to the last game of the season, he faced Tom Zachary of the Washington Senators. The Babe had socked 3 homers in the last three games to reach 59. Zachary pitched to him cautiously.

Tom Zachary: "I was pitching my best. After I served him four balls in the first inning, I said to myself, 'Well, Babe, if you want to hit any homers today, you'd better start swinging.' I had made up my mind I wasn't going to give him a good pitch all afternoon. The ball Babe hit for his sixtieth homer was the kind of ball no other batter would even have tried for. It was a curve ball, high, straight at him. You might call it a bean ball. The score was tied. There was one out and a man on third. I wanted to get the Babe away from the plate. Instead of stepping back, he waded right into the ball. He lunged for it before it ever got over the plate and pulled it around into the stands. I don't see yet how he did it. He never hit a worse ball in his life. Not one that would be more difficult to hit into the stands."[3]

Benny Bengough: "See, the funny thing about it is, we never figured 60 was going to stand. We felt Babe Ruth might hit 65 the next year because, see, he was the only real home run hitter. And Babe never really thought about it. He never figured I'll hit 90 home runs this year or 60 or whatever. He just hit the home runs. He hit 60 and I imagine the next year Babe figured, well, I'll probably hit 65 or 70—who knows?

He never hit that many again, but we thought he might. So it wasn't that important.

"The 60 didn't mean that much to me at the time because I caught that game and I didn't remember that until years later when someone mentioned it to me. We didn't have a big celebration because he was only breaking his own record. Babe never bothered about it. He figured, if I played tomorrow I might hit another. He had no one to battle."

FOUR STRAIGHT

The mighty Yanks took Pittsburgh four straight in the 1927 World Series, but first, before they beat them, they scared the Pirates to death. Or so the story goes.

Babe Ruth: "We won the World Series before it even started. The Pirates were the other club, and the first two games were scheduled for Forbes Field. Naturally we showed up a day early and worked out in the strange park—and we won the Series during that workout.

"You see, the Pirates had held their own practice first, and then they had had a little pep meeting and started back to their homes and hotels.

"But by the time they came out of their dressing room, to start away from the park, the Yankees were taking batting practice. Most of them had never seen us, so they draped themselves here and there in the empty stands and took a look. Manager Donie Bush should have insisted that they go right home.

"The 1927 Pirates had some darn good ball players: the Waners, Pie Traynor, Glenn Wright, old Joe Harris, and a good pitching staff. But you could actually hear them gulp while they watched us.

"We really put on a show. Lou and I banged ball after ball into the right-field stands, and I finally knocked one out of the park in right center. Bob Meusel and Tony Lazzeri kept hammering balls into the left-field seats.

"One by one, the Pirates got up and left the park. Some of them were shaking their heads when we last saw them."[4]

Lloyd Waner: "Of course everybody knows that the 1927

Yankees are supposed to be the greatest team ever put together, what with Babe Ruth, Lou Gehrig, Earle Combs, Bob Meusel, Tony Lazzeri, and the rest of them. The famous story that has come out of the 1927 World Series concerns the first day, when we were supposed to have watched the Yankees taking batting practice.

"According to the story, which I have read and heard so many times, Paul and me and the rest of us were sitting there watching those big New Yorkers knock ball after ball out of sight and became so discouraged that we just about threw in the sponge right then and there. One story that I've read I don't know how many times has me turning to Paul and in a whispery voice saying, 'Gee, they're big, aren't they?'

"That was the story. Well, I don't know how that got started. If you want to know the truth, I never even saw the Yankees work out that day. We had our workout first and I dressed and was leaving the ballpark just as they were coming out on the field. I don't think Paul stayed out there either. We never spoke of it. I know some of our players stayed, but I never heard anybody talk about what they saw. I don't know where that story came from. Somebody made it up out of thin air, that's all I can say. Every time I hear that story I tell people it's not so, but it just keeps on going. I don't think Paul ever saw anything on a ball field that could scare him anyway. He was such a great hitter in his own right that he never had to take a backseat to anybody.

"This is not to say we weren't impressed by those Yankees during that Series. We sure were. They were just a fine ball club. . . ."[5]

1928, THE GREATEST TEAM—TAKE TWO

With virtually the same players as the great 1927 team, the 1928 Yankees took their third straight pennant. But they were not quite as devastating. Connie Mack was building another great team in Philadelphia, and the Yankees edged out the A's by two and a half games for the title.

It would have been asking a lot even for the greatest team of all time to match their magnificent '27 season, and, though it was another formidable year, most of the Yanks were off just a bit. Gehrig hit .374, a point higher than in 1927, but his homer production dropped from 47 to 27. His staggering total of 174 RBIs came down to a more human 142. Ruth had another Ruthian year, but how could he have matched 1927? Still he chalked up 54 home runs, hit .323, and drove in 142.

The rest of the lineup, however, was off more markedly. Injuries to Dugan (who was eventually shipped off to the Boston Braves in September) and Lazzeri, who missed forty games, hurt the infield. A rookie named Leo Durocher helped fill the defensive gap at second and short, but his batting was anemic. Combs suffered a sprained wrist, and Meusel was also hurt.

The pitching also fell off. Pipgras had his first great year, winning 24 games, and Hoyt added 23 more. But the magnificent years of Herb Pennock were behind him. Pennock notched 17 wins in '28 but he struggled throughout the year with an arm injury and would never pitch with his old brilliance again. Also Wilcy Moore, whose miracle season of a year before was the talk of baseball, hurt his arm, cooled off, and was just another arm in the bull pen. Worst of all, however, was the fate of Urban Shocker. Shocker developed a serious heart condition and went home in July to recuperate. He died before the season was over.

Despite their season-long struggle to win the pennant, the Yankees ripped through the St. Louis Cardinals in the World Series, winning four straight for eight World Series victories in a row. It was sweet revenge for the defeat the team had suffered to those same Cards in the '26 Series.

Ruth hit .625, a Series record, and belted three homers in one game. Gehrig hit .545 and smashed four homers. Together the two sluggers drove in fourteen runs and scored thirteen more. They were the whole show.

Babe Ruth: "I doubt if there ever was another train ride to match our wild ride out of St. Louis on the night of our great triumph. This wasn't a usual victory. When you win two straight World Series without the loss of a game it calls for something special.

"By midnight we were as crazy as a bunch of wild Indians. We paraded through the entire train and everyone had to sacrifice his shirt, if he was still up, or his pajama coat, if he had gone to bed. Not only the ball players were in this victory jamboree, but I remember Ford Frick, my ghostwriter, and Dick Vidmer were right up at the head of the parade with Lou and myself.

"Ruppert locked himself in his drawing room, but it was no go. He had another old geezer with him, a guy with a little goatee who we used to call Colonel Wattenburg. He was about the same age as Colonel Jake. We knocked at their door, and Jake called out, 'Go away; I've already turned in and want to get some sleep.'

" 'This is no night for sleeping,' I yelled through the door.

" 'Go away, "Root," ' Jake said.

"I gave Lou Gehrig a signal. We put our shoulders to the door and pushed right through the panel. I reached through, unlocked the door, and a moment later Lou, Pat Collins, several others, and myself tumbled into the room. I got away with Jake's lavender pajama coat and Gehrig undressed Wattenburg, carrying off the top of his pajamas as a souvenir.

"Little Huggins wasn't a drinking man. His digestion was bad and he couldn't stand hard liquor. But even he broke down on this night of nights, and the next morning he went through the train asking over and over again, 'Did anybody see my teeth?' "[6]

9

McCarthy

THE DEATH OF MILLER HUGGINS

The 1928 World Series was the last hurrah of the first great Yankee era. They had captured pennants six out of the last eight years and won three World Championships. But the Yankees would win only one more pennant in the next seven years.

Except for Ruth and Gehrig, who were still pounding the ball all over the lot in 1929, the only bright spot was the emergence of rookie catcher Bill Dickey. Dickey was a marvelously gifted athlete who would put in All-Star performances behind the plate for the Yankees for the next fifteen years. But the rest of the Yankee lineup slumped miserably, and the pitching staff, once the pride of the American League, sputtered rapidly downhill. Hoyt and Pennock were getting old and Koenig and Dugan were through. Huggins shuffled the infield around constantly, searching for a winning combination. Even rock-steady Bob Meusel, showing his years, hit a tired .261 and played in only 100 games that year and was sold the following year.

For some time Miller Huggins had been suffering from

neuritis, and due mostly to the pressures of trying to rally a fading Yankee team, he exhausted himself. In his weakened state erysipelas (blood poisoning) rampaged through his body. On September 20 he showed up at Yankee Stadium with an ugly blotch under his right eye. Feeling "rotten," he decided to skip the game and go home and rest. It was the last time his Yankee players ever saw him. The doctor took one look at Huggins and checked him into the hospital, but Hug was too far gone. He was dead five days later, at age forty-nine, leaving the Yankees bereft and without a great manager to lead them out of their doldrums.

Art Fletcher: "When Miller came into the clubhouse that morning he looked bad. He was laying under a heat lamp trying to bake this sort of boil out from under his eye. I swear he looked dead already. But none of us thought he'd die. We knew he hadn't been feeling so hot but we just didn't think. . . .

"We were right in the middle of a game at Fenway Park when we found out. They lowered the flags out in center, then Barrow came into the dugout and told us Hug had died. Well, that was maybe the saddest day I had in baseball. You gotta understand that team was a pretty hard-boiled bunch and it just shook 'em. We sat there a minute and then Combs just broke down and started crying and that broke the dam. There wasn't a dry eye in the dugout.

"I remember some writer came down and tried to ask Babe a few questions and he about tore his head off. Finally, after five, ten minutes we all just decided to get on with the game and we went out and beat the Red Sox. That was something. I remember it wasn't like we wanted to kill them. It was just a bunch of professionals doing their job the way Hug would have liked to see it done."

McCarthy TAKES OVER

Ruppert and Barrow chose Bob Shawkey to replace Huggins. Shawkey had been a steady performer on the mound for the Yankees until his retirement in 1927, but he was overmatched for the job as manager of the team. He had to follow the legendary Huggins and also, until only recently, he had been a teammate of most of the players. Discipline broke down early on the team as players defied Shawkey's curfew and ignored his rules.

The Yanks finished the 1930 season in third place, and though many people in baseball thought Shawkey had done a good job, third place was not good enough for Ruppert and Barrow. They decided to approach Joe McCarthy, who had only recently been fired from his position as manager of the Cubs.

After kicking around the minors as a player and manager for fifteen years, McCarthy won his first pennant in Louisville in 1921 and repeated in 1925. He then signed with William Wrigley, Jr., to manage the Chicago Cubs in 1926, and by 1929 he had brought Chicago the pennant. But the Cubs fell to second in 1930, and Wrigley fired McCarthy and promoted Rogers Hornsby, the veteran Cub second baseman, to manage the club.

McCarthy was bitterly upset by his dismissal. But in retrospect it was the best thing that could have happened because it left him free to take over the Yankees.

Joseph Vincent McCarthy was what the Yankees needed. He wanted to murder the opposition every time he got on the field. While Huggins took it easy on his players during spring training, McCarthy drove them mercilessly right from the start. McCarthy's teams were drilled in fundamentals. They made the double play, hit the cut-off man, and the pitcher fielded his position like a fifth infielder. If they made a mental error they were gone in short order.

And they knew their places off the field as well.

Lefty Gomez: "I think a lot of the Yankee success in those days was due to McCarthy's leadership. He was a tough guy but he really knew the game. We went through a lot of schooling with him. He was always trying to be perfect in everything, on and off the field. He didn't let guys smoke a pipe, and you had to wear a shirt and tie with a jacket on the road. He wouldn't let you get away with things like dungarees and T-shirts, the way some of the players come to the park these days. He couldn't stand shirts unbuttoned and hairy chests showing. He could really get on you for an open shirt. 'You don't go in a bank and see people with shirts unbuttoned and hairy chests,' he would say. He thought playing for the Yankees called for being the same kind of gentleman who would work in a bank."[1]

Tom Meany: "I was sitting with Joe one night in the lobby of the Hotel Hollenden in Cleveland, while a Yankee pitcher, of no particular skill, by the way, was wandering about the newsstand, examining the magazines and engaging in light chitchat with the girl behind the counter.

"'See him?' remarked Joe, pointing with his cigar to the pitcher. 'He's going to make a great show of buying a couple of magazines and then he's going to walk past us so I'll be sure to see him and he'll make some remark about getting caught up on his reading. Then he'll take the elevator to his room. Then he'll come down the service stairs and stay out half the night.'"[2]

Earle Combs: "That first spring when Joe took over in 1931 we got a good idea the way it was going to be. We played some minor league team at Waterfront Stadium the first game of spring training and we just ripped 'em up. It was like an execution. Gehrig put one over the centerfield wall, then Lazzeri put one out in right. Ruth came up the next inning with the bases full and hit one off the right field fence that bounced all the way back to the infield. The second baseman had to field it. By the time we were through we beat them 19 to 1—something like that.

"Well, after the game when we got on the bus we were feeling pretty good and Jimmy Reese, a second baseman just up from Triple-A, yells over to Joe.

"'Well, Joe, how'd you like that one?'

"And McCarthy turned around and looked at the whole damn bus-load of us like we were a troop of Girl Scouts out selling cookies and he about chewed Reese's head off.

"'Against a bunch of bums like that, you should have scored fifty runs!'

"That shut us up. No one said boo the whole ride. We just looked at each other. We knew right then there wasn't going to be no nonsense."

* * *

Tommy Henrich: "He had a phenomenal memory for facts and figures and for a ball player's strengths and weaknesses. I don't think that guy ever forgot anything. He told me a story one time, after he'd retired. Red Rolfe was managing the Tigers and Joe was managing the Red Sox. The Tigers were doing all right, but they might have been doing better. The Red Sox came in for a ball game and Rolfe invited McCarthy into his office to sit down and talk a little bit. Rolfe idolized McCarthy.

"'So I went over to his office,' Joe said, 'and we sat and chatted for a while. Then I noticed he had a lot of clipboards hanging around the office. I asked him what they were. He said they were records he was keeping. Records of what, I asked. Oh, he said, various things that had happened in ball games during the year. He liked to keep those records so he could refer back to them.'

"After telling me that, McCarthy looked at me and said, 'That's what his trouble is as a manager.'

"'What?' I asked.

"'He's got a lousy memory.'

"McCarthy didn't need any clipboards; he had it all upstairs, all the time. Remember Jimmy Wasdell? He came up to the major leagues with Washington in 1937, in the middle of the season. Now, I knew him; I'd played with him in the Mid-Atlantic League in 1935. He hit .357 that year. That guy could hit. He was a good friend and I was delighted when he came up.

"The next time we played Washington Charley Ruffing was the pitcher. He's sitting in the clubhouse looking at the Senators' lineup.

"'Who's this guy Wasdell?' he says. 'What do we know about him?'

"Well, as far as I knew, I was the only one on the club who had ever played with Wasdell, who knew anything about him. But I'm not that dumb; I'm not going to tell these wise guys how to pitch to Jimmy Wasdell. I've seen too many outfielders give well-meaning advice that exploded in somebody's face. But while I'm keeping quiet, McCarthy says, 'I know who he is. He's that kid that pinch-hit against us in Chattanooga when we came through there in the spring. He can't hit a change-up.' This is what McCarthy says.

"I looked at him. I couldn't believe it. To this day I can't believe he's that sharp, that he could size up and remember a man in one appearance in an exhibition game. The truth was, Wasdell *couldn't* hit a change-up. But I still don't believe a man can have that kind of memory. He *must* have called and got a scouting report on Wasdell when he heard Jimmy was joining the Senators. And if he did do that, then he was shrewd enough to sell us on the idea that he did indeed remember Wasdell from one at-bat in the spring."[3]

Tommy Henrich: "He knew everything that was going on, and when he didn't want you to know something, well, you just didn't know it. Art Fletcher was our third-base coach in those days and McCarthy would flash signs out to him. And do you know that no Yankee ball player ever knew what those signs were? Now, on any ball club, after a while the players know what signs the manager is using with the coaches. Not only did we never know them, but he never told anybody what they were and I don't suppose he ever will.

"Now, Gomez was pretty cute. You know all about the Great Gomez. One day he's sitting a few feet down the bench from McCarthy, watching out of the corner of his eye to see if he could pick up those signs. All of a sudden, without even looking at him, McCarthy says, 'Gomez, pay attention to the ball game. You can't get my signs.'"[4]

Earle Combs: "The first day he put me in center field I was so nervous I could hardly see straight—and I muffed the first ball that was hit to me. Joe never said a word to me when I went to the bench at the end of the inning, and he didn't say a word when, a couple of innings later, I booted a single into a couple of extra bases for the hitter. Finally, in the eighth inning, with the score tied and a couple of men on the bases, a hitter singled to center. As I saw the ball coming out to me, I said to myself, 'I will stop this ball if it kills me.'

"Well, it didn't kill me. But it went through my legs to the fence. As I went after it, I was tempted to keep right on going, climb the fence, and not stop running until I got back to Pebworth. But I couldn't do that. I had to get the ball, throw it in, finish out the game—and then go in the clubhouse and get dressed. But my mind was made up. I was through. If

McCarthy didn't fire me, I'd quit.

"He didn't say anything to me until I reached the clubhouse after the game. I guess he could tell how I felt by the way I looked. He came over to me and said, 'Forget it. I told you today that you were my center fielder. You still are.'

"And then he laughed and said, 'Listen. If I can stand it, I guess you can.'

"I think I can say that from that minute on I was a ball player."[5]

Joe Paparella: "I'll never forget something that happened in my first year [as umpire] in Yankee Stadium. I called a Yankee out at second, and out came Joe McCarthy, the manager. It was a Sunday afternoon, and there were probably fifty thousand fans there. He said, 'You know, young man, I've been telling the fellows what a hell of a chance you got of staying up here. You're going to be one of the greatest umpires. For God's sake, I don't know how you could miss that play.' Then he walked away. That's all he said, but the fans were really yelling and screaming at me. McCarthy didn't say anything, but he did put on a show to get them worked up. With his arms flapping and all, it looked like he was eating me alive. He got away with it, but if he had done that later in my career, I would have done something about it."[6]

Joe McCarthy: "No, I didn't get thrown out of many ball games. I learned early on that you couldn't do your ball club much good if you weren't there. I generally got along okay with the umpires. I remember one time I pulled a good one on Bill McGowan. We were playing Washington and Arndt Jorgens was catching—I used to put him in once in a while to give Dickey a rest. A runner slid into the plate and Jorgens tagged him and thought he had him, but McGowan called the man safe. Jorgens jumped up and pushed McGowan. Naturally McGowan ran him out of there.

"So I went up there and said to McGowan, 'Mac, what the hell did you put him out for?'

"'You saw what he did, didn't you?' he said.

"'Why, he just gave you a little push like that,' I said, and demonstrated it by giving him a push.

" 'Isn't that enough?' he asked.

" 'You mean to tell me,' I said, 'if a fellow gives you a little push like that'—and I demonstrated it again—'you're going to run him out of the game?'

"By this time the crowd was yelling like crazy. They didn't know what we were talking about. All they knew was that I was standing there pushing McGowan, and he wasn't doing anything about it. But then he got wise to it and said, 'Goddamnit, don't do that again.'

" 'Okay, Bill,' I said and winked at him and walked away. For the rest of the game, the fans were on him something awful for not having thrown me out. McGowan never let me forget that. Years later he'd say to me, 'You put one over on me that time, didn't you?' "[7]

Ben Chapman: "McCarthy was standoffish. He drew the line between the players and himself but he also knew when to cross over it. I'll tell you, if you left McCarthy alone he was easy to get along with. I left him alone. I let him and the Babe go ahead and have their own little discussion, and boy, did they discuss things. But to tell you the truth, though, their fights, like most of the Babe Ruth stories, are a figment of some writer's imagination."

The way McCarthy dealt with the problem of Ruth was probably the best example of his shrewd handling of men—he ignored it.

Ruth was furious that McCarthy had been hired to manage the team. The Babe had his own choice for Yankee skipper—himself. He had approached Ruppert in the off-season and asked for the job as player-manager. Rogers Hornsby, Ty Cobb, even Tris Speaker had been player-managers in the twilight of their magnificent careers. Why not the great Ruth?

But Ruppert, backed by Barrow, almost laughed the Babe out of his office. Ruth couldn't take care of himself; how was he going to manage thirty other men? Ruppert and Barrows wouldn't even consider Ruth, and the Babe never forgave them for this insult. He resented McCarthy and tried his best to undermine the manager's authority with the other players. But McCarthy stayed out of the Babe's way and, in fact, was popular with most of Ruth's teammates. Even Lazzeri, a good friend of Ruth's and one of the old-schoolers, played hard for McCarthy.

Despite the antagonism, Ruth had another superhuman year in 1931, hitting .373 and tying Gehrig for the home-run championship with 49. Gehrig, in addition to the homer crown, won the RBI championship with 184—an American League record that has stood for over fifty years. The Yanks, however, finished second to the mighty A's. Ruppert and Barrow were satisfied for the time being, but McCarthy was disappointed. He thought he should have won in 1931 and he vowed to bring home the pennant in 1932.

He was as good as his word.

10

The Called Shot

The 1932 Yankees were ready to knock the A's from the top spot. They captured first place in mid-May and never fell out of the lead, winning 107 games and finishing 13 games ahead of Philadelphia.

The Babe was now thirty-eight, and his legs had gone bad. He was slow in the field and he missed more than twenty games, but he could still pound the horsehide. He hit .341 with 137 RBIs and 41 homers, but for the first time since 1925 he lost the homer crown. Jimmy Foxx of the A's hit 58 that year, the closest anyone came to topping Ruth's 60 for forty years.

The Yankees were strong at nearly every position. McCarthy put the brilliant twenty-one-year-old rookie Frank Crosetti at shortstop, where he patrolled steadily for seventeen seasons. Lazzeri had 113 RBIs, and Ben Chapman, a swift, hard-hitting rookie who replaced Meusel in left field, drove in 107.

Ben Chapman: "The '32 team was a great team, but did you know that the team with the best average the Yankees ever had was the 1930 team and we finished second. We hit .309 and nobody knows that. Gehrig hit .370-something. Ruth hit .359. Heck, I hit .316 and I was only a rookie. The next year I hit .316, drove in 125 runs, and scored 120. I even stole 61 bases. See, I could run and nobody knows that either.

"One thing I could never figure out, though. How in the hell I drove in 125 runs when Gehrig drove in 150 and Ruth drove in 150 and Dickey drove in 120. They must have been walking those guys to get at me and I just plum surprised 'em.

"I started out as a third baseman and I led the league in errors, so when two or three of the outfielders got hurt they put me in the outfield. I played all the positions out there. See, the Babe wouldn't play the sun field. We played day ball back then, of course, and if the sun was in the left fielder's eyes, ol' Chapman played left field. If it was in the right fielder's eyes, ol' Chapman played right field.

"I'll tell you, if you don't have enthusiasm for living you're in bad shape. But that was one of my problems. I was too enthusiastic. I was always getting in trouble. I got kicked out of more ball games than you can shake a stick at. I'd slide into second base and I was out by ten feet but I'd start hollerin', 'No! No! No!' when I was halfway there.

"But I had a lot of fun. If you can't have fun when you're participating in athletics or anything else—you can't have fun, then get the hell out of it."

Bill Dickey was emerging as one of the game's greatest catchers. He batted over .300 in ten different seasons and ended with a lifetime mark of .313, and in 1936 he had the highest batting average ever recorded by a catcher when he hit .362. He could hit for power, too, slugging 212 homers— the record for catchers until Yogi Berra came along. Dickey also collected 1,969 hits and 1,209 RBIs, again both records at the time for a backstop.

Beyond his potent batting talents, Dickey was a natural behind the plate. He was a big man, but his agility and quickness around the batters' box were well known and he had an arm runners feared. Many still consider him the best all-around catcher ever.

Tom Henrich: "Dickey was one of your best money players. Take that first game of the 1939 World Series, against Cincinnati. We're tied 1–1 going into the last of the ninth, Derringer against Ruffing. Charlie Keller hits a ball between Harry Craft and Ival Goodman into right-center field. Either one could have caught it, but they couldn't get together and it drops. So Keller's on third, one out, and up steps DiMaggio, followed by Dickey and Selkirk. What do you do? Walk DiMaggio? Never a bad idea, and that's what they did. Then what do you do, walk Dickey to set up a force at any base and pitch to Selkirk? You don't like to pitch to Dickey in a spot like that, but you don't like to pitch to Selkirk, either.

"So they pitched to Dickey. When I saw that—and this is the absolute gospel truth—I turned and picked up my glove, because I knew the game was going to be over right now. And it was. Dickey singled into center field. One way or another, he was going to get that run in. No doubt about that."[1]

Ben Chapman: "Dickey was my first roommate. He was a great guy. I can't say anything bad about any of those Yankees and, I'll tell you, I would, too, if it was true.

"Dickey was just one of the greatest catchers baseball ever knew. He could do everything. He could throw. He could hit. Of course, he couldn't run a hundred yards in a hundred minutes. But then he didn't have to. He was a catcher."

Bill Dickey: "A catcher must want to catch. He must make up his mind that it isn't the terrible job it is painted, and that he isn't going to say almost every day, 'Why, oh why, with so many other positions in baseball, did I take up this one?'"

Burleigh Grimes: "At the very end of my career I went over to the Yankees, and one of the best things about that was I had an opportunity to pitch to one of the greatest catchers of all time—Bill Dickey. Which brings to mind an incident that tickled me at the time. I'd been there just five days when they put me in for the first time in relief of Johnny Allen. There was a man on first base—Heinie Manush, I believe—and no outs. I'd had five days' rest, so I had pretty good stuff warming up.

"I went into the game, and Bill signaled for the spitter. I broke off a good one, low and away, and it bounced off the edge of his mitt and rolled away. Manush advanced to second. Then Bill gave me that spitter sign again. Ball got away from him again, and Manush moved over to third. Still nobody out.

"So I called Bill out to the mound and asked, 'What're we gonna throw him now?'

"Bill said, 'Throw that same goddamn thing and cover the plate.' "[2]

Bill Dickey: "That was the first time I ever caught Burleigh, and he had the widest breaking spitter I'd ever seen. Also, I'm not offering any alibis, but it was getting dark—I believe it was the ninth inning—and the ball was hard to see. But Burleigh didn't tell you the end of the story. We got the man out. And we won the ball game."[3]

Lou Gehrig had another banner year in 1932, driving in 151 runs and batting .348 with 208 hits including 42 doubles and 34 homers. The Iron Horse also hit four consecutive homers in one game, to become the first player in modern era baseball to perform that feat. Only one other man, Bobby Lowe of the Boston Nationals, way back in 1894, ever hit four consecutive homers in a single game. One other man, Big Ed Delehanty of the Phils, had hit four in a game but not in consecutive at-bats.

Bill Dickey: "I'll never forget the day Gehrig hit four home runs in a game in Philadelphia—one in left field, one in left-center, one in right-center, and one in right—and in that order. All well-hit balls. Just went around the horn with it. That day made me very happy. We did have a disappointing moment in that game because the fifth ball he hit looked like it was going into the lower left-field seats and Al Simmons boosted himself up on the left-field fence and made the greatest one-handed catch you ever saw on it. Lou very easily could've had five homers in one game."[4]

George Earnshaw: "Do I remember the day Gehrig hit four homers off me? No, I don't. Because he only hit three off me. The other he hit off Roy Mahaffey. Connie Mack always liked Mahaffey, so after Gehrig hit his third off me, he brought in Roy to cool 'em off. Boy, he sure did cool 'em off. Scored twenty runs that day and they only got me for seven of them. Roy came in for one inning and he gave up something like six straight hits. The funny part, though, was I was ready to head into the shower after Connie took me out, only Gehrig was coming up again and Connie says, 'Wait a second. I want you to see how Mahaffey pitches to Gehrig.'

"So Gehrig steps up and kills Roy's first pitch, a real screamer, right out of the park.

"'I see what you mean,' I said. 'May I go now?'"

The pitching staff on the 1932 team was superb. Pipgras and the aging Pennock, now thirty-eight, pitched solidly throughout the year, and the Yanks landed Red Ruffing from Boston and he starred for the Yankees for a dozen years.

Ben Chapman: "Ruffing was a less-than-five-hundred pitcher when the Red Sox had him. Then he came over to the Yankees and he had the good fastball and he was a hell of a competitor. He deserves to be in the Hall of Fame just like Gomez. But it wasn't until he got to the Yanks that he became great. He got a good team behind him and he couldn't lose. And he got into a big ballpark too. That makes a hell of a lot of difference. There's a lot of difference between pitching in Fenway and pitching at Yankee Stadium."

The star of the staff in 1932, however, was a loose-armed, loose-lipped character named Vernon "Lefty" Gomez, who racked up twenty-four wins for the Yanks.

Gomez was one of the finest pitchers in Yankee history and certainly the wittiest. Fireballing Gomez won 189 games as a Yankee and was undefeated in World Series competition with a 6–0 record. He won 20 games in each of four different seasons for the Yankees, a team record, and twice led the league in strikeouts, wins, and ERA. Gomez was a seven-time All Star and finished third on the Yankee all-time list in wins and strikeouts and second in complete games.

Despite his heroics on the mound, everybody first of all

remembers that Gomez wit. A tall, lanky customer, Gomez just looked the part of a wisecracker. He had a long nose and an elastic face that he could change into a thousand screwball expressions. And he was always ready at any moment to shoot off a zinger or tell a good one.

Lefty Gomez: "Casey Stengel was managing the Braves when I joined them. He had me whipping back the ball harder in the back part of my delivery than in throwing it forward. Everything he told me was, 'McGraw did it this way,' or maybe it was, 'McGraw did it that way.' I stood as much of it as I could, until Casey asked me what was the difference between the National and American leagues. That did it.

"'Case,' I told him, 'the trouble with this National League of yours is that they don't know McGraw's been dead for ten years.'

"Five days later I got my release."

"I always admired Lefty Grove so I thought I'd ask him for some advice on how to pitch one time.

"'Say, Lefty, what do you do in the eighth inning and you're in a tight spot and you've really got to get somebody out?'

"'Oh,' Grove tells me, 'in that kind of situation I just give it a little extra.'

"'Ya, well, what do you do in the ninth inning and you've really got to get an out?'

"'In the ninth inning I just rear back and blow it by 'em.'

"So I tell him, 'Thanks, Lefty, now I'm a smart pitcher.'"

"I was pitching one day when my glasses clouded up on me. I took them off to polish them. When I looked up to the plate, I saw Jimmy Foxx. The sight of him terrified me so much that I haven't been able to wear glasses since. . . ."

"When Neil Armstrong first set foot on the moon, he and all the space scientists were puzzled by an unidentifiable white object. I knew immediately what it was. That was a home run ball hit off me in 1937 by Jimmy Foxx."

"My manager spent ten years trying to teach me a change of pace. At the end of my career that's all I had. . . ."

"I'm throwing just as hard as I ever did. The ball's just not getting there as fast."

"I want to thank my teammates, who scored so many runs, and Joe DiMaggio, who ran down my mistakes. . . . All I ever saw of Joe on the field was the back of his uniform. I wouldn't have known what he looked like except we roomed together. . . . I'm responsible for Joe DiMaggio's success. They never knew how he could go back on a ball until I pitched."

"A lot of things run through your head when you're going in to relieve in a troubled spot. One of them was, 'Should I spike myself?'"

THE BATTLE OF CHICAGO

Over in the National League that year the Cubs had finally won their pennant. William Wrigley, owner of the Cubs, had fired McCarthy because he wanted "somebody who can get me a World Championship." Now McCarthy had a chance for some very sweet revenge.

McCarthy held a pregame meeting with the club before the first game, and for the first and only time in the players' memory he asked them to go out and *kill* the other team.

THE CALLED SHOT

Joe Sewell: "It was a rough-going Series, I can tell you. There was a lot of bad feeling on both sides and it just kept on getting worse. You see what happened, late in the season the Cubs lost their regular shortstop, Billy Jurges, to an injury. So they bought Mark Koenig to fill in. Mark did more than fill in; he played great ball for them. He hit over .350 and pulled their infield together. A lot of people said the Cubs wouldn't have won the pennant that year without Mark Koenig. But when it came to dividing up the World Series money, the Cubs voted Koenig just a half-share.

"Now, Koenig used to play for the Yankees and he still had a lot of friends on the club. So when it came out in the newspapers what the Cubs had done, you should have heard the talk in the Yankee clubhouse. The Cubs were called every kind of cheap, no-good so-and-so's you could imagine. 'If it hadn't been for Koenig they would be dividing up second-place money.' That was the feeling in our clubhouse.

"The Series opened in New York. After we'd taken batting practice on the first day, Ruth went and sat in the dugout near the runway where the visiting clubs came out. In those days the visiting club had to come through the Yankee dugout to get to the field. But they had to be steaming.

"We beat them two straight in New York, pounding them round pretty good. Naturally that didn't improve their disposition any. They had started yelling back and we knew that when we moved on to Chicago it was going to be a rough time, because the newspapers were in on it now. A feud had started between the Yankees and the Cubs and it wasn't going to get any better.

"By the middle of the third game, in Chicago, it had got just plain brutal. I'd never known there were so many cuss words in the language or so many ways of stringing them together. But I'll tell you where it was all heading—right for the history books.

"In the top of the fifth inning the score was tied, 4–4. I was batting in front of Ruth and I led off that inning. I grounded out. I went back to the dugout and sat down. Babe stepped up, and just the sight of him was enough to set that place to jumping—the Cub players, the fans, everybody. Charlie Root was the pitcher. The Babe took one strike. Then two strikes. With each pitch the yelling was getting louder and louder. Babe? He was just as calm as could be. He was enjoying it all, that son of a gun. You couldn't rattle Babe Ruth on a baseball diamond. No sir!

"After the second strike Babe backed out and picked up some dirt. He rubbed his hands, looking square into the Cub dugout. What was coming out of there was just turning the air blue. He looked at Burleigh Grimes who was cussin' at him, and Babe cussed him right back. Burleigh had a towel around his neck, which he took and started to wave. Then Babe raised two fingers and pointed to the center-field fence.

After doing that, he got back into the box and set himself.
Charlie Root delivered the next pitch. The ball was just
above Ruth's knees. A good pitch, a strike. Babe uncoiled
one of those beautiful swings. *Crack!* I can still see that ball
going out of Wrigley Field. Have you ever seen a golf ball
take off? That's the way that ball shot into the air, just like a
golf ball. It got so small in such a hurry it looked like it was
shrinking as it went. It traveled out of the ballpark and
through a high tree standing out beyond. That tree was full of
little boys and maybe some men, too, watching the game.
When the ball went through the tree every one of them just
rained out of there, dropping down to run after it.

"By the time Ruth rounded third base it was something to
see. The fans were throwing whatever was handy at him—
cabbages, oranges, apples, just everything. What a show!
What a circus! Babe Ruth. My heavens, that was some Babe
Ruth.

"Do I believe he really called it? Yes sir. I was there. I saw
it. I don't care what anybody says. He did it. He probably
couldn't have done it again in a thousand years, but he did it
that time."[5]

Babe Ruth: "We were givin' them hell about how cheap
they were to Mark Koenig, only votin' him a half-share in the
Series, and they were callin' me big belly and balloon-head,
but I think we had 'em madder by givin' them that ol'
lump-in-the-throat sign . . . you know, the thumb and finger
at the windpipe.

"I told Hartnett: 'If that bum [Root] throws one in here,
I'll hit it over the fence again,' and I'll say one thing for
Gabby, he didn't answer, but those other guys were standing
up in the dugout, cocky because they'd got four runs back
and everybody hollerin'. So I just changed my mind. I took
two strikes and after each one I held up my finger and said:
'That's one' and 'That's two.' Ask Gabby . . . he could hear
me. Then's when I waved to the fence!

"No, I didn't point to any spot, but as long as I'd called the
first two strikes on myself, I hadda go through with it. It was
damned foolishness, sure, but I just felt like doing it and I felt
pretty sure Root would put one close enough for me to cut at,
because I was showin' him up. What the hell, he hadda take a

chance as well as I did or walk me?

"How that mob howled. Me? I just laughed . . . laughed to myself going around the bases and thinking: 'You lucky bum. . . .'"[6]

Ben Chapman: "He was cursing Charlie Root, the pitcher. He didn't point for a home run. He came in the dugout and I was at the bat rack and somebody said, 'Did you call your shot?' And he said, 'No, but I called Root everything I could think of.'"

Billy Herman: "He didn't point, don't kid yourself. If he'd pointed do you think Root would've thrown him a strike to hit? I'll tell you what he would've done. Remember he was ahead on the count. Right, you guessed it—Ruth would've been sitting in the dirt, maybe rubbing himself where it hurt."[7]

Gabby Hartnett: "Babe waved his hand toward our bench on the third-base side. One finger was up, and he said quietly—and I think only the umpire and I heard him—'It only takes one to hit it.' Root come in with a fast one, Babe swung, and it landed in the centerfield seats. Babe didn't say a word when he passed me after the home run. If he'd pointed out at the bleachers, I'd be the first to say so."[8]

Bill Dickey: "I know the true story—I was in the on-deck circle with Gehrig at the time—but I'm gonna hold my tongue.

"I used to get in arguments with Gabby Hartnett. He'd say, 'Ruth did *not* point.' And I'd say, 'Oh, yes he did, Gabby. Oh, yes he did.' And he'd get so mad at me he couldn't see.

"Let's leave it just like that."[9]

"Of course, Ruth got all the headlines in the Series, but the real hitting star was Gehrig. Lou followed Ruth's "called shot" with a towering blast of his own, but hardly anyone noticed because the fans were still cheering Ruth's audacious feat as Lou's ball was flying into the stands. Gehrig batted .529, hit three home runs, and drove in eight as the Yankees wiped out the Cubs in four straight. And yet all the talk, all the ink throughout the years has always focused on the way the Babe pointed to center and then parked it right where he said he would.

Counting the 1927 and 1928 Series, the clean sweep of the 1932 Series meant that the Yanks had won twelve consecutive Series games—three sweeps in a row. Another one for the record books. And another team to add to the list of "Greatest of Them All."

Joe Sewell: "I'll never forget I was watching the World Series in 1978 and comparing the modern Yankees to the champs of 1932. Do you know how many boys on that '78 team would've made our team in '32? I might be a little prejudiced now, but I say *two*. That's right, two. Guidry and Munson. Both of them in the bull pen!

"Go back and check the records. I believe our team batting average was around .300, and our pitching was *strong*. Gomez, Ruffing, Johnny Allen, Pennock, Pipgras—those boys knew what they were out there for. Look at the records and decide for yourself, but for me, I've seen every good team in the last sixty years, and I never saw a better one than the '32 Yanks."[10]

THE DECLINE OF THE BABE

The 1932 season was the last great year of the Ruth era. After that the Babe declined sharply, hitting only .301 in 1933 and then dropping below .300 with only twenty-two homers in 1934. He slowed down markedly in the field as well. The Babe was thirty-nine now, and his great belly ballooned as his weight went up to 280 pounds. Even though he still was a potent gate attraction, it was obvious Ruth was more of a detriment to the Yanks than a help.

Just as the Yankees had ascended on the power of the mighty Babe, they fell in the standings as he declined. They finished second to the Senators in 1933 and second to the Tigers in 1934.

On February 25, 1935, Ruth was gone, released outright to the Boston Braves, who made him a vice president, assistant manager, and part-time player. They also made him a lot of empty promises. Braves owner Emil Fuchs implied that Bill McKechnie, the Braves manager, had a year to go on his contract and then the Babe would take over as manager of the team.

This looked like Babe's big chance. But all Ruth's dreams disintegrated with all the promises. What Fuchs actually wanted was a drawing card to prop up his dying franchise. The Braves were sinking fast, and Babe Ruth, even though his skills had deserted him, could resurrect the interest of the fans.

After hitting a pathetic .181 with four homers in two tedious months with the Braves, Ruth decided to retire. But before he did, Ruth, the Sultan of Swat, the Titan of Terror, the Great Bambino, the one and only Babe, had one last glorious day. In Pittsburgh, on May 25, 1935, he hit three towering homers, the last of which measured more than six hundred feet.

Beans Reardon: "I was behind the plate the day Babe Ruth hit three home runs in Forbes Field. He was with the old Boston Braves then. One of them went out over the third deck. I had never seen that before, and after the game they said it was the first time a ball had been hit out there. I didn't know at the time that it was the last game he'd get a hit in. He played only four more games. The Babe could have played a little while longer, but you could tell he didn't have much left."[11]

Guy Bush: "I never saw a ball hit so hard before or since. He was fat and old, but he still had that great swing. Even when he missed, you could hear the bat go swish. I can't remember anything about the first home run he hit off me that day. I guess it was just another homer. But I can't forget that last one. It's probably still going."

That was Ruth's swan song. On June 2, 1935, a leg-weary, sore-all-over, forty-one-year-old Babe Ruth, the greatest and most colorful slugger the game has ever seen, retired. He had played in 2,503 games; stepped up to the plate 8,399 times; ripped 2,873 hits; scored 2,174 runs; had a lifetime average of .342; and, of course, banged 714 home runs.

As his reward, the Braves immediately fired him as vice president and assistant manager, dumping him unceremoniously from the game he had built almost single-handedly into a national pastime. He was signed briefly in 1938 by the Dodgers to coach for half a season. But again he was hired primarily as a drawing card to bolster the attendance of a comatose franchise.

Ruth repeatedly sought managerial positions in baseball but was turned down every time, the door slammed in his face by the game he had saved.

PART III

The
Great DiMaggio

11

The Voyage of the Yankee Clipper

When Babe Ruth left the Yankees in 1935, no one could imagine a star of his magnitude ever again playing the game. But in 1936 a twenty-one-year-old kid from San Francisco burst like a supernova over New York. And suddenly a new era of Yankee dominance began.

Joe DiMaggio—Joltin' Joe, the Yankee Clipper, Joe D., The Great DiMaggio—took over in center field and was a star before he stepped to the plate for his first at-bat as a Yankee. In the Pacific Coast League the nineteen-year-old DiMaggio had hit .398 with 34 home runs and 154 RBIs and put together a gaudy 61-game hitting streak. Everyone predicted stardom for the young slugger, but DiMaggio became more than a mere star. He became a legend as mighty as the Babe.

There were never two men more different than Ruth and DiMaggio. Joe was quiet and reclusive; Ruth was loud and uninhibited. Yet DiMaggio attracted just as much attention, was adored with just as much fervor, was followed about by crowds, talked about and written about and dreamed about with the same passion as the Babe.

In the end, DiMaggio may have shaped the championship mystique of the Yankees more profoundly than Ruth did. The Babe established New York's winning tradition, but DiMaggio made it an institution. He created the Yankee image of indomitable will, of quiet confidence that bordered on arrogance. The Yankees were going to win because it was their birthright. And with the lordly DiMaggio in center field, the Yankees won like never before. In Ruth's fifteen seasons the Bombers took away seven pennants and four World titles. In DiMaggio's thirteen seasons the Yankees won ten pennants and an astounding nine World Championships.

During his magnificent career Joe DiMaggio won three MVP awards, batted .325 (.422 in Series play), hit 361 home runs and, in the memorable 1941 season, hit safely in 56 straight games, one of the most hallowed and untouchable records in all of sport. He has been called the greatest all-around player that ever lived. Joe D. did everything—hit, field, throw, and run—with a superlative ease and majestic grace that has never been seen on a ball field before or since.

Joe DiMaggio: "I went to spring practice in 1934 with the San Francisco Seals of the Pacific Coast League and they couldn't find a position for me. They knew I could hit the ball but they also knew I surely was not an infielder because they had tried me at shortstop and every time I wound up with the ball I could never find the first baseman.

"Anyway, the Seals had a great big left-handed hitter who was having a great spring training—hit like a bull and he played the outfield—and they brought a left-handed pitcher in to pitch against him and the manager sent me up there to hit against him. Now this really surprised me because we had several good right-handed hitters on the club, like my brother Dom, Jerry Donovan, and a fellow named Hank Awano. But the manager singled me out and I went up there and walked on four pitches.

"Well, we had another inning to play and I thought I was all through because I was known as an infielder, so I started up the runway because the game was over as far as I was concerned and the manager came up to me and said, 'Get out there in right field.' And that's the first time I ever played the outfield and, of course, I stuck there. And later on when the Yankees bought me they requested that I stay there another year and possibly to play me in center field because they had future plans for me to play center for them."

Lefty Gomez: "You know it's about forty years ago but I remember the first time I ever saw DiMaggio. I had a big year with the Yankees, won twenty-six games, and now I was back in San Francisco for an exhibition game. They used to play a lot of postseason games out there in those days before the major leagues moved to the Coast. Well, I'm the big-shot local guy pitching in this exhibition game against the Seals. I think we had a team of major-league players from the San Francisco area against the Seals. Lazzeri, Crosetti, and a few other guys were on the team, and now I'm facing this kid DiMaggio for the first time. I don't know who he is and I don't care. I was the star attraction because I had the big year, and the people had come out to see me. Now the first time up this big kid gets ahold of my best fastball and whacks it like a bullet off the wall in right field for a double.

"The next time up I figure I'd better be a little more careful with him, so I get a pitch a little lower and a little more inside on him, and he hits that one on a line off the wall in right center field for another double.

"Now I'm steaming pretty good. I don't like a kid outfielder from the Seals treating the great Lefty Gomez from the Yankees that way. I look up and our manager, Earle Mack, Connie's son, is coming out to the mound.

" 'Do you know who that kid is?'

" 'No, does he know who I am?'

"Earle tells me his name is DiMaggio, he is the hottest thing in the Coast League, he once hit in sixty-one straight games, and I better work on him like he's a big-league hitter because he will be a big-leaguer very soon. I think I finally got him out the next time, on a ball that he hit near the wall.

"Years later he used to kid me about that game. 'You had a big year with the Yankees; you won twenty-six games. I was just a kid and I got two doubles off you. You couldn't have been so good, Lefty, if a kid like me could get two doubles off you.'

"'Yeah, Dago, but you couldn't have been too good either. You didn't pull the ball against me.'"[1]

Joe DiMaggio: "My first year at spring training when I came to bat we had an intersquad game and Luke Hadley was pitching against me and he hit me on the fists with the first pitch and I hit a real weak grounder to shortstop, so naturally the press said, well, there's another San Franciscan that's gonna bite the dust. See, Paul Strand was from the Coast League and had gone to the majors and he was a big flop. So they predicted the same thing for me. One time at bat and they had me sized up and sent back to the minors.

"But, of course, McCarthy would have none of that. He kept playing me and eventually I got hot and the rest you know."

Ben Chapman: "In 1936 a young man came in and played left field for about two weeks. Then they traded me and put him in center. Nobody's heard of him since—name of DiMaggio.

"Most people don't know that he didn't break in as a center fielder. He was a left fielder. Once they found out how good he was, they got rid of me real quick."

Joe McCarthy: "He looked real good in spring training that first year—what was it, '36—and then he burned his foot in that machine. [DiMaggio, hobbled by an ankle injury, was burned by a malfunctioning diathermy machine and missed the first sixteen games of his rookie season.] Well, we knew he could play so we just waited for him to get well. Ben Chapman was my center fielder then and he was a pretty good one. He could really go get a fly ball. DiMaggio had never played center field. I watched him go back on a ball and I knew he could play it. I started him in left field after his foot got better and then I moved him over to right field for a while. I wanted to make sure he was comfortable before I put him in center field. Finally I decided he was ready so I moved him into center field. He never would have become the great outfielder he was if I hadn't moved him. He needed that room to roam in Yankee Stadium. That's the toughest center field in baseball and only the real great ones can play out there. That's a lot of ground for a man to cover."[2]

Eddie Lopat: "I guess you'd call DiMaggio a perfectionist. I faced him for a couple of years when I was with the White Sox. I got him out with the screwball for a while. That's a tough pitch for any right-hander. Then he studied me and after a while the screwball was no problem for him. There was no way to pitch him and get away with it regularly. He was just too smart for that. He knew the ins and outs like nobody else."

Casey Stengel: "Joe DiMaggio was the greatest player I had. That was myself, Stengel. I'll say he was the biggest man we ever had on the Yankees. He was the best player because he could execute all the plays. He could play center field, get a start on a ball; he could field, throw. On base he used good sound judgment.

"He was the greatest."

Allie Reynolds: "DiMaggio wasn't nearly as fast as Mickey Mantle but Joe was the best base runner I've ever seen. He stretched routine singles into doubles all the time. See, Joe was always going all out every play of every game. He'd come flying around first all out and he'd make his turn and go about halfway to second and if that outfielder just hesitated for a moment he'd take that extra base. And if the guy got cute and tried to go behind Joe to first to get him, he'd just head for second. He put a lot of pressure on those outfielders. They had to field the ball perfectly every time or they knew it was two bases."

Ernie Sisto: "I can still see DiMaggio out there in center field. I saw him play so many games, almost every game he played in New York. When he was out there in center field it was like a song, he had that graceful rhythm. A guy would hit a ball. He'd take a look at it and then he'd turn away and he'd run to a certain spot. Then he'd turn around and be ready. He knew where that ball was gonna go before the ball got there. He made it look so easy. It was uncanny, the naturalness. It seemed like he was made for the game. I don't know how to explain it, maybe it was the other way around, like the game was made for him.

"I can still see him running out to his position. He used to step on second base all the time when he went out to the field and when he came back into the dugout. But he had another little thing. It wasn't a superstition, but every time he went out to center field and got ready to play his position he'd spread his legs far apart and then pull down on the visor of his cap, sort of getting himself all set. He did it every time. I still see that picture of him out there."[3]

Phil Rizzuto: "I mean, he did things so easily that people thought that everything came easy to him. He was the most graceful outfielder I've ever seen. You got spoiled playing with DiMaggio in back of you. Never once when a ball was hit would I look around and not see him on the move— sometimes even before the ball was hit. And I never saw him make a running, diving catch, or lose his cap, or make a circus catch, if he didn't have to. He made it look so easy out there."

Oscar Vitt: "Everybody talks about Joe DiMaggio's hitting. But Joe won more games with his glove and arm than with his bat. When I was managing the Indians we were playing the Yankees one day in that big Municipal Stadium in Cleveland. We had the bases loaded with two out and Hal Trosky, our first baseman, cow-tailed one out of sight. I waved our runners around. 'DiMaggio,' I said, 'get that one!'

"He did! He went back to the wall, over four hundred feet away, and speared it one-handed. So okay, I figured, Di-Maggio can play deep. The next time up Trosky took his usual toehold and DiMaggio was in deep center. But Hal hit the ball on his fists for a blooper behind short. 'Okay,' I muttered, 'get that one, DiMaggio.' He did—raced in and took it off his shoe tops. After that I was through challenging DiMaggio. I never did it again."[4]

Casey Stengel: "Now wait a minute for crissakes, you're going into too big a man. Maybe he woulda been an astronaut if he wanted. He could hit some balls off the moon and see if they'd carry. There were a lot of great ones, and Ruth could pitch, too, but this fella is the best I had.

"He started in with a bang and never stopped. Of course when he played for me he was handicapped, but you wouldna knowed it if you didn't see him limping in the cabs and in the clubhouse.

"The best thing he had—and I'll give you a tip—was his head. He saw some of the faults of the pitcher and he would hit the ball, and he didn't hit it just on Sunday, neither."

Eddie Lopat: "I was pitching against Cleveland in Yankee Stadium and we're ahead 3–2. It's about the fifth or sixth inning and Boudreau's the hitter. I sorta turned around to center field, trying to make up my mind what I wanted to start Boudreau with, and I noticed Joe was playing Boudreau straight away in dead center.

"So I turned around, got the sign, threw my pitch, and it was a ball. So I turned around to center again to think what I was gonna do with the next pitch and DiMag is still in dead center and I went back to the rubber and got the sign and missed again. Now I'm 2 and 0 and I'm really peeved and this time I don't turn around. On the next pitch Boudreau hits a frozen rope over Rizzuto's head right in the gap and as I turned to follow the ball I'm thinking, 'Oh, my God, there goes a triple, at least.' As I followed the ball out to the outfield, Joe was standing right there. Never moved. I was shocked. So when the inning was over I went over and sat down next to him. 'Joe,' I said, 'I noticed on the first two pitches to Boudreau you were playing dead center. How the hell did you get over in the hole waiting for the ball?'

"He says, 'Well, I seen you pitch enough to know if you were even up or ahead of him you wouldn't let him pull the ball. But when you got behind two balls and no strikes I just moved over seventy, eighty feet in the hole.'

"That's when I said to myself, 'Now I know what makes that guy great.'

"That's one of the reasons you rarely saw DiMag make a sensational catch. He knew who was pitching and who was batting and moved accordingly."

Phil Rizzuto: "I'll never forget holding DiMaggio's glove. I don't think anyone else could catch a ball with that glove. He didn't break in his glove the way most ball players break in a glove. Most ball players form a pocket, a deep groove. Joe would fold his glove lengthwise in half, just in half. He was one of the first ones to use sticky stuff on his hands at bat. Most ball players used rosin but Joe would mix it with something that would make his hands really grip that bat, and as a result he would get the sticky stuff on the palm of his glove. And his glove was so hard, I couldn't believe it. It almost cracked from folding over with that hard stuff in there. And nobody could catch a ball with that glove, I'm sure. I put it on a couple of times but you wouldn't dare use it in a game."[5]

DiMaggio's contribution to the club went beyond his potent bat and his great fielding. He was a born leader—the "unspoken captain" of the Yankees who led by example, not words. A superstar from his first day in a Yankee uniform, DiMaggio nevertheless was never a prima donna. He hustled for every fly ball, ran out every pop-up, and never complained.

Eddie Lopat: "If he went 0 for 4 and we lost, he'd sit there in front of his locker for thirty, forty minutes and never move. He felt he'd let the club down. No man can carry a club by himself. But that's just the way he felt. He hadn't done the job that day. He'd let his teammates down."

Johnny Murphy: "I remember many a day Joe would be the third hitter in a close game and McCarthy would call him back. 'Now, Joe,' he'd say, 'don't forget. I'd rather you'd hit at a ball over your head than get a base on balls because you can drive that run in, even on bad balls over your head. So don't get a base on balls.' And Joe never did. He'd swing at many bad balls to get a run in. He'd give up his time at bat to get a run in, and wouldn't think anything about it."[6]

Phil Rizzuto: "The way they would work it [at spring training], they had the eight regulars of the previous year take hitting practice. Joe McCarthy had said to me, 'Now, Phil, you hit at batting practice with the regulars.' So I was supposed to be hitting in the number-nine spot. Well, it seemed like after the eighth man hit, the first man would jump back in and of course, being a rookie, I couldn't say, well, it's my turn. And they just wouldn't let me in there at bat.

"DiMaggio saw what was going on immediately but didn't say anything until his third day in camp. That morning, after the eighth man in the lineup had hit and the number-one man was about to jump back into the batting cage, DiMaggio, standing close by, hollered, 'Rizzuto, come on; get in there and hit. We want to see what you can do.'

"That's how DiMaggio was a leader. Joe didn't go to the other guys and say, 'Let this kid hit.' He just did it by indirection, by example. After that, he began to help me out a little and he sort of broke the ice. And so when the other fellows saw Joe do that, then little by little they came over and started to joke with me, and from then on it was more relaxing."[7]

Charlie Silvera: "DiMaggio was the epitome of perfection. The Yankees didn't have a captain but he was the unspoken captain. He commanded so much respect. In the clubhouse and on the field.

"Hank Bauer and Billy Martin and I roomed together at the Concord Plaza up in the Bronx and Joe would come by and we'd hang around two, three hours just talking baseball and listening to what Joe had to say. We'd learn so much just being around that great man."

DIMAGGIO, THE MAN

If you had one word to describe DiMaggio the player and the man, the word would have to be *graceful*. A supremely private person, Joe lived his life and played baseball with a grace that exuded class.

A shy man by nature, his fate, ironically, was to live his life in the glare of spotlights and flashbulbs. He fell in love with and married two movie stars—Dorothy Arnold (with whom he had his only child, Joe Jr.) and, of course, the legendary Marilyn Monroe. His marriage to Monroe provoked Joe to utter perhaps the greatest understatement in the history of our galaxy: "It's got to be better than rooming with Joe Page."

Monroe's tragic death only heightened DiMaggio's own legend. Until recently he had fresh flowers placed on Marilyn's grave twice weekly. In that gesture we've glimpsed the heart of this private man, and he has become ours even more.

Joe DiMaggio: "Frankie Crosetti and Tony Lazzeri, fellow San Franciscans and already established Yankee stars, agreed to chaperon me across the country to St. Petersburg, Florida. After all, I had never been east of the Rockies and they weren't so certain that I was bright enough to buy a ticket, get on a train, and reach St. Pete all in one piece. I was grateful for their solicitude because it would save me from entering the Yankee camp cold. Their presence would give me some moral support when I reported to Joe McCarthy.

"I was really seeing America for the first time on that trip. Any ball player is likely to remember always his first trip to a big league training camp, but this one stood out in my mind because of its accent on silence. I already had been called Dead Pan by a couple of sports writers, and neither Crosetti nor Lazzeri was exactly a barber. We went two or three hundred miles at a clip without any of us saying a word.

"Near the end of the first day, Tony asked me to relieve Frankie at the wheel.

" 'I'm sorry,' I said as meekly as I could, 'but I don't drive.'

" 'You don't what?' screamed Lazzeri.

" 'Let's throw the bum out,' said Crosetti.

"They didn't, of course, but they gave me a couple of twelve-pound looks from time to time during the remainder of the trip."[8]

Arthur Daley: "His shyness was mistaken for sullenness by some and for swellheadedness by others. The DiMaggio of 1936 was silent and uncomfortable. He was monosyllabic and uncommunicative with writers. He was ill at ease with all strangers."

Joe DiMaggio: "I saw New York in the movies, and as I got glimpses of the skyline, of all those tall buildings, of big crowds hurrying through busy streets, I got a little scared. . . .

"I can remember a reporter asking for a quote, and I didn't know what a quote was. I thought it was some kind of soft drink."

Lefty Gomez: "Everybody who knew Joe in those days knew he didn't talk. I remember a two-week road trip—New York, Chicago, Detroit, Cleveland, and St. Louis. Two weeks, not one word. I'll tell you what he did do. He would take along one of those small radios on the trip and listen to the radio, the big-band music and those old quiz shows, Dr. IQ and things like that. He'd read the sports pages and he'd read—well, he'll probably kill me for this but he loved to read Superman comics.

"One day we were walking down the street of some town and he suddenly turns to me and says, 'Lefty, you know what day today is?' I say, 'Yeah, Wednesday.' Then he says, 'No, no, today is the day the new Superman comes out.' Every Wednesday there was a new issue. So now he sees this newspaper stand and looks to see if they got comic books. He points to it and wants me to get it for him. He stands off to the side. Hell, he was Joe DiMaggio and if the newsstand guy saw him buy Superman comics it would be all over the world. I got one of those faces nobody could ever recognize so he wants me to buy it for him. 'Joe, is this what you want, the Superman comics?' He looks around at a couple of people there and he says, 'No, you know I wouldn't buy that.' Then I walk away and he motions again. I finally buy it for him and he stuffs it into his pocket. He spends the night with Superman."[9]

Bill Bevens: "DiMaggio wasn't quiet exactly. See, everybody knew him. With his features you couldn't miss him. So they wouldn't leave him alone. That's what made him withdrawn and quiet, made him want to get away from people. With his teammates, though, he was very friendly. Heck, I go back to the old-timers' games and he treats me just like an old lost friend and I only played with him a few years. He wasn't no big shot to the ball players. Just a regular guy."

Pete Sheehy: "When he first broke in he was very shy and people might have thought, you know, that it was a little high-hattedness. But it was shyness. Later on, when he came to spring training, he would sit down and talk to the reporters and it was just like John F. Kennedy the way he handled everybody. . . ."[10]

"I can describe Joe in one word: *class*. He was the most perfect ball player I ever saw. Joe was a shy fellow but he loosened up. He would come in early and stay late. Ruth used to stay late. Not Gehrig. He'd be the first one dressed and on home to his momma. DiMaggio would sit down at his locker and say, 'Pete, half a cup of coffee.' Never a full cup. Just half a cup. He must have drunk thirty half-a-cups of coffee a day. Funny, now he doesn't touch coffee. Just tea. He used to smoke a lot too. Joe was a nervous sort. It was all inside him. He was intense. He would smoke a pack of Camels every day before the game. Sometimes during the game he would sneak under the stands and have a smoke in between innings. Now I think he's stopped smoking.

"He wasn't no problem. He didn't ask for special favors. He wore regular-size clothes: 44 shirt, 36 pants. They weren't made to order and tapered like they are now. He always looked good in his uniform—in his street clothes too. We were good friends. He invited me to his wedding when he married Dorothy Arnold in San Francisco. I met Marilyn a couple of times too. She seemed like a very nice girl. Now sometimes before Old Timers' Day he calls me up and asks me to get him a pair of shoes or something he might need. I always get what he wants. Joe always took good care of me, a real good tipper. I look forward to seeing him every year at Old Timers' Day. It seems like all the players do. When he comes into the clubhouse they all jump up and greet him, 'Hi ya, Joe. How you doin', Joe?' and like that. He seems to enjoy it. I'll tell you something else. When Joe DiMaggio walks into the clubhouse, the lights flicker. He's the star."[11]

Phil Rizzuto: "When Joe walks into a locker room—even an all-star locker room—it's like a senator or a president coming in. There's a big hush. The respect for this man is amazing."

Pete Sheehy: "I remember one time I made Joe really laugh. He had this big red welt on his backside. The players had gone on the field and DiMag stood near a long mirror and examined the mark. 'Hey, Pete, take a look at this.' I walked over and saw the red mark. 'Yeah, Joe, there's a mark there all right. It's from all those guys kissing your ass.'"

In no time everyone in America knew who DiMaggio was. He had taken Ruth's place as the most famous and most revered man in America, on or off a playing field. But while Ruth loved the spotlight, DiMaggio shrank from it. He went to great lengths to guard his privacy, but he rarely found peace. His personal magnitude and his movie star looks attracted attention DiMaggio never wanted.

Joe DiMaggio: "The games were the easiest part. It was the constant calls from fans and well-meaning friends and news-papermen. Every church in every town wanted me at a banquet and every organization requested a speech."

Toots Shore: "If the Yankees had won, he would come into the place and sit at his regular table and I'd eat with him. Nobody bothered him. Everybody would look at him, but nobody would bother him. In our joint if a guy wants to give autographs, fine, but if he doesn't, we don't let the customers bother him. All the waiters knew how to handle that. If the Yankees won and he had a good day and was feeling all right physically—Joe was hurt a lot because he played so hard—some of the sportswriters would come over. He never pushed himself on them; they would just come over. See, that's what changed in New York. They had day ball, and they would all come in after they had written their stories and have a few belts before going home, and sometimes maybe they didn't go home. Joe would sit there, he wouldn't say much, just listen to those lies. He loved Looie Effrat from the *Times*. Looie made him laugh a lot, and Jimmy Cannon was probably his closest friend—they would spend a lot of time together. He admired Bill Corum and Granny Rice and

Arthur Daley and Red Smith. He used to love to sit and listen to Red talk. He never had to be afraid of those guys: they would never write anything he told them in the joint. He knew they were off duty and he was off duty.

"I remember one time little Frankie Graham from the *Journal* was in the joint. He had an appointment to interview Alex Webster. He was the running star of the Giants then, and DiMaggio happened to be in the place. Graham came in and Alex was sitting at a table over on the side and he kept looking at DiMaggio. Finally Graham asked Webster who he was looking at. Webster said he was looking at DiMaggio and he had always been his hero, and he asked Frankie if he knew him. So Frankie took him over to meet Joe. His eyes were popping out of his head. Alex was the biggest football player in New York then, but when he was introduced to Joe he was like a little kid. He was everybody's hero. Still is. When he walks into a restaurant or a room now, everything stops."[12]

Phil Rizzuto: "For one thing, he was instantly recognizable. There'd be forty-five players down on the field and you could just look down and pick out DiMaggio without any trouble. The way he was built and his facial features and his hair and the way he'd walk and the way he'd run to his position. And he was just as easy to pick out on the street. As a result, he hardly ever had a moment to himself unless he was in his room, and that's one of the reasons he kept to himself a lot.

"We'd be on the road, and he'd say to me, 'Let's go to a movie.' That was about the only spot where he wouldn't be bothered for autographs. But even in the movies, sometimes, when a shot would come on the screen and would lighten up the place, you'd hear somebody say, 'There's DiMaggio over there.' Man, they could pick him out just in a second."[13]

Johnny Murphy: "We sat up in the balcony. We were in the front part and I happened to look around and in the very last row of the balcony I see Joe DiMaggio, all alone . . . I walked up to him. He said, 'Well, I knew somebody who got me in through the back elevator. It left me off right behind the balcony. I just stayed here in the last row to see the movie. It's the only place I have peace and quiet. . . .'"

"It must have been tough for him. He could never go anywhere in public like the rest of us without being bothered. He just couldn't drop into a restaurant, he'd be swamped, they'd tear off his clothes. The autograph seekers would annoy him so much that it took all the fun out of going anywhere."[14]

Eddie Lopat: "I think DiMaggio was the loneliest man I ever knew. He couldn't even eat a meal in a hotel restaurant. The fans just wouldn't let him. He led the league in room service."

Joe DiMaggio: "Some days I would open my hotel door and there'd be fifty kids waiting outside my room for autographs. I bet I got to know more back exits from hotels than any man in the world.

"It got so that the only place I could relax was at the ball park.

"Being there was like a haven. That was the best place to hide. Nobody could catch me there."

12

Four in a Row

THE FIRST OF FOUR IN A ROW

The team that DiMaggio joined in 1936 was one of the most powerful in history, winning four straight World Championships. They clinched the pennant that year on September 9, earlier than any other club ever, and finished 19½ games ahead of second-place Detroit.

The 1936 Yankees had five players who drove in at least 100 RBIs, and the team set a record for the most homers in a season—182. They also had 2,703 total bases—nearly 18 a game—and hit over .300. Red Rolfe at third hit .319; George Selkirk, Ruth's replacement in right, hit .308. Bill Dickey belted 22 homers and hit .362.

Gehrig had another MVP season with a .352 average, 49 homers, and 152 RBIs. But even with Ruth out of the way, Gehrig still did not get the headlines. It was the smooth-fielding, elegant man of supreme class—the one and only Joltin' Joe DiMaggio—everyone was talking about. DiMaggio was Rookie of the Year with a .328 average, 206 hits, 29 homers, and 125 RBIs.

Lefty Gomez: "Joe became a big star almost as soon as he joined the Yankees. The man I felt sorry for was Lou Gehrig. He had always played behind Ruth and finally Ruth quit and he had it all to himself in 1935. Now in '36 Joe comes along. Lou had another big year but Joe was the rookie sensation so he got all the attention.

"The relationship between Joe and Lou was very good. They never had a cross word that I know of. They were both quiet fellows and they got along. But it just seemed a shame that Lou never got the attention he deserved. He didn't seem to care but maybe he did. Anyway, I always felt a little sorry for him because of it."[1]

In the first game of the 1936 Series the Giants, behind Carl Hubbell, beat the Yankees 6–1. But in the second game the Yankees showed the National Leaguers who was boss, clobbering the Giants 18–4. The demoralized Giants managed to eke out one more victory in the Series (an extra-innings 5–4 win), but the Bombers put their crosstown rivals out of their misery in the sixth and final game 13–5, to take home their first World Championship since 1932.

THE BOMBERS WIN AGAIN

The 1937 season was a repeat of 1936. The Yanks won 102 games and clinched the pennant in early September, then went on to take the Giants in the Series, four games to one.

DiMaggio was not bothered by a "sophomore slump" like so many other rookie phenoms. In 1937 he bettered his Rookie of the Year performance, tagging 46 home runs, batting .346, knocking in 167 runs, and scoring 151. His 418 total bases still stands as an American League record. Only Jim Rice's 416 total bases in 1978 approaches DiMaggio's lofty stat.

Gehrig and Dickey supported Joe with brilliant seasons of their own. Dickey had 29 homers, 133 RBIs, and hit .332. Gehrig had 159 RBIs with 37 homers and hit .351. Red Ruffing notched 20 wins and Lefty Gomez had 21 wins with two victories and a 1.50 ERA in the World Series.

As if the Yankees weren't powerful enough in 1937, they picked up a slick-fielding, good-hitting outfielder named

Tommy Henrich, who batted .320 that season and would occupy right field for the next thirteen years.

Tommy Henrich: "I joined the Yankees at the beginning of the season in '37, stayed with them for two weeks and then was shipped to Newark. I was there for about ten days and was hitting around .440. Then McCarthy got rid of an outfielder and I was recalled.

"I'll never forget the bellboy who showed me to my hotel room. He really gave me a hard time. 'So you're Henrich,' he said. 'The papers say you're going to break into the lineup right away. Hey, wait till you see DiMaggio and Hoag and Selkirk. You ever seen those guys play?' I wasn't going to let him walk all over me, so I said, right back at him, 'You ever see Henrich play?'

"After a while they started calling me Old Reliable. I always got a kick out of that. Russ Hodges, the broadcaster, gave that one to me. We were playing a game against the Athletics at the stadium and were leaving after the game to make a train and go on a Western trip. We were ahead by a run in the ninth inning. We had two out and Buddy Rosar was up. He hit a pop-up right behind the plate. Ken Silvestri missed it. As those things happen, Rosar hit the next pitch into the seats, and we were all tied up. Now it looks like we are going to blow our train. Rizzuto leads off the bottom of the ninth and hits a triple. Now the winning run is on third, time is getting close for making the train, and I'm up. I hit the first pitch up the alley in right center field and we win the game. Hodges is on the air and he's yelling, 'Henrich did it again, Old Reliable that he is, and the Yankees will make the train.' After that they started calling me Old Reliable."

SNOW WHITE AND THE SEVEN DWARFS

The Yankees won their third straight pennant in 1938, clinching it on September 18. DiMag hit .340 and drove in 140 runs. Dickey hit .313 with 27 homers and 115 RBIs, and Henrich, a fixture now in right, added 91 RBIs and 22 homers. Ruffing had 21 wins, his third year in a row as a

20-game winner. Gomez added 18 wins, and Monte Pearson chipped in 16.

The Yankees fielded the same lineup as the two previous blockbuster years except for Joe Gordon, a flashy rookie who replaced Lazzeri at second base.

Gordon hit only .255 his rookie year, but he belted out 25 home runs and 97 RBIs, a tremendous total for a second baseman, and just that quickly Lazzeri was a memory shipped off to Cleveland.

Frank Crosetti: "Both Gordon and Lazzeri were really great second basemen. Tony might have been the better hitter for average and driving in runs. But Gordon was an acrobat in the field. He made tremendous plays. He was just a jumping jack. He was an acrobat in college and a tumbler and he was really quite a fielder."

Spud Chandler: "I was with the Yankees the year before Gordon came up and he came in and took over second base. McCarthy put him in to pinch-hit one day and he just hit a home run and the next day he was in the lineup and they never got him out of there.

"It was good having him backing me up. He was always in position and he was good for at least one or two of those spectacular plays a game. Joe was a good hustling ball player."

The Bombers were so dominant over the rest of the league in 1938 that one writer dubbed the American League "Snow White and the Seven Dwarfs." Said one manager, "If the Yankees don't win the pennant by August first, there should be a grand jury investigation."

The Yankees made short work of Chicago in the World Series, sweeping the Cubs 4 games to 0. McCarthy had now led the Yankees to three straight World Championships.

SEASON OF TRIUMPH, SEASON OF SADNESS

The 1939 Yankees easily won their fourth pennant in a row, setting an American League record and tying the major

league mark held by John McGraw's great Giant teams of the
1920s. Their 106–45 win-loss record gave them a winning
percentage of .702, second only to the .714 mark of the 1927
Yankees. In the 1939 Series McCarthy's Yanks clobbered the
Reds 4 games to 0 to win an unprecedented fourth straight
World Championship. And no one—not McGraw's Giants,
not Connie Mack's A's, not even Huggins's Yankees—had
ever accomplished that feat.

The season was highlighted by DiMaggio's year-long assault on the magical .400 batting average. On September 8
DiMaggio was at .408 and it looked certain that he would be
the first player since Bill Terry in 1930 to reach that lofty
plateau. Then DiMag came down with a nagging cold that
persisted until the end of the season. But McCarthy, who was
from the old school, refused to let DiMaggio rest even for a
day, though the Yankees had long since nailed down the
American League flag.

Joe DiMaggio: "I remember I was batting more than .400,
then I got this terrible allergy in my left eye, my batting eye,
and I could hardly see out of it. Joe McCarthy didn't believe
in cheese champions, so he made me play every day. I went
into a terrible slump. McCarthy had to know the agony I was
going through, but I'll never understand why he didn't give
me a couple of days off. I guess it was the rule of the
day—you played with anything short of a broken leg."[2]

The Clipper, badly disappointed, ended the season at .381,
still easily winning the batting championship. DiMaggio was
named the MVP that year, belting 30 homers with 126 RBIs.
Charlie "King Kong" Keller, a rookie out of Newark, joined
DiMaggio in the Yankee outfield, and along with Tommy
Henrich constituted one of the best outfields baseball had
ever seen. Keller hit .334 in '39 and in the World Series he hit
.438 with 3 homes. One sports writer quipped after the Yanks
massacred Cincinnati, "Break up the Yankees? Hell, I'll be
satisfied if they break up Charlie Keller."

THE FINAL DAYS OF THE IRON HORSE

One of the most bittersweet of all Yankee seasons was 1939. In January, 1939, Colonel Jake Ruppert, whose money and wisdom built the Yankee dynasty, died. Ruppert, a lifelong bachelor, had said, "Men marry only when they are lonely or in need of a housekeeper—I'm neither." But ironically, in his will he left the love of his life, the Yankees, to three women—Mrs. Hellen Holleran and Mrs. Ruth Maguire, his two nieces, and Mrs. Helen Winthrope Weyent, a family friend. Soon after, these three women wisely named the shrewd, unsentimental Ed Barrow as Yankee president. Shortly after Colonel Jake's passing, Barrow issued the following statement:

"Business will go along as usual. We will miss the Colonel, of course. But we'll try to carry on the way we know he would want us to carry on. Right now, I'm busy getting things ready to mail contracts to the Yankee players."

Then, another tragedy. In fact, probably the greatest tragedy, the saddest story in the long history of baseball. On May 2, 1939, Lou Gehrig, the Iron Horse, after playing 2,130 consecutive games, took himself out of the lineup, and one of the enduring, truly unbreakable streaks of all time came to an end. Replaced by Babe Dahlgren, it was the first time in 5,082 days that another man had started at first base for the Yankees.

Gehrig's streak eclipsed the old major league mark of 1,307 games by Everett "Deacon" Scott by better than 800 games, or more than five full seasons of everyday baseball.

The year before Gehrig hit .295 and blasted 29 homers and 114 RBIs. It is a measure of Gehrig's greatness that people were badly disappointed by those numbers. He had not hit below .300 or had so few RBIs since 1926!

Mrs. Eleanor Gehrig: "The trouble started in 1938, when his batting average slipped 56 points to .295. . . . Nobody touched off any skyrockets. He was in a 'slump,' so they just looked the other way. Then, that winter, there were times when he stumbled over curbstones, and maybe I looked the other way. When we went ice skating, Lou started to fall down more than usual, too. And at home, he began to drop things, as though he'd lost some of his reflexes. He was in a slump?"[3]

Jim Kahn: "I think there's something wrong with him. Physically wrong, I mean. I don't know what it is. But I am satisfied that it goes far beyond his ball playing. I have seen ball players 'go' overnight, as Gehrig seems to have done. But they were simply washed up as ball players. It's something deeper than that in this case, though.

"I have watched him very closely and this is what I have seen: I have seen him time a ball perfectly, swing on it as hard as he can, meet it squarely—and drive a soft, looping fly over the infield. In other words, for some reason that I do not know, his old power isn't there. He isn't popping the ball into the air or hitting it into the dirt or striking out. He is meeting the ball, time after time, and it isn't going anywhere."

Bill Dickey: "I knew there was something seriously wrong with him. I didn't know what it was, but I knew it was serious.

"We were in the room one day . . . and Lou stumbled as he walked across the floor. I was reading a paper and looked up to what he had stumbled over, but there was nothing there. I was going to ask him what had happened, but he had a strange look on his face and I didn't say anything. . . . A few days later he was standing looking out the window and I was sitting behind him, talking to him, and I saw one leg give way, just as though somebody had tapped him sharply at the back of the knee joint. He looked around, quick, to see if I had noticed, I guess . . . but I didn't say anything.

"So I knew it was something serious but I didn't know it was as bad as this."

Lou Gehrig: "They don't think I can do it anymore. Maybe I can, maybe I can't. But they're talking about it now, they're even writing about it. And when they're not talking, I can almost feel what they're thinking. Then, I wish to God that they would talk—you know, say anything but sit there looking.

"One day I made a routine play on a ground ball and Murph, Gordon, and Dickey all gathered around me and patted me on the back. 'Great stop,' they all said together, and then I knew I was washed up. They meant to be kind, but if I was getting wholesale congratulations for making an ordinary stop, I knew it was time to fold."

Joe DiMaggio: "Gehrig was always a very, very slow starter in spring training. He'd take at least ten swings before he'd even foul a pitch. So that was common for him.

"The year he was sick it just took a lot longer. He was down there three weeks in spring and he wasn't even fouling the ball. The balls that he finally did hit were just little weak grounders toward second. He just couldn't break a piece of glass. It was that bad.

"It was pretty depressing for all the ball players to see this man who used to hit balls harder than any man I ever saw. He'd hit balls to left center as hard as I could hit 'em, and he was a left-hander. He hit the most devastating line drives that would tear the gloves off the infielders. Then to see this man weakly hit ground balls was awful.

"So we're on a road trip playing our way up north to start the season. And McCarthy was that type of fellow he wouldn't take Lou out. We only found out something was wrong when he finally went to a doctor."

Joe McCarthy: "We had an off day, going from New York to Detroit, and I stopped off in Buffalo, where my home was. When I rejoined the team in Detroit the next day, Art Fletcher, my coach, came up to me and said, 'Lou is looking for you. He wants to talk to you.'

" 'Send him up to my room when you see him,' I said.

"A little later there was a knock on the door and Lou came in. I told him to have a seat. He was troubled, I could see that.

" 'Joe,' he said, 'how much longer do you think I should stay in this game? When do you think I should get out?'

" 'Right now, Lou,' I said.

"He didn't say anything right away, just sat there. Then he said, 'Well, that's what I wanted to know.'

" 'That's what I think,' I said.

" 'That's the way I feel too,' he said. 'I'm not doing the ball club any good.'

"I told him that maybe some rest would help and then we'd see what was going to happen. Then we went out to the ballpark. Lou was the team captain, you know, and it was his job to take the batting order up to the umpire. Well, just before he did that, the public address announcer got on his microphone and announced that Lou Gehrig was breaking his string today, that he would not play. There was a big crowd in the stands, and when Lou took the batting order up, they all got to their feet and gave him the damnedest ovation I ever heard.

"I knew there was something wrong with Lou, but I didn't know what it was. His reflexes were shot. I was afraid of his getting hit with a pitched ball. He wouldn't have been able to get out of the way, that's how bad it was. That was my chief concern, to get him out of there before he got hurt."[4]

Tommy Henrich: "He went up to home plate to hand in the lineup, then came back to the bench and sat down and began bawling. There was a tremendous ovation for Lou, while he was sitting there bawling. Now, what do you do? That's a very sad and delicate situation. Well, here's what happened. After about fifteen seconds Gomez got up and walked down past Gehrig, looked at him, and said, 'What the heck, Lou, now you know how we feel when we get knocked out of the box.' Everybody laughed, including Gehrig, and that broke the tension."[5]

Lou Gehrig at the press conference following the game: "I decided last Sunday night on this move. I haven't been a bit of good to the team since the season started. It wouldn't be fair to the boys, to Joe, or to myself. It's tough to see your mates on base have a chance to win a ball game and not be able to do anything about it. McCarthy has been swell about it all the time. He'd let me go until the cows came home, he is that considerate of my feelings. But I knew in Sunday's game that I should get out of there. I went up four times with men on base. Once there were two there. A hit would have won the game for the Yankees, but I missed, leaving five stranded.

Maybe a rest will do me some good. Maybe it won't. Who knows? Who can tell? I'm just hoping."

Babe Dahlgren: "Lou had a very slow start in spring training. We started working our way north into Norfolk, Virginia, where he had a four-for-four day, which cheered everyone on the ball club. But we didn't lose sight of the fact that it was a small ballpark and that the balls would have been caught in the bigger major league parks.

"We moved up to Washington and New York after that and I think Lou had about four hits in twenty-eight times. There were rumors that he was gonna take himself out but after such a long span you just couldn't believe these things until it actually happened. Old Art Fletcher came into the clubhouse and reached over and told me I was playing first. It was rather a shock because although everyone had dreams of becoming a major leaguer on that Yankee ball club in that era . . . , well, see, to me Lou had been an idol of mine in high school and I didn't want the job.

"Anyhow, before no time the park was full of photographers, taking Lou's picture and taking mine. When he took the lineup up to the umpire it was pretty well known that he wasn't going to play. As he walked back to the bench, you could see tears in his eyes. The fellows tried not to look as he went over to the fountain to get a drink and someone threw him a towel and he stayed there a long time.

"Later on a photographer asked Lou and me to go out to first base. Lou said, 'What kind of a shot do you want?' He said, 'Well, we'll have Babe stretching for a ball and you stand behind him cheering him on.' And Lou said, 'No, I'm not going to be cheering him on. That's my job and I'm going to be back!' At the time I was temporarily hurt. But then I could see this was one of the attributes that made him a great man. He was a great competitor."

Lou was thirty-six years old, and it appeared that age, as it does to all athletes, had slowed him down. But the troubles were much more serious than fading youth. Gehrig checked into the Mayo Clinic, and after a battery of tests, the diagnosis was amyotrophic lateral sclerosis, a chronic form of infantile paralysis or poliomyelitis—forever after to be known to the layman as Lou Gehrig's disease. It was Lou's death sentence. The doctors gave him two and a half to four years to live. He lasted barely two.

Bill Dickey: "After that—this was in 1939—Lou went out to the Mayo Clinic, and they told him what disease he had and told him that he would reach a low before he would begin to come back. A lot of people thought Lou didn't know he was gonna die. Well, the first year he stayed with the ball club and continued rooming with me. The second year, of course, he was too sick to travel. But I remember once during that first year, we were on the train, going to Washington to play the Senators the following day. It was late in the afternoon. Lou and I were the last players to get off the train. And there was a bunch of kids waiting for us, so we stood out there and signed autographs for twenty or thirty minutes. Finally we got into a cab, and this was the only time I ever saw that Lou knew that he didn't have too much longer. He said, 'Look at all the happy kids, and here I am dying.'"[6]

On July 4, 1939, the Yankees honored Lou Gehrig. It was a day baseball has never forgotten, as an overflow crowd jammed the stadium. Ed Barrow arranged to bring back as many of the old Yankees as possible. Ruth was there, Bob Meusel and Wally Schang, Waite Hoyt, and Herb Pennock, Joe Dugan, Benny Bengough, George Pipgras, Bob Shawkey, Tony Lazzeri, and Mark Koenig. Also Wally Pipp, whose job at first base Lou had taken, and Everett Scott, the old Yankee shortstop, whose record for consecutive games Lou had broken.

Finally, after many speeches of praise to Gehrig, the Iron Horse stepped to the microphone before a hushed crowd.

Lou Gehrig: "Fans, for the past two weeks you have been reading about a bad break I got. Yet today I consider myself the luckiest man on the face of the earth. I have been in ballparks for seventeen years, and never received anything but kindness and encouragement from you fans.

"Look at these grand men. Which of you wouldn't consider it the highlight of his career just to associate with them for even one day?

"Sure I'm lucky. Who wouldn't consider it an honor to have known Jacob Ruppert; also the builder of baseball's greatest empire, Ed Barrow; to have spent six years with that wonderful little fellow, Miller Huggins; then to have spent the next nine years with that outstanding leader, that smart student of psychology—the best manager in baseball today, Joe McCarthy.

"Sure I'm lucky. When the New York Giants, a team you would give your right arm to beat, and vice versa, sends you a gift—that's something! When everybody down to the groundskeepers and those boys in white coats remember you with trophies—that's something.

"When you have a wonderful mother-in-law who takes sides with you in squabbles against her own daughter—that's something. When you have a father and mother who work all their lives so that you can have an education and build your body—it's a blessing! When you have a wife who has been a tower of strength, and shown more courage than you dreamed existed—that's the finest I know.

"So I close in saying that I might have had a tough break; but I have an awful lot to live for."

Babe Dahlgren: "On July Fourth they had a day for Lou and it was this day I realized there was something seriously wrong with him. As Lou was receiving all the gifts from the fans, Joe McCarthy came up to about four of us on the third base side and said, 'Watch for Lou. He's liable to fall in the excitement.'

"That's the first time that I realized the man was really sick. I watched him and as he was talking, the lower part of his body was trembling and I could see what McCarthy meant. He sat out the rest of the year. The following spring he greeted us in the clubhouse when we came up. From a man who had played the previous spring to then he was kind of like a baby. The last thing I remember was down in the runway he asked me for a cigarette and I reached in my back pocket to hand it to him and I flipped one out and he leaned over and took it with his mouth. And looking away, he said, 'Light it for me, wouldya, Babe?' I struck the match and it

was a terrible thing to realize that this man couldn't even
strike a match.

"It was a year, the following June, that Lou died."

On June 2, 1941, Lou Gehrig died. Four days later,
between games of a doubleheader at the stadium, Joe
McCarthy and Bill Dickey, his closest friends on the Yankees, unveiled a granite bust of Lou out in the far reaches of
center field. The inscription on the monument read:

"June 19, 1903: Henry Louis Gehrig—June 2, 1941. A
man, a gentleman and a great ballplayer whose amazing
record of 2,130 consecutive games should stand for all time.
The memorial is a tribute from the Yankee players to their
beloved captain and former teammate."

13

The Streak

In 1940 the Yankee domination ended with Gehrig's career, and the New Yorkers dropped to third place. But the following season, led by Joe DiMaggio, the Yanks were once again on top in a big way. The 1941 Yanks clinched the pennant earlier than any other club in history when, on September 4, they went up by twenty games over second-place Boston.

The pitching and the infield were, as usual, strong and consistent. Ruffing and Gomez each managed 15 wins and Johnny Murphy in the pen chipped in 15 saves and had a minuscule 1.98 ERA. Joe Gordon at second hit 24 homers and 87 RBIs, and rookie shortstop Phil Rizzuto batted .307.

But the real power of the Yankees was their outfield of Joe D., Tommy "Old Reliable" Henrich, and George "King Kong" Keller. Keller had joined the Yankees in 1939, and his potent stick made the Yankee outfield the best in baseball for over a decade.

In 1941 DiMaggio won the MVP and batted .357 with 30 homers and 43 doubles. He also led the league in runs batted in with 125 and total bases with 348. Keller hit .298 with 33 homers and 122 RBIs. Henrich added 31 home runs and 85 RBIs.

THE ANATOMY OF THE STREAK

The big story of 1941—and one of the biggest stories in baseball ever—was "DiMaggio's Streak," in which the Clipper hit safely in 56 consecutive games and 72 of 73. Before DiMaggio went on his hitting binge, the Yankees were playing .500 ball. During his skein, however, the Yankees had an overwhelming 55–16 record (including two ties) and a winning percentage of .775. After his streak ended they settled down to a more human .600. But by August, when DiMaggio's hitting orgy finally ended, so had the pennant race.

For the record, during those fifty-six games, which lasted more than one-third of the season—from May 15 in Yankee Stadium to July 17 in Cleveland—DiMaggio batted .408 with 91 hits, including 16 doubles, 4 triples, and 15 homers. He also scored 56 runs, drove in 55, and struck out only seven times.

DiMaggio started it all against Edgar Smith, a stocky left-hander for the White Sox, when he went 1 for 4. By June 10 he had hit in twenty-four straight games, but that day against Chicago he went hitless until the seventh. Then he hit a rocket at third baseman Dario Lodigiani. Lodigiani knocked it down but couldn't get DiMaggio at first and it went for a hit.

Phil Rizzuto: "That was the way he was hitting in that streak. He always hit a ball well. Very seldom, if ever, would he hit a ball on the handle or on the end of the bat, like most of us 'normal' ball players. Every time he hit it, it was almost always good wood. But now he was outdoing himself. Everything he hit was a bullet. I'll never forget Joe telling me once—and he's the only man that ever said it, the only man who could ever say it—that he could hit a ball with the third baseman playing deep and still handcuff him. In other words, if he hit a low line drive and that third baseman had his

hands on his knees, the ball would be by him before he could
actually get set to field it."

That was game number 25, and by then the New York
scribes had rummaged around the record books and dug up
the longest Yankee hitting streak to date—29 in a row, held
by Roger Peckinpaugh, and Earle Combs. "That's when I
became conscious of the streak," said DiMaggio, "when the
writers started talking about the records I could break, but at
that stage I didn't think too much about it."

Joe surpassed the Yankee record on June 17 in Chicago,
but it wasn't easy. He came to the plate in the seventh still
hitless and tapped a routine ground ball to Luke Appling at
short, but the ball took a bad hop and hit off Appling's
shoulder, and DiMaggio beat the throw to first. The crowd
and DiMaggio's teammates waited for the call from the
official scorer, Dan Daniel, who, after a long, suspenseful
delay, indicated a hit.

Joe DiMaggio: "There was only one scorer's decision
involved, in Chicago. I hit a ball deep to Luke Appling at
short and he had a little trouble getting the ball out of the
webbing of his glove. It was scored a hit, and I honestly
believe I would have beaten it out even if Luke had made the
play without delay. I hit a home run the next time up and that
took the curse off it.

"The only blooper I hit in the entire string was also against
the White Sox. I hit one off my ear against Thorton Lee,
which just looped into the outfield. However, later in this
game I also hit a home run, so in each instance, the string
would have kept going without the benefit of the infield hit or
the blooper."

The Clipper had broken the Yankee record. His next goal
was Rogers Hornsby's National League record of 33, and he
breezed easily by the great second baseman, going 4 for 5
against Detroit to tie and 1 for 4 the next night against
"Dizzy" Trout to pass Hornsby.

DiMaggio was now shooting for what was thought to be the
longest hitting streak in history—George Sisler's 41 in a row.
But five days later, on June 26, the streak was once again in

jeopardy. In game number 38 at Yankee Stadium against St. Louis, the Yankees led 3–1 going into the last of the eighth. DiMaggio was scheduled up fourth that inning, and that meant if the Yankees went down in order, the Clipper's streak was through.

Joe DiMaggio: "That was the trouble at the stadium. On the road I knew I always had nine innings, so I was almost sure to get up at least four times. But at home, if we were winning, I only had eight innings. I was fourth in the lineup in the last of the eighth, and we were leading. The first man got on and the second man popped out. Tommy Henrich was the next batter and decided to call time and he ran over to McCarthy for a moment. Then, after getting Joe's okay, he went up and bunted in order to eliminate the possibility of the double play and to give me another chance to keep my streak alive. And on the very first pitch, a low and inside ball, I managed to get around on it and hit it by the third baseman for a two-base hit. And that kept my streak alive."

On June 28, in game 40 against the A's, Joe ran into his toughest opponent yet—Johnny Babich.

Phil Rizzuto: "There were so many great games in the streak. I guess I remember best the hit he got off Johnny Babich of Philadelphia. Babich was another Sal Maglie. He would knock his mother down. He really threw hard and could intimidate a hitter. He announced in the papers about three or four days before we played the A's that he would personally stop the streak. He was going to get Joe out the first time and then walk him the next three times."

Joe DiMaggio: "I don't think that Babich was really a loudmouth. See, he was with the Yankees at spring training in 1940 and he felt that he didn't get a fair chance. He was traded to the Philadelphia Athletics and he went on to beat us that year five times—knocked us out of a pennant. He was delighted about that.

'"I knew Babich had great control because he pitched against me in the Coast League. The first time I went up there he threw so wide I looked down at Art Fletcher coaching third base to see if they wanted me to take the walk because it was obvious that he was going to put me on. But McCarthy gave Fletcher the hit sign to give to me. The next pitch was just as bad. There was no way to hit the ball. The next pitch was pretty much the same thing. I had the hit sign flashed to me at 3 and 0 again and this time the ball was thrown not quite as far outside and I reached out and swung and hit the ball right between his legs and Babich went down on all fours.

"That was one of the most satisfying hits I ever got because Babich had great control and he wasn't even going to give me a chance to hit.

"He was out to stop me. Even if it meant walking me every time up. After I took my turn at first, I looked over at him. His face was white as a sheet. McCarthy was great to me. He let me hit the 3–0 pitch quite a few times, but that's the one I remember best."

"Bobo Newsom was a good-natured guy and he was pitching for Washington and he held a press conference before his game against us. 'Tonight,' he says, 'I'm going to stop that kid. I know how to pitch to him. I pitched against him in the Coast League and I know what his weakness is.'

"So the game started and the first time I came up I hit a double to center. The second time I came up I hit one to right center for two bases, and the third time I hit a double to left center to knock him out of the game.

"After the ball game the press walked in all in one gang and surrounded Bobo. 'Hey, Bobo, you said you knew DiMaggio's weakness. So what's his weakness?'

"Bobo looks at 'em all and says, 'Doubles.' "

The next night, June 29, the Yankees were scheduled to play a doubleheader against Washington, and DiMaggio could tie and then break Sisler's all-time record in one night. He singled off Dutch Leonard in the first game, and then as he sat in the locker room between games, the news came over the wire that Sisler's was not the all-time record. A reporter named Jack McDonald had unearthed an even longer streak. In 1897 Wee Willie Keeler, the old Yankee from the High-lander days, had hit in forty-four straight games for the old

Baltimore Orioles then in the National League. Even though Keeler was aided by the ancient rule that foul balls were not counted as strikes, the record was there.

Joe DiMaggio: "When I read that I almost fell over. I believed that once I beat Sisler's record I could relax. I was at forty now and I expected it to be finished one way or another the next afternoon. Now I had four more to go."

There was more bad news that day, however. Between the two games of that doubleheader, while DiMaggio was digesting his first piece of hard luck, a kid reached over the rail at the Yankee dugout and snatched Joe's favorite bat.

Joe DiMaggio: "I went to the bat rack the first time up in the second game, and the bat rack was right alongside the stands. Anyone could have reached in and grabbed a bat and took off. I'm looking for my bat and don't find the one I usually used throughout that whole streak. I got a little panicky about it.

"Tommy Henrich, who was the batter before me, used to use my bats on occasion. I gave him a couple and he had great success with them. So I yelled out to him while he was on the on-deck circle. 'Tommy, you have my bat?' He looked down and said, 'No, I don't, Joe. But if you can't find yours, use one of these.' And that's exactly what I did and with Henrich's bat I got my hit and extended the streak.

"Well, it turned out a guy from Newark stole it out of the rack. I had a lot of friends in Newark. There's a lot of Yankee fans in that town, you know, and, of course, it didn't take too long before word got out that this fellow had my bat. The following day I had my bat back."

On July 1, against Boston in a doubleheader, DiMaggio caught Keeler, but not without a little helping hand from the Almighty.

Joe DiMaggio: "There's an element of luck in any batting streak. When I hit in my forty-fourth straight game, which tied Willie Keeler's record, it was the second game of a doubleheader against the Red Sox. I got a first-inning single against Jack Wilson, my only hit, and the game was called because of rain at the end of five innings. Had the first-inning single been an out, my streak would have ended at forty-three games."

Now it was back to New York. Fifty-two thousand fans turned out at the stadium on July 2 to see DiMaggio set a new record. In the first inning he drove a long, towering drive to the left field stands and it looked like Joe had bested Keeler, but Stan Spence leapt up and snagged the sure home run ball. In his next at-bat DiMaggio smacked another hard drive for what looked like the record breaker, but his brother Dom DiMaggio, of all people, made a spectacular catch to rob him.

In the fifth inning DiMaggio finally ended the suspense with a long home run.

Joe DiMaggio: "It was Dutch Leonard who I faced that day to break the record and he was a knuckleball pitcher who was known to throw a spitter. Well, I managed to get my hit. But it wasn't until about three years ago, just before he died, that he told me, 'You know, Joe, I've been an admirer of yours for years. I tried to stop you that day. I gotta tell you I threw my best spitter at you and you hit that spitball to break the record.'

"My teammates never mentioned the streak. They'd never say, 'Come on, Joe, get that base hit,' or anything like that. You knew all the time they were pulling for me, though. Finally, in the game I did break the record, the whole bench ran out to congratulate me. That was a real thrill—the fact that the players themselves were excited about it."

He had hit in forty-five straight games to set an all-time record. The only question that now remained was: How long could he keep it up?

Joe DiMaggio: "When I started this streak I had no idea I was going to last anywhere near as long as this. When I got up around thirty straight games, I was almost indifferent about it, figuring that if I gave it too much thought I might start pressing and not be natural at the plate. I even told one reporter I hoped I would go 0 for 4 if I was going to cause all that commotion. But when I got up to thirty-five games I really got interested in it myself. I said to myself, just like the human fly when he got up to the thirty-fifth floor of the Empire State Building, why not go farther. And that's when I started bearing down.

"I felt great when I equaled George Sisler's record of forty-one straight games, but when you step out and tie one of those Baltimore Orioles, you're just flying high. . . .

"It's all over now and I'm sure glad of it. How far can I go? I don't know, but I'm not going to worry about it now. It got to be quite a strain in the last ten days. Now I can go back to swinging at good pitches again—if I get them. I'm kind of sick of going after anything they throw up there—just so I wouldn't be walked."

THE NIGHT THE STREAK ENDED

On July 17, 1941, the streak ended in front of 67,468 fans in the stands in Cleveland's Municipal Stadium, setting a new major league record for a night game. They were there for one reason, of course—to see if DiMaggio could keep it up. That's the way it was all over America in the summer of 1941. Scoreboards kept track of how DiMaggio did each night, and when he got a hit in Boston or Philadelphia or St. Louis or Chicago, they cheered in every ballpark, in every bar, in every living room where a radio was tuned to baseball.

Lefty Gomez: "Joe didn't talk much about the streak while it was on. He just went out and got a hit day after day. The night it ended in Cleveland, we jumped into a cab before the game and the driver recognized Joe and told us he had a premonition the streak would end that night. That really burned me up, especially considering how superstitious ball players are. People ask me if Joe had any superstitions during the streak. I don't think so. I did. I don't think I changed my underwear for two months.

"Joe hit three balls as good as you could hit balls and he didn't get a hit. Ken Keltner made two great plays at third base and Lou Boudreau handled a hot grounder at short. One of the balls to Keltner was a line drive that really exploded just back of the bag and Keltner made the play, beat Joe by a hair. What really beat Joe was the fact that he didn't get away from the plate. For some reason or other, maybe he hit the ball so hard, he got a little tangled up and was late out of the box. That cost him the hit."[1]

Joe DiMaggio: "Well, to get to the final day in Cleveland, I remember this quite well, it was a night ball game and it had rained the day before, which made the field very soggy. I came to the plate the first time against Al Smith and he walked me on four straight pitches. The second time I came to bat, why, I hit a ball down the third base line on which Kenny Keltner made a great fielding stop. He knew I wasn't going to bunt so he played deep in left field, and actually when he fielded the ball he was in foul territory and he straightened out and made that long throw to first base and it just nipped me. It was one of those nip-and-tuck plays where the umpire called me out. However, it was very heavy going to first base due to the rain and that's one of the reasons I wasn't able to beat the play.

"Of course, the next time I came to bat, I hit pretty much the same kind of a ball where he caught it on kind of a half hop, brought it into foul territory, and straightened up and threw me out again.

"My last time at bat we managed to get Al Smith out of there and Jim Bagby came in to relieve. This time the bags were loaded and I hit a ground ball to Lou Boudreau, the shortstop, and as it was approaching him the ball took a bad hop, bounded up, and he caught it along his chest. He whipped it over to second—and that was it.

"The following day I started another streak. I went on sixteen more games, and I want to tell you something, I could never have stood that pressure again.

"Strangely enough, I wanted to keep on going. I felt a little downhearted. I was stopped, but I quickly got over that. It was like going into the seventh game of the World Series, and losing it. That's how I felt. But I did want to keep going. I wanted it to go on forever."[2]

Joe McCarthy: "There was a tremendous crowd out to see the game, close to 70,000, I'll bet. They were there because of Joe. After the game I saw the president of the Cleveland ball club, and he was so happy and excited that his pitchers had stopped Joe. He was congratulating everybody in sight. But the next day, you know what happened, don't you? The park wasn't half-filled. He was glad they'd broken the streak, but the next day he was wondering where everybody was. That's what happens."[3]

Phil Rizzuto: "Finally the streak was over in Cleveland. Keltner made those two plays, Boudreau fielded a hard ground ball, and that was it. After the reporters left, Joe asked me to wait for him. I don't know why, I guess to keep some fans away. Lefty had pitched the game and he was gone. Now Joe gets dressed and we walk out of the gate together. He doesn't say a word. We just start walking back toward the Cleveland Hotel. We go about two blocks. I don't know what to say to comfort him so I say nothing. Finally he looks up at me with a little smile. 'Do you know if I got a hit tonight I would have made ten thousand dollars? The Heinz 57 people were following me. They wanted to make some deal with me.' Then he reached into his back pocket. 'Son of a bitch. I forgot my wallet. I left it in the park. Phil, how much money you got?' I reached into my pocket and pulled out my wallet. I had eighteen dollars. 'Let me have it.' I gave it to him and he turned toward a bar. I started in and he turned back toward me. 'No, you go on back to the hotel. I want to relax a bit.' I just left him and walked back.

"The next day he was at the ball park and never said a word about what happened the night before. He never discussed anything about it and I never brought it up. I'll tell you something else. He forgot about the money. I never asked for it and he never returned it. That's probably the most famous eighteen dollars I ever had."[4]

THE 1941 WORLD SERIES—A GIFT FROM MICKEY OWEN

In the 1941 World Series the Yankees met the Brooklyn Dodgers led by Leo Durocher. The Bums had just taken their first National League pennant in twenty-one years and, if not for two catastrophic breaks, the Dodgers might well have beaten the Yankees and captured their first World Championship ever. Apparently it was not meant to be.

Red Ruffing outdueled the Dodgers' Curt Davis 3–2 in the opening game of the Series, but the Dodgers came back to even things in the second game, this time getting themselves on the right end of another 3–2 ball game.

Then, in the third game at Ebbetts Field, Brooklyn fell victim to their legendary bad luck. In the seventh inning Marius Russo of the Yanks smacked a hard line drive off the right knee of Brooklyn pitcher Fred Fitzsimmons, and Fitzsimmons, who had held the Bombers in check in a scoreless tie, was unable to return to pitch in the eighth. The Yankees immediately jumped on Fitzsimmons's replacement, Hugh Casey, for two runs and won it 2–1 for a two-games-to-one lead.

Then utter calamity struck. In game number four Hugh Casey had a 4–3 lead in the ninth inning, with two out and nobody on. Casey struck out Tommy Henrich on a wicked breaking ball to even the Series two games apiece. . . . Well, not quite.

What happened next is deeply etched in baseball lore.

Tommy Henrich: "I was up at bat when Mickey Owen let that third strike get away. Is that the most famous strikeout in baseball history? I don't know; it could well be. Hugh Casey threw me a heck of a pitch. Everybody says it was a spitter, but I don't buy that. I listened one time to Mickey Owen describe what he thought the pitch was and he described it exactly as I remembered it. He said it was the best curveball Hugh Casey ever threw. It looked like a fastball. Then when it broke, it broke so sharply that it was out of the strike zone. So I tried to hold up, but wasn't able to.

"But even as I was trying to hold up, I was thinking that the ball had broken so fast that Owen might have trouble with it too. Yes, sir, that went through my mind. And I saw that little white jackrabbit bouncing, and I said, 'Let's go.' It rolled all the way to the fence. I could have walked down to first."[5]

Mickey Owen: "No, it wasn't a spitter. It was a curveball. It was as good a curveball as Casey had ever thrown, and it was my own fault. Casey had two curveballs, a big curveball and a short quick one. He'd been throwing the short quick one for five innings. We had just one sign for a curveball. I gave him the sign and he threw the big curveball instead, and I crossed myself up.

"No excuse. It was my fault. It was a great breaking ball. I should have had it. It got away from me and by the time I got hold of it near the corner of the dugout, I couldn't have thrown anyone out at first."

Phil Rizzuto: "I was in the dugout at the time holding a bunch of gloves—DiMag's, Keller's, Henrich's, and my own. I knew it would be a madhouse when it was all over and we didn't want to lose any of them. When Tommy swung and missed, we all got up and started toward the runway that led out of the dugout. Some of us were already in it, including myself. Then we heard all that yelling and we hurried back. There was Tommy running down the first base line with Owen chasing the ball. The fans were pouring on the field and the umpires and the cops had to get them back.

"And after that, you never saw such shots in your life. DiMaggio gets a hit, Keller hits a double off the wall, Dickey walks, and Gordon hits a wall. We get four runs and it's over the next day."

Leo Durocher: "Owen cried. He took it real hard. The writers gave him a real going-over. They compared his muff with boners in previous World Series.

"It wasn't fair and I told the writers so. Owen didn't commit a boner. It was a mechanical error; errors happen all the time. . . .

"I told the writers if they really wanted to get the reason why we lost the game, they should blame me, not Owen. After Henrich got on, DiMaggio singled and Keller doubled off the screen to score two runs. That's where I pulled a rock. Casey got two quick strikes on Keller and again we were only one strike away from winning.

"My mistake was, for the first time in my life, I was shell-shocked. I should have gotten off the bench and gone out to the mound to talk to my pitcher. In a spot like that, especially after what happened, I've got to go out there and talk to the pitcher, slow him down. I've got to say to him,

'Look, you got him where you want him. Take your time. Waste a couple of pitches; maybe he'll go after a bad one.' Instead, I just sat on my ass and didn't do anything. I let Casey come right back with the pitch that Keller hit for the game winner. So, I told the writers, if you want to criticize anybody criticize the manager."[6]

Joe DiMaggio: "Well, they say everything happens in Brooklyn."

Down three games to one, the Dodgers were finished. They lost the next day, 3–1, and that made it eight successive World Series championships in a row without a defeat for the Yankees, dating back to 1927. McCarthy himself had managed six in a row.

Two months later the Japanese attacked Pearl Harbor, and suddenly life was never the same again.

14

The War Years

In 1942, instead of rewarding DiMaggio for his MVP year and his incredible feat that drew huge record-breaking crowds wherever he went, the Yankees, headed by the penurious Ed Barrow, actually tried to cut DiMaggio's salary.

"There's a war on," Barrow told DiMaggio. "The country's in bad shape. We're going to have to cut you $2,500." Then he told the press, "Soldiers are making $21 a month but DiMaggio wants a big raise."

Joe DiMaggio: "Eventually I signed for $43,750; but while I was battling for it, the Yankee front office put out a lot of propaganda about boys being in the army at $21 a month, the insinuation being that I was lucky to be playing ball. I don't think anything burned me up as much as that.

"What letters I got after Barrow mentioned the soldiers! Baseball owners ruled with an iron hand then. Now, with the free-agent situation, the shoe is on the other foot. And deservedly so.

"There were times when it was plain hell. I'd read in the papers the next day that the cheers offset the boos, but you

166

could never prove it by me. All I ever heard were the boos.

"At first I thought it would wear off, but it didn't and every town I went into I'd get a fresh batch of raspberries right between the eyes. And it didn't seem to make any difference whether I had a bad day or a good day. Pretty soon I got the idea that the only reason people came to the game at all was to give DiMaggio the works.

"I remember I was going to St. Louis and we played a Monday game there, and there were only a few scattered hundreds in the stands. It was practically an empty house. That was one day I wasn't bothered much. There weren't enough people in the stands to get up a real good boo. It was the first time I ever enjoyed playing in what practically amounted to privacy."

It seems odd in this era of multimillion-dollar contracts that the man who had just set an unbreakable record would be shamed for demanding merely a $6,000 raise. But those were the days when the owners handed out take-it-or-leave-it contracts. And the players took them. Not DiMaggio. Though quiet, DiMaggio was a man of high principles, and he held out nearly every year for the salary he believed he deserved.

In the winter of 1938, for example, he asked for a $40,000 contract, and when Ed Barrow laughed him off, eventually offering only $25,000, DiMaggio stayed in San Francisco to tend his new restaurant, claiming, "The restaurant is going good. For what the Yankees are offering, I can't afford to leave."

"Young man," Barrow told DiMaggio, "do you realize that Lou Gehrig is only making $43,000 after thirteen seasons?"

"Then, Mr. Barrow," DiMaggio shot back, "Mr. Gehrig is a very underpaid ball player."

Joe DiMaggio: "I held out for the first eight years I was with the Yankees. They ruled with an iron arm. If you didn't play with them you played with nobody else.

"I was always sending contracts back with the help of Ty Cobb, who helped me during my contract negotiations with Ed Barrow, who was a very difficult man. Every time we'd send a contract back, I'd get a contract for a five-hundred-dollar raise. That was all we were getting. So I sent back about five letters and each one came back with a five-hundred-dollar raise.

"Cobb dictated the letter for me to Barrow and in it I said, or rather Cobb said, 'I don't care if you trade me to the St. Louis Browns.' And I looked up at Cobb and said, 'I don't want to go to the Browns.' He said, 'Don't worry. This is just to get them to give you some money.'

"So I got a letter back that said, 'We're going to give you another five-hundred-dollar raise. And don't ever talk about where you want to be traded because when we want to trade you we'll tell you what club you're going to go to.'

"Oh, my goodness, that Barrow was tough."

After his bitter contract dispute, DiMaggio had what for him was an off-season in 1942, hitting .305 with 114 RBIs. Joe Gordon, the jumping-jack second baseman, took up the slack, however. He hit .322, smacked 18 home runs, drove in 103, and was named the league's MVP.

The Yankees won the pennant easily by nine games over the second-place Red Sox. But in the World Series the heavily favored Yanks were ambushed by the Cardinals. The Yankees won game one behind a great pitching performance by Red Ruffing. But St. Louis, led by two future Hall of Famers—Stan "The Man" Musial and the hustling future Yankee Enos "Country" Slaughter—took the next four games and the Series.

Enos Slaughter: "That was my first World Series in 1942. Anybody who tells you he's not nervous going into his first World Series is lying to you. Why, being nervous is part of it. If you're not nervous, then it isn't important, and to a ball player the World Series is the most important thing there is.

"We opened in St. Louis against the Yankees. Red Ruffing was pitching for them, and he showed us something. He had a no-hit, no-run game for seven and two-thirds innings before Terry Moore finally got a base hit and broke it up. We went into the last of the ninth getting beat, 7–0. Well, something happened then. We knocked Ruffing out and scored four runs and had the tying run at the plate before they stopped us. That rally, even though it fell short, was the turning point for us. It made us feel real good. We went into the clubhouse and said, 'Well, we gave them one hell of a scare.'

"Everybody said what a great upset it was, us beating that Yankee team. But I don't think it was such an upset. Those 1942 Cardinals were a great ball club, that's all."[1]

DIMAGGIO GOES TO WAR

On December 7, 1941, Joe DiMaggio was in the stands enjoying a ball game at Spartanburg, South Carolina, when the Japanese attacked Pearl Harbor.

Joe DiMaggio: "You could hear the buzz through the stands. People who had come out with portables knew what was going on. Finally we asked someone with a radio nearby what it was all about. He told us. It took the edge off the game all right. Suddenly it was a solemn occasion. It was on all our minds, but what could we do about it?

"Up until that time everything was a joke. The army was a joke. I think we had one rifle for our whole platoon. We used the ends of broomsticks and everybody thought it was a big game until that day. And then all our attitudes changed. We became men overnight."[2]

In February of 1943 Joe DiMaggio volunteered for the draft and went from a $40,000-a-year outfielder to a $50-a-month private.

DiMaggio was far from alone. The ranks of every major league team were seriously depleted as ball players entered the armed forces. Along with DiMaggio the Yankees lost stars such as Rizzuto, Ruffing, Henrich, and Selkirk. To fill the roster the Yankees brought players up from the minors or traded for such luminaries as Nick Etten, Bud Metheny, Ken Sears, and Charley Wensloff. Regulars in the Yankee lineup included Mike Milosevich, Oscar Grimes, Russ Derry, and Mike Garbark.

Joe DiMaggio: "I was in this hotel in town and the next thing I knew the MPs were coming around and, boy, this was something like the movies. I mean they had drawn their guns. They told us, 'Okay, get your clothes on, get downstairs.' I said, 'What the heck's going on?' They said, 'Shut up, boy.'

And we didn't know what had happened.

"Next thing we knew there were trucks down there. They loaded us into the trucks and brought us into the camp, under armed guard. Word got out and there was a feeling that a lot of youngsters, guys my age, would be going over the hill. So they brought us all to camp under armed guard and the next thing we knew there were no more passes issued. The next day we were on the firing range."[3]

Enos Slaughter: "Then one day they called us all together and an officer spoke to us.

" 'Boys,' he said, 'if you'll volunteer to go out to the islands and play some ball for the fellows there, we'll see you get shipped home real fast when the war is over.'

"We said we'd go. We were all willing, and anyway nobody wanted to take a chance on saying no. So we got our shots and they boarded us onto a ship—the PA-101, I'll never forget it—and we landed in Saipan on July 4, 1945. Then they divided us up. I was assigned to the B-29s of the Fifty-eighth Bomb Wing on Tinian. We had two teams there and one over at Saipan in the Mariana Islands. A long way from Roxboro, North Carolina.

"The first thing we had to do was build diamonds. I got in working with the Seabees, running a bulldozer, helping to carve out the ball field. They did the same thing on Saipan, and we played back and forth: The bleachers were built out of empty bomb crates and sometimes we had as many as fifteen thousand troops at a game. We were drawing better crowds on Saipan than they were in Philadelphia.

"You've heard what great baseball fans the Japanese are. Well, when we got to Saipan there were still quite a few of them holed up in the hills. I'll be damned if they didn't sneak out and watch us play ball. We could see them sitting up there, watching the game. When it was over they'd crawl back into their caves. But they could have got themselves killed for watching a ball game. Talk about real fans!

"A lot of times we'd go out and sit on the edge of the runway and watch those B-29s taking off, one after the other. You know, we were on Tinian when that plane took off to drop the atomic bomb on Hiroshima. Of course, nobody knew what was up. That was the best-kept secret of the war.

Later on we met the crew that dropped the bomb. They were a pretty quiet bunch of boys."[4]

Baseball continued unabated throughout the war, but with most of the major and minor leaguers in the service, the brand of ball being played was decidedly subpar. In 1944 Ed Barrow received the following letter at the Yankee offices, and it was a graphic indication of the dire situation that faced baseball.

"I am ready to play left field for the Yankees," the letter read. "I am a fine fielder and a good hitter and could easily make good. I also am free from the draft or war work because I have a recent discharge from the state hospital for the insane at West Haven."

Said Ed Barrow, "If this man still were at West Haven I would write him to move over. The situation in baseball is enough to drive anybody daffy."

The quality of play sank to such awful depths that when a Chicago sportswriter was asked who would win the 1945 World Series between the Cubs and the Tigers, a Series that has been dubbed the World's Worst Series, he answered, "Which team will win? I don't think either one of them can win."

The Tigers, known as The Nine Old Men, won the pennant, but one sportscaster noted, "Most of the Tigers were war veterans and were playing their positions from memory. Some of them didn't remember very well. Thank heavens, though, no one was killed. There were some mighty close calls."

Ben Chapman: "I played seventeen years and yet I probably got the biggest kick out of pitching when I went over to Brooklyn in '44 and '45. I won eight and lost six. Then I got to be manager and I said, 'No more pitching for you.'

"Of course, that was during the war and the play wasn't so good. The war affected play like the expansion—it was a question of supply and demand. And the supply sure wasn't there."

Paul Waner: "With the war and all, they couldn't get young players, so I played until I was forty-two, and then my legs just wouldn't carry me anymore.

"I remember one day when I was with the Boston Braves in 1942. Casey Stengel was the manager. I was supposed to be just a pinch-hitter. But in the middle of the summer, with a whole string of double-headers coming up, all the extra outfielders got hurt and I had to go in and play center field every day. Oh, was that ever rough! One doubleheader after the other.

"Well, that day—I think we were in Pittsburgh of all places—in about the middle of the second game, one of the Pittsburgh players hit a long triple to right center. I chased it down, and came back with my tongue hanging out. I hardly got settled before the next guy hit a long triple to left center, and off I went after *it*. Boy, after that I could hardly stand up.

"And then the next guy pooped a little blooper over second into real short center field. In I went, as fast as my legs would carry me. Which wasn't very fast, I'll tell you. At the last minute I dove for the ball, but I didn't quite make it, and the ball landed about two feet in front of me and just *stuck* in the ground there. And do you know, I just lay there. I *couldn't* get up to reach that ball to save my life! Finally one of the other outfielders come over and threw it in.

"That's like in 1944, when I was playing with the Yankees. I finished up my career with them. Some fan in the bleachers yelled at me, 'Hey, Paul, how come you're in the outfield for the Yankees?'

"'Because,' I said, 'Joe DiMaggio's in the army.'"[5]

The depleted Yankees, behind the sterling pitching of Spud Chandler, won again in 1943, finishing 13½ games ahead of second-place Washington. Chandler posted a 20–4 record and a microscopic earned-run average of 1.64, the lowest ERA recorded in the American League since 1919. He was voted the league's Most Valuable Player, the third year in a row a Yankee player had been given the honor.

Spud Chandler: "I broke in 1937. Ruffing, Gomez, Pearson, and Broaca were already there when I came up, so you can see it wasn't going to be easy. The first game I started was in Chicago and I lost it 1 to 0 on three hits. Then Cleveland came into the stadium and I shut 'em out. Chicago came in and I shut 'em out. The Athletics came in and I gave 'em one run. So I made my letter right there.

"I went along and developed four or five different pitches. I had different pitches to suit any occasion and it all worked out pretty good. Of course, my big year was 1943. That was a terrific year as far as winning and losing is concerned. I think I reached my peak that year. I was just so confident in winning that I knew every time out there I was gonna win. After that I went in the army for two years and when I came out in 1947 I still won twenty games."

In the 1943 Series the Yankees again tangled with the Cardinals, but this time they bested the scrappy Redbirds, four games to one. The clincher came on a two-run homer by Bill Dickey as Chandler was shutting out St. Louis in game five, 2–0.

Spud Chandler: "I didn't have too good a stuff in that fifth game but I guess I was lucky. I had what I call just average pitching. My control was a little shaky. My arm had gotten tired. I was just lucky to win 2–0.

"The Cards had a great team back then, remember, with Enos Slaughter and Stan Musial. But I still managed to get them all out that day somehow. Then, Dickey come up in the seventh or eighth and just put one out and just like that we were World Champs again."

After three consecutive pennants the 1944 Yanks finally felt the heavy toll that the war effort had exacted on their roster. They sank to third place that year, then finished fourth in 1945. Most of the stars—DiMaggio, Keller, Henrich, Gordon, and Rizzuto—returned from active duty in 1946 but, almost to the man, these rusty veterans had poor years. DiMaggio hit below .300 for the first time in his career, Gordon hit an abysmal .210, and the Yankees finished in third place, a distant seventeen games behind Boston.

TOPPING, WEBB, AND MACPHAIL

In January, 1945, the Ruppert heirs sold the Yankees to Dan Topping, a wealthy playboy; Del Webb, who'd made a fortune in Arizona construction; and the iconoclastic, bombastic Leland Stanford "Larry" MacPhail. The price was $2.8 million and, considering that Yankee Stadium alone had cost $4 million to construct, not including millions spent for improvements throughout the years, it was quite a bargain.

Since MacPhail was the only one of the three who had any experience in running a baseball team, Topping and Webb put him in charge of directing the club. MacPhail was a baseball renegade and a brilliant innovator who had introduced night games to the majors a decade earlier while running the Redlegs. At Brooklyn a few years later MacPhail built the Dodgers into a winner. As president of the Yankees, he immediately alienated Ed Barrow, the long-time Yankee general manager. Barrow was a crusty old-schooler who never had much use for renegades, visionaries, or anybody else for that matter. When MacPhail quickly announced that lights would be installed in Yankee Stadium and then sent the team down to Panama for spring training, Barrow vehemently opposed both moves. MacPhail blithely ignored him. That was more than the old tyrant could take. Barrow resigned, and another era had passed.

As general manager and later president of the club, Barrow had helped direct the Yankees to fourteen pennants and ten World Championships. Before Barrow came over from the Red Sox in 1920 to help Miller Huggins stock the team with stars, the Yankees had been losers.

Joe McCarthy didn't get along with MacPhail, either. MacPhail had to have his nose in everything, and when he meddled with the on-field running of the club, McCarthy resigned in May, 1946. He left as baseball's most successful manager, winner of eight pennants and seven World Championships in fifteen years at the helm.

MacPhail hired Bill Dickey, then thirty-nine and at the end of his brilliant playing career, to take McCarthy's place. But by September Dickey had also resigned and was replaced by interim manager Johnny Neun for the last few weeks of the 1946 season.

After some secretive shuffling mixed with the loud denials that were typical of him, MacPhail named Stanley "Bucky" Harris to manage the Yankees in 1947. Harris was the "Boy

Wonder" who had led the Senators to two pennants back in 1924 and 1925 while Ruth was having his famous bellyache. However, Bucky was no longer a boy or a wonder. Since his early success he had managed the Tigers, the Red Sox, and the Phillies with dismal results. But he was a sound baseball man with a soft-spoken, low-keyed approach, and he turned the Yankees once again into a winning team.

Joe Collins: "Bucky was a man who'd leave you to yourself. In '48 I don't think he said five words to me all year long. Now some of the players felt bad about it. They'd think, 'He's not talking to me, I'm in the doghouse.' You'd have to tell 'em, 'No, that's the man's nature.'

"He had a favorite expression. The only time he'd raise his voice is if we were playing an opposing pitcher he didn't like. When we'd start getting to him with a couple runs, he'd yell out at him, 'Slap a little color in his face.' That's about the only thing he'd ever say.

"The difference between Casey and Bucky was for example in '48 [Joe] Page was the guy who hurt us. He had an off year but Bucky said, 'He won it for me last year. I'm going with him this year.' Now Casey would have never done that. Casey woulda got somebody else. No sentiment with Stengel."

THE YEAR OF JOE PAGE

Jackie Robinson broke the color barrier in major league baseball in 1947 when he joined the Brooklyn Dodgers. It was also the season the Yankees climbed back on top again. Led by Bucky Harris, New York captured the pennant by twelve games over second-place Detroit. The returning war veterans had taken a year to play themselves back into the groove. Rizzuto and Henrich had good years and DiMaggio was once again magnificent, batting .315 and taking away his third MVP award.

The pitching staff also had a good year. Allie Reynolds had nineteen wins and rookie Frank Shea added fourteen. But the big story on the mound in 1947 was a fireballing left-handed reliever who had had only modest success as a starter for several years. He was so mediocre, in fact, that Bucky Harris was about to send him back to the minors.

Eddie Lopat: "In the forties there was a pitcher who was a starter. He started for four years and he couldn't make good. He was too wild. And Bucky Harris decided to make a reliever out of him. Now this all sounds like a real fantastic Hollywood story.

"He was brought in with the bases loaded with one out against the Red Sox. He walked the first fellow, Rudy York, and forced in the run. He walked the next guy and forced in another run. The third hitter, he had 3–0 on him. And Bucky Harris grabbed the phone and said, 'If it's ball four, he's going to Newark.'

"Well, the young pitcher struck out that hitter and the next guy. His name was Joe Page and the rest is history.

"He was sensational. If any one of the starters looked like they woulda stumbled over a blade of grass in the seventh inning, we were outta there and Page would come in. We didn't mind it. Hell, he'd get in there for two, three innings and we knew he'd win the game.

"In '47 Page had 14 wins, 17 saves, and a 2.49 ERA and then he starred in the World Series. Then in Casey's first year in '49 Page was 15–5 with 27 saves. That accounts for 42 wins. That's one hell of a season."

Bill Bevens: "The Yankees in those days were looking for big guys to throw the ball. Rawboned, hard throwers. You look back at the club. They were all big guys. Joe was six foot two or three and 210, 215. He was a big boy. He could throw hard and his ball moved around a lot. And he had one of those rubber arms—never got sore. They'd call on him all the time. And he'd pitch all day if you let him.

"But Joe, he liked the nightlife."

Allie Reynolds: "Joe Page could have been a great pitcher. But Joe just wasn't of the nature to take care of himself and get in condition. He hated to run but he could throw that ball. So when he found out he didn't have to be a starter, just come in and pitch an inning or so, he liked that real well. And he was tough. He could come in there and throw like hell."

BABE'S FAREWELL

Commissioner Happy Chandler proclaimed April 27, 1947, "Babe Ruth Day." Ruth had recently left the hospital diagnosed as having terminal throat cancer, and it was obvious that the Babe had only a short time to live. Ceremonies were held simultaneously at every major league game in the country, and a coast-to-coast hookup would carry a special nationwide broadcast of the ceremonies at Yankee Stadium.

It was a sad occasion when Ruth, dressed in his familiar camel's hair cap and coat, stepped to the microphone. His face was gaunt, his body horribly shrunken, and his voice was a low, rasping croak.

Typically Ruth's last words in public were about the people he had always cared for the most and who, in return, had idolized him—kids.

Babe Ruth: "Thank you very much, ladies and gentlemen. You know how bad my voice sounds. Well, it feels just as bad. You know, this baseball game of ours comes up from the youth. That means the boys. And after you've been a boy, and grow up to know how to play ball, then you come to the boys you see representing themselves today in our national pastime. The only real game in the world, I think, is baseball. As a rule, some people think if you give them a football or a baseball or something like that, naturally, they're athletes right away. But you can't do that in baseball. You've got to start from way down, at the bottom, when you're six or seven years old. You can't wait until you're fifteen or sixteen. You've got to let it grow up with you, and if you're successful and you try hard enough, you're bound to come out on top, just like these boys have come to the top now.

"There's been so many lovely things said about me, I'm glad I had the opportunity to thank everybody. Thank you."

Yogi Berra: "When he was finished talking the Babe waved a salute and turned around and walked back to the dugout. Nobody made a move to help him. I remember one of the ball players saying, 'Do you think we ought to go out and give him a hand?' And somebody said, 'Leave him alone. He knows where the dugout is.' "[6]

Bill Bevens: "I was just happy to be a Yankee. As a kid, that's what I wanted to be. And I wanted to meet Babe Ruth. He was my idol. Just before he died I got a chance to meet him. They gave him that day there in the stadium when he couldn't talk. He was taking pain pills to keep himself going. He was in awful pain but he was nice as hell to me. Took time to talk.

"I didn't go to the funeral. I wanted to remember him the way he was."

Babe Ruth died on August 16, 1948. At the Babe's funeral on an oppressively hot and humid New York summer day, Joe Dugan leaned over to Waite Hoyt and whispered, "I'd give a hundred bucks for a beer." Hoyt nodded over at Ruth's casket and answered, "So would the Babe; so would the Babe."

THE 1947 SERIES—BEVENS'S ALMOST NO-HITTER

In the 1947 Series the Yankees faced the Brooklyn Dodgers, who were led by the sensational, controversial, history-making Jackie Robinson. It turned out to be one of the most exciting fall classics ever played. The Yankees jumped off to a quick two-games-to-one lead, and when Yankee pitcher Bill Bevens waltzed into the ninth inning of game four with a no-hitter, the Bums looked to be had once again.

Bevens, an erratic right-hander who had joined the Yankees in the war years and pitched with only moderate success, had had a terrible season, finishing 7–13—tough to do on a club that had won 97 games. But pitching a no-hitter in the Series can make people forget all about a bad season.

Bill Bevens: "You only get one chance. See, I had a sore arm during the season so I never pitched too well. But at the end my arm came around and I started pitching good and that was the main reason Bucky gave me a shot at starting.

"I felt great in that game. My arm felt very strong and

that's probably what made me wild, because I was a little too strong. In fact, I set a record for most walks in a Series game—ten I think it was. You want to make a good impression, especially in the World Series. A lot of people only get one chance so I wanted to do the best I could. And it turned out to be my first and only Series game."

With two out in the ninth inning Bevens still had his no-hitter, but he had already walked eight men and clung precariously to a 2–1 lead. With Carl Furillo on first with a walk, Burt Shotten, the Dodger manager, put Al Gionfriddo in to run for Furillo. Gionfriddo promptly stole second. With pinch-hitter Pete Reiser at the plate, Bucky Harris made the fateful decision to intentionally walk Reiser, who was then replaced by another pinch-runner.

Shotten, playing this game of chess to the hilt, then put in Cookie Lavagetto to pinch-hit for Eddie Stanky. Lavagetto was a veteran infielder at the end of a good career, but in 1947 he was only a part-time player hitting .261 and an unlikely candidate for history-making heroics. On paper it wasn't a very smart move. So much for paperwork.

Lavagetto swung and missed badly on Bevens's first pitch, and then with a packed, rowdy Ebbets Field crowd struck quiet with the high-tension drama of the moment, Lavagetto hit a drive to right field.

Bill Bevens: "I rolled right along into the ninth without giving up a hit and I walked Gionfriddo and got a couple guys to pop up. Then we walked Reiser intentionally, which put the winning run on. That's when they put Miksis in to run for Reiser. See Reiser was crippled at the time—he ran into a wall chasing a fly ball—but nobody knew it.

"Anyway, Gionfriddo had stole second and that's why we walked Reiser. Actually, I still think Gionfriddo was out stealing. Yogi threw him out. Got him clean. And Rizzuto and Sternweiss both said they had him. I've watched it over and over on TV and it looked to me like we had him. That would have been the last out, you know, and I would have had the no-hitter but . . .

"Then Lavagetto came up and I got a strike and a ball on him. Charlie Dressen had been with him at Brooklyn and he was our pitching coach then and he said pitch him high and away. So that's what I done and he hit it against the right-field fence, which isn't too far. It was only about 290 feet down the line there at Ebbets Field. See it was just an ordinary fly ball in most ballparks.

"Lavagetto told me afterward he always hit to the opposite field. He said, 'I don't know how come Dressen said to pitch me away. That's where I hit.' So I was pitching to his power. The next day Frank Shea struck him out on a ball inside because I told him what I'd thrown Lavagetto.

"Even when he hit it I thought Henrich was gonna catch it the whole time. It just looked like a high fly ball. It wasn't no line drive or anything. Tommy backed up to the fence, stood there a second waiting, and then he jumped and the ball hit not more than a foot or two above his glove. And then it bounced off the fence and he had to chase it down and that's the reason both runs scored.

"And that's all there was to it. I'd like to had it. But, what the heck, I think I got more recognition by losing than if I woulda won. I sure woulda liked to win it though. Sure woulda."

Tommy Henrich: "I can tell you what happened the next day. We're in Ebbets Field. Frank Shea has them beat 2–1 in the last of the ninth. There's a man on first and two out, and we know that Lavagetto is going to pinch-hit. You wonder: Can that guy do it again? I was standing near DiMaggio in the outfield, and we look at each other. Would you believe that he said to me, 'For Christ's sake, say a prayer'? That's exactly what he said. DiMaggio.

"Shea strikes Lavagetto out. We run into the clubhouse and I go over to Crosetti. 'Get a load of this,' I said. 'What do you think the big guy said when Lavagetto came up?' And I tell him. Crosetti's reaction is, 'Why didn't you tell him to pray?' That's pretty good, right? So I go over to DiMaggio. 'What do you think Crosetti said?' And I repeat it to him. And Joe says, 'I was praying. I wasn't sure if I was getting through.' "[7]

Joe DiMaggio: "After the game I was in our dressing room at Ebbets Field when Bob Cooke, a baseball writer on the

Herald Tribune and since sports editor of that paper, came over to speak to me.

" 'Tough break for Bev, wasn't it, Joe?'

" 'It's always tough to lose a World Series game, especially a close one, Bob,' I answered, none too brightly, I guess.

" 'I don't mean losing the game so much. I mean losing the no-hitter,' explained Cooke.

" 'No-hitter?' I shouted. 'Do you mean to tell me that Lavagetto's hit was the first Brooklyn made?'

"That was the first time I knew Bevens had almost pitched a no-hit game. The fact that Brooklyn had scored a run and that Bill had walked a lot of batters, ten, had thrown me off, but I was so wrapped up in the game that I hadn't noticed that the Dodgers hadn't made a hit until Cookie's ninth-inning pinch double."[8]

The Yankees went on to win game five, and the Dodgers came back to tie the Series once again by taking game six, thanks to a famous game-saving catch by Al Gionfriddo of a sure-thing homer by DiMaggio. Gionfriddo went back to the 415-foot sign on the dead run and hauled the ball in just as it was leaving the park. In frustration the usually emotionless DiMaggio kicked the dirt as he rounded first base, after Gionfriddo robbed him of a homer that would have locked up the game and the Series for the Yankees.

Allie Reynolds: "Gionfriddo made an incredible catch. I didn't think he could catch the ball but he did. He turned and went back just as far as he could go and turned and stuck his hand up and the ball hit in his glove. I think he was as surprised as the rest of us.

"It was over his head and he caught it right over the gate to the bull pen in Yankee Stadium, which is 407 feet away. It was a line drive, a real shot that got over him fast. I didn't think he could get to it, it was hit so hard. I'd say the pitcher hadn't fooled DiMaggio greatly. Joe jumped all over it."

Bill Bevens: "You remember the old Yankee Stadium where the gate was out there by the bull pen? He just went back to the gate and kinda leaned over it. It woulda been a home run if he hadn't caught it. It was gone. He didn't have to jump or anything. He just got back there, leaned over, and got it.

"It looked like it was a homer the whole time. Everybody in the dugout said it was outta there. Joe thought it was gone too. He said it felt good when he hit it. He kind of circled around and gave the bag a kick when Gionfriddo caught it, and that was unusual for Joe."

The Yanks came back the next day to win the Series behind five innings of overpowering one-hit pitching by Joe Page. The Yankees were champions of the world once again.

MACPHAIL TAKES THE MONEY AND RUNS

Larry MacPhail walked into the Yankees' tumultuous postgame locker room after the last game of the 1947 Series and announced he was selling his interest in the club. It was a typical grandstand play by MacPhail, and the players were miffed because they thought MacPhail was trying to upstage their victory. They weren't *too* upset, though, because it meant they were getting rid of him.

Eddie Lopat: "Larry MacPhail was a tough man. Had a short fuse and wanted to get in a fight with the owners. You don't fight with the owners. But he was no dummy. He came in that deal when Topping and Webb bought the Yankees. His share was $150,000 and when he left he got a million and a half tax-free. Not bad for three years' work!"

Topping took over the chores as president of the Yankees and named George Weiss, who had headed the Yankee farm system for Colonel Ruppert for years, as the new general manager. Topping gave Weiss the same unlimited powers over player acquisitions and salaries that Ruppert had given to Barrow. And Weiss, in turn, left his field manager alone to handle the team the way he saw fit. It was a very effective policy. Under Weiss's leadership the Yankees would win five World titles in a row and ten pennants in thirteen years, a mark no other general manager in baseball has ever matched.

Joe Collins: "The genius behind the Yankee success in the fifties was George Weiss. He ran the minor leagues when Ruppert was still alive, then MacPhail got in that hassle with Topping and Webb. So they paid him off and brought in George Weiss. He was general manager there from about '48 to '60. Thirteen big years.

"He was a cold fish—a tough man to deal with. He was from the old school. Tried to keep the players down as much as he could. To get four, five thousand dollars out of him was a tough deal."

Mickey Mantle: "The thing is, I was only makin' $32,000 in '56. We didn't have no long-term contracts, either. So, after my Triple Crown, the first contract they send me for '57 is for a little $5,000 raise. I ended up with $65,000, but in '57 I hit .365—three-six-five! And they tried to get me to take a $10,000 cut. They said I didn't have as good a year as before because I only hit thirty-four home runs. That Weiss was mean, boy, mean. He even had a private eye on me. Threatened to show the report to my wife. Hell, the only thing on it was that I was comin' in at one in the morning, and she already knew that. I finally got up to $100,000 and stayed there—no raise, no cut."

Allie Reynolds: "Weiss was tougher than gangbusters. In '51 I pitched two no-hit ball games. First time in the history of the American League. I came in that fall to sign a contract and he looked at me and said, 'Well, Allie, you didn't finish many games this year but I'm not going to give you a cut.'

"And I went right through the ceiling and when I came down I called him a nasty name like S.O.B. I said, 'You just made me mad. I'm going to go back over to the hotel. If you want to see me, call me. I'll come back at ten tomorrow morning. If you don't want to see me, don't call me and I'll get on the plane and go home and you can pay me another airfare up here.' We finally got together and I got my raise. But it was like dating a scorpion.

"I was nineteen and eight in 1947 and there was still about two weeks to go before the World Series and you know I never started another game. See, they were great about keeping you from winning twenty because you could demand a lot more salary if you reached the magic number. I thought it was pretty chicken myself. Hell, they'd have a federal investigation if you did that to a ball player today. They just said we're going to save you for the Series and that was that. It comes under the heading of good business.''

Bob Cerv: "I went in a lot of times and, hell, they'd have an attorney there. They'd have a business manager. They'd have a general manager. They'd have the president. And there you sat by yourself. If you'da gone in with an attorney you wouldn't of had a job. So it was kinda one-sided."

Bob Grim: "The Yanks were a first-class organization but the salaries were ridiculous. But what the hell you gonna do? You don't like what they offered you, what could you do? I win twenty games as a rookie, I'm making $6,000 and they jump me to $13,000. Twenty wins! Nowadays a guy like Valenzuela wins nineteen games as a rookie and they jump him to $800,000. It was ridiculous. The owners had the players by the short hair. Now it's the other way around."

Bob Cerv: "Really I always say the Yankees were a great team as long as George Weiss was there. He was one of the best, if not the best general manager ever. Just look at his record. Won umpteen championships with the Yanks, then he went to the Mets after that and most of the kids he signed were the ones that come up and eventually won the World Series for that club. The Amazin' Mets. Hell, they were just good ball players. Weiss could always spot a good ball player."

Casey Stengel: "We fought over some things but he never stopped paying me. If your checks don't bounce, why wouldn't you like the man?"

Highland Park

Hal Chase

Jack Chesbro

Miller Huggins

The Babe

Babe Ruth, Colonel Ruppert, Edward Barrow

Casey Stengel

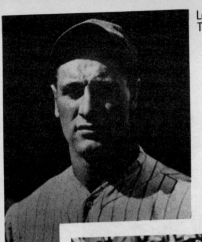
Lou Gehrig,
The Iron Horse

Bill Dickey

Babe Ruth

Bill Dickey, Lefty Gomez, and Lou Gehrig

Lou Gehrig and
Babe Ruth

Joe DiMaggio,
The Yankee Clipper

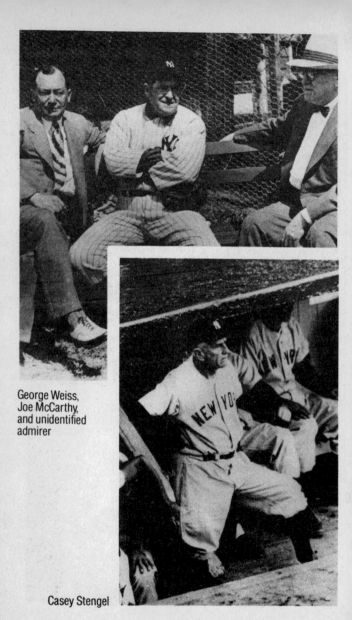

George Weiss,
Joe McCarthy,
and unidentified
admirer

Casey Stengel

Billy Martin

Yogi Berra

Phil Rizzuto

Mickey Mantle,
The Mick

Don
Larsen's
perfect
game

Whitey Ford

Elston Howard

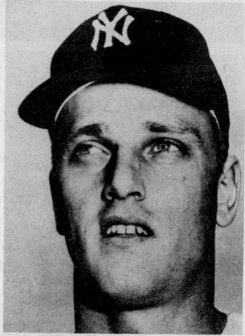

Roger Maris

Billy
Martin
and George
Steinbrenner

Tony Kubek

Jim
"Catfish"
Hunter

Reggie!
Reggie!
Reggie!

Richard
"Goose"
Gossage

Graig
Nettles

Thurman Munson

Ron Guidry

PART IV

Casey, Yogi,
and the
Mick

15

Casey

The Yankees did not repeat as American League champs in 1948, finishing third behind Cleveland and Boston, and just like that, Bucky Harris was gone. Harris was a MacPhail man and it was likely he would have been fired even if the Yanks had won the championship in '48. The Yankees were eager to sweep away any remnant of the tumultuous MacPhail, and Harris was the primary casualty. George Weiss ran the Yankees now, and he would get his own man to manage the club.

Topping's announcement that Charles Dillon "Casey" Stengel would become the new Yankee manager was met with an incredulous silence and then a loud skepticism by the press, the fans, and the players. In the first place, Stengel had never had much success as a manager. In nine years with the Dodgers and the Braves, his clubs had never finished in first. At age fifty-nine Casey would get his third chance to bring home a winner, but things didn't look too promising to Yankee die-hards.

Even more than his mediocre record, what seemed to bother his critics most was Casey's image as a clown. Who could take Stengel seriously? There was no doubt that Casey was a lovable guy who could make everyone laugh. But did the Yankees, who wielded their mystique of invincibility like a cudgel, really want a buffoon to spearhead their charge?

Lee MacPhail: "The general consensus was that Stengel simply didn't fit in with the Yankees, that image of dignity, class, refinement. Everybody knew Casey Stengel, he talked a lot, he was loud, and he drank publicly. When we heard it, there were a lot of people around the Yankees who said in one way or another, 'My God, we've hired a clown.'"

Dave Egan (in his Boston sports column): "Well, sirs and ladies, the Yankees have now been mathematically eliminated from the 1949 pennant race. They eliminated themselves when they engaged Perfesser Casey Stengel to mismanage them for the next two years, and you may be sure that the perfesser will oblige to the best of his unique ability."

Eddie Lopat: "I think a lot of guys looked at him as an interim manager. We all knew about him. When you thought about Casey Stengel taking over, all you could do was smile."

Casey Stengel: "Well, I guess I've been doing things that were a little out of the way for most of my life in baseball. It gave some people the idea that I was just a comedian. When I was signed to manage the New York Yankees after the 1948 season, many of the writers couldn't understand why I was brought in to handle such a big job. They had watched some of my work, evidently, as a manager at Brooklyn in the thirties, and at Boston later on. They thought that I wasn't very serious, and that I never cared very much about winning games, and that I was too easy to get along with, and so forth.

"But half the time I was too serious, maybe, with my work. When I don't win, I'm good and mad at night. But if you think you're going to do better just by being serious all the time, and never telling any stories or doing any kidding around—why, you're a little mistaken. Some people never could understand that."[1]

Stengel's considerable reputation as a joker started in his playing days. He played several years for McGraw's World Champion Giants in the early 1920s and starred in the 1923 Series in a losing effort against the Yankees. But before his career was over, Casey had bounced around quite a bit. "Every time two owners got together with a fountain pen, Casey was being bought or sold," said Quentin Reynolds.

Casey Stengel: "I played in professional baseball for twenty years but a lot of people seem to remember some of the stunts I pulled better than they do the ball games I helped to win.

"The one that's remembered the most was the time I came back to Ebbets Field in 1918 after being traded from Brooklyn to Pittsburgh over the winter. Those Brooklyn fans were riding me. They cheered you as long as you were playing for them, but when you went away you weren't any good, see.

"One of my old Brooklyn buddies, Leon Cadore, was out in the bull pen. He was a cutup—loved to do card tricks, loved to do coin tricks. He was very agile with his hands, and he'd caught this young sparrow in the bull pen that day. Just before my first time at bat I got it from him and put it under my cap. I could feel it moving, you know, inside there on my scalp.

"So I walked up to the plate swinging three bats very hard. And the crowd yells, everybody gets excited, and they're booing me to death. Then I threw the bats down and grabbed my eye as if something was in it, and said, 'Time.' Cy Pigler was umpiring behind the plate, and he called time. Then I turned around to face the crowd and lifted my hat off and made a big bow. And when the bird flew out, the crowd just went, 'Oh-h-h-h-h-h-h-h.' "[2]

"How'd I get my name? Well, you know my hometown is Kansas City, Missouri. So a number of people when I started out in baseball called me K.C. for Kansas City. And there was the old story of Casey at the bat and I struck out a number of times my first two years in baseball and I received the name Strikeout Casey.

"I was a high school star in several sports in Kansas City. And I found out that baseball paid a little money in those days. About the size of army pay. So I decided I'd go to Illinois and try my luck in professional ball. My dad when he found out I was thinking of baseball as my career said, 'Son, what are you going to do laying idle in the winter?'

"I said, 'I don't know.'

"'Well,' he said, 'you're not going to be a pool hall bum, son. So you better come back home. And save your money because you're going to go to work and quit baseball if you don't.'

"So when I went home I went to dental college. But the first few plates I made convinced me that I was not a dentist. The first person I made a plate for never talked for about ten days. So that's when I decided I was a ball player.

"Later on I played with Racine in the Wisconsin-Illinois League. The league blew up July the Fourth and I had to go with it. I remember the day I played in Racine and I went behind the umpire that called a strike out on me and I sneaked up and hit him with a bat on the fanny. And after that they wanted to turn me out of baseball and I had to go on up to Chicago or they woulda run me outta baseball for sure."

George Weiss: "I've been in this game a long time and I never knew a man who could talk baseball all night the way Casey can. He is a dedicated baseball man. You can ask him anything about any move he makes in a game and he'll always have an answer. Casey never makes a move without knowing why he does it. He isn't a clown. He's a great baseball man."

All Stengel did was win a record five straight World Championships from 1949 to 1953. It took 111 wins by Cleveland in 1954 to stop the Yankee string of titles, but the "slump" was short-lived. Under Casey the Yanks won pennants again in 1955, 1956, 1957, and 1958, dropped to third in 1959, and then won again in 1960, including two more World Titles. But even after all his success they never could figure Ol' Casey out. And that's the way he liked it.

Joe Collins: "Casey was very flamboyant. In spring training every evening Casey closed the cocktail lounge in the hotel. Every evening! Casey would have all the newspaper boys down there. He'd have an audience down in the bar till four o'clock in the morning. He'd be up at eight. Used to wear those sportswriters out. They were all afraid to go to bed in case he told something at four in the morning and they'd miss a story. That's a fact."

Bob Cerv: "Funny thing about Case, he'd tell you something and you'd have to get out of there and kind of go back later because he'd start a story on something and pretty soon he'd be onto something else, pretty soon something else, then something else. Then, he'd be back to the first story and finish 'em all. A lot of the writers didn't understand if they just waited long enough they'd get all the answers. They'd leave and they never did know what was going on.

"I remember one time in 1956 it was one of those terrible hot muggy days in New York. I was there early and I did some hitting and I threw some batting practice and I was beat. There was water just pouring off of me and I came over to the bench to cool off. Stengel's there and he starts going on about Slaughter and Ford and this and that and on and on and, finally, he said, 'And, by the way, one of you guys is going to Kansas City next year.' And I'm the only one sittin' there. So that's how I knew I was going to Kansas City.

"So if you listened hard enough and long enough to Casey he'd tell you everything you needed to know. So, guess what, come November—BOB CERV TRADED TO KANSAS CITY.

"I think Larsen was supposed to go, too, but damned if he didn't pitch that perfect game of his. They sure couldn't trade him after that, now could they?"

George Weiss: "I suppose I have stayed up later and talked longer—or, rather, listened longer—with Casey than anybody else in baseball. He'd talk all night and if you weren't a baseball man you'd think the guy was crazy. But if you were a baseball man, well, by the time you finally got to bed—and the chances were he'd be sitting on the other bed still talking—you discovered you were really learning things. I mean, you'd quit second-guessing him."

Joe Collins: "I was with Stengel for nine years and I could never figure out why he did some things he did. But every time he made a move something good came of it. I don't know why. To me and everybody else on the ball club, well, we'd shake our heads and say, 'Hell, I wouldn't do it!'

"He would pinch-hit in situations that were ridiculous. He'd have two runs in, bases loaded, nobody out, and he'd pinch-hit Bauer for Woodling in the first inning when Woodling was on a hitting tear. And I'll be damned if Bauer didn't get a double or a triple about every time and, suddenly, we're ahead by five runs. It could just as easily have been a double play, but instead we're up five–nothing—and the game's over real quick like.

"Up in Boston, Mel Parnell used to beat us every time we went there. He musta beat us a minimum of fifteen, twenty times over a period of three, four years. We always loaded our lineup with right-handed hitters—big, strong, right-handed hitters to take advantage of that short left-field wall. That's how you're supposed to play it in Fenway. So one day Casey came up with the idea he's going to put all left-handers in the lineup. From that time on Mel Parnell never beat us one time. He couldn't pitch to left-handed hitters."

Eddie Lopat: "He did certain things at certain times which always panned out. Of course, he had some horses that could produce.

"One time we had Jackie Jensen who was a young kid and we're playing in Detroit and Jackie's first time up in the ball game he hits a home run. Second time up he hits a home run. The third time he came up with the bases loaded and Casey took him out for a pinch-hitter and Bauer, the hitter, got a long single and drove in three runs.

"About three or four weeks later we were on a train, which is how we traveled at the time, so we tried to pin him down as to why he made those moves.

"'You know,' he says, 'I've seen a lot of guys hit two home runs in a row but very few hit three.'

"How can you argue with that kind of logic?"

Moose Skowron: "I had a hell of a year in '53. Minor League Player of the Year. Come up in '54 with the Yankees. I'm hitting fourth against Billy Heft playing the Detroit Tigers at home with 55,000 people there. It's in the first inning, bases loaded and no outs. And I hear a whistle and I says, 'You gotta be kiddin'!' I never got taken out for a pinch-hitter in the bottom of the first inning.

"He took me out, put in Eddie Robinson. I was so angry I went into the clubhouse, didn't even shower, put my clothes on and went back to the hotel. Eddie Robinson hits a double and he drives in all three runners and we win 3–0.

"The next day I come out to the ballpark and Casey's waiting for me. He said, 'Moose, come to my office.'

"Well, you know he dealt out a lot of doubletalk to sportswriters but when he talked to me he talked in real plain English. I'll never forget the words he said.

"'Don't tell me. I'm out to win a pennant and I don't give a damn how you feel. I want to win a ball game.' I never challenged him again.

"Then, in the World Series he almost took me out with the bases loaded in the seventh game against the Dodgers in '56. I hear a whistle and I come back to the dugout.

"'Moose,' he says. 'Take a shot to right field.'

"'Okay.'

"First pitch was low and away and I pulled the ball into the left-field stands, hit a grand slammer, and I come into home plate and Casey yells, 'That's the way to hit that ball to right field.'"

Eddie Lopat: "They didn't have all those stats that they have today. He had a wonderful memory. He knew every hitter that was sitting on that bench—how he executed against whoever was pitching. He didn't have to whip out the stat sheets and read data. He had it on his fingertips. That was one of his big assets."

"I would have to say that in my eight years I played with Casey he was the greatest psychologist I ever saw. In 1953 we had gone through a streak in which we won 18 in a row and everybody was hoppin' around, skipping. We were 13½ games in front. This was like the tail end of June. But there's always a letdown when you run a streak like that, and consequently, after they broke the streak we lost the second and third and fourth game and we weren't too concerned about it. Then, all of a sudden nobody could make the right play and we lost the fifth in a row.

"Then we were saying to ourselves, 'Casey's got to have a meeting and really chew us out.' And we lost the sixth and we're waiting for the meeting. Nothing. So we go out and play the seventh game. Got beat again. Waiting for the meeting. Nothing. Now we're in Boston, Friday night, we lose. That's eight. Then Reynolds is pitching the Saturday game and he's got two outs in the ninth and we're winning 3–2. There's nobody on and he walks the next batter. Then White, their catcher, homers against the screen and we lose that one. And now it's nine in a row!

"Finally, the next day Raschi won 5–2. So we had the next day off and came back Tuesday night and before the game as we were dressing, Crosetti says, 'Skipper wants to hold a meeting.' And he really jumped on us. He chewed us from top to bottom.

"There was another incident that will help explain this one. We were in Detroit for a doubleheader one day and we played sloppily and terribly and we gave the first game away. And the second game starts and in the fifth inning we're leading 16–2 and Casey is ranting and raving in the dugout like a maniac. We're all thinking the man's losing his marbles. What the hell's he raving about? We're winning 16–2 and he's raising hell with everybody.

"Like I said, a couple weeks later on the train we pinned him down. 'What's going on with you, Casey? We lose a sloppy game and you go in the clubhouse singing, and we win 16–2, you go crazy.'

"'Well,' he says, 'I found out one thing. I know I got some guys that know how to play. They know when they make mistakes. They're mad. And you try to talk to a worked-up man and you're liable to get punched right in the mouth. When you're ahead they laugh at it and you can call 'em anything. They can take more than when they're mad.'

"That was his psychology."

Casey Stengel: "The first fifteen guys on a club you don't have to bother with. They're always playing and don't need the manager. The next five play once in a while, so you gotta spend some time buttering them up. The last five you gotta be with all the time, because they may be plotting a revolution against you.

"The secret of managing a club is to keep the five guys who hate you away from the five who are undecided.

"What do I say when I go out to take the pitcher out? I usually say, 'Hello, darling. How are you this evening?' He's only walked two, three weak hitters. And I say, 'Well, you're such a lovely fellow and this and that but it'd be grand if you'd get out of this hole. Now just relax.' And I say, 'Tra-la-la-la-la, relax. Don't get tight now. You've walked all these men. You get the side out I will raise your salary.'

"And sometimes they do it and I usually raise their salary. I have so much money now. I played so many years in baseball I give 'em a raise."

Yogi Berra: "You never could tell when Casey was going to start psychologizing you. I remember once he came out of his private office into the clubhouse before a ball game and started giving it to me about the way I had called the pitches the day before, when we had lost. I didn't mind at first but he kept it up, and he got pretty personal and I finally blew my stack. 'So if I'm doin' so bad,' I told him, 'why don't you catch?' He didn't say anything to that; he just walked back into his office. But after we won the game that day, and I got three for four, he came over to my locker and gave me one of those sly grins of his and said, 'Got you mad, didn't I?' "[3]

Casey Stengel: "I had this player in Brooklyn and you could ask him for a match and find out what bar he was in the night before. After we traded him to another club I always went up to him before the game with a cigarette and asked for a match. If he pulled out a match from some bar, I knew he had been out late and I could pitch him fastballs."

STENGEL-ESE SPOKEN HERE

Despite Stengel's unmatched success as manager of the Yankees, despite his seven World Championships and ten pennants, he is still best remembered and loved for his zany brand of witticism, double-talk, off-the-wall one-liners, and run-amok monologues known affectionately as Stengel-ese.

Academy award-winning actor Charles Durning said about portraying Stengel, "It's the first role I've ever played in a foreign language."

Casey Stengel: "With the salary I get here, I'm so hollow and starving that I'm liable to explode like a light bulb if I hit the ground too hard."

"I was such a dangerous hitter I even got intentional walks in batting practice."

"They brought me up to the Brooklyn Dodgers, which at that time was in Brooklyn."

"Take those fellows over to that other diamond. I want to see if they can play on the road."

"Jerry Lumpe looks like the best hitter in the world until you put him in the lineup."

"It's like I used to tell my barber. Shave and a haircut but don't cut my throat. I may want to do that myself."

"What's the secret to platooning? There's not much to it. You put a right-hand hitter against a left-hand pitcher and a left-hand hitter against a right-hand pitcher and on cloudy days you use a fastball pitcher."

"People ask me, 'Casey, how can you speak so much when you don't talk English too good?' Well, I've been invited to Europe, and I say, 'They don't speak English over there too good, either.'"

"It ain't sex that's troublesome, it's staying up all night looking for it. You gotta learn that if you don't get it by midnight, chances are you ain't gonna get it, and if you do, it ain't worth it."

"Now there's three things you can do in a baseball game: you can win or you can lose or it can rain."

"There comes a time in every man's life and I've had plenty of them."

"Old-timers' weekends and airplane landings are alike. If you can walk away from them, they're successful."

"Most people my age [75] are dead at the present time, and you could look it up."

"When I played in Brooklyn, I could go to the ballpark for a nickel carfare. But now I live in Pasadena, and it costs me fifteen or sixteen dollars to take a cab to Glendale. If I was a young man, I'd study to become a cabdriver."

"I stayed up last night and watched the Republican Convention all night long. I watched all of them talk, and listened to them and seen them and I'm not interested in politics. If you watch them and listen to them you can find out why you're not."

"The way our luck has been lately, our fellows have been getting hurt on their days off."

"Once, someone in Washington gave me a picture to autograph and I wrote, 'Do good in school.' I look up, this guy is seventy-eight years old."

"I love signing autographs. I'll sign anything but veal cutlets. My ball-point pen slips on veal cutlets."

"Kansas City wasn't the fun spot in my day that it is now."

"Look at Bobby Richardson. He doesn't drink, he doesn't smoke, he doesn't chew, he doesn't stay out late, and he still can't hit .250."

"Whenever I decided to release a guy, I always had his room searched first for a gun. You couldn't take any chances with some of them birds."

CASEY GETS HIS HORSES

Casey had always said, "If you give me the horses, I can win a pennant." And in 1949, riding precariously astride a herd of galloping stallions known as the Yankees, Stengel finally had his stable of thoroughbreds. But best of all, he had the one thing every manager prays for—a great pitching staff. In fact, one of the best ever. Eddie Lopat, Allie Reynolds, and Vic Raschi won 307 games and lost 143 (a .682 percentage) for the Yankees between 1949 and 1953, during which time the Yankees won five straight World Championships.

Tom Sturdivant: "It was Raschi, Reynolds, and Lopat who brought Stengel up. They already had the greatest staff of all time when Stengel came over to the Yanks. So they all broke Casey in. He was a great manager the moment he set eyes on those three guys."

Eddie Lopat: "In his last days they asked Branch Rickey who he thought was the greatest pitching staff that he ever saw and he said, 'Raschi, Reynolds, Lopat, and Ford.'

"So they asked him how can you say that with all the great pitchers in all those years you were in baseball. That covers quite a few years.

"He said, 'Well, to make it short and sweet, you name me another staff that won five straight pennants and five straight World Series. When it got toughest they always won.'

"Coming from a man like Rickey that was quite an accolade.

"Raschi was a power pitcher. He threw a fastball and a slider. He was what you call a bulldog on the mound. He went after you. Everything was all business. He'd battle you tooth and nail.

"Reynolds was on the same pattern. I still claim as far as I'm concerned Reynolds threw harder than anybody I ever saw. Some days he was impossible to hit and his record shows that. During his years with the Yankees he relieved twenty-two times and he was 22 for 22.

"He could throw as hard as Gossage and he had a good curve to go with it and a slider to go with that. He relieved

me in a Series against Brooklyn in '49 with the bases loaded
and two out. The last seven men he faced, he struck out five
of them. Then in the '50 Series, he came in to relieve against
Philadelphia. The batter was Lopata—a damned good hitter.
He threw three fastballs by him. Lopata didn't know what
was going on.

"Feller had a good fastball but on a given day for three,
four innings Reynolds could throw the ball harder than
anybody I ever saw. . . .

"In the spring of '48 I was traded to the Yanks and, funny
thing, I was born and raised in New York City and was a
Yankee rooter as a kid growing up, but I guess I'd gotten
acclimated to Chicago, met a lot of people and the players
there were great to me. So when they first told me I was
traded I sorta felt bad.

"Then the more I thought about it I realized I'd fulfilled
my dream, being a kid going to Yankee Stadium, rooting for
the Yankees all the time and here I am. Plus, I was going
from a seventh-place ball club to a champion. So it was a
great thrill for me when it finally dawned on me.

"You know, they used to call me the Junkman because I
had four or five different pitches and I threw them all with the
same motion. My style was deceptive. I was famous for
throwing junk but anybody that knows anything about baseball knows you can't just throw slow stuff up there. You've
got to be able to set a batter up with the fast stuff first.

"I'll give you an example. One day we were playing in
Cleveland and it was hot as heck. The hotel where we were
staying wasn't air-conditioned, so instead of staying in our
room and boiling I asked Johnny Sain if he wanted to go on
down to the ballpark with me and wait around there.

"When we got over to the ballpark we could hear someone
in there taking batting practice, which was odd because it was
only about three or four in the afternoon. So we were
wondering what was up.

"So we went inside kind of quiet like and stood at the back
and checked it out. The Cleveland ball club was out there
taking batting practice. They had a left-hander, Sam Zoldak,
whose style was similar to mine and they had him throwing
junk up there—those big slow curves—and the Cleveland
batters were standing in the box flat-footed and just slapping

the ball to the opposite field.

"They were getting ready for me, see. So I told Yogi before we went out there that night that the first time through the order we weren't going to give them anything slow. Just fastballs in. So we did that for about four or five innings and they didn't know what to do. They were all looking for the slow stuff and they were getting jammed. They broke two or three bats in the first couple innings.

"After that I went back to my old style and we beat them pretty easy. The next day I went over during batting practice and talked to Tony Cucinello, one of their coaches, who I'd played with on the White Sox. 'Hey, Tony,' I said. 'Next time you have one of your secret batting practices, get out there before noon. I don't get up that early.'"

Casey Stengel: "Lopat looks like he is throwing wads of tissue paper. Every time he wins a game, fans come down out of the stands asking for contracts."

Charlie Silvera: "They'd put Lopat in between Raschi and Reynolds, who could really throw smoke, and Eddie would feed 'em his junk. That would screw 'em up. Eddie threw a screwball, curve, slider. Great motion. He'd come at you with his jerky type of shoulder motion and all. People would be swinging at the ball before it got to the plate."

Allie Reynolds: "Me and Eddie had one problem. He was so different from me. He threw a lot of finesse balls mostly out of the strike zone. Looked big as watermelons coming up there. I made a bad pitch one time in Detroit and came into the dugout after the inning and he said, 'How in the hell could you make a pitch like that?' And I said, 'I don't need no soft-throwing son of a bitch telling me how to pitch.'"

A PENNANT ON THE LAST DAY OF THE SEASON

Despite the superlative battery corps, 1949 was anything but a cakewalk for Stengel and the Yankees. The Yankees were decimated with injuries. Henrich went down with a back injury, Yogi Berra broke a finger, and Johnny Mize tore

a muscle in his shoulder. In all, the Yankees suffered
seventy-two injuries that kept players out of the lineup. They
should have limped home in fifth or sixth, but they battled
down to the last day.

Casey Stengel: "There was a time when I thought I
wouldn't have nine men to put on the field. I would say to
myself, 'This was the greatest club in baseball. What's
happened to it?'"

Gus Mauch: "We had seventy-two injuries that season.
And when Henrich caught the foul ball that ended that last
game and gave us the pennant, Bill Dickey jumped up in the
dugout and cracked his head on the roof. That made seventy-
three.

"That was the most fighting team I ever saw.

"Every day I'd walk into Stengel's office and I'd say, 'Your
star outfielder is hurt and can't play.' And he'd say, 'Thank
you, doctor.' He never blinked an eye. He grew tougher
later, but that year he was gentle. If the team was on a
winning streak, he might howl and shout, but he was mild
when we were losing or when we were hurting.

"It was hard to believe, but Casey would take a guy out of
the lineup and the substitute would do better than the
original. He moved players around, he switched positions, he
did everything, and everything seemed to work."[4]

Vic Raschi: "In 1949 the Red Sox came into New York to
close out the season with a two-game series, leading us by
one. All they had to do was win once to take the pennant.
They had a rookie pitcher, whose name I forget at the
moment. Well, just before the Saturday game we overheard
some of the Red Sox talking about starting this rookie on
Sunday. In other words, they were so confident of beating us
on Saturday that they were looking forward to relaxing in the
last game, figuring they'd have wrapped it up by then. This
was the way they felt. I suppose they were entitled to feel
confident; but it made us kind of mad and gave us some
added incentive—not that we weren't primed for those games
to begin with.

"Well, they did jump off to a 4–0 lead in that game. But we

tied it and then won it on Johnny Lindell's home run and some great relief pitching by Joe Page. So we went into Sunday's game tied for first place, and I guess they forgot about starting that rookie.

"Ball games just don't come any bigger than that, do they? Not only are you tied for first place on the last day of the season, but you're playing the team that you're tied with.

"To make things just a little more difficult for us, Joe DiMaggio had been sick for about a week with a virus and wasn't up to full strength. He couldn't run too well, but he was in there, and we wanted him in there.

"I had a pretty good idea that I would be pitching that game and I was pleased about it. You have to get back to pride again; everything was riding on this one game, and the team was entrusting me to win it for them. I knew that as long as I stayed in baseball, no matter how many times I went to the mound, I would never pitch a game bigger than this one.

"I never talked too much before I pitched, because I had a lot of thinking to do. You've heard of pitchers psyching themselves before a game; well, it can help quite a bit, but I think it helps even more if you get a kind of sweaty feeling in the palm of your hand. That's anticipation. I had never experienced a buildup and an anxiety before a game to such an extent. And they can say what they want to, but they all get it. I wouldn't give one penny for any ball player who didn't get that anxiety; I wouldn't want him playing beside me.

"I think it was fitting that it turned out to be a close, hard-fought game. We scored a run in the bottom of the first inning. Phil Rizzuto hit a triple and Tommy Henrich brought him in with a ground ball. After that it was nip and tuck all the way. Nothing but zeroes up on the scoreboard, and that big, big Sunday crowd sitting back and watching.

"So we went into the ninth inning leading by five runs. It should have been easy, but it wasn't. The Red Sox still had some kick left in them. They got two men on and Bobby Doerr hit one into deep center. Normally DiMaggio would have caught up with it. It fell in for a triple. Joe took himself out of the game, right then and there."[5]

Joe DiMaggio: "I should have removed myself on Vern Stephens's single in the ninth. I had terrible pains in my shinbones. And when I didn't catch Bobby Doerr's triple, which was catchable, I didn't hesitate any longer and walked off. Gosh, we had only a three-run lead and I didn't want to hurt the club by falling on my face if another fly had been hit to me."

Tommy Henrich: "Cliff Mapes took his place in center. Somebody flies out to Mapes for the second out. I'm playing first base and I position myself at the mound to take the throw in. Mapes throws it over my head to Yogi at the home plate. Raschi is backing up Yogi. So I'm standing at the mound. Yogi comes out and we wait there for Vic. And here he comes, scowling; he's all business. Vic Raschi was always all business. I know Yogi is going to give him the old, 'Come on, Vic old boy, just one more.' That's what I'm going to say, too. As Vic gets close to us he says, 'Give me the damned ball and get the hell out of here.' We left. And as I walked to first base I said to myself, 'We're in.'

"Birdie Tebbetts is the batter. He hits a foul ball in the air down to first base. I didn't have to move more than a few feet. But I hear Jerry Coleman yelling behind me: 'I got it! I got it!' Jerry called for everything. 'Get out of here!' I yelled. He wasn't taking that one. That was my ball. That was the one I'd been looking for all year long.

"So we went into the Series, against the Dodgers. That first game was as good a pitching duel as you'll ever want to see. Allie Reynolds against Don Newcombe. Nobody got close to a run until the bottom of the ninth. I led off that inning. Newcombe tried a fastball and missed outside. Then he came back with kind of a slider and missed outside again. Now it's two balls and no strikes. He hasn't walked anybody all game, and nobody wants to start an inning with a base on balls. So I say to myself, 'This is going to be a good ball.' I was ninety-nine percent certain he was going to throw his fastball and that it would be over the plate.

"So I'm geared for the right speed now. Everything was my way, right? Hitting the ball was something else again, but at least I knew I had every advantage. If I had been anything less than positive about it I would have sacrificed part of that advantage. Newk came in there with it and I tagged it good and solid. I knew it was hit hard enough, but sometimes that kind of ball sinks before it has a chance to go out. As I ran down the line, I looked at Furillo and as soon as I saw his head go up a little bit I said to myself, 'That's all.' I knew it was going to go out. That got us going in that Series. We won it in five games. You know, I participated in eight World Series, as a player and a coach, and was never on a loser. Never saw the losing side of a World Series. That's pretty good, isn't it?"[6]

16

Yogi

Along with great pitching, Stengel inherited a great catch-er. In fact, he may have been the greatest catcher that baseball has ever seen—Lawrence Peter "Yogi" Berra.

Berra eventually won three MVP awards and hit more home runs—313—than any other catcher until Johnny Bench bettered his mark in 1980. He also holds the record for a catcher of most games without an error (148) and most chances without an error (950). His World Series credentials are unmatched, having played in more Series games than any player in history—75—with the most at-bats—259—and the most hits—71.

Bill Dickey: "Yogi was a great kid and a good learner. He was very shy, I remember, and quiet, but he listened real well. It was really my job to work with him and make a judgment whether he should catch or play the outfield.

"The Yankee staff would hold a meeting every week and talk about the club, and every week they'd ask me, 'You gonna make a catcher out of Berra?' And I kept putting them off because I hadn't seen enough of him. Finally, I gave them their answer. 'I think he ought to make a pretty good catcher.' And a pretty good decision that was! I think most of the others thought he should play the outfield, but he convinced me that he could handle catching. And I think Berra improved more as a defensive catcher, not just that spring but over the next few years, too, than any catcher I ever saw. He became one of the truly all-time great catchers of baseball history.'"[1]

Spud Chandler: "Yogi came in and it so happened that the first game Yogi ever caught, I pitched. I told Yogi, 'You won't have a tough time catching me. Just be in position. That's all I ask. I know what the story is.'

"But me and Yogi had a problem. See, his little fingers was so short that he got down and gave the signs and they were hard for me to see and he accused me of crossing him up. I said, 'Yogi, I haven't crossed you up.' He said, 'Yes you did. I gave you a curveball sign and you give me the fastball.' I said, 'No you didn't. I didn't see but one finger.'

"So we was in the dugout, see, and I says, 'Get down and give me a curveball sign.' And he got down and I says, 'Yogi, look down there at the way you're givin' the fingers for the curveball sign. Your fingers ain't spread. They're frozen together. You've got to separate them a little so I can see two of those little stubs that you're puttin' down.'

"And we got along real good after that."

Allie Reynolds: "Yogi sure wasn't a great catcher to begin with. He didn't have a very good arm. His arm got better and he learned. Problem was he just hadn't played much baseball. When a man got on first he got a little nervous. He wanted you to throw everything high and outside so he could throw it easier. I said, 'Yogi, that's not very good pitching. You gotta throw it over the plate if you expect to get anybody out.'"

Eddie Lopat: "Berra wasn't a very good catcher when he first came up. But nobody is. He had trouble when he first came up throwing runners out. He had a good arm but he didn't know how to get in position to throw. He was terrible in blocking balls, throwing runners out, and we had a tough time winning.

"It got so bad in '48 that we told Bucky Harris to get him out of there. We couldn't win a close game 'cause a guy would get on first and run to second. Yogi'd throw the ball into center field, the guy would be at third. Then, you'd drop a curveball in front of the plate and it would go through his legs because he didn't know how to block it and the guy would score. So consequently the pitchers were afraid to throw that kind of ball so you'd hang one and the guy would hit it out.

"So Dickey eliminated all that in '49. And Yogi kept working at it and got better and better and better. By '52, '53 he'd become a good defensive catcher—a really good one.

"Plus you couldn't take him out of the lineup because he had that good bat, so he played right field. He was a good athlete, too, because he went out in right field and he played that thing like he was playing it all his life. He even played third base later on in his career a couple of times and he did a hell of a job at it. The good athlete can adapt himself."

Bob Grim: "Yogi was a smart catcher. His arm was just adequate, but by God, he got the job done. They didn't steal much on him. Oh, he had that one bad Series against the Dodgers in '49, I think it was, when they ran wild on him.

"Of course, that's when he first came up, but then Dickey got ahold of him and made him a hell of a catcher. They never stole on him much after that. He didn't have the great gun but he could get rid of the ball very quickly."

Bill Kinnamon: "Yogi Berra was as good a receiver as I ever worked behind. He had as good an arm as I've ever seen and an innate ability to catch the ball. He was the best ever on a bouncing ball in the dirt. He absolutely never gave you that nonchalant swipe at the ball. He'd be down right in front of it. I never saw a ball hit the dirt and get by him to the backstop. If the ball was close, he would get it. He was so quick back there—not fast, but quick.

"To illustrate the point, Bert Campaneris was on first base in Kansas City one day. Campy could fly, and he got a jump on a pitch like you couldn't believe. The batter foul-tipped the pitch, and I'm telling you before it ever got to Yogi's glove, he opened the glove. The ball hit right in that glove and fell to the ground. I'll swear on a stack of Bibles that if Campy hadn't been running, Yogi would have caught that ball. Catching a foul tip is pure reflex; you can't control it. Now Yogi didn't catch the ball because if he had, I would have left Campaneris at second base. He didn't catch the ball, and I swear he did it on purpose.

"Of course, Yogi was not the most delightful guy to be behind because he chattered all the time. Every time his pitcher threw the ball it was a strike, and when he was hitting, every pitch was a ball. I mean every pitch. One time a pitch bounced up there, and he said, 'Wasn't too bad, was it?' Fortunately, when he was batting, he swung at an awful lot of bad pitches. He was such a good hitter he could pick them out of the dirt and double them off the wall."[2]

Berra may have had to learn to catch, but he was a born hitter. He had one of the purest swings baseball has ever seen. He could hit anything, and that was the problem. He may have hit as many bad balls as strikes. Yogi was a notorious bad-ball hitter, but that seemed to fit his image.

Ben Chapman: "Yogi was a reasonably good catcher but mostly Yogi could hit. He could hit wild pitches over his head and lose 'em so fast the pitcher'd be out there wonderin' what the hell happened."

Yogi Berra: "I can't deny that I've always been a bad-ball hitter. I like to swing at anything that looks good to me, as long as I can reach it. I've always figured I'm not getting paid to get bases on balls. Bobby Brown used to say I had the biggest strike zone in baseball, from my ankles to a foot above my head, and I guess that's right. The coaches were always getting on me about it, and I remember once, in '47, I hit a home run with the bases loaded, and when I came around third Chuck Dressen shook his head at me. 'It was a bad pitch!' he yelled at me. I hollered right back. 'Nah!' I said. 'It was a good pitch, right where I wanted it,' and I put my hand out in front of the letters on my shirt to show him where it was. The point is, it might have been a bad pitch, but not for me; I like that kind.

"A bad pitch isn't a bad pitch anymore when you hit it into the seats."[3]

Allie Reynolds: "Yogi looked less like an athlete than anybody I ever saw, yet he was one of the best. He could do everything. Yogi made more good pitchers blink their eyes than anyone I ever saw. Some of 'em thought nobody could hit their curveball. He broke them of that habit pretty quick. If he could reach it, he could hit it. He could hit anything. His only problem was he swung at some he couldn't reach."

Hector Lopez: "Yogi had the fastest bat I ever saw. He could hit a ball late—that was already past him—and take it out of the park. The pitchers were afraid of him because he'd hit anything. So they couldn't set him up by throwing the ball outside or try and waste one 'cause Yogi might reach out and hit it off the fence. So they didn't know what to throw him. Yogi had 'em psyched out and he wasn't even trying to psych 'em out."

Yogi Berra: "I think maybe that's my trouble, the reason why I had such a bad year last year. Maybe that's the trouble, I'm getting too many good balls. I should start swinging at the bad ones again."

No matter what he did on the diamond, Yogi's personality always seemed to get as much press as his hitting. A shy, awkward, truly nice guy whom everyone found lovable, Yogi was not blessed with movie star looks, and he always seemed to get himself into one verbal cul-de-sac after another.

He was, as Casey Stengel put it, "a peculiar fellow with amazing ability."

Yogi Berra: "The best thing that happened to me when I was a kid was being asked by Leo Browne, the commander of the Stockham Post, to play on their ball team in the American Legion tournament.

"When I was fourteen the manager, Jack McGuire, was a scout for the Cardinals. He had a boy on the team, Jack Jr., who later played shortstop for the Giants for a little while.

Young Jack was the one who hung the name Yogi on me. I was always called Lawdie by my family as a sort of endearment for Lawrence, until one day the team went to the movies and saw a short subject that was a travelogue about India. One of the people in it was a Hindu fakir who was called a yogi. The yogi was sitting with his arms folded and his knees crossed, looking very sad. Jack thought he looked just like I used to look, sitting down after a ball game or killing time outside Riva's at night. 'You know,' he said when we walked out of the movie house, 'you look just like a yogi. I'm going to call you Yogi.'"

Bobby Brown: "You know what I'd do if I were a writer? I'd dog Yogi Berra's steps all through spring training and all through the regular season, too. I'd jot down every remark he made and I'd write a book about him at the end of the season. There's never been anybody like Berra in baseball."

Charlie Keller: "I'm gonna have a picture taken of me and Yogi. Then I'm going to take it home and tell my wife anytime she thinks I'm not so good-looking, she should take a look at you."

Lefty Gomez: "Yogi's the only catcher whose looks were improved with his mask on."

Casey Stengel: "Yogi Berra's one of my only players that's never been booed but once in his life. He's an odd character. He looked like a wrestler but he wasn't a wrestler. He's a good ball player. He's one of the greatest catchers now in the present-day era.

"Also, he has some way about him. When he gets on the ball field he has the feminine appeal of the ladies and he also has the male appeal of the men. They say, 'Now look at that boy that looks like a wrestler.' He doesn't look like a graceful fawn or a deer that goes sprinkling around on the field. He just goes out and does his work and he always has good results.

"Everybody talked about his intelligence but in baseball you have to have something besides intelligence. You have to be sharp and see what'll weaken a man. It's just like if a man is a thief he has to be able to steal or he's caught immediately. It's just like if you're in baseball and you're a catcher, you've got to find out the weakness of the man."

Bill Johnson: "I guess Yogi was Casey's favorite, his assistant manager. He always made fun of him, kidded him, but he really loved him. One time Casey was doing an imitation of Yogi on the bench while he was batting. He stuck out his lower lip and talked funny like Yogi and did some of Yogi's bouncy, walking steps. Then Yogi homered and when he came back to the bench I said, 'To me you look like Tyrone Power,' and Yogi said, 'I don't hit with my face,' and Casey just fell off the bench."[4]

Frank Graham: "Casey did more than that for Yogi. Aware, as no one before him had been, that here was a truly sensitive young man who was hurt by many of the quips made about him, yet had the guts to smile through them, Casey acted as a buffer between Berra and those on his own club who poked fun at him. It wasn't long before the slower thinkers among the Yankees gained a realization of what Yogi meant to them."

Moose Skowron: "Berra was funny on the bench, say a lot of different things and everybody understood Yogi. When he said something, we all listened. A lot of people they all think Yogi didn't hit the books, but he didn't miss a trick on the ball field. He knew everything that was going on."

Joe Garagiola: "One year he wasn't hitting well, and people kept making excuses for him. The papers talked about an allergy on his hands. Allergy, hell. That was a case of nerves. And there wasn't anything wrong with him that year except that his mother was dying of cancer and he couldn't concentrate on playing baseball. That's the kind of guy he is. He'd do anything for you. He'd give you half of whatever he had. If he hit a double, he'd gladly give you a single. He's a man who's good to his family, a sensitive man, not a guy who's going to do lines for you. He's not a funny guy and he shouldn't be depicted as a funny guy."[5]

Mel Allen: "Yogi, a bad-ball hitter who hates to pass up the first pitch thrown to him no matter where it is, had no trouble at all passing up the first contract mailed to him by the Yankee front office. He waged his first serious holdout in the spring of 1950, and it was a lulu. Shortly after the contracts were put into the mail that February, a reporter hungry for a scoop asked Yogi if he had signed his yet. 'Nope,' Yogi said cheerfully. 'What did you do? Send it back?' 'Yeah, I sent it back,' Yogi said. 'Wasn't it for enough money?' 'No, it wasn't.' 'How much was it for? Are you far apart?' 'I don't know.' 'What do you mean, you don't know? Didn't you look at it?' 'No, I didn't. I just told my wife to mail the first one right back to them. I knew it wouldn't be for enough.' And that's when the Yankees first discovered what they were up against in Yogi Berra."[6]

Yogi Berra: "I'd rather be a Yankee catcher than the president, and that makes me pretty lucky, I guess, because I could never be the president."

"I want to thank everyone for making this night necessary."

"[When introduced to writer Ernest Hemingway] Yeah, what paper you write for, Ernie?"

"A nickel ain't worth a dime anymore."

"You can observe a lot just by watching."

"If the people don't want to come out to the park, nobody's going to stop 'em."

"It gets late early out there."

Tom Seaver: Hey, Yogi, what time is it?
Yogi: You mean now?

Larry Berra to his father: Hey, Dad, the man is here for the venetian blind.

Yogi: Well, go in my pocket and give him a couple of bucks for a donation and get rid of him.

Carmen Berra: Yogi, I went to see *Dr. Zhivago* today.
Yogi: Now what's wrong with you?

"[Wiring Johnny Bench after Bench broke his record for career home runs by a catcher in 1980] Congratulations on breaking my record last night. I always thought the record would stand until it was broken."

"Nobody goes to that restaurant anymore, it's too crowded."

"Baseball is ninety percent mental. The other half is physical."

"You give a hundred percent in the first half of the game, and if that isn't enough, in the second half you give what's left."

"I usually take a two-hour nap, from one o'clock to four."

"How can you think and hit at the same time?"

"Slump? I ain't in no slump. I just ain't hitting."

"I never blame myself when I'm not hitting. I just blame the bat and if it keeps up I change bats. . . . After all, if I know it isn't my fault that I'm not hitting, how can I get mad at myself?"

Lefty Gomez: What's your cap size, Yogi?
Yogi: How do I know? I'm not in shape yet.

"It ain't over till it's over."

RIZZUTO'S YEAR

The Yankees won the World Championship again in 1950, but this time it was a little easier, as Stengel's team finished three games ahead of Detroit. Then they swept the "Whiz Kids" of the Philadelphia Phillies in four straight in the Series.

A healthy DiMaggio hit .301 with 32 home runs and 122 RBIs. Berra, a regular now behind the plate, hit .322, with 28 homers and 124 RBIs. Hank Bauer, a tough ex-Marine, played alongside DiMaggio in the outfield and hit .320. Raschi, Reynolds, and Lopat, as usual, were the big winners on the mound. But they got help from Tommy Byrne with 16 wins, and from a cocky twenty-one-year-old New Yorker named Edward Charles "Whitey" Ford, who was called up for the last half of the season and won nine big games for the Yanks.

The big story in 1950, however, was the long-underrated Phil Rizzuto. For a decade after he joined the team in 1941, Rizzuto was undeniably the finest shortstop in the game. He was the supreme glove man. He made the impossible look easy and he played so spectacularly for so many years that he was taken for granted. His string of 289 consecutive chances without an error was a record for shortstops, and he led the league in fielding twice and was a four-time All Star.

Never a power hitter, Rizzuto was obscured by the might of the Yankee lineup. He had his best year in 1950, however, hitting .324 and winning the MVP award.

Spud Chandler: "Scooter came up and took Crosetti's place. He did a hell of a job. He was a great little ball player. A great fielder. He could run, steal bases. He could make the double play like a top spinning. And he wasn't a bad hitter. He didn't have the home run power that some of the players had and that probably was the reason he didn't get the attention he deserved."

Casey Stengel: "Every year I get these young shortstops and they always tell me they're ready for the Yankees. And I say, 'All right, let me see you lay down a sacrifice bunt or drag one and beat it out or hit behind the runner the way Rizzuto did. Let me see you come in behind the pitcher and pick up that ball that's bounced over his head and throw the runner out the way Rizzuto did. Let me see you go into short left field or center field or cross the left field foul line and catch that pop fly the way Rizzuto did.'

"They all say they can do it like Rizzuto did but you know something? There ain't a one of them can."

Ty Cobb: "One of the few scientific hitters left in baseball today is Phil Rizzuto. He's small, he's frail, and there are a hundred players in the big leagues who can hit a longer ball. But he can lay down a perfect bunt and poke his hits in any direction, and he gets results. Pound for pound he's the best baseball player alive today. I like to watch him field as well as bat. He picks off grounders like picking cherries, and he has the opposition jittery every time he comes to bat. They don't know what to expect. If it were not for Honus Wagner, who was a superman in every respect, I would make Phil Rizzuto my all-time, all-star shortstop."

Bucky Harris: "I wouldn't trade Phil for any shortstop in baseball. He pulls a miracle out there every day. I don't care if he hits .250, it's what he does with his glove—the way he saves our pitchers—that makes him so great. And he's great to have in the clubhouse. He's always kidding around, full of fun. It's impossible to stay down with Rizzuto around. He's the pepper guy. He keeps everyone hopping."

Charlie Silvera: "You'd have to say that Rizzuto should belong in the Hall of Fame 'cause you can't live without a good shortstop. But you look back and see who he played with. He was on a team of Hall of Famers and he was just overlooked. But he should have been one too. He could do everything. He could go in the hole better than anyone I ever saw. And he was a magician with that glove. And he could hit, too—just not the long ball. But, hell, in 1950 he hit .320. That's stickin'."

Bob Cerv: "I thought one of the best shortstops of all time was Phil Rizzuto. Hell, he was better'n Pee Wee Reese or any of 'em in those days. Rizzuto did everything. He could bunt like a demon. Never had a great arm but he just got you every time—bang-bang! He just threw it as hard as he had to. Funny thing is he hit ten, twelve homers a year.

"Hey, no doubt about it, Rizzuto belongs in the Hall of

Fame. But you go back and look how many Yankees made it to the Hall that played during those years. You got Ford, Mantle, Berra, and that's about it out of that crew and you gotta realize, hey, there's no Raschi or Reynolds in there. Those are Hall of Fame-type players. They were class people all the way. Remember for four, five, six years they just dominated everybody. Five World Championships in a row! Five! Nobody else has ever done that.

"But one of these days they'll have to get to some of these people. How the hell can you have a dynasty like the Yankees and have so few pitchers in there? There is no reason why Allie Reynolds is *not* in the Hall of Fame.

"You know it's like they're afraid to put Yankees in the Hall. The Yankees have dominated baseball since 1920 but they don't dominate the Hall of Fame. Explain that. There's a definite prejudice there. No doubt about it. The Yankees couldn't have done all those great things without great players. So why aren't they in the Hall of Fame?

"I heard a rumor that Steinbrenner won't take the Yankees to Cooperstown for that Hall of Fame game until they get Rizzuto in the Hall of Fame. So they said, 'Well, as long as he threatens us like that we'll never put him in.' And if that's the kind of committee that's running the thing, then they should shut her down! Just shut her down!''

THE LAST HURRAH FOR THE YANKEE CLIPPER

The Yankees captured their third pennant and third World Championship in a row in 1951. The hitting star was Yogi Berra, who led the team with 88 RBIs and 27 home runs and won the first of his three MVP awards. Newcomer Gil McDougald hit .306, fielded spectacularly at second, and was named Rookie of the Year. Raschi and Lopat both had 21 wins in 1951, but the pitching performance of the decade was given by the third member of the Yankee pitching triumvirate, Allie Reynolds. "Superchief," a half-blood Cherokee from Oklahoma, pitched two no-hitters in 1951, matching Johnny Vander Meer's stunning feat. Reynold's last gem clinched the pennant for New York.

Eddie Lopat: "The first one he threw was against Bob Feller in Cleveland—a 1–0 game. The funny thing about that one was the last hitter up was Bobby Avila, who was a pretty good hitter. And Allie had two strikes and no balls on him. He tried to throw that last pitch so hard that he lost his balance and fell like a guy doing a swan dive. He fell flat on the mound and lay out spread-eagle. That's how hard he threw it. The next pitch he kept his balance and got him out."

Allie Reynolds: "It was a real tight ball game. Feller was pitching and we never did exactly desecrate Feller. About the fifth inning Ben Chapman hit one off me that I thought was gone. The wind kind of caught it though and Hank Bauer hauled it in right at the fence. And in the seventh inning Woodling finally hit one out for the only run of the game.

"I finally got down to the last inning and I pulled something that got me into a little trouble later on. My roommate Eddie Lopat was a very temperamental guy. So just for the heck of it I walked up to him just before the start of the ninth inning and said, 'Ed, you think I can pitch a no-hitter?' It upset him so much he ran into the locker, changed his clothes, and left the park.

"He was really superstitious. Of course that got out and I got at least one letter from every person in the United States that I was a smart aleck trying to tear up baseball, and really that wasn't in my mind at the time. I just wanted to see what ol' Eddie would do—he ran like hell.

"Anyway, I got the first two fellows out easily in the ninth. I ended up facing the batting champion, Bobby Avila. I got him to two strikes and a ball and I was standing out there and I said to myself, 'Well, I'm going to throw this ball harder than anybody ever threw one and strike him out.'

"Well, anyway, Feller dug a big hole in the mound whenever he pitched. He was a little taller than I was and I was hitting short of it when I was throwing within myself. But when I really tried to let out, I overstrided and hit this big ol' hole and my feet went out from under me and I hit on my fanny and I tried to squirrel around there so I could see where the ball went 'cause it was close to the plate. In fact, the ball should have been called a strike. I just laid there and I didn't get up. I was just laying there saying to myself, 'I wonder what all these people are thinking about me out here laying on my butt.' There was about seventy thousand in Cleveland that day.

"Anyway, the pitching coach, Jim Turner, came running out there. He said, 'What's the matter? Are you hurt? What are you laying there laughing for?'

"And I just looked up at him and said, 'You imagine what all these people are thinking?' So then he got to laughing too. So there we were the last out of a no-hitter out on the mound laughing our asses off.

"The next pitch Avila swung at a bad pitch and that was it."

Eddie Lopat: "The second no-hitter was in New York against Boston. They had some great hitters on that Boston club. Dom DiMaggio, Williams, and Pesky. Pesky used to get two hundred hits a year, just a slap hitter. Then there were Bobby Doerr, Vern Stevens, and Walt Dropo. One year Dropo and Stevens had 144 RBIs apiece! They had some guys who could really wallop that ball.

"Anyway, it was the ninth inning and still no hits and Ted Williams was up. He hit a big pop fly which Yogi chased to the stands and it hit in his mitt and dropped out. Yog later told us when he came back to the plate, Williams really gave him hell. He says, 'You really put me in a hell of a spot. What am I supposed to do now? I get a base hit, I'm a bad guy. Allie pops me out and then I get a lucky hit.'

"So the next pitch the Chief fired another fastball up and Ted hit it exactly the same way—popped it up. Hell, it must have gone up two hundred feet high and almost in exactly the same place between home plate and third base up against the stands. And with that Reynolds was right over next to Yog then. He figured if Yogi dropped it, he'd grab it.

"That was a great day and Yog got a chance to redeem himself. We used to kid Yogi. We called him the luckiest man that ever stepped in a pair of baseball shoes. He got a chance to redeem himself on the very next pitch. That's a one in a million."

Allie Reynolds: "The second no-hitter came on the last day of the season. The fact is we had a doubleheader that day.

We needed one game to tie for the pennant against Boston and two to win.

"I had something funny happen to me that day too. When I was at the hotel gettin' ready to go to the park, my wife fell over on the floor. I was on the phone and I said, 'Just a minute. My wife fell over!'

"I went over and picked her up and she said she just fainted. So I called some friends in town and gave them the name of the doctor and so I took a cab out to the stadium. And I got out there and pitched the first inning and the second and the third and she still hadn't come into the park. And finally she came in so I kind of relaxed.

"I got three or four pretty quick runs and I went along in pretty good shape until the ninth inning and I said to myself, 'If I can get the first three guys out I won't have to pitch to Ted Williams.' But darned if I didn't walk Dom DiMaggio so I ended up pitching to Ted and I ended up doing something I hadn't done with him in all the years I'd pitched to him. I threw him three fastballs in a row. He popped the first one up and I thought, 'Well, it's over!' Danged if Yogi didn't drop the ball. It was a tremendously high pop-up and the currents in that stadium make it difficult. They're not a cinch by any means.

"I stepped on Yogi's hand when he fell down because I tried to catch it too. I asked him if I'd cut him and he said no. So I said, 'Well, let's try it again.' So we did and he popped it up again and this time Yogi caught it and I told him, 'That was your last chance. I was going to take the rest of 'em.'"

In the 1951 Series the high-flying Giants, fresh from their thrilling playoff victory over the Dodgers in which Bobby Thompson hit his "Shot Heard Round the World" (a last inning homer that won the pennant for the Giants) took a two-games-to-one lead over the Yankees. But the Yanks, behind the pitching of "Steady Eddie" Lopat, who won two one-run games, swept the last three games for the title.

JOLTIN' JOE RETIRES

Despite their triumphant season, 1951 was a sad year for New York because Joe DiMaggio ended his magnificent career. Injured much of the year, the Jolter slumped to .263 and hit but 21 homers. DiMag, a proud man, could not stand to see himself play except at his best. Although Topping offered him the same $100,000 salary if he would come back in 1952 as a part-time player, DiMaggio declined and called it quits.

Joe DiMaggio: "You start chasing a ball and your brain immediately commands your body to 'Run forward! Bend! Scoop up the ball! Peg it to the infield!' Then your body says, 'Who me?' "

Billy Martin: "It was a tough year for Joe DiMaggio. Joe was depressed quite often. Injuries and age began taking their toll, and it was a well-kept secret, but for the last couple years Joe couldn't throw. No one said anything, he kept playing, with the second baseman running as far out into right field as possible to take the throws. Everyone admired his arm so much from before that they never caught on that his arm was bad. He was also starting to struggle at bat. His back muscles were hurting him, and he was having a hard time holding his bat up, they hurt so much, so he had to drop his bat down a little, and he was hitting balls to the opposite field, which he never did before. When he hit a home run to right field, he would complain about his 'piss home run.' He'd say, 'Anybody could hit a piss home run to right.' I knew '51 would be his last year. He didn't feel he was Joe DiMaggio playing anymore.'"[7]

Joe DiMaggio (announcing his retirement): "I told you fellows last spring I thought this would be my last year. I only wish I could have had a better year, but even if I had hit .350, this would have been the last year for me.

"You all know I have had more than my share of physical injuries and setbacks during my career. In recent years these have been much too frequent to laugh off. When baseball is no longer fun, it's no longer a game.

"And so, I've played my last game of ball. Since coming to New York I've made a lot of friends, and picked up a lot of advisers, but I would like to make one point clear—no one has influenced me in making this decision. It has been my problem and my decision to make. I feel that I have reached the stage where I can no longer produce for my ball club, my manager, my teammates, and my fans the sort of baseball their loyalty to me deserves.

"I have been unusually privileged to play all my major league baseball for the New York Yankees. But it has been an even greater privilege to be able to play baseball at all. It has added much to my life. What I will remember most in days to come will be the great loyalty of the fans. They have been very good to me."

17

The Mick

In 1951, the same year the great DiMaggio announced his retirement, a green kid named Mickey Charles Mantle burst out of a tiny Oklahoma mining town, headed for overnight stardom for the Yankees of New York City. During his spectacular career Mantle ripped out 536 homers, won three MVP awards, hit for the Triple Crown in 1956, played in twenty All-Star games, and left behind a towering list of World Series records, including 18 homers.

The torch of greatness belonging to the legendary Yankee superhero had been passed with barely a flicker from Ruth to DiMaggio to Mantle.

When nineteen-year-old Mantle moved to the majors from "D" ball in one enormous leap, he was a shortstop, but he didn't remain a shortstop long—not with MVP Rizzuto staked out at short. But there's always a place for a kid who can hit the ball five hundred feet from either side of the plate. In no time his tapemeasure home runs were part of Yankee lore.

Bill Dickey: "I was pitching batting practice when he took his first swings. The kid hit the first six balls nearly five hundred feet, over the lights and out of sight. He hit them over the right-field fence batting right-handed and over the left-field fence batting left-handed. And remember, Mantle was only eighteen at the time."

"I played with Gehrig and with Ruth and I've seen fellows like Jimmy Foxx and they hit prodigious home runs in their day but I have to say Mantle hit more tapemeasure home runs consistently than any of those players. Mantle outdrove them all."

Charlie Silvera: "I'd heard a lot about Mickey. People around New York had all heard about him and Willy. Mantle and Mays. Everybody was buzzing about those two guys. 'Well, wait until you see Mantle.' 'Wait'll you see Mays.' And then these two future Hall of Famers came up in the same year. Two of the best who ever played the game. It was incredible.

"Mickey was just unbelievable. He came up in spring training and whistled balls out of the park. Balls we didn't realize could be hit that far.

"I was there when he hit most of his long ones. I saw the one he hit off the facade in Yankee Stadium off Robertson and a couple he hit into dead center beyond the monuments. But the best one that Mickey ever hit was in Washington. The old park is gone. That was back in '52, I guess it was. He hit the ball and they said it ricocheted off the scoreboard and bounced into the street. But, hell, I was in the bull pen and I saw it. It went clean over everything—the bleachers, the twenty-foot scoreboard, everything!

"Red Patterson went out there and measured it: 565 feet! The first tapemeasure job. And, tell you the truth, I think it was farther than that. I was standing right on the left-field foul line and it was still taking off when it cleared the scoreboard. What a shot!"

Joe Collins: "Mickey tried to hit every one like they don't count under four hundred feet."

Mickey Mantle: "My father was the one who wanted me to switch-hit. I started at six or seven and when I first started I couldn't hit as good left-handed so it was tough for me to stick with it because I could hit the ball a lot farther right-handed and I got a bigger kick out of hitting the ball a long ways than just trying to hit for average. But my father told me that someday baseball was going to be a two-platoon system where left-handed hitters would hit against right-handed pitchers and right-handed hitters would hit against left-handed pitchers. So if you could hit both ways you could play in more ball games and be more valuable to the club.

"So I kept trying and by the time I got out of high school I could hit just about as good left-handed as I could right. The only thing is I strike out a little more left-handed and I don't have quite as much power.

"I just got up there and swung for the roof every time and waited to see what would happen."

Whitey Ford: "I just wanted to know how it felt to pitch against him, just in case I ran into another Mantle, heaven forbid, somewhere along the line. So there he was, right-handed, and there I was, left-handed. I decided to give him my best in five swings at me.

"I threw him three fastballs and two curves. Mickey got good pieces of the quick ones, all being long drives, but they remained in the park and probably would have gone for extra bases. He murdered my curves. Mantle could always hit breaking stuff when batting right-handed. He follows a sharp curve (my best, anyway) right down to his knees.

"But I finally got him. He turned cutie and switched left-handed against my left-handed stuff. This was an insult. I set him up with a fastball that didn't bother him. Then I let him have a sidearm curve. He took a wild cut that made him look like the world's worst batter. But you didn't get this from me."

Mantle was more than a big, strong kid who could poke the ball a country mile. He was a supremely gifted athlete and the fastest man in baseball during his time—perhaps of all time. He also had a rifle arm and an instinct for the game of baseball that put him on a nonstop trip to the Hall of Fame.

* * *

Eddie Lopat: "In his peak years he was an outstanding center fielder because he could take off and run. He didn't study the batters like DiMag. DiMag was a more astute student of the game than Mickey was. If Mantle would have had DiMag's attitude and his makeup he'd have been the best player of all time, hands down.

"He was a much better athlete than DiMag. He could run faster than DiMag, and Joe could run! He could hit a ball farther than DiMaggio could from *either* side of the plate. His arm was the equivalent of Joe's, and Joe had a great arm.

"He had a tremendous body. He was really strong. He looked like a weight lifter. When he was in clothes he didn't look that big, but the more clothes he took off the bigger he got. Mantle had small hands but his forearms were like Popeye's. He worked in the copper mines as a kid and that's why that head and neck looked like a fullback's. He had a small waistline. Really an athlete. Fantastic!

"If you had a player to mold right from scratch—you took Jimmy Foxx's power, Cobb's speed, this guy's arm, and you molded those five or six players into one player—that player would be Mantle. That's the kind of ability he had. If Mickey hadn't been hurt there's no telling what he could have done."

Bill Dickey: "Mickey didn't impress me as being particularly fast when he was playing short, but when we divided the boys into groups for a series of seventy-five-yard sprints, he won his heat looking back over his shoulder, as if to see what was keeping the others. Then we had a sprint for the winners, and Mantle won that, too. Then he became sick and apologized, explaining that he wasn't in shape!"

Charlie Silvera: "He was the fastest I ever saw in a baseball uniform. The thing about Mickey is he could lay down a bunt from the left side and get to first base in 3.1 seconds. So if you played in shallow and got right on the ball when he laid it down and you fielded the ball perfectly and really gunned it, you'd get him. But, of course, the infielders didn't want to play in close on Mantle because he'd tear their heads off if he ever hit one. That's like standing in front of a firing squad just before they offer you a cigarette. Hell, he could only hit the ball six hundred feet from either side.''

Casey Stengel: "My God, the boy runs faster than Cobb.''

Mantle may have been the greatest athlete ever to wear pinstripes. He may also have been built like a god, but his knees were mortal. In the 1951 World Series Mantle and DiMaggio roamed the outfield together—Joe a few days from retirement, Mantle a rookie. Then, on a routine fly ball, Mantle's career was almost wiped out.

Monte Irvin: "You know, there was a play in that second game that was of some interest, especially if you like to think about baseball history, which I do. It happened in the fifth inning. Let me set it up for you. That was Willie Mays's first World Series and Mickey Mantle's first World Series—they were both rookies that year—and it was Joe DiMaggio's last World Series. Joe retired a few weeks later. I guess you might say that Series saw a changing of the guard, the great center fielder of the past going out and the two great center fielders of the future coming in, all on the same field at the same time.

"Mickey, of course, was playing right field. Well, a ball was hit to right-center in the fifth inning. Joe and Mickey went for it and at the last minute Mickey lay back and let Joe take it. But in doing so, Mantle stepped on something in the outfield —I think it was a loose drainage cap—and went down like he'd been shot. He hurt his knee badly and had to be taken out of the game. He didn't play again in the Series. That was a bad injury, one of several that I believe bothered him throughout his career and impaired his effectiveness. And do you know who hit that fly ball? It was Willie."[1]

Eddie Lopat: "Mantle never ran the way he ran that first year, because the first year he came up he was an eighteen-year-old kid, weighed 178 pounds. Then he hurt himself in the '51 Series when he stepped in a water sprinkler hole. I was the pitcher that ball game and DiMag caught the ball because he was backing Mickey up. When Mantle went down, DiMag caught it and if he don't catch it, we lose the game because the bases were loaded.

"After he wrecked his ankle Mantle played at 190, 192 the rest of his career. He could still run but nothing like the first year. He was unbelievable. He was just like a sprinter. On a drag bunt he could get to first in 3.1 seconds. On the left side he'd get there in 3.4 or 3.5. Right now there's no one as fast as Mantle was. Not Ricky Henderson. Not Vince Coleman. The only guy equal to Mickey was Vada Pinson. He could fly too."

Mickey Mantle: "My whole baseball career terminated almost on that one play. . . . I thought I'd broken my leg in two and my career was over right there. But they carried me off and took me to the hospital and operated on me. That was the first of four knee operations over the next fifteen years. I was never right again. It still just flops around to this very day. All of my other injuries, and I had them every single year, came from favoring that knee.

"So as far as I'm concerned that was the worst thing that could ever have happened to me. It forced me to retire early, and I know I could have set a lot of records that I didn't get a chance to because of my legs. They still cause pain and problems today, and I'm just hoping they don't get worse."

Whitey Ford: "If I have any lasting picture of Mickey myself, it's probably a picture of a really strong, powerful guy with all these muscles—and with two of the worst knees you ever saw. Sometimes we'd be sitting and talking or having dinner, and he'd be there sort of rubbing his knees with his hand, and then when it came time to get up and leave, he'd take a long, long while just lifting up out of his chair. I think he was in pain all the time I knew him."[2]

Dick Young: "Mantle ran into the training room after a bad day like a rat running back into a hole."

Charlie Silvera: "I used to drive Mickey to the ball park and after the game I dropped him at his home and Mickey was only twenty-two, twenty-three at the time and we got to his house and he said, 'I'll see you tomorrow, Charlie.' And he had to lift his legs out of the car with his hands one by one to get out."

Moose Skowron: "I'll tell you who I admired the most on the team—Mantle. He played when he was hurt. I had the pleasure of being between Yogi and Mantle in the Yankee locker room and I'll never forget days where he had bad days he'd cry and say, 'I let people down. People paid a lot of money to see me perform.'

"He took the game serious. He played when he was hurt. We all did because it was the reputation of the Yankees to win."

MANTLE, THE MAN

Mickey was an easygoing, fun-loving kid who had the mantle of greatness thrust upon his shoulders. He stepped immediately into the limelight, but unlike Ruth, who sought publicity, who flourished in the glow of all that attention, and unlike DiMaggio, who could protect himself with his stoic silence, Mantle remained vulnerable.

Though he quickly became a legend, Mantle was, of course, human and he had neither the sophistication nor the hard edge to protect himself from his own publicity. But beyond that, his father, who was his idol, was dying of Hodgkin's disease, and Mickey's deep fear was that, like several other male members of the Mantle clan, he, too, would succumb to the fatal disease.

Mickey Mantle: "The idol of my early days was definitely my dad. He was the bravest man I ever knew. He never complained, and he never acted scared even when he was dying of Hodgkin's disease in 1951 and 1952. No boy ever loved his dad more than I did. I'd do anything to make that man happy. All it took from him was a sharp look, and I knew what was right and what was wrong.

"His real name was Elvin, but they called him Mutt. He was a damned good ball player, but he had to work in the mines all his life to support our family during the Depression in one of the poorest parts of the country—in Dust Bowl country out in Oklahoma. I know that's why he felt so strongly about my making good in baseball. And that's why I'm glad he had a chance to see me play with the Yankees before he died. . . ."[3]

Joe DiMaggio: "Mickey is one of the great players of all time. Unfortunately, he came up from "D" baseball to the Yankees and he had a dad who really was one hundred percent all Mickey. He lived for him. He taught him an awful lot when he was a kid and it bothered him to see his boy not hitting as well as he thought he could hit. He went to Casey Stengel and Casey said, 'Well, go talk to Joe and he'll give you a little insight about your boy.'

"So he came to me and I tried to explain to him that this game from "D" to the major leagues is quite a jump. We know he has all the ability but it might take a little time.

"I tried everything possible to help him but he was a fresh kid at the time and you couldn't convince him that he didn't know everything about the game.

"Well, I think the Yankees gave him a lot of time. But they waited about as long as they could and then sent him down to the minors to get his confidence back and he just tore up that minor league and came back to the Yankees in time to play in the World Series."

Mickey Mantle: "[July of Mickey's rookie year] I was batting lead-off and was driving in quite a few runs—even hitting a few home runs—but I was striking out too much. . . . I was getting mad and losing my confidence, hitting water coolers and all. Casey called me in when we got to Detroit and said he was going to send me back to the minors. Of course, I started crying, and he started crying. You know, he was like my Dad by that time. He felt like he had took me in and brought me up. I felt like I could play because I had signs of being a 'phenom' like they were saying. I could hit a couple of home runs or steal second or score from first, but I just wasn't doing it like I thought I was going to, and I was losing my confidence. So Casey *had* to send me back.

"I went back to the minors and joined Kansas City, and the first time up, I bunted. George Selkirk was the manager at Kansas City then, and he called me over after the inning and said, 'Look, we know you can bunt; we didn't send you down here to learn how to bunt. We want you to get your confidence back and start hitting the ball again.'

"But I didn't get another hit in my next twenty-two times at bat, and that's when I called my dad and said, 'I don't think I can play ball anymore.'

"He was working in the mines in Oklahoma and he came to Kansas City the next day, and he came right into my hotel room and I thought he was going to say, 'Geez, you're all right.' But instead, he walked in and got my suitcase and started throwing the stuff into the suitcase. I said, 'What's the matter?' And he said, 'Hell, you ain't got no guts. I thought I raised a man. You're nothing but a goddamned baby.' And I said, 'What're you doing?' And he said, 'Packing! You're going home. You're going to work in the mines, that's what we'll do, you can work back down there. . . .'"

"He had tears in his eyes; he was really hot. And when he said he thought he'd raised a man and all he had was a baby—well, that really curdled my guts.

"Then he just threw the stuff down and said, 'Get your ass on the ball. Shit, you ain't no baby, you can do it.' And he just turned and walked out.

"He stayed for the game that night, and I got a couple of hits, and then I wound up hitting something like .360 for Kansas City—drove in a lot of runs, hit a lot of home runs. And the Yankees called me back up.

"I think that speech my dad gave me really did it. . . . It was the turning point in my whole life."[4]

Mantle was the quintessential farm boy come to the big city. He was a kid from Oklahoma and he acted just like a kid from Oklahoma—he horsed around with his buddies and drank a lot and chased girls and with that cowboy twang he came off sounding like a hick to the sophisticated New York scribes. Mystified by all the bad press, by the boos of the fans, Mantle often showed his frustration.

Casey Stengel: "Sure I've heard about Mantle's being called dumber than Ned-in-the-third-reader. If that's so, I could use a few more like him around. The feller is the second-best man on the club when it comes to stealing signs and he knows what's going on, with or without the bubble gum."

Joseph McBride: "It was said that the first book Mickey Mantle ever finished reading was his own autobiography."

Mickey Mantle: "Yep, I've heard rumors how some of the folks rate me in the thinking league. Well, I never did claim to be smart and never was much, I guess. I'm sorry some of 'em call me a dummy. But to tell you the truth, it doesn't bother me anymore and I'm not going to holler. What the writers write and what the fans say are their privilege. I'll admit when they started booing me a couple of years ago, it upset me. But then I noticed they also booed Ted Williams and it didn't seem to bother Ted any. So I decided to take the same attitude. From the way Ted concentrates at the plate, I don't believe he hears them anyway."

Casey Stengel: "The only thing the feller does that makes me mad is the way he acts after he strikes out or fails to get a hit. See that water cooler, notice those dents. He put 'em there punchin' and kickin' that iron with his fists and feet. It's a wonder he isn't crippled all over, besides having those legs that bother him all the time."

Mickey Mantle: "They'll boo the ass off anybody sometimes. I used to get it . . . and in Yankee Stadium besides. They'd get on me for not going in the army or not being able to run so fast if my legs were bad. . . .
"Sometimes you even get it from the family, and that's when it really hurts. Once I struck out three times in a game, and when I got back to the clubhouse, I just sat down on my stool and held my head in my hands, like I was going to start crying. I heard somebody come up to me, and it was little Timmy Berra, Yogi's boy, standing there next to me. He tapped me on the knee, nice and soft, and I figured he was going to say something nice to me, you know, like 'You keep hanging in there,' or something like that.
"But all he did was look at me and then he said in his little kid's voice, 'You stink.'"[5]

"The newspapers were nearly my undoing. The writers . . . probably felt that they were doing me favors by writing me up as if I were already ticketed to the Hall of Fame. The result was that many of the home fans resented me right from the beginning, or resented my not delivering immediately on my newspaper promise. It may have been, too, that the write-ups had an effect upon me, scaring me with the goals they set for me.

"It took me a while to learn to be wary of writers. At first I thought you could talk to them just the way you might talk to any of the guys in the clubhouse—none of whom would think of running out and repeating some dumb thing you said, trying to make it sound dumber. It was a real shock to me to discover that when I said something in front of a writer, I was shouting it from the New York rooftops. . . ."[6]

Hank Bauer: "I gave Mantle his first drink. We had come back from the ball park and I asked him if he would like a drink. I put a bottle down on the table and went to get him a glass. When I looked back he had the bottle right up to his lips glugging the stuff down. Just like a big farm kid from Oklahoma, I guess."

Casey Stengel: "When Mr. Billy Martin and Mr. Mickey Mantle came to me they were such kids in their hotel rooms they were having pretend gunfights with toy guns, which they would draw on each other and then argue who was the fastest on the draw."

Jerry Coleman: "You have to remember how young Martin, Mantle, and Ford were. They just wanted to enjoy every aspect of playing baseball, on and off the field. They would do anything to entertain and kid each other. They had this favorite trick of scaring the hell out of each other with a hose of ice water. First they started attacking each other with the ice water in the shower. Then they began attacking everybody else. Have you ever been hit by an ice water attack? It will shake you up. I don't know about the other guys on the team, but I started to wait until the three of them had gotten out of the shower before I would ever get in."[7]

Billy Martin: "One day we were going hunting. He said, 'We're going down to south Texas, about a five-hour drive. I have a friend I went to school with there. He has a big ranch, and we can go deer hunting.' I said great. We made the trip, got down there, and Mickey said, 'You stay in the car. I'll go in and talk to my buddy, and we'll go right out and hunt.' Mickey went into the house. I didn't know this, but the owner said to Mickey, 'Heck, Mickey, you can hunt all over my place, but would you do me a favor? I have a pet mule who's going blind, and I don't have the guts to kill the poor fellow. Would you kill him for me?' I didn't know he had asked Mickey to kill it.

"Mickey came out, and he slammed the door like he was mad. I said, 'What's the matter?' Mickey said, 'He won't let us hunt here.' I said, 'You got to be kidding.' He said, 'No, I'm not, and I'm so mad that I'm going to go by the barn and shoot his mule.' I said, 'Mickey, you can't shoot that man's mule.' He said, 'The hell I ain't. I'm gonna kill that mule.' We drove through the barnyard, and there was the mule. Mickey got out of the car with his rifle, and crack, he shot the mule and killed it. He turned around, and he saw that my rifle was smoking. He said, 'What the hell are you doing?' I said, 'I got two of his cows.'

"Ahh, that cost us some money."[8]

Whitey Ford: "Marvin Miller was over at the clubhouse talking about the players' pension plan, how you could start collecting when you got to be fifty. And Mickey kept saying, 'Get it down to forty. . . .'

"He always had it in his mind that he wasn't going to make it to forty because of his uncles and his father. . . .

"I really think that's why Mickey acted a little crazy at times. It wasn't what Toots Shor said when we got voted into the Hall of Fame: 'It shows what you can accomplish if you stay up all night drinking whiskey all the time.'

"It wasn't that. I think Mickey acted a little crazy at times because he just figured he was only going to be around a little while and he might as well enjoy it."[9]

Mickey Mantle: "My new book [*The Mick*] makes me sound like an alcoholic. I'm not sure why there's so much, well, emphasis on it.

"When I went to play pro ball at seventeen, my daddy said, 'Whatever you do the rest of your life, just act like I'm sittin' near you.' I hoped he couldn't see me some of those times because I'm not sure he would have been happy with the way I ended up. I blew God-given talent to be the best there ever was. Because of the way I lived, I was over the hill at thirty-three.

"I worked in the lead mines outside of Commerce when I was a kid. They went straight down into the ground four hundred feet, not into the side of some hill. I had to go down there. My father was the ground boss. Worked the mines all his life. He died when he was thirty-nine. Grandfather and uncles the same thing. Early. Hell, I only figured to live till forty. That's why I had as much fun as I could while I was young. You know the old saying, If I'd known I was gonna live this long, I'd a taken better care of myself. That's me all right.

"If I could do everything over again, I'd be like Willie Mays or Pete Rose. They took care of themselves all year long. I was stupid. I thought it was never going to end. . . . I was thirty-six years old when I had to quit—which is practically the prime of life. And that hurts—when you have to quit doing the work you love at an age where other men are just hitting their prime.

"If I miss anything today it's the atmosphere of the clubhouse. You live with those guys for eight months every year; and when you've finally got to leave them, a part of you dies.

"You know, people come up to me and tell me about some great thing they saw me do in some game in 1957. They tell me every last detail about it. It's like the whole thing happened to them instead of to me."

Tom Tresh: "I played with Mickey the last seven years of his career until he retired. He was a really fine person. He had pressures that you and I will never know but he handled them pretty darn well. He's a special person. He was born to be a great hero. I believe that. Certain players have this magnetism—you can't train it. He was just this kid who came out of Oklahoma with blond hair and looked like what America was supposed to be."

18

Billy and Whitey

The 1952 campaign was again a struggle for the Yankees. The team fought off a good Cleveland club that boasted three twenty-game winners—Early Wynn, Bob Lemon, and Mike Garcia. But when the Yankees won nine out of their last ten games, the Indians couldn't keep up with the pace and finished two games back.

Mantle, in his first full season, led the way, hitting .311 with 23 homers. Berra hit 30 homers, a new American League mark for a catcher, and Gene Woodling, platooned with Hank Bauer in the outfield, batted .309. Allie Reynolds had his first twenty-win season, and Raschi added sixteen victories.

The Yankees and the Dodgers met again in the 1952 World Series and it was a battle to remember. The Dodgers bolted to a three-games-to-one lead, but the Yankees won game five and evened things up in game six on homers by Mantle and Berra.

In the decisive seventh game, Casey started Lopat for three innings, then used Reynolds for three. With a 4–2 lead he brought in Raschi to pitch the seventh inning, but Vic quickly loaded the bases and Casey waved in Bob Kuzava for his first and only appearance in the Series.

Kuzava got Duke Snider to pop up for out number two in the seventh. Then, with the bases still loaded, Jackie Robinson hit another routine pop-up for what looked like the inning-ending out. But first baseman Joe Collins, who was supposed to take it, lost the ball in the sun as the Dodger runners wildly circled the bases. Billy Martin realized at the last second what was happening and began a desperate charge from his second-base position to try an impossible game-saving catch.

It appeared that the Yankees had made one of the biggest bone-head plays in all Series history. A routine pop out would suddenly turn into three runs for the Dodgers.

Hank Bauer: "I shifted over toward right center, where I always played Jackie. Jackie took his usual quick swing and the ball went straight up—a pop-up to the first-base side of the pitcher's mound. I slapped my glove, happy that we were out of trouble. It was a routine pop-up, usually a sure out.

"I still shudder when I think what almost happened to that 'sure' out. Joe Collins, our first baseman, lost the ball in the sun. He stood there frozen. Bob Kuzava, our pitcher, didn't move after the ball. Neither did Yogi Berra, our catcher. I couldn't believe it. There were four Dodgers tearing around the bases and nobody was close enough to the ball to wave hello to it.

"From nowhere Bill Martin, our second baseman, came racing across the infield. Billy charged in like a runaway truck, holding his glove out. He lunged forward at the last second and the ball fell into his glove, about six inches off the ground. I still don't know how Billy got there that fast. But we knew that nothing the Dodgers did after that could keep us from winning."

Casey Stengel: "We had this left-hander, Gazzara [Kuzava], and they had that brilliant Mr. Rob-A-Son at the plate and all of a sudden, whoops, here comes a slow ball when you expect a fastball, and why wouldn't you tap it into right field if you wuz right-handed, but Mr. Rob-A-Son tried to hit the ball over the building and instead he hit a ball up the shoot and Mr. Collins, which was my first baseman, was counting his money so he never seen it and Mr. Berra, my catcher, is standing with his hands on his hips yelling for Mr. Collins and Mr. Gazzara did the pitching and he ain't about to do the catchin', so that leaves the second baseman, and you know who that is, to come in, lose his cap, and get it before it hits the grass, which if he did would be kicked because he was runnin' so fast and almost tripped over the mound which was a mountain in Brooklyn to help them sinker ball pitchers, Mr. Erskine and them and McGraw used to do that, too, and why wouldn't ya, if you had spitters in the staff, but my rooster caught it and it didn't hit off his schnozz like a lot of them would have."

Series hero Billy Martin was a tough, wiry Italian kid from Oakland, California, who grew up on the wrong side of town and had to fight for everything he got, on and off the field. Martin was brash and fearless, and his frequent on-field fights became legendary. His battles with Clint Courtney and Jimmy Piersall, in particular, made headlines everywhere.

Allie Reynolds: "Clint Courtney? Did Billy get the credit for that one? Heck, I was the one who K.O.'d Courtney. You know, Clint was a hell of a nice guy off the field but on it he was a son of a bitch.

"See, what happened was the day before a couple of their guys got brushed back, so Courtney goes around telling everybody first chance he gets he's gonna cut one of our players up. Well, when I heard that I told him, 'You do and you're going down.'

"So sure enough the next day I was pitching and he gets on and when he went into second he spiked Rizzuto but good. Well, I went runnin' over there and knocked him out cold with one punch. And then all hell broke loose. The whole Yankee team come out and in the mess I got knocked out cold too. By one of my own teammates. It had to be Joe Collins because that's the side of the head I got hit on. The first-base side. Besides, none of Clint's teammates came out there to help him 'cause they knew he was wrong. So it had to be a Yankee.

"Hell, Billy wasn't anywhere around. He was out in center field chasing the ball Courtney knocked out of Rizzuto's glove. But the next day it's all over the papers about Martin fighting with Courtney. And Billy gets fined $150 along with Courtney and they only tag me for $100. And Billy comes up to me and says, 'Hey, what's this? You punch Courtney and I get the big fine?' I told him, 'It's simple, Billy. Your reputation preceded you.'

"The funny thing was the next day I went on out there before the game and Clint was standing by the batting cage. And hell, I didn't feel like getting into it again. Besides, that maniac had a couple bats in his hand. But I had to go that way to get to the dugout so there was no way out of it. So, anyway, I walked on over and he looked over at me and said, 'Ain't you gonna say hello?' I said, 'Sure. How's it going?' And he said, 'Oh, I'm doing all right. But man, that Martin's got one hell of a punch, don't he.' And we laughed our asses off.

"Now that fight of his with Piersall wasn't no fight. Hell, those two guys were too little to hurt each other. They got into it in the runway between games of a doubleheader. I was supposed to pitch the second game and when I headed out there to warm up they were rolling around on the floor near the locker room and Bill Dickey was down there with them and when he saw me he yells, 'Reynolds! Help me separate these two guys!' And I said, 'Aw, hell, let 'em fight. They're too damned little to do any harm.' And I stepped on over them and went out and warmed up."

Bob Grim: "I played with Billy in Cincinnati and they had a little gym there off to one side of the locker room and they had a punching bag in there and I used to go in there and play around with it a little bit. So one day Billy came in and he said, 'Hey let me take a whack at that bag.' And boy he just made that sucker talk. Hit it with both hands and his elbows and even his head. Billy fought a little pro when he was seventeen, eighteen years old, I understand, and when he hit that punching bag, whew! I don't know, maybe he was sneaking in a little on the side practicing but he made it sing just like you see the pros do. So when he's in there up against one of those marshmallow salesmen it's a mismatch.

"Billy used to go down to Key West every so often and I was buddies with a couple of bartenders that knew him down there. They told me he got into an argument with three big guys from the navy one time in a bar down there and Billy tells them, 'Let's just step outside. I'll take all three of you on.' And they all went on outside and Billy mopped 'em up because he was the only one who came back into the bar. He could handle himself."

Martin came up with the Yankees in 1950, and on April 30, 1952, when Jerry Coleman was called back into active duty with the marines, Martin took over second base for the Yankees.

Casey and Billy the Kid hit it off from the beginning. A man with no children and a fatherless boy, they were both cocky and loud, harsh and aggressive. And they both had a maniacal passion to win.

Phil Rizzuto: "The funniest thing was watching him and Stengel together. They really got on each other. Most of the other players never talked back to Casey. Billy always did. In a loud voice, too. Holy cow, they could really shout at each other. I remember Lefty Gomez getting on Joe McCarthy that way. He was the only player I ever remember talking back to McCarthy or kidding him. Billy always talked back to Casey, always kidded him, and always fought with him. Casey made one thing clear to the rest of us very early. He was a Billy Martin fan."[1]

Eddie Lopat: "There was this one game in Washington. The Old Man had had a bad night. You know, his eyes were all bloodshot, his head was down on his chest, he wasn't saying a word. Billy went up to hit and popped up. He comes back to the bench steaming and smashes his bat against the bat rack. A lot of those bats fly all over the dugout, and Casey is really jarred. He grabs Billy and tells him to watch that stuff. We're winning big, so the Old Man falls off again. Now Billy is at bat for a second time. This time he takes a called third strike and he's really mean coming back to the bench. He smashes his bat against the top step of the dugout, and the Old Man is jolted awake. He reaches over into the bat rack, picks up a fungo stick, and starts chasing Billy with it. When I last saw them Casey was running up that ramp, Billy was only a couple of steps in front of him, and he was screaming, 'No, Casey, no.' "[2]

Moose Skowron: "Played with Billy for three years. He was great. If we were in a slump, Casey would tell him if a guy slid into second base, start a fight to motivate the Yankees. Somebody threw at his head as a knockdown pitch and he'd start a fight and we'd start getting all hepped up and we'd start playing great ball.

"Casey and Billy were very close. Billy always said Casey was like a father to him, took care of him. Billy lost his father at a young age and he always respected Casey."

Ty Cobb: "If I were managing a ball club I certainly would do everything within my power to keep from losing a player like Martin. He's a winner. I think of him as a throwback to the old days when players were supposed to fight for every advantage. Sure there are better hitters, better fielders, but for fight, spirit, and whatever it takes to win a game, Martin is something special."

Bob Cerv: "I played with Billy in Kansas City and New York. He wanted to win. That's the name of the game. Anybody can lose. It takes a little effort, a little harder work to win.

"Martin was a damn good athlete, too, but he never got the credit he deserved either. They used to always compare the lineups of the Yankees and Dodgers every year. Catcher was a toss-up between Campanella and Berra. First was pretty even. Shortstop—Reese and Rizzuto about the same. The outfield they had Snider and Furillo so it was pretty even. But second base they'd always say, 'No comparison. Jackie Robinson is better all around than Martin.'

"But hell, when the Series got over guess who always had the best Series—Mr. Billy Martin. Why, he'd just outplay Robinson something awful. It was embarrassing. And who caught Robinson's pop-up to save the Series for us that year—Billy Martin. For a guy who supposedly wasn't a very good athlete, he sure played great."

A CADILLAC OF A FORD

The Yankees won the 1952 Series and with it Casey tied Joe McCarthy's record of four World Championships in a row. Could they make it five? Billy Martin would have a lot to say about that one, too.

The Yankees were the favorites again in 1953 and they disappointed no one. They cruised to an 8½-game finish over second-place Cleveland, thanks in part to an 18-game winning streak that buried the rest of the league.

No Yankee batter hung up any really big numbers. Woodling hit .306. Mantle was at .295 with 21 home runs, although one of Mantle's blasts was walked off at 565 feet. Lopat came back from his physical miseries to win 16. Raschi and Reynolds had 13 wins apiece and Johnny Sain added 14.

The big gun for the Yankees that year, though, was Whitey Ford, just back from a two-year stint in the service. Ford was 18–6 and would be the Yankee ace for the next eleven years while pitching himself to Cooperstown. Ford won 236 games in his Yankee career (a Yankee record) while losing only 106. That figures out to a .690 win-loss percentage, the best ever recorded by a pitcher with over 200 wins. Only fellow Yankee Spud Chandler had a better percentage—.717—but Chandler's all-time mark was made with only 109 wins. Whitey had nearly that many in five seasons.

Ford, though not equipped with a speed-of-light fastball, was acknowledged to be one of the smartest pitchers ever to play, and his 2.74 ERA and ten World Series wins add weight to that claim.

Fresco Thompson: "Ford would have been a bargain at a bonus of fifty thousand. Everybody in the business is so hipped on getting big rookies who can throw the ball through a brick wall that we overlook kids with qualifications that are a hell of a lot harder to find. Ford had the guts of a burglar and the curveball of a mature pro who had been pitching for ten years."

Moose Skowron: "Ford was the best left-handed pitcher I played with or against. I judge pitchers after they pitched, say, ten years. That's the way I judge these modern ball players. I don't care if he's a phenom his first two years. After ten years I wanna see his stats. Then, I make my decision.

"It's who wins the most, who's on the most pennant winners. That's the name of the game. The Yanks with Ford on the team won a lot of championships.

"And it was great to play behind him because if you won or lost he was the same person after the game. Some pitchers on the club, you make an error, they get mad and all this stuff. But Whitey was great. If I made an error he came up and said, 'Moose, listen, get the next one.' Built up my confidence. I didn't want to make an error."

Bill Kinnaman: "Whitey Ford was a great pitcher. He wasn't a big man, but he could hum it pretty good. And he had perfect control. He was one of the smartest pitchers who ever played the game; he'd take advantage of any edge you gave him. Also, he was one of the nicest ball players I have ever known. He never said a word to an umpire when he pitched.

"Whitey loved to throw that dirty ball. One day, late in his career, after he had had surgery and was trying to hang on, he came off the mound in the second inning and said as he walked by, 'Hey, don't throw them out too quick. It's going to be a long day.' I think umpires went along with him a little bit because he had been such a great performer. You wouldn't intentionally allow anything other than what you normally would, but there were times when you might give him another pitch with a ball that is just a little bit dirty or something along that line.

"Whitey dirtied the ball on only one side. That meant that when the ball was rotating on its way to the plate you had an optical illusion—you saw only half of the ball. Once, after we had thrown out three or four balls on Whitey in an inning, I told Bobby Richardson that I didn't think there was another human being on earth who could get a ball dirtier than Whitey Ford. Bobby looked at me and said, 'You know, I've been playing with him a long time, and I don't really know how he does it myself. Just about the time I think I know exactly what he's doing, he'll change and do something else.'

"My first year in the big leagues I threw a new ball out to

Whitey in Yankee Stadium. Yogi went out, Richardson and Tony Kubek came in, and they had a little conference out there, all the time rubbing the ball. I didn't know what was going on. Finally, they went back to their positions, and Whitey got ready to pitch. The batter, Charlie Maxwell, Always on Sunday they used to call him, stepped out and asked me to look at the ball. I said, 'I just threw him a new one.'

"He said, 'Yes, but I know this guy better than you do. Check it.'

"When that ball came in, I could not believe it. In a matter of a minute or a minute and a half at most, he had gotten that ball so dirty you couldn't possibly play with it. I had to throw it out and give him a new one. He just stood there, grinning and rubbing it up again."[3]

Jimmy Dykes: "I know he throws a spitter. Someone on his own team told me he does. He throws it with two strikes, the batter swings and misses, then the ball goes around the infield and comes back dry as the Sahara."

Whitey was born and bred in New York, a kid whose cherubic looks belied his cocky, streetwise personality. Along with Martin and Mantle, he formed a trio of fun-loving pranksters whose rounds of partying and drinking gave the Yankee front office nightmares. Stengel, however, laughed off their rowdiness as boyish exuberance. Besides, Casey had been a bit wild as a kid himself, and as long as you produced for Stengel, he didn't care what you did. Mantle, Ford, and Martin kept him smiling on and off the field for years.

Whitey Ford: "When I first reported to the Yankees, the team was in Boston. I arrived at seven in the morning, and the first thing I did was call Billy Martin, whom I'd known in the minors. I woke him up, in fact, but Billy didn't mind; he said, 'I've got two girls who are going to have breakfast with us.' And, sure enough, when we went downstairs, there were these two girls in the lobby. One of them had been living near Billy in New Jersey, and she knew some of the ball players. But it looked pretty funny, a couple of rookies walking into the Kenmore Hotel dining room at breakfast time with two blondes, and we took a bit of heat from the rest of the players for that little entrance. . . ."[4]

"They played the All-Star Game in San Francisco in 1961. . . . They played the game on Tuesday and we got there on Monday, so Mickey and I headed right for the golf course. It was a place where the owner of the San Francisco Giants, Horace Stoneham, was a member, and we played with his son, Peter. But we didn't have any equipment with us so Pete Stoneham said, 'Just sign my father's name,' and that was the best offer we'd had in a long time.

"We didn't go so far as to buy golf clubs, but we did get new shoes, a pack of sweaters, balls, and shirts; and the whole bill came to something like two hundred dollars. But Pete Stoneham insisted, 'Just sign my father's name to it,' and so we signed.

"Well, Toots Shor had a suite over in one of the big hotels in San Francisco, and he invited me and Mickey over for a little cocktail party he was having that night. . . .

"So we were there telling everybody about our golf game, and while they were all talking I went over to Horace Stoneham to pay back the two-hundred-dollar tab that we ran up at his club.

"Horace is a nice, generous man . . . and he didn't want to take the dough back. You know, he looked sort of amused at the way we took him up on his offer. So he said, 'Look, I'll make a deal with you. If you happen to get in the game tomorrow and you get to pitch to Willie Mays, if you get him out we'll call it even. But if he gets a hit off you, then we'll double it—you owe me four hundred, okay?'

"So I went over to Mickey and told him what Horace said, but Mickey wouldn't go for it. No way. He knew that Mays was like nine for twelve off me lifetime, and he didn't have any reason to think I was going to start getting Willie out, not especially in his own ball park. But I talked him into it. . . .

"Sure enough, the next afternoon in Candlestick, there I am starting the All-Star Game for the American League. . . . Willie's batting cleanup, and in the first inning I got the first two guys out, but then Roberto Clemente clipped me for a double—and there comes Willie.

"Well, I got two strikes on him somehow, and now the money's on the line because I might not get to throw to him again.

"So I did the only smart thing possible under the circumstance: I loaded the ball up real good. You know, I never threw the spitter—well, maybe once or twice when I needed to get a guy out really bad. . . . But this time I gave it the old saliva treatment myself, and then I threw Willie the biggest spitball you ever saw.

"It started out almost at his chest and then it just broke down to the left, like dying when it got to the plate and dropping straight down without any spin. Willie just leaned into it a little and then stared at the ball while it snapped the hell out of sight, and the umpire shot up his right hand for strike three.

"Okay, so I struck out Willie Mays. But to this day people are probably still wondering why Mickey came running in from center field now that the inning was over, clapping his hands over his head and jumping up in the air like we'd just won the World Series—and here it was only the end of the first inning in the All-Star Game and he was going crazy all the way into the dugout. It was a money pitch, that's what, and we'd just saved ourselves four hundred dollars."[5]

Mickey Mantle: "After the game, most of the time we'd go out and have a few drinks and a dinner.

"What I really liked about Whitey, and what he liked about me, was we didn't talk baseball very much.

"It bugged me more than it did him—the games did. If I had a bad day it really stayed on my mind.

"I don't think I ever remember him worrying about his game. I mean, he always knew he was going to come back out and win the next one. Whereas, if I went into a slump, I imagine it got pretty quiet in the room. I'd worry about it a lot more, it seemed, than he did. And he was good to be around when you were going bad.

"He wasn't tense before he pitched, but he was maybe different then. He'd never go out the night before he pitched. Most of the time, if he was pitching the next day, he'd even leave the game a little early and go home and go to bed. I wouldn't bother him then. If he hadn't gone to bed when I got home, we might watch the late-night movie on TV or something. I didn't ever ask him to go out with me those nights, I just figured he didn't want to.

"But when Whitey pitched he always felt like unwinding that night after the ball game. I always felt good, too, especially if he won the game. I was always ready to celebrate it with him."[6]

Whitey Ford: "Gomez had a rule that we all had to be in our rooms by ten o'clock every night, and you don't have to be a genius to see trouble right there. We tried, though. But one night about nine-thirty one of my roommates and I decided to go to a carnival in town; we wanted to take a ride on the Ferris wheel. You know, we figured about five minutes of that and we'd be back in our room on time. So we got on and rode for about ten minutes, but then we couldn't get off. Every time it came our turn to get off, the guy running the ride would pass us, and he kept doing this till ten o'clock. I didn't know why, then.

"We finally got off and ran back to our hotel, which was only about two blocks away. We got there about five minutes after ten, and there was Gomez in the lobby. I said, 'Skip, you'll never guess what happened, you'll never believe it. We got on the Ferris wheel and the guy wouldn't let us off.'

"And Gomez said, 'You're fined five bucks each.'

"Years later Dizzy Dean had Gomez as a guest on his after-the-game television show from Yankee Stadium. And Lefty tells this story how he'd given this guy a couple of bucks to keep us on the Ferris wheel. Now I'm in the clubhouse watching the show, and when it's over Lefty comes into the clubhouse and I say: 'You son of a bitch. All these years you never told us.'

"So I say, 'Give me my ten dollars back.' Now he's laughing his head off but gives me ten dollars. Then I say, scoring big, 'Good, you son of a bitch, you only fined me five.'"[7]

Bob Cerv: "Roger Maris and I never did much when we were roommates. We weren't like some of the Yankees. We all know who they are. Oh, we'd go out and have a party every once in a while if we had a day off.

"But really the press blows these things out of shape. If you played nights you didn't get through until midnight. Then, you had to go find something to eat because you hadn't eaten since afternoon. That's what people could never understand. They all thought you'd get there an hour before the game. If you had a night game usually you were there before three or four o'clock. It was like a full-time job and then some.

"So before a game we'd have a great big breakfast—only late, more like a brunch. Then before the game you'd have maybe a sandwich. Then you'd have to have a big meal after the game. That was your schedule.

"Oh, I used to chuckle at the writers. They'd say, 'Hey, I saw so and so out at two o'clock in the morning.' What the hell did they think he was going to do? Go right home and jump in bed? Ball players would get home at four and sleep until two in the afternoon."

NUMBER FIVE

The Yankees met the Dodgers in the 1953 World Series. The Dodgers had a powerful crew that year, with Roy Campanella knocking in 142 runs (a major league record for a catcher), Duke Snider hitting .336 and 42 homers, Carl Furillo leading the league in hitting at .344, Jackie Robinson averaging .329, and Gil Hodges hitting .302 and smacking 31 home runs.

Despite the Dodger firepower, the Yankees downed Brooklyn four games to two, thanks mostly to Billy Martin. Billy the Kid clobbered the Dodger pitching, hitting .500 including 2 home runs, 2 triples, a double, and 7 singles. He drove in 8 runs and eclipsed Babe Ruth's record of 19 total bases in a six-game Series with 23. His 13 hits were also a record. He capped off his incredible performance by driving in the winning run in the ninth inning of game six to give the Yanks the victory.

The Yankee triumph gave Casey his fifth World Championship in a row, a feat no other manager had ever accomplished —not the great Connie Mack, not John McGraw or Miller Huggins or Joe McCarthy.

Eddie Lopat: "In those five years, ninety-six players went through that club. People say how can you win a pennant five years in a row with ninety-six players going through a club. Well, the nucleus of the club was there the whole time and they just filled in around it where they needed. Actually of the five World Series we won there were only twelve of us who were on that club through it all: Berra, Joe Collins, Rizzuto, Gene Woodling, Hank Bauer, Raschi, Reynolds, and myself, and Charlie Silvera, who didn't do much catching but he was there those five years. Johnny Mize we got in the middle of '49 so he was there the whole time.

"Mize was a fantastic part-time player and pinch-hitter. Then we picked up Enos Slaughter and you got a couple Hall of Famers like that sitting around and you get in a tight spot and the opposing pitcher has to see two of those guys in a row. Well, you got trouble.

"We also had Bobby Brown and Bob Cerv and either one of those guys could go out and knock your brains out."

Bob Cerv: "The Yankee dynasty was no accident. See, years ago each organization had different types of personnel. Nowadays you don't have that. The Yankees had a certain type, Cleveland had a certain type, Detroit—all of them. They'd go out and say this is the type we want. Nowadays with free agency they're like gypsies. The Yankees now have started to bring young guys up through their organization again and they're sticking with them and they're really starting to do something again.

"It's the character of the players that makes a winner. I was on other clubs. Hell, I could never understand how they could beat someone 14–1, then lose for the next three or four days resting on their laurels. They'd fattened up their average. They could coast. The Yanks never worked that way. They played just as hard as they could every day. When we crossed that white line we went to work. We'd always say, 'Well, let's go to work!' And boy did we!

"Another thing that made those teams great—we were much closer. See, we used to ride trains back in those days. From St. Louis all the way to New York. It wasn't until '55 that we started flying. We went to Japan in '55 and we said, 'Hell, if we can fly halfway around the world I don't know why we can't fly from town to town.'

"We'd be clickety-clacking down the rail and it wasn't the greatest sleeping. You'd have to be pretty danged tired to go to sleep with that clicking. We'd always have our own private dining car and, consequently, you'd usually end up in there playing cards. What else was there to do? So you'd get real close that way. Play cards, stand around, and shoot the bull.

"And then go out and win a lot of pennants!"

19

Five More Pennants for Casey

When Roger Bannister broke the four-minute mile in 1954, the Yankees had another great year winning 103 games—the highest total since Stengel took over the Yankees. Only Joe McCarthy's 1932 team and Miller Huggins's 1927 power-laden juggernaut had more victories. But the Yankees did not win the pennant in 1954. The Cleveland Indians set a new major league record for wins with 111, eclipsing the record set by the 1927 Yankees.

Even though his team failed to win the pennant, the Yankees' Yogi Berra won the MVP award, hitting .307 with 125 RBIs. Bob Grim, a hard-throwing right-hander, finished with a 20–6 record and was named Rookie of the Year.

Bob Grim: "I was Rookie of the Year in 1954, won twenty games, eight of those in relief. After that I was kind of top dog out of the bull pen with the Yankees for a little while but deteriorated rapidly. Some calcium deposits developed on my elbow but it never showed and I kept having trouble with my arm. I had a good year in '57 out of the pen. In fact I was

12 and 2 until September and then I couldn't get anybody
out. I had nothing and when I walked out there I knew I
didn't have my stuff, so it wasn't any surprise when they hit
the ball all over the park. I was 12 and 2 and ended up 12 and
8.

"I came to spring training in '58 and it was the same thing
and I was gone. You don't produce for the Yankees, you
don't stay around long. But you can't blame them.

"But I gotta tell you about my home run. One year the
Red Sox were breathing down our necks and they came into
the stadium. It was the bottom of the ninth with two outs and
very late in the year—every game counted. Anyway, it was a
tie game and two men on and two outs and the Sox brought in
Russ Nixon, the Yankee Killer, to relieve. He used to just
mow us down.

"Hell, I was a terrible hitter. I'm a right-handed hitter and
I couldn't hit a ball even in batting practice to right field. So I
hit the first pitch into the bull pen in right field. You figure
that out. Just swung and closed my eyes and the next thing I
know I'm running the bases.

"Now comes the embarrassing part. I swung and the next
thing I know I'm rounding second base and I looked up at
Crosetti coaching at third and he says, 'Come on. It's all
over.'

"So anyway, as I'm rounding third base I wanted to shake
hands with Crosetti so I stuck out my hand. But, see, Crosetti
never shakes hands. Only in the excitement I forgot that.
That was the tradition with Crosetti. He never shook hands
with anyone after they hit a home run. And the only time he
ever broke that tradition was when Maris hit number 61. He
shook Roger's hand then but he sure wasn't going to shake
mine after one lucky home run.

"Man, that was embarrassing."

The Yankees came back in 1955 to win their twenty-first
pennant, but not without some changes. First of all, Stengel
had to overhaul the Yankee pitching staff, one of the oldest in
baseball. Gone were Raschi, Reynolds, and Lopat. To replace them the Yankees obtained two flamethrowers—Bob
Turley and Don Larsen from the Orioles. With rookie Johnny
Kucks, an injury-free Tommy Byrne, and the ace of the staff,

Whitey Ford, the Yankees again had one of the most formidable mound crews in baseball.

The hitting was plentiful and potent as usual, with Mantle, Berra, Bauer, Skowron, and Collins able to put one out of the park at any time. The Yankees also added rookie Elston Howard, a catcher-out-fielder who was the first black player in Yankee history. Billy Martin was back from the army, and with Billy back, Stengel had the guy who could ignite his explosive lineup. Martin hit a surprising .300, Mantle slugged thirty-seven homers, and Yogi won his third MVP.

In the 1955 Series the Yankees met the Dodgers, and for the first time in their long, ill-fated history the Dodgers won the World Series. The Yankees took the first two games handily. But then the Dodgers won three in a row and the Yankees evened things by winning game six.

In game seven the Dodgers went ahead 2–0, and Yogi Berra stepped to the plate in the sixth inning with nobody out and Martin on second and McDougald on first.

Bob Cerv: "Hell, the Dodgers never won a championship until 1955 and that's when they put Amoros in the outfield and he didn't know where to play so he caught Berra's ball down the line—made an ice-cream catch.

"The Dodgers put Amoros in left field in the sixth because Gilliam had come in from left to play second. So in the bottom of the sixth Billy Martin and Gil McDougald get on. Yogi steps up with nobody out. Now Yogi never, never hit the ball down the opposite line to left field. He was one of the deadest pull hitters ever played the game. So what's he do? He hits it down the left-field line. Looks like two bases for sure. So Martin and McDougald take off. No way Amoros could get to it. But danged if he doesn't catch the thing.

"If Sandy had been right-handed, he never would have caught it. But he was left-handed. Everything was just right. If Gilliam was still out there, he's right-handed and he don't make the catch. Plus, Gilliam knew how to play. He wouldn't have been out of position and Yogi'd had a stand-up double and two RBIs and we win the game."

Bob Grim: "I never thought Amoros had a chance for the ball because it was right down the line. He just kinda stuck out his glove and there it was. Give the man credit. He had to come a long way and he backed off at the last second and kinda stuck his hand out and it just kinda fell right into his glove. It was a good catch but I still think there was a little bit of luck involved. Coming from that far and catching it right by the fence and, hell, Yogi don't hit a ball that way—never in a million years. So, first off, he was out of position. If Yogi hits it in the gap where Amoros is supposed to be, Yogi gets a triple.

"That killed us right there. McDougald got doubled off first and instead of two runs in, we got two outs. Podres shut us down after that and the Dodgers won their first Series. That was a tough one to take."

DON LARSEN'S PERFECTO

The year 1956 was good to the Yankees as they blasted their way to the American League pennant with 190 home runs, breaking the 1936 Yankee record of 182. Mantle hit 52, Berra 30, Bauer 26, and Skowron 23. It also was the year Mantle fulfilled his gargantuan potential by winning the Triple Crown. In addition to his 52 homers, Mickey hit .353 and drove in 130 runs. Only six other players had ever done it before—Rogers Hornsby, Jimmy Foxx, Chuck Klein, Lou Gehrig, Joe Medwick, and Ted Williams.

Whitey Ford again led the team in victories with nineteen, and young Johnny Kucks had his best year, winning eighteen. But 1956 was the year of Larsen. While Don had only a fair regular season, winning eleven games, the 1956 World Series would etch his name indelibly in baseball history.

The Series was tied two games apiece when on October 8 Larsen took the mound for game five before 64,519 fans in Yankee Stadium. Larsen was a wild character whose drunken brawls were notorious. In spring training that year he had demolished his car against a telephone pole in St. Petersburg at five-thirty one morning. Said one Yankee wit, "Anybody who can stay out until five in the morning in a town like St. Petersburg, where the young people are seventy, is a man you've got to admire."

Larsen and Sal Maglie of the Dodgers both pitched flawlessly into the fourth inning. Maglie retired the first eleven batters he faced until Mantle homered in the fourth. But Larsen, using his unique no-windup delivery, continued to cut down Dodger after Dodger. No one reached first base for six, then seven, then eight innings as the drama mounted.

There had never been a World Series no-hitter, and no one had pitched a perfect game in the majors in thirty-four years. In fact, there had been only four perfect games in the history of the game.

Bob Grim: "Larsen? He was a sweetheart. Just a big pussycat. Hey, he liked to have a good time and that reputation followed him from St. Louis and Baltimore.

"I was in the bull pen for Larsen's no-hitter, and from the seventh inning on everybody started to get a little jittery. That's generally the time you get a little pumped up about it.

"From the bull pen it was a little hard to see the kind of stuff he had, but from the way the hitters were swinging at it, they really weren't doing much with him that day. Oh, they hit a few balls. Mickey made a hell of a play on one ball. And Carey made a hell of a play at third.

"You know, there's a lot of luck in a no-hitter but you gotta give Mr. Larsen a lot of credit. He could throw hard but he just had an exceptional once-in-a-lifetime day.

"I'm just glad I was a part of it."

Bob Cerv: "I'd tell you where Don and I were the night before but you better ask him."

Don Larsen: "No comment."

Bob Cerv: "I left him about four o'clock in the morning and he got to the ball park about nine-thirty the next day. I called that morning at the hotel and said, 'Larsen, you better get out of bed. The white rabbit's in your shoe.'

"He said, 'Nooooooooo!' And sure enough he looked down and there it was. He staggered to the park and took a whirlpool bath, a shock shower, a rubdown, and went out and pitched a perfect game.

"We knew it was a no-hitter the whole time. Hell, you can see the scoreboard. I always chuckle about it. They say, 'Don't talk about it. Don't talk about it.' Hell, the pitcher can see what the hell he's doing.

"Around the seventh I had to go out to the pen and warm up pitchers 'cause Howard got called in to pinch-hit. The only other guy out there catching was Charlie Silvera.

"I was catching somebody and I nearly got hit in the damned head 'cause I heard this cheer and somebody hit that long fly ball that Mantle ran down and I turned around to see what was up 'cause I knew the no-hitter was on the line and 'pfffft,' I heard this pitch go right by my ear. And I said, 'Oooops! I gotta tend to my business here or I'll get hit right on the nose.' "

Tom Sturdivant: "My claim to fame is I pitched the day before Don Larsen's perfect game. I was sitting out there in the bull pen sunnin', you know what I mean, because I'd pitched the day before and we were ahead and it didn't look like he was having too much trouble. So we just sat there. Then in the ninth inning with one out somebody just happened to say, 'God, look at the scoreboard!'

"And I looked out at the scoreboard and I started going down it: 2 and 0, 0, 0! And I said Jesus Christ!

"I gotta be truthful with you. That was really when I first knew about it. I was more intent on watching him pitch, helping him get 'em out, than I was worrying about whether they had any hits, because I needed that World Series check.

"He was really throwing hard that day. Don had fantastic stuff. He was probably one of the better athletes that I've ever seen. He couldn't run with Mickey—who the hell could! But he was probably the third fastest man on the club and he could hit a ball as far as anybody. Two or three times he pinch-hit against left-handers. And a couple other times, he played in the outfield.

"Don was a lot like I was. We got extremely nervous. Pressure affects different people different ways. But that day it didn't seem to affect him too bad, now did it? He just had one thing in mind—throw the ball as hard as he could for as long as he could. And, boy, he did."

Shirley Povich: "He did it with a tremendous assortment of pitches that seemed to have five forward speeds, including a slow one that ought to have been equipped with backup lights."

Babe Pinelli (Umpire Pinelli called balls and strikes for Larsen's perfect game): "He was a master of control that day. His change of pace, particularly to the right-handed hitters, was great, because it kept curving away from them, but the biggest thing is the way he was pinpointing his pitches. He wasn't an overpowering pitcher that day, but he was making them hit his pitch.

"The atmosphere carries you right along. You can tell by the way the players act and the noises from the fans when you've got a no-hitter going."

Casey Stengel: "I never had so many assistant managers in my life. Every time Larsen got ready to throw a pitch, the guys on the bench were hollering out to the fielders, telling them where to play the hitter."

Don Larsen: "I don't know what I was thinking about. I was thinking about a million things and nothing, really. It was little things that popped into my mind here and there. I couldn't believe it. I was shaking a little bit, and I was so excited I could hardly talk.

"I started to get nervous around the seventh inning. I went over to Mick and gave him a little nudge and he wouldn't have anything to do with me. Everybody clammed up on me. I didn't like it. Everybody was nervous and it made me nervous.

"My legs were rubbery, and my fingers didn't feel like they were on my hand. I said to myself, 'Please help me out, somebody.'"

When Carl Furillo flied out and Roy Campanella grounded to Martin for out number two in the ninth inning, Larsen stood only one out away from history. Then Larsen faced Dale Mitchell, a dangerous left-handed hitter who could slap the ball to all fields. With the count three and two, Mitchell watched Larsen's pitch sail into Berra's glove and waited for umpire Babe Pinelli's call.

Babe Pinelli: "What a spot for the plate umpire to be in. If I called a base on balls, it would go down in history as the Crime of the Century."

Bill Kinnamon: "Another example of a veteran umpire at work is the call Babe Pinelli made to end Don Larsen's perfect game in the 1956 World Series. If that pitch was a strike, I'm a monkey's uncle. I was there, and I know that ball was higher than Pinelli's strike zone. And I know a lot of other people who have seen that picture a thousand times who say the ball was high. But Pinelli got away with it; no criticism was ever voiced about the fact that the ball could have been high. It was the last pitch of a perfect game, and wherever Larsen threw it, it was strike three if the batter didn't swing. Dale Mitchell should have never taken the pitch. Pinelli knew that, and he called it exactly the way he should have. In other words, he handled it just like a veteran umpire would have. Babe Pinelli has all the respect of me and every other umpire because of the way he handled the situation."[1]

Don Larsen: "Mitchell really scared me up there. Looking back on it, though, I know how much strain he was under. He must have been paralyzed. That made two of us."

Reporter: "Was this the best game you ever saw Larsen pitch?"
Casey Stengel: "So far."

In game six Bob Turley and Clem Labine dueled to a nothing-nothing tie into the tenth inning. Then Jackie Robinson hit one off the wall to even the Series. The next day in game seven Johnny Kucks, capping a brilliant season, shut out the Bums and the Yankees had won their seventeenth World Title.

Bob Cerv: "The day after that Labine and Turley tangled. Everybody forgets about that 'cause of what Larsen did. But they went 1–0 in about eleven innings. The first hit they got was a ball down the left-field line that we all thought Slaughter shoulda caught. I was out in the bull pen right there. It was a line drive that just got over his head somehow."

Joe DiMaggio: "Did you see what I saw? It looked like that fly ball took a bad hop."

Bob Cerv: "In fact, Turley woulda had another no-hitter. That woulda been two no-hitters in a row. So actually the Dodgers didn't get a hit for like twenty straight innings. They won that one, though, in the eleventh, like I said. But the next day Kucks won like 8–0. Berra creamed Newcombe that day. He always had Don's number. He just hit him like he owned him."

THE COPACABANA INCIDENT AND A PAIR OF SERIES WITH MILWAUKEE

Billy Martin was traded to Kansas City on June 15, 1957. General manager George Weiss had branded Martin a troublemaker and he had been looking for an excuse to unload the cocky second baseman. Weiss got his chance when Martin and several other Yanks got embroiled in a nightclub brawl that has become known as the Copacabana Incident.

On May 16 Billy Martin, Yogi Berra, Mickey Mantle, Whitey Ford, Hank Bauer, and Johnny Kucks celebrated Yogi's and Billy's birthdays at several places in New York, ending up after midnight at the Copacabana Club in New York City to catch Sammy Davis, Jr.'s late set.

A group of men on a neighborhood bowling team were sitting at the next table making lewd racial remarks at Davis. Hank Bauer, who had fought side by side in Korea with many blacks, took exception. Eventually a fight ensued in which Bauer may or may not have hit one of the bowlers.

Bob Cerv: "I woulda been there. Irv Noren and I were with Kansas City at the time so we were at Danny's Hideaway. They were all in there. Berra was having his birthday and they said, 'Hey, why don't you go with us to the Copa?' And we said, 'Nah, we're headed back to the hotel.' It was getting kinda late by then. That's how close we came to getting into that mess. The next morning we read all about it in the papers and me and Irv looked at each other and said, 'Thank God we didn't go.' That little fiasco probably woulda cost us some pretty good dough."

Whitey Ford: "I think what started the entire thing was this one guy leaning over to Hank Bauer and saying, 'Do you like listening to Little Black Sambo?' Hank turned to the guy and told him to shut up and that was all there was."

Billy Martin: "We never did find out who hit the guy. Hank didn't hit him, never touched him, and I certainly didn't. I was talking to his brother. We think that a bouncer must have decked him.

"The next day it came out in the papers, YANKEES IN BRAWL AT COPA, and it wasn't true. Not one Yankee was involved.

"We all had to testify before the New York Supreme Court."[2]

Hank Bauer: "Remember the Copa thing? Well, that really had me worried for a while. Everybody made such a big deal out of it. The next day they had these television cameras all over me as I took batting practice. They were trying to find bruises and breaks on my knuckles as evidence that I hit that guy. You would have thought that I was John Dillinger. The papers really treated me like I was a criminal. When Dan Topping asked me if I hit the guy, I said I hadn't, which I hadn't. I also said I wanted to, which I did. George Weiss just sat in Topping's office looking down at the ground. I don't know if George ever saw anybody's eyes. About a month later the grand jury hearing came up and they had all the guys there. They all were called to testify—Whitey, Mickey, Billy, Yogi, and Kucks. Then the buzzer sounded in court for the end of the session. I said, 'What the hell is this? Don't I get to testify?' They called a recess and I was real scared of the outcome. I looked over at the lawyer representing the district attorney and I was frightened. He was wearing a blue suit, black tie, argyle socks, and loafers. He looked like all those toughguy lawyers in the movies who sent you away for thirty years. Then the recess is over and the court clerk looks over at me and gives me a big wink. That made me feel optimistic. Then the judge announces that there is no case and this court clerk rushes up and asks for my autograph. 'Hank, you're my favorite player.' I was never so happy to sign an autograph in my life."[3]

George Weiss, however, was not pleased with the incident, regardless of whether the players were guilty or not, and he fined everyone involved. But he blamed Martin, whom he had tagged a "bad influence" on other members of the team. Weiss had been trying to get rid of Martin for years, but Billy was Casey's boy and he stayed. After the Copa mess, however, Weiss had his excuse, and Martin was traded to Kansas City within a month.

Phil Rizzuto: "They got on Billy later for being a bad influence on Mickey and traded him. They said he was a bad influence on all the guys on the club. All I know is the year he roomed with me I was the MVP, the year he roomed with Yogi he was the MVP, and the year he roomed with Mickey he was the MVP. Some bad influence."

Bob Grim: "Billy and Mickey were very close and they thought Billy led Mickey astray. But Mickey didn't have a ring in his nose. He liked to have a good time just as much as Billy.

"Whitey was in on it too. But Whitey was a little more discreet. He knew when and where to have a good time. After he'd pitch, he'd go out, but a couple days before he was scheduled to pitch, he'd back off. Billy and Mickey never backed off from anything."

Mickey Mantle: "The Yankees always claimed they traded Billy because he was a bad influence on me. Hell, they traded him in 1957, the year after I won the Triple Crown. Lessee, I hit .353, had 52 home runs, and drove in 130 runs. Billy told George Weiss, our general manager, 'If I'm a bad influence, just look what the guy did. How much better do you think he can get?' Three years later they found it wasn't Billy who was the bad influence, anyway. It was Whitey Ford."

Billy Martin: "I have to admit that trade hurt me badly for years. I expected Casey to fight hard for me and keep me.

Casey didn't fight hard enough to keep me and that hurt. I didn't talk to him for five years. People were trying to get us together. Mickey and Whitey also said I was Casey's boy and I should talk to him. Finally, I was scouting for the Twins and he was with the Mets, and he was seventy-two or seventy-three and I saw him in a hotel at the winter meetings. I looked over and he was surrounded by sportswriters and I thought, 'I won't be able to live with myself if he dies before I can talk to him again.' I went over like nothing happened, said, 'Hi, Casey,' and he looked at me, winked, and said to the writers, 'Let me tell you about this here fella, he caught a fly ball for me. . . .' We never mentioned it again."[4]

Even without their pepper guy Martin, the Yanks won the pennant again in 1957. Mantle won the MVP trophy for the second straight year, and Tony Kubek took the Rookie of the Year award. Tom Sturdivant was the workhorse on the mound that year. He went 16–6, recording the best winning percentage in the league, but he came in second to teammate Bobby Shantz in ERA.

Tom Sturdivant: "The first thing I remember was when we came into New York for spring training in '55 they parked the train at 158th Street and I got off the train and walked up to 161st Street and they were cleaning out the stadium. I walked out on the mound and I had accomplished my first goal, to be a Yankee pitcher. My second goal was to win a World Series game and in '56 I did that, and my third goal was to be the best pitcher in the American League. In '57 I went 16–6, had a 2.50 ERA, second to Bobby Shantz and he had a 2.49. I pitched 220 innings and he pitched 150-something—just enough to qualify for the ERA championship.

"The last day of the season he had 149 innings and the Yankees pitched him the last day so he'd have enough innings. That way he'd beat me out of the ERA championship and the Yanks wouldn't have to pay me what I was worth. So Shantz went out there and just lobbed it up there. And every ball they hit, they hit it at somebody. He tried his best when he saw what they were doing, to give the ERA championship to me.

"See, Shantz had been down the road pretty good. He'd been over with Connie Mack and he'd found out how low the Yankee salaries were under Weiss. Shantz knew if I won the most ball games and had the best won-lost percentage and ERA title, I would have deserved some money. I could have gone into that stingy bastard Weiss and demanded more money. And Bobby was just trying to see that I got it. He was a fantastic gentleman and a great pitcher."

Allie Reynolds: "Sturdivant came from around my neck of the woods in Oklahoma and he was a third baseman in our farm system originally. I was the one who talked him into becoming a pitcher. He had a good arm but I told him he wasn't going to make it at third base.

"'What makes you think that?' he said.

"'Hell, I can hit better than you and I would never try to make my living hitting.'"

In the 1957 Series Milwaukee Braves pitcher Lew Burdette, backed by the heavy hitting of "Home Run" Hank Aaron, Eddie Matthews, and Red Schoendienst, won three games and just about single-handedly sank the odds-on Yankees. Burdette hurled two shutouts and went twenty-four consecutive innings without giving up a run to the Yankees' fearsome lineup.

Bob Grim: "Burdette handcuffed us in that Series. He wasn't an overpowering pitcher. He just kept the hitters off-stride. He had a pretty good sinker and, of course, some of 'em thought he was throwing a spitter. Who knows? It certainly wouldn't be the first time.

"But, basically, he kept the ball down. He threw hard enough and had a decent breaking ball. But what it was mostly was at that time the Yankees loved those hard throwers and he was a finesse pitcher. Berra and Mantle and those guys all liked to slug the ball, and the harder they threw it, the farther they hit it. If anyone was going to get the Yankees out it would be a type like Burdette.

"Another thing you gotta remember, when a pitcher gets on a roll like that they generally have two or three good games. Burdette happened to hit his stride during the Series and that was all she wrote for the Yanks.''

The Yankees sewed up the pennant early the next year when they went up by seventeen games on August 2. No other team in the league was above .500, and the Yankees strolled to their twenty-fourth pennant in thirty-eight years.

Bob Turley was the pitching star that year, easily winning the Cy Young Award as the major leagues' best pitcher. Turley, who had a big, hopping fastball, was 21–7 and pitched six shutouts in 1958. Mantle again led the offense with 42 home runs.

In the 1958 Series the Yankees got their revenge on the Braves in a monumental struggle. Milwaukee went up three games to one and it looked bad for the New Yorkers. Only one other team, the 1925 Pirates, had ever come back from a 3–1 deficit to win the Series. But that's exactly what the Yankees did, beating first Lew Burdette, their nemesis of the year before, then the immortal Warren Spahn, to even the series at 3–all. In game seven the Yanks again beat Burdette on the strength of a three-run homer by Bill "Moose" Skowron.

A tremendously strong yet gentle man, Skowron was a five-time All Star who hit over .300 five times for the Yanks. In 1960, his best year, he hit .340 with 26 homers and 91 RBIs. Moose was overshadowed by the Yankee stars like Mantle, Berra, and Maris, and was never given full credit for his accomplishments. He also suffered an endless string of nagging injuries that kept him from reaching his full potential.

But Moose had one thing no one could take from him: He had his name.

Moose Skowron: "How'd I get my name? Well, when I was about eight years old living in Chicago, my grandfather gave all the haircuts to his grandchildren. He shaved off all my hair. I was completely bald. When I got outside all the older fellows around the neighborhood started calling me Mussolini. At that time he was the dictator of Italy. So after that in grammar school, high school, and college everybody called me Moose.

"My grandfather never saw me play major league baseball. But I always wanted to thank him because when I'd strike out or hit into a double play in a game, I couldn't separate the *Moooooose* from the *booooooooos*.

"People have said for years, 'Smile, Moose.' I say I'm not mad, I'm not mean, so what's the big deal? But everybody always says I'm scowling. 'Skowron is scowling again.' What are you gonna do?

"I don't know. I'm ugly, I guess. Me and Yogi and Hank Bauer. Mickey Mantle says all the time that I look like I got run over by a train.

"The Yankees was the team I always wanted to play for. But I didn't always want to be a ball player. When I was young I was gonna be a priest, but one day I walked into the priests' house and I saw one of the priests comin' out of a dark room with these two women and there was lipstick all over his face. From then on I wanted to be a Yankee.

"I remember when I first went to camp with the Yankees—1954. You know, I'm nervous and all of that, and Hank Bauer, a veteran, comes up to me right off and says, 'Don't mess with my money, Skowron. I'm used to winning. I'm used to driving a new car every year, my wife likes a mink coat, you understand? I want you to remember that. We play as a team here. When Joe Collins is at first base, I want you to cheer for him. When you're at first base, I want Joe Collins to cheer for you. You understand what I'm saying?'

"I did. I was always in the shadows with Mickey and Roger around. But we won. All I know is that I was a winner. I did what Hank told me to do. I didn't mess up his money.

"One of my biggest highlights, of course, was hitting that homer to win the '58 World Series, but my biggest highlight was just putting on a Yankee uniform. Everybody on the team felt the same way. Nobody wanted to get traded. It was a privilege to play for the Yankees."

THE LAST PENNANT FOR CASEY

In 1959 the Yankees had their first bad season since Stengel had taken over the club. The team had failed to win the pennant only one other time, in 1954, but that season they won 103 games. In 1959 the Yanks won only 79 and finished a distant third.

Mantle had a nightmare of a year—for him—hitting only .285 with 75 RBIs. Bob Turley, who was 21–7 in '58, won only eight games in 1959. The Yankees hit the cellar on May 20, the first time they had been in last place in nineteen years. They never recovered.

The Yankees came back to win the pennant again in 1960, but in the end it was not a happy season for the team. In one of the most exciting and dramatic of all World Series, the Yankees lost a heartbreaker to the Pittsburgh Pirates. To add to this disappointment, the beloved Casey Stengel was forced to retire after the Pittsburgh Series. Suddenly another of the fabulous Yankee eras was over. The Ol' Perfesser was gone.

Stengel fielded a powerful team in 1960. Moose Skowron, Bobby Richardson, Tony Kubek, and Clete Boyer made up an airtight infield. Yogi Berra and Elston Howard were behind the plate and they took turns in the outfield alongside Mantle and a new face acquired from the Kansas City A's—Roger Maris. All Maris did that season was win the MVP award with 39 homers and 112 RBIs.

The Yankees manhandled the Pirates in the 1960 World Series, batting .338 as a team—the highest in Series history. Bobby Richardson batted .367 (he hit .252 during the season), hit a grand slam, and drove in 12 runs—almost half his total of 26 RBIs for the entire season. Mantle hit 3 homers and had 11 RBIs, and Whitey Ford hung two shutouts on Roberto Clemente and the rest of the Pirates. The Yankees won three games in embarrassing romps—16–3, 10–0, and 12–0—and outscored the Pirates 55–27. It was a massacre. Except that Pittsburgh won three squeakers, and after six games the two teams were even at three games apiece.

Game seven was a masterpiece of suspense, a seesaw struggle that wasn't settled until the last swing. Down 4–1 in the fourth, the Yankees scored four runs to go ahead and added a couple more to take a 7–4 lead into the eighth.

Bobby Shantz: "You remember that Series against Pittsburgh in 1960, don't you? That was something. We did all the hitting but they came out on top. I can't figure out how we lost it. But the whole thing turned around in the seventh game because of a damned pebble or something.

"Everybody remembers the ball that hit Kubek in the throat. But do you know who was pitching for the Yankees when it happened? Yours truly. I came in in the third inning and was really mowing them down. Shut them out for five innings while we caught up and went ahead. We were winning 7–4, going into the bottom of the eighth. Gino Cimoli came up to pinch-hit and he got a single. Still nothing to worry about, right?

"Bill Virdon was the next hitter. I threw him a good pitch and got him to hit it on the ground to Kubek at short. A sure doubleplay ball. Richardson was running over to cover second. I turned around and could just see that double play being executed. But it never happened. The ball hit a pebble or a clod of dirt or something, took a wild bounce and got Tony right in the throat. He went down and lay there gagging. I'll never forget it. He had to leave the game.

"Boy, that was a lousy break if there ever was one. Instead of two out and nobody on, they had two on and nobody out. I left the game at that point and Jim Coates came in. He gave up a base hit to Dick Groat but got the next two guys out. Then Clemente hit a little roller down the first-base line and beat it out when Coates didn't cover the bag. Skowron was mad as hell. That should have been the third out. Instead, Hal Smith came up and he hit a home run and we were down, 9–7.

"We came back and tied it in the ninth, but all that did was set the stage for Bill Mazeroski. He was a fastball hitter, and Ralph Terry, who was in there then, threw one right up his alley and he really tagged it. I felt sorry for Ralph. I felt sorry for me, too. As soon as I saw Mazeroski hit that ball, I knew it was going to be a long winter."[5]

Mickey Mantle: "I think when we lost the 1960 World Series to Pittsburgh was about the worst I ever felt. That was about the only time I ever felt like the best team lost. You know Pittsburgh was good and they weren't just a lucky team. You don't get into the World Series on luck. But in that seven-game Series, every break went their way. We won our three games by scores like 10–0 and 15–3, scores like that. All their wins were real close games. And then in that last game when that ball took that bad hop and hit Tony Kubek in the Adam's apple and then Mazeroski hit that home run—we just sat there in the locker room afterward. Nobody could believe it. I could barely get out of my uniform. That one hurt all winter. In fact, it still hurts. Twenty years later I still can't believe they beat us in that Series."[6]

Bob Cerv: "Pittsburgh was a no-comparison team. But we still got beat. We were down the last day and we came back and had it won. But we had some inexperienced kids come in and make some dumb plays and that cost us. Coates forgot to cover first base on a ball hit at Skowron. Kubek got the bad hop. Ralph Terry was a young pitcher and he threw a dumb pitch. It was mistakes. Young kids' mistakes.

"See, another thing is I hurt my ankle and sat out that last game and Berra played left in my place and Howard caught. If Berra woulda caught maybe we would have won. You never know, but Berra could control those young pitchers better than Ellie.

"I remember I was sitting in the dugout with Joe Cronin, the American League president, and it looked like we had it sewed up and he leans over to me and says, 'Well, it looks like we're gonna win this.' And just then—*boom!* Mazeroski hits it and I turned back and said, 'See you next year, Joe.' When Mazeroski hit it I can tell you there wasn't any doubt. When you play as long as I had you knew by the sound it was gone. The ball was up and he lost it."

Hector Lopez: "We outplayed them and they got lucky. We set all kinds of World Series records. We should have won easily but Casey was makin' some kind of moves I didn't think should have been done.

"Like when Ralph Terry threw up that home run we had guys like Turley, Ryne Duren, Arroyo, and all those guys on the ball club. Ralph Terry wasn't a relief pitcher and he put Ralph in to pitch. The reason why I don't know.

"When Mazeroski hit that homer, we felt cheated. We had all kinds of bad breaks. We had a bad hop at shortstop. Bill Virdon hit a doubleplay ball to Tony Kubek and it hit him in the throat and he was out. Then a guy comes up, hits a three-run homer that put them right back in the ball game. We were thinking World Series check and then all these bad breaks come out of nowhere.

"But like Yogi says, 'It ain't over till it's over.'"

20

The Great Race

1961

The Yankees were again entering a new era. Shortly after the 1960 World Series ended, the Yankees dropped the biggest bombshell in decades. Dan Topping fired Casey Stengel and named Ralph Houk, a favorite of Topping and Webb's, to replace him. The reason given for Stengel's so-called resignation was "advanced age." But when a reporter at the news conference announcing Stengel's dismissal asked Casey, "Did you resign or were you fired?" a bitter Stengel blew the cover off the charade.

"I couldn't be a yes-man. I never was and I never will be. I commenced winning pennants when I came here but I didn't commence getting any younger. . . . They told me my services were no longer desired because they wanted to put in a youth program as an advance way of keeping the club going. I'll never make the mistake of being seventy years old again.

"I worked for the Yankees for twelve years. When you work for people twelve years they have to have some idea that you had good value or you couldn't have stayed with them those twelve years. Very seldom has anyone stayed with the Yankees twelve years. Berra's the only man on the team that stayed there as a player. So maybe the Yankees don't want a manager to stay any longer than that.

"I haven't made up any ideas. I haven't decided for myself and I don't think anybody can change my mind. I'll do what I want to do at this here time. I might wait a while longer. I might wait a month. I might wait two months. I might not play baseball."

This was not what Topping had in mind when he set up his little whitewash news conference, and the press crucified the Yankee owners in the papers.

"Casey imparted warmth to a cold organization and gave it an appeal that it couldn't have bought for millions of dollars," wrote Arthur Daley. "He was priceless. From a public relations standpoint the Yankees have done great damage to themselves. . . . It's a shabby way to treat the man who has not only brought them glory but also has given their dynasty firmer footing than it ever had. So long, Case. You gave us twelve unforgettable years."

"Twelve years ago we were ridiculed when we hired Casey Stengel," Topping shot back. "Today when Casey is leaving, we are ridiculed again."

The firing of Casey was actually part of a general house-cleaning by Topping and Webb. George Weiss was also sent packing after thirteen brilliant years as general manager. He was replaced by Fred Hamey, a long-time assistant to Weiss. Hamey lasted two years and eventually handed the job over to Ralph Houk.

Eddie Lopat: "I was sorry to see Casey go because if he'da stayed I'da stayed because I was his coach in '60. So I got it too.

"Topping and Webb also let George Weiss go that year. As soon as Weiss went, Casey was gonna go. The writing was on the wall. We won a pennant that year but we lost in the World Series to Pittsburgh. But that wasn't the reason they let him go. If he'da won it, he'd still been gone.

"They wanted to bring Ralph Houk in. They'd been grooming him. He managed the Denver club for two or three years, then they brought him up as a coach under Casey a couple years."

Clete Boyer: "I think a lot of it had to do with the way Ralph took to the young players and Casey didn't. One day, I was on third, Kubek was on short, and Richardson was on second. We all made errors in the same game. Stengel called us an air-conditioned infield. The next year Houk called us his million-dollar infield."

Ralph Houk was a paternal, easygoing man, full of praise and good judgment, whom the players and front office loved and admired. In 1961, under Houk's gentle hand, the players responded by winning 109 games and the pennant. The 1961 Yankees may have been the equal of the 1927 team, and at least in the matter of hitting home runs, they were unquestionably superior. The home-run hitting of the '27 team was considered awesome, but the 1961 team hit 80 more homers than the Ruth-Gehrig-Lazzeri congregation. In fact, no team has ever hit as many home runs as the '61 Yanks. They obliterated the record books when they walloped the prodigious total of 240 home runs, easily breaking the major league record of 221 shared by the '47 Giants and the '56 Reds.

In all, six different players hit more than 20 homers that season for the Yanks. The two-man punch of Maris with 61 and Mantle with 54 hit 115 homers between them—more than any other twosome in history; better than Ruth and Gehrig, Foxx and Simmons, or Kiner and Greenberg. Skowron added 28 homers, Berra 22, and Howard had 21. But perhaps the greatest long ball feat of all time was given that year by third-string catcher Johnny Blanchard. He hit 21 home runs in only 243 at-bats, including 4 in a row off four straight pitches! That's a home run every 11.5 times at bat—many of them as a pinch-hitter coming in cold off the bench.

The pitching was similarly spectacular for the Yankees that year. Whitey Ford was almost untouchable, winning 25 games and losing only 4. Ralph Terry had 16 wins and Bill Stafford had 14. The Yanks also had Luis Arroyo, a portly left-hander who turned in one of the finest relief performances baseball has ever seen. Arroyo was 15–5 with 29 saves for the Yankees that year.

Tom Tresh: "The day I came up to the big leagues in 1961, we played a four-game series in Detroit as the Yankees swept the Tigers and went on to win 14 in a row. So for the first 14 games I didn't know what it was like to enter a Yankee locker room after you'd lost. You just walk in, have a good time. Hey, this is great! You never lose here.

"It was a great ball club. In a game where statistics play such an important role, you have to equate teams by statistics. And the '61 Yankees certainly had a lot of good stats.

"I was in such awe getting called up anyway, getting your dream come true. Looking down the bench and seeing all those great players, one after another—Whitey Ford, Elston Howard, Yogi Berra, Mickey Mantle, and it went on and on."

M & M AND THE RACE FOR 60

Babe Ruth (after hitting his sixtieth homer in 1927): "Let's see some other son of a bitch match that."

Though it was a tightly contested pennant race most of the year, the real focus of the entire baseball world was on the "M & M Boys," Mickey Mantle and Roger Maris, and their magnificent assault on the Everest of baseball records—Ruth's 60.

What made the effort to surpass Ruth even more dramatic was that Mantle and Maris were taking aim simultaneously at the Babe's hallowed mark. It was a race to immortality. Maris would knock one out to go ahead of Mickey by a couple of homers, and Mantle would whack a pair the next day to stay even.

On July 1 Mantle hit home runs number 26 and 27, and Maris hit his twenty-eighth, putting him five games ahead of Ruth's 1927 pace. The next day Mickey caught Maris, but then Roger hit two himself, numbers 29 and 30, to go eight games ahead of Ruth. By the end of July Mantle had 38,

Maris 40, and Roger had built a twenty-three-game advantage on the Babe.

With a month yet to go, the record was well in view. On August 31 Roger was up to 51 and Mickey had 48. They were getting very close and they still had plenty of time. Then trouble began. Mantle was forced to the bench with leg injuries and his quest ended at 54 home runs. But Maris still had a decent shot at it. There was a good chance he could reach Babe's mark if he could survive the pressure of all the attention he was receiving, of the press asking over and over the same questions, of the fans booing him and cheering him and hanging all over him everywhere he went, dogging him, driving him crazy.

Maris was a smalltown boy from North Dakota who was uncomfortable with the big-city whirl of New York. He abhorred dishonesty, exaggeration, and anyone on the hustle, and he instinctively turned away from the glaring spotlight and grew sullen and moody. He began avoiding the press and stopped answering questions. Then he turned his back on the New York fans—always a fatal mistake.

Roger Maris: "They are a lousy bunch of front runners, that's what they are. Hit a home run and they love you, but make an out and they start booing. Give me the fans in Kansas City anytime. There's no place where the fans can compare to the people out there.

"There are a few faces you see all the time. I know who they are . . . the same ones always give me a hard time. As long as they leave me alone outside the park I don't care. They never say anything to you face to face.

"I didn't ask them to come. If they keep giving me a hard time, I'll do my job on the field and give them what they pay to see. But they better not come around after the game bothering me for autographs. I can walk through fifteen million of them and never look at one of them."

Bob Cerv: "Roger would get to the stadium and the press just wanted him to stay forever and he didn't want to be there forever being interviewed and interviewed and interviewed. Same question, same question, same question. What pitch did you hit? Hell, I always say I wished Skowron woulda been the one that hit sixty because he never knew what he hit anyway. He'd say he hit a fastball and everybody knew it was a change-up. If it was a fastball, he'd say he hit a curve. Hell, all he ever said was, 'I hit the ball.' Maybe that's the best way to hit. Just hit what you see.

"Probably the worst of the bunch was Howie Cosell. I always remember Howie. He used to come pounding on your door at eight o'clock in the morning after a night game and you'd say, 'Get the hell out of here, Howie.' And he'd say, 'Someday I'm gonna be the top dog.'

"There he'd be at eight, nine o'clock knockin' down your door, wakin' you up. I thought he should show a little more respect than that. But not Howie. Some of them birds never change."

Tom Tresh: "The press and fans just ate up all his time. He was the first one in the locker room in the morning and the last one to leave. He had maybe thirty, forty sportswriters around his locker. Once he hit the clubhouse he had no privacy whatsoever. He started losing hair in the back of his head from nerves.

"Consequently, from the pressure of him trying to answer all those questions and then being misrepresented— misquoted—in the papers, he got a little hard. He was giving all this time trying to answer all those questions, trying to earn a living for his wife and six kids, and he's still getting rapped in the paper. Then the fans read the paper and the fans started getting on him. So sometimes if you're under all that pressure you don't handle things maybe with the fans the way you would normally. It was just tremendous pressure.

"Roger is a tremendous individual. No one in this world can understand the pressure that he had. Babe Ruth didn't have that pressure. Nobody pressured Babe Ruth. Ruth was breaking his own records. Here's a record nobody expected to be broken and here Rog has a shot at it.

"Roger is a top person. If you talk to any player that played with him, they'll tell you he was a great player. He wasn't just a homerun hitter. He was one heck of a defensive outfielder. Great arm, had no fear of the fence, went into the stands after balls. He didn't just lay his glove down when he was a big slugger. He was out there playing both ends of the game.

He'd take guys out at second base on double plays. He was always hustling."

Hector Lopez: "The next year they said he went in a slump, didn't do anything, but he had 33 home runs the next year. Well, after hitting 61, that's a slump. But still 33 home runs is a lot of home runs.

"It was very tough for him. I can remember Maris during that period when he hit all those home runs he had no time to rest. Everywhere he'd go they'd ask him, 'What do you think about breaking Babe Ruth's record?' He didn't have time to concentrate on baseball. Most of the time he'd check in one room and live in another so when they called, no one was home."

Mickey Mantle: "Once, when Roger was taking all that heat, he even got a big list of questions that was sent to New York from some paper in Japan by cable, and he said, 'No wonder I'm going nuts.' Another time, some writer asked him, 'What's a .260 hitter like you doing hitting all those home runs?' And Maris just looked at him and said, 'You've got to be a fucking idiot.' After a while he came to me and said, 'I can't take it anymore, Mick.' And I had to tell him, 'You'll have to take it, you'll just have to.'"

Roger Maris: "Don't ask me about that fucking record. I don't want to talk about the record. All I'm interested in is winning the pennant. The only time I'm by myself is when I'm taking a crap.

"Some people want autographs on demand no matter what you're doing. They think they have a right to order me around. It's just a matter of courtesy."

But something else blocked Maris's drive to break Ruth's record. Mickey Mantle was the favorite of New York fans and they pulled for him and against Roger to shatter 60. If Ruth, the national treasure, was to be brought to his knees, at least let it be done by another Yankee hero.

Tom Tresh: "As he was getting closer, it appeared that a lot of people, fans and press, did not want him to break the record. If they had their choice they would rather have Mantle break the record. Mantle had been there a lot longer and Rog hadn't. Rog was a great player but all of a sudden he was hitting 60 home runs very early in his career. A lot of people just didn't know him.

"It was a tremendous thrill to be there watching Mantle and Maris both going after the record. They weren't going at each other. They were both going after the record. So it was two guys both having a good year.

"But neither one of them tried to zero in to hit a home run every time out. We had a pennant to win—we had to win ball games. Of course, after the pennant was sewed up and Rog was taking the lead and had a chance to go for it, then yes, he tried to take the ball out when he could.

"That's the toughest time to try to hit home runs."

Roger Maris: "They were really rooting for Mantle to break the record that year, not me. Not just the fans, but the ball club itself. How could I have any respect for them? I could only respect what respected me. I was an outsider to them."

Jimmy Cannon: "The community of baseball feels Mantle is a great player. They consider Maris a thrilling freak who batted .269."

Mickey Mantle: "When Roger Maris and I got in that race for home runs, somehow I became the underdog in that contest, and fans stopped hooting at me. People booed Roger and cheered for me. It's sort of an American tradition to root for the underdog and boo the frontrunner. If there are three people out on a field, you can bet one of them is going to be booed. And I don't care who you are, you hear those boos."

Roger Maris: "One evening Mickey was reading the papers, when he leaned toward me and said with a grin, 'I hate your guts.'

"This had become a running gag between us by this time. When he said that, it was a signal to me that there was another gossip item about our rumored feud in the paper.

It got to the point where we just had to find a release. One

day Mickey came over to me, smiled and said, 'I just want to
warn you that if it's the last day of the season and I'm ahead
of you, or we're tied, watch out. If you hit a home run, I'll
stand at the plate and, just before you cross, I'll hit you with
the bat.'

"I went along with the gag. I told him, 'That's all right,
Mick. If I'm on base and you hit one, then I'll turn and run
the wrong way, and you'll pass me on the bases and won't get
your homer either.'"

Bob Cerv: "I know everything that happened that year.
People don't know that Maris, Mantle, and I roomed together in an apartment out by Forest Hills. I probably knew those
two that year better than anyone including their wives. I
know we spent more time together.

"I always laugh because they say they had a battle all
season long to see who would break Ruth's record. Heck,
there wasn't no battle. Those two were the best of friends on
and off the field. We roomed together all gol-darned summer.
When we left Yankee Stadium and got into a car we never
talked ball until the next day heading back to the ball park.
Just put it out of our minds. We'd go home and one of us
would throw together some supper and have a few beers and
a few friends would stop by or not. There wasn't no battle. It
was just good hard baseball.

"I wished Mickey wouldn't got hurt though. They no doubt
both woulda hit 60.

"You know, the Yankees could have helped Roger more.
They had P.R. people. But in my mind I always said the
Yankees—the guys in the front office—didn't really care for
him to break the record. If it was Mantle then fine. They'd
rather had an organization man do it.

"See, I was an organization man, played with the Yanks'
Kansas City AAA club. But Maris wasn't. He came up with
Cleveland. Then he went to Kansas City, then the Yanks.
Naw, they didn't really want him to do it. It was politics. I
can't figure that kind of thinking. Hell, his first two years with
the Yankees he was MVP. Hey, not many guys make MVP.
And two in a row. I don't care if Roger was an organization
man or not. You make MVP, you're good enough to be a
Yankee."

Then in early September with the pressure already crushing Maris, Commissioner Ford Frick upped the ante. Since the American League had expanded to ten teams that year and, in the process, enlarged its season to 162 games, Frick declared that if Maris was to break Babe's record it would have to be done within 154 games. Or no record. That was the final blow.

Roger Maris: "Ford Frick said the record had to have an asterisk because I had the advantage of a longer schedule. By doing that, he was telling everybody, the sportswriters and the American public, 'Whatever Roger Maris does, we are not going to accept it.' Frick never did mention that when I hit number sixty I had four fewer at-bats than Babe Ruth."

Despite Frick's pronouncement, Roger kept hitting them out. On September 20, before game 154 of the season, he had 58 home runs. He needed to hit two to tie Ruth, three to break the record within Frick's limit.

Roger Maris: "In the dugout the other players started coming up to wish me luck. I was so fogged in that I don't even remember who said what. In the third inning I swung and I knew it was gone as soon as I hit it. As I ran the bases I thought, this is great. That's 59. Now I'm maybe going to get up three more times."

But in three more trips to the plate that day Maris couldn't manage to put another one out. He had hit 59 home runs in the first 154 games of the season.

Bob Cerv: "We were in Baltimore when he hit number 59. That was a big night. It was the hundred fifty-fourth game so he had only a couple more at-bats to break Ruth's record within the time limit Frick put on him. So he came up later in the game and hit one even better than he hit number 59, but the wind had changed and it hung it up there and they caught it against the wall. I used to kid Roger, 'That was the ghost of Ruth that blew that ball back in.'

"Actually, it really was Ruth's ghost that stopped Roger. See, Ford Frick was against him. I used to tell him, 'Ah, don't worry. Frick was Babe's ghostwriter.'

"Frick was Babe's ghost. That's why he did it. Boy, it took a long time, though, before people started writing, 'Oh ya, Frick was his ghost.' But, hell, we knew it right off. We never liked him as commissioner anyway. He was too much front office. You go back to Landis. He didn't care if you were an owner or a player. You had just as much right as the next guy. Not with Frick. He was the owner's man."

Roger Maris: "I can't lie about it, I would have loved breaking or tying Ruth's record. But I wasn't really too disappointed. I knew that now the pressure would start easing off and I could start learning to live like a human being again.

"As I ran off the field the guys ran around me and shouted, 'Nice going, Roger. You've had a helluva year.' Things like that. I had to believe them. I made a pretty good run at Ruth's record so I still figure I'm one of the luckiest guys in the world."

On September 26, 1961, in game 159, Maris tied the Babe.

Roger Maris: "Jack Fisher was pitching for Baltimore. I got a single in the first inning. In the third Fisher started bearing down, trying to get me out. Then I saw it coming, it was a high curve. I swung, connected, and heard the roar of the crowd. I stood at the plate watching. It hit the upper deck about four feet in fair territory and then bounced back onto the field. As I trotted around the bases I was in a daze. . . . I couldn't believe it had happened. . . .

"I came off the field and found myself on television. I was surprised to see Mrs. Ruth there. She had said all along that she hoped the record wouldn't be tied or broken. I knew how she felt. I admired her for being honest.

"Mrs. Ruth took my hand and I think I kissed her on the cheek. . . . 'You had a great year,' she said. 'I want to congratulate you, and I mean that, Roger, sincerely. I know that if Babe were here, he would have wanted to congratulate you too.'

"I told her, 'I'm glad I didn't tie the Babe's record in 154 games. This is enough for me.' I meant it then. I mean it now."

Then Roger came to the last game of the season still tied with the Babe.

Roger Maris: "The sections in right field were crowded because of the reward of $5,000 that had been offered for the person catching the ball. On one occasion, all the players and members of the ground crew in the bull pen stood up and put on gloves as I came to bat. Everyone wanted to make a $5,000 catch.

"The score was 0–0 when I came up in the fourth. . . . It was between Tracy Stallard and me. Every eye in the stadium was on us. In the first inning he had pitched to me, and I had hit an easy fly ball. Would he pitch to me again? He knew what was riding on each pitch. His first serve was a ball. The crowd booed. The second pitch was another ball. The boos grew louder. Perhaps the booing made Stallard mad. He's a proud young man and was only doing his job.

"He wound up and delivered the next pitch. It was a good fastball. I was ready, and I connected. As soon as I hit it, I knew it was number 61."

Tracy Stallard: "I have nothing to be ashamed of. He hit sixty others, didn't he?"

THE LEGACY OF ROGER MARIS

Roger Maris died in St. Louis in December, 1985, after a long, courageous battle against cancer. There was a deep sadness to his passing that went beyond the loss of a great ball player. Roger Maris was ultimately a sad figure to the true fans of sport—unappreciated and underrated, almost as if he had broken some sacred trust when he unseated Ruth as the homer king. But beyond his immortal feat, Roger Maris was a good man. That's what everybody says who knew him.

George Steinbrenner: "Roger was a most misunderstood young man. In my mind the Yankees treated him shabbily. He should have been a hero."

Ken Harrelson: "When I was a rookie in '63 and he was a star, he'd come up to me and ask me how things were going and did I need some help. One time I was holding him on first base, and he said to me, 'Hawk, what are you doing after the game?' and I said, 'Nothing, just going back to my hotel.' He said, 'No, you're not, you're going to meet me in the tunnel after the game and we'll go out and have a few beers.' And we did, and I'll always remember that a star was nice to a rookie."

Mickey Mantle: "The greatest single feat I ever saw was Roger Maris hitting 61 home runs to break Babe Ruth's record. I was with him practically every step of the way, and I know the dues he paid to get there."

Bob Cerv: "Just before Christmas I went up to Fargo to Roger's funeral. Blanchard, Mickey, Duren, Boyer, Ford, Skowron were all there along with Richardson and that announcer for the Cardinals, Mike Shannon. He played third base for the Cards and was a real close friend of Roger's. Funny thing, though, the only front office guy from the old days who was there was Bob Fishel. Of course, most of those front office guys are dead now.

"But it wasn't just a bunch of baseball players. The people who were there thought a lot of him. See, what people don't realize—that was his hometown and the people just thought the world of the man. Forget he was a great ball player. Hell, in North Dakota he was just thought of as the greatest guy that ever walked around. He did a lot for them. He started the Roger Maris tournament up there. He was going back there every year. He was getting a lot of people to come up. That's his hometown. They even got a museum up there of all of Roger's stuff.

"Hell, I'll tell you what kind a guy Roger was. See, I got laid up with a bad knee the last week of the '61 season. I was in the hospital the day he hit number 61, and after the game he came over to see me. The day he breaks Ruth's mark he don't go out and get tanked. He comes over to see his buddy in the hospital.

"Why, heck, when Roger come to the Yankees everybody said after spring training, 'Well, hell, we got something here,' I knew what he could do because I'd played with him for a year and a half at Kansas City. It wasn't no surprise to me. I knew exactly what he could do.

"Roger was just a fine athlete. Not many could field better than he could or throw. He had above-average speed, knew how to run bases. He was just a total ball player. He had such a great swing. I could never understand why he didn't hit for better average. The only thing I could figure out was he did hit well when men were on base because he concentrated more. I always told him he didn't concentrate. If you were ahead four or five runs, why, he'd say, 'Let's get the heck outta here. We got 'em beat. Why rub it in.'

"Well, you know Maris went over to the Cards and, guess what, they won the pennant the first two years he was there. You realize from 1960 to 1968 Roger was in an awful lot of World Series.

"I'll tell you what really happened to Roger. He told me a damn umpire stepped on his hand in 1965. And he broke it and the Yankees told him nothing was wrong with it. But he just couldn't do anything with it. Then finally at the end of the season they told him, 'Hey, you know you had a broken hand.' Oh, that really perturbed him. Anything like that got to Roger. He was a very honest man.

"So anyway he had three options. They told him, 'Your hand can be normal, crippled for life, or your finger'll be turned up.' You know, the tendons would curl his little finger up crooked. So that's what happened—it curled his little finger up. Consequently, after that he never had the strength he once had.

"He said, 'The first year I went to the Cardinals they threw me curveballs and I managed to hit the ball real well. The next year they started smokin' 'em at me and I just couldn't wield the bat anymore with that hand.' He said, 'I always thought the top hand didn't have anything to do with hitting. That's not true. I learned that both hands are important with hitting the long ball. I could still field and run and hit but I just couldn't pop that ball anymore.'

"So I guess he made the deal with Busch and got the beer distributorship and then he just got out. He wasn't that old, you know. That was 1968, I think. Seventeen years ago. He was fifty-one when he died. So let's see, that means he was thirty-four when he retired. That's a young man."

THE '61 SERIES—THE YANKS CRUSH THE REDS

In the 1961 World Series the Yankees pounced all over a cocky bunch of Cincinnati Reds, winning the Series four games to one. Whitey Ford was the Series hero. He shut out the Reds in the opener and pitched 5 more scoreless innings in game four before he was forced to retire in the sixth inning due to an ankle injury suffered earlier in the game. Jim Coates came in to replace Ford and he completed the shutout of Cincy. Counting his two shutouts of the Pirates in the 1960 Series, Ford had pitched 32 consecutive World Series innings without giving up a run. That broke Ruth's record of $29\frac{2}{3}$ innings that had held up for forty-two years. As Ford said after the game, "It was not a good year for the Babe."

While Ford was mowing them down on the mound, the '61 Series batting hero was an unlikely, soft-spoken Panamanian named Hector Lopez. Lopez came off the bench to bolster the injury-riddled Yankee assault.

Hector Lopez: "In '61 we played Cincinnati. They beat us the second game at Yankee Stadium. At that particular time they had Robinson, Pinson, Kluszewski—a good team.

"They beat us and they kinda popped off and made us mad. They were saying, 'The Yankees ain't nothing. We can beat 'em.' But after that we took 'em four straight ball games. We finished them right there in Cincinnati.

"What I remember best is the fifth game of the Series. I didn't play much that year. And in the fifth game a lot of guys were hurt. Mantle was out, Maris played center field. They moved Johnny Blanchard to right field and Yogi was in left. Early in the ball game Yogi dove for a ball and he ended up with a big gash across his nose. He had on sunglasses and they jammed right into his face. He couldn't play, so I went in.

"So the first time at bat I came up with the bases loaded

and I hit a triple. The second time at bat I hit a two-run homer. The third time at bat I had a bunt single. I drove in six runs that day and all total 7 RBIs for the '61 World Series.

"That was one of the nicest experiences I ever had."

THE 1962 WORLD SERIES—THE NEW YORK YANKEES AND THE GIANTS OF SAN FRANCISCO

The powerful Yankees were picked to win the 1962 pennant and they did, but they weren't as devastating as in 1961. Mantle won his third MVP award even though he had tailed off badly from 1961, hitting only 30 homers and driving in 89 runs. Those figures were deceiving, however, since Mantle, injured most of the year, had only played in 123 games.

Maris's numbers also fell off considerably from his history-making year of 1961. That magical year 1961 was a once-in-a-lifetime season, but that didn't make any difference to the press and the fans. In 1962 Roger hit 33 homers and batted .256 and everyone called Maris a fluke. He'd only won the MVP award two years in a row and hit 133 homers in three years with the Yankees—an average of more than 44 a year.

The man who took up most of the hitting slack was rookie Tom Tresh. Tresh took Tony Kubek's place at shortstop when Kubek went into the service and had a sensational rookie season. He made the All-Star team and was named Rookie of the Year.

Tom Tresh: "Phil Linz and I broke in about the same time in the minor leagues and we kind of followed each other up the ladder. In 1961 I lead the Carolina League in hitting and Phil led the Texas League that year.

"So when Kubek went in the service the stage was kinda set for the battle between us because we really had to be considered the two best shortstops in the organization. I had a little bit of an advantage because I'd been called up to the Yankees at the end of the 1961 season and was the only minor league player to be called up that season.

"So we hit spring training and the press was building up this big battle for who was going to get the job. Well, Phil and I had been friends all through the minor leagues so we sat down together one day and decided we weren't going to play their game. So we decided that anytime they asked me about Phil, I would build Linz up, and whenever they asked him about me, he'd build me up. We did that all spring and they were so frustrated because they thought it was a mutual admiration society. Every time they talked to me I said I thought Phil Linz ought to be our new shortstop. Everytime they talked to him he'd say, 'Tresh has more power than me.' I'd say, 'Well, his hands are quicker than mine.'

"We ended up leading the Yankees one and two in hitting that spring. I was lucky enough to get a starting job and Phil became the utility player.

"Stepping in for Kubek at short was a very important position to play for a World Champion. There's more right-handed hitters and more balls are hit on the ground than in the air, so short is the area where most balls are hit. Plus, you've got to be in on double plays and steals at second, you've got all the cutoffs to make. So as a rookie thrown into a Yankee pennant race it was a thrill, believe me.

"But I was ready. My dad was a major leaguer for twelve years and that's an advantage because you grow up in an environment where you meet a lot of players and the experience doesn't seem so distant, so unattainable. You know, 'My father did it, why can't I?' But for other kids it's such a faraway dream that it may be harder to believe they can get there.

"It was quite an experience growing up in major league ball parks. Of course, the only food I knew were hot dogs and ice cream. I guess I had a lot of soda pop in there too.

"I used to get out on the field with my father and shag fly balls. They never let me in the infield. I got some great instruction from the players. The great Luke Appling was my father's roommate and a close friend of mine.

"It's an advantage to have grown up in baseball because I knew not only what the game was about out on the field but also what the life was like outside the ballpark."

Hector Lopez: "Tresh was a hustler. He played hard baseball and he was a fine fielder. He knew the game well and he was a team man. Of course, in those days there were nothing but team men on the Yankees. Or they weren't a Yankee."

The 1962 World Series between the Yankees and the San Francisco Giants went down to the final pitch in the seventh game. In game one Whitey Ford beat the Giants 6–2, but San Francisco evened things in game two, 2–0 on a three-hitter by Jack Sanford. The loser was Ralph Terry, a twenty-three-game winner that year, who had always had a rough time in the Series. He had now lost four straight games in Series play without a win. That jinx was broken in game five, however, when Terry won to put New York up three games to two. The big blow in the game was a three-run homer by Tresh.

Billy Pierce beat Whitey in game six, to even the Series once again. Then Houk called on young Ralph Terry for the third time in the Series, and Terry, who had been the best pitcher in the majors all season long, delivered one of the finest and most dramatic performances in Series history.

Ralph Terry: "It had rained so long there in San Francisco that it enabled me to get three starts in the Series. Of course, I was pitching against Jack Sanford for the third time and he'd really shown great stuff in the other two games. I felt kind of like some of these astronauts probably do the night before they go up. Strangely enough, though, I got a good night's rest and I was real thankful I had a chance to redeem myself in the seventh game of the World Series because I'd been a loser in the seventh game in Pittsburgh in the 1960 World Series.

"So anyway I warmed up and I had my good stuff and I felt it right away. Mayo Smith had given me an outstanding scouting report on every one of the Giant hitters. He gave me a little extra insight and that helped me a lot. My slider and all my pitches were working good. And Elston Howard caught a good game.

"Funny thing, the first hit they got was with two men out in the sixth and it was the pitcher, Sanford. Ellie signaled for a breaking pitch and I shook him off and threw him a fastball and he got a single to right field. That was the only time I shook him off the whole ball game. Isn't that funny?

"Then we got down to the latter stages of the ball game. I

felt like we were gonna open the game up. We had the bases loaded a couple times and none or one out and they pulled off a couple double plays, keeping it real tight.

"So at the end I wanted to get them one, two, three in the ninth. I wanted to get Alou, Hiller, and Alou, then I wouldn't have to face Mays and McCovey with anybody on. But Alou hit a little pop fly that fell just off the edge of Ellie's mitt by the dugout. So then he comes back and lays down a perfect bunt and gets on first. The next thing I did in that inning was stop Alou and Hiller from bunting. I struck them out and kept the guy on first base.

"Then Mays! Well, I threw him two fastballs inside, trying to keep the ball in on him because the wind was blowing in real strong from left field so if he hit the ball I wanted him to drive it into that gale at Candlestick. And after two pitches inside I figured I better not stay in there because he's strong enough he can still knock it out of anywhere. So I decided to go away and I made a super pitch, low and away about knee-high on the corner and I felt like I had real good stuff on it. Anyway, he opened up and just hit it with his hands. He wristed the ball and just hit a shot into right field. And Maris made a fine retrieve of the ball and perfect relay to Richardson and they held Alou at third. Whether he could have scored or not is conjecture. I was running to back up home plate and it was muddy and I slipped and fell down. The ball took a big hop in to Howard. If it got by him Alou would have scored because I was flat on my back.

"So now runners are on second and third with two out and McCovey is the hitter. Howard comes out to the mound and says, 'How do you feel? How's your control?' And I knew what he was getting at. He was wondering if I walked this guy and pitched to the next guy, Cepeda, if I'd walk him.

"But I kept thinking I could get McCovey out. I felt like I had a pretty good line on him. I hadn't faced Cepeda but this one game and I felt like pitching to McCovey. Pitching my very best stuff, pitching spots, inside and outside. Instead of worrying about a base on balls, trying to pitch careful, then if you miss a couple then you really have to give in and come down Broadway.

"Others look at it different. Some infielders say you got to set up the force. Maybe I was overconfident. I threw him a slow curveball that was down and away and he hit it kind of on the end of his bat to right field. Maris was moving in for the ball and, oh boy, this looked like the last out. Then, all of a sudden that damn wind at Candlestick took the ball and lifted it foul way up over the bull pen.

"So then I've got to come back and I figure I better not give him another one. So I gave him a fastball inside and it had my very best stuff on it and he hit a bullet. I saw it go by me and right at Richardson. I didn't have time to worry about anything. I knew I had a man over there somewhere. He hit my best pitch very hard and it went right at Bobby.

"I felt fortunate to win. It was a shame that with two clubs so evenly matched throughout the Series that one had to lose."

Houk won his third pennant in a row in 1963. His Yanks won 104 games and finished 10½ games ahead of Chicago. There were a few new faces on the club. Moose Skowron was traded to the Dodgers and a brash young wisecracker named Joe Pepitone took his place at first. Pepe hit 27 home runs his first full year with the club. Bobby Richardson, Tony Kubek, and Clete Boyer filled out a leak-proof infield. Tresh, Maris, and Mantle composed the power-hitting outfield—though Maris hit only 23 homers that season and Mantle broke his foot and played just 65 games.

Whitey Ford had another great year, winning 24 this time around. Jim "Bulldog" Bouton went 21–7 and Al Downing was 13–5. Behind the plate was Elston Howard, by now a master of his craft. He hit .287 with 28 homers and 85 RBIs and was named MVP, the first black man in the American League so honored.

George Weiss had excluded blacks from playing with the Yankees. When Jackie Robinson broke the color barrier in baseball in 1947, the Yankee general manager at the time, Larry MacPhail, had seen the wealth of talent available in the Negro Leagues and he was determined to mine this treasure of talent. MacPhail wasted no time in signing a number of talented blacks to play in the Yankee farm system, including Ruben Gomez, Vic Power, Artie Wilson, Frank Barker, and Elston Howard.

When Weiss took the reins of the Yankees upon MacPhail's

retirement, he quickly traded or sold all the black ball players
in the organization except for Howard. Elston had simply had
too outstanding a season in the minors (he hit .330, 22
homers and drove in 109 runs at Toronto of the International
League) to justify shuttling him off to another club. In 1955
Howard was brought up to the Yankees, but no other black
ever made his way through the Yankee farm system to play
for the parent club while Weiss was general manager.

Once he was with the big club, however, Howard's recep-
tion by the players and Stengel was always warm. As long as
he could do the job, they didn't care if he was purple. And
Howard could do the job.

Elston Howard: "I remember everybody tried to make
everything pleasant for this black guy who was the first one
with us. I remember Bill Skowron and his wife came to pick
me up at the train station, which I'll never forget, and Phil
Rizzuto, goddamn, he was great. I'll never forget him. I give
Phil the most credit of anyone. He would call me up during
the day and take me out to various places, go to the movies,
meet people around the league. I would call him the Great
White Father. He was the type of man I respected, and I gave
him a lot of credit. Also Hank Bauer. Another friend of mine
was Andy Carey. The whole ball club was great. I remember
one day the first year I was there I hit a triple that won a ball
game. My biggest ball game. I won the ball game for the
Yankees in the bottom of the ninth, and I was outside doing
an interview. I came into the locker room, and they had
towels lined up from the door to my locker. Joe Collins,
Mickey Mantle—they lined the towels up. It was like a red
carpet. Laid out for me. I was surprised. And when they did
that, I figured I was accepted just like everyone else."[1]

"I never felt any prejudice around Casey. He treated me
the same as he did any other player. . . . I had stayed in a
black hotel the first time in Kansas City. Now this second
trip, Casey came to me in the lobby and said, 'Just get your
key like everybody else.' Then I was so frightened I double
locked my door and put a chair against it. The phone rang
and it was Phil Rizzuto, my great white father. 'Come down
and have dinner with me in my room.' After that it was all the

same for everybody. I asked Casey about it later. He said he went to George Weiss and said, 'Howard's one of my players, ain't he? If he don't stay here, we don't stay here.' That settled it."[2]

Howard spent several years in the minors learning how to catch. But when he finally made it to the Yanks he found himself playing behind the great Yogi. Howard soon became a man for all reasons—a utility man par excellence. "You can substitute but you can rarely replace," said Stengel. "With Howard I have a replacement." Whether relieving Yogi at backstop or roaming the outfield, Howard played brilliantly, making the All-Star team eight straight years from 1957 to 1964.

Elston Howard: "I played outfield in high school and when I came to the Yankees I played left field and caught. I used to fill in because Yogi at the time was the best catcher in baseball. I had to adjust myself. I wasn't a very good outfielder because I had a tendency to get a slow start on the ball. But when I'm catching everything is natural. It's my normal position. I don't worry about other things.

"Also, I used to be strictly a pull hitter. Casey used to talk to me about hitting the ball to right field a great deal. So I picked up a heavier bat and by using that bat I could hit the ball to right field. And that helped me a lot.

"So it took me a while, I think, before I developed fully as a player and was appreciated fully for my ability. By 1963, of course, I had taken over full-time for Yogi and I won the MVP. That's the Nobel Prize of baseball."

The 1963 Series was a disaster for the Yankees. For the first time ever in World Series play, they were humiliated in four straight. There certainly wasn't any big mystery about what happened to the Yankees. They simply ran into perhaps the greatest pitching machine in history—Sandy Koufax, Don Drysdale, and Johnny Podres. When these starters couldn't do the job, like when Koufax took the day off for Yom Kippur, the Dodgers had Ron Perranoski, the best reliever in baseball. Perranoski won 16 games, saved 21, and had a 1.67 ERA.

Koufax set a Series record with fifteen strikeouts in game one, and the Yanks hit a sickly .171 for the Series.

Yogi Berra: "I see how Koufax won twenty-five games. What I don't understand is how he lost five."

Tom Tresh: "Actually, they were all close ball games. They didn't blow us out in any ball game. They just beat us. They had great pitching. We just didn't produce. Or we couldn't produce maybe. We didn't hit much of anything. They just beat us. It was as simple as that."

Hector Lopez: "In the first game I pinch-hit against Koufax and I struck out. Believe me, I wasn't alone. He struck out fifteen of us. Then the fourth game I started, went 0 for 4 and made the last out of the Series. It wasn't the best day for me or the Yankees.

"We were never blown out of the ball games. We lost 2–1, 3–2, 1–0. It was very close. A base hit here and a base hit there and it might have made a difference. But we just couldn't get those big base hits against a guy like Koufax."

YOGI TAKES OVER AND A HARMONICA WINS THE PENNANT

After three straight pennants Ralph Houk was promoted to general manager in 1964. Houk was replaced as manager by long-time Yankee hero Yogi Berra, one of the most popular men ever to wear pinstripes.

Berra led the Yanks to their fifth pennant in a row, but from the beginning the players were unhappy with Yogi. Berra had been the object of a lot of wisecracks over the years, and now the master of malaprop was going to be the man who ran things. When the Yankees, who were plagued by injuries in the first half of the season, got off to a rocky start, the players voiced their discontent to Houk. And he listened.

Bill Veeck: "The decision to make Yogi Berra, of all people, the manager of the Yankees was admittedly one of the more moonstruck episodes in baseball. So moonstruck that nobody will ever be able to convince me that Yogi was ever anything more than a handy stopgap Houk latched onto in order to boost himself up in the front office."

Tom Tresh: "Yogi's not a hard-driving personality. He's a real fun-loving person. A gentle type of guy. So that's the way he has to lead. When you have a bunch of guys who've all played together it's hard for one person to suddenly say, 'This is what we're going to do.'

"It was just a very hard situation for Yogi. I liked Yogi a lot. Here's a guy who's been a teammate of many of the players for a lot of years and all of a sudden he's a manager. How do you say to your friend, 'Hey, you didn't run your ball out, for crying out loud.' Or 'Hey, I think you ought to be getting in earlier.' That wouldn't be the case today after the experience he's had, but that was a tough situation. Anybody who would have been put in there one year being a player and the next a manager would have found it tough.

"It was a hard situation and yet we won it and got beat in seven hard games in the Series. He certainly couldn't be embarrassed."

By mid-August the Yanks were struggling along in third place, behind Baltimore and Chicago. But then the Bombers exploded, and it is now part of the Yankee lore that the team was ignited by a harmonica rendition of "Mary Had a Little Lamb."

The club had just lost ten out of fifteen on the road, including four straight losses to Chicago. On August 20, after the final game in the White Sox sweep, on the bus going from Comisky Park to O'Hare Airport, Phil Linz took out his harmonica and began to blow.

Tom Tresh: "Phil Linz should have been a starting shortstop or second baseman for someone. He had a lot of talent. But back in those days the Yanks were real talent-heavy. So anyway Phil became the supersub. Did a heck of a job for us.

"Well, anyway, Kubek had been hurt and Linz was playing short and we'd lost seven in a row and we were going into Chicago and Yogi inserts Kubek back in the lineup at short. And Phil had done a great job at short. Even though we hadn't been winning, he was playing very well. So Phil was kinda miffed when they sat him down.

"Anyway, I had a guitar and harmonica and I'd play in my room. And Kubek, who I was good friends with, would come up to my room and borrow my harmonica. So I said, 'When we get to Chicago we're going to buy you a harmonica.'

"So we get off the bus in Chicago and Phil sees us taking off and he says, 'Where you going?' And we said, 'We're going over to Marshall Field's to buy a harmonica.' So Phil says, 'That sounds like fun.' So we all go over to the music department and Kubek picks out a harmonica. And we started to walk out and Tony takes out the harmonica—this is one of the gutsiest guys you ever want to know—and he starts playing it right there in Marshall Field's. 'Streets of Laredo.' It's the only song he knew. So Phil says, 'Boy, that sounds great. I think I'll buy me one. How much does it cost, Tom?' 'Two and a half,' I said. So he went back and got one.

"Well, Phil did not start the next four games and we lost all four games to Chicago. After the last game we got on the bus and Linz whips out his harmonica. Phil's got no ear for music whatsoever but he's got the little card they give you with it—'Mary Had a Little Lamb.' You toot here and you suck in here, whatever.

"So he's sitting in the back of the bus. He's got his card out there and he's just playing the hell out of 'Mary Had a Little Lamb.' Crosetti was on the bus and Yogi had just gotten on and Yogi didn't say anything. Pretty soon, though, Crosetti got up and told Phil where he should stick the harmonica. Phil, of course, was a real fighter all his life and you don't want to challenge Phil 'cause he really could fight. Then, Yogi gets up and Phil told Yogi, 'You show me where to put the harmonica.'

"So Yogi comes walking down the aisle. Phil throws him the harmonica and says, 'Here, take it!' Yogi's mad and he wheels the harmonica at the back of the bus and Joe Pepitone's sitting in the back aisle between the two rows so he can stretch his legs out in the aisle and it hits him right in the shins. So here's Pepitone jumping up and down, yelling and screaming, 'I'm wounded! I'm wounded!' And Yogi and Linz going head to head. It was a madhouse.

"So Phil gets fined $250 and Phil says to me, 'I thought

when you said this damn thing was gonna cost two and a half you meant two dollars and fifty cents.'

"But the funny thing was that after all the publicity that incident got, Phil ended up signing a $20,000 contract with Hohner Harmonica."

The harmonica incident fired up the complacent New Yorkers. From that day on the Yankees put on a ferocious surge, winning thirty out of their last forty games. By September 17 they had regained first place. Then they won nine in a row, to sew up pennant number twenty-nine in their illustrious history. It would be their last pennant for over a decade.

In the 1964 World Series the Yanks faced the St. Louis Cardinals, managed by Johnny Keane. Ford pitched the first game. It was the great lefty's eleventh World Series and his twenty-second Series start—both records for a pitcher. He also owns the record for most Series wins, most innings pitched, and most strikeouts. But he lost this opener 9–5, retiring with a sore arm in the sixth inning. It proved to be Ford's last Series appearance ever. He was unable to pitch again that year and, sadly, the Yanks never won another pennant during Whitey's career.

Mantle also put another notch in the Series record book by blasting three homers in the Series, to eclipse Babe Ruth's record of sixteen Series homers. Mantle's eighteenth and last Series home run came in game seven against "Bullet Bob" Gibson in the sixth inning, to cut the Cards' lead to 6–3.

The score was 7–5 with two out in the ninth when Bobby Richardson stepped to the plate against Gibson. Mantle kneeled in the on-deck circle, waiting for one more crack at tying the game. But Richardson popped up to end the game, and St. Louis was the World Champion.

PART V

A
New Dynasty

21

The Decline and Fall of the Yankees

In August of 1964 Columbia Broadcasting System bought the Yankees from Dan Topping and Del Webb for $13.2 million. Another Yankee era had begun, but instead of another string of championships, the leadership of CBS produced the bleakest decade in Yankee history. In the eight years CBS owned the Yankees, the club never won a pennant, finished higher than fourth only once, and saw attendance plummet below the one million mark for the first time since 1945, when most hard-core baseball fans were off fighting a war.

CBS named Mike Burke as president of the Yankees. Burke possessed no baseball knowledge whatsoever, but he kept Ralph Houk as his general manager and baseball confidant. Houk's first move was to fire manager Yogi Berra. Houk replaced Yogi with Johnny Keane, the manager of the World Champion St. Louis Cardinals. It was the first of a long list of bad decisions, bad luck, and bad timing that would plague the once-proud Yankee organization.

Jim Bouton: "Yogi was very blunt, but a good man nevertheless and a good manager. The Yankees won the pennant under Yogi. How bad could he have been, for Christ's sake? But Houk didn't think that Yogi was a good manager. Houk never backed Yogi up. Houk wanted to get rid of Yogi so he could get his own man in there. All the time the players would come into Houk's office and complain that Yogi did this or did that, and 'Why can't you come back?' Houk never kicked those guys out of his office."[1]

Tony Kubek: "It was a difficult position for him. He had been the butt of our jokes for so long, and then he was our leader. We respected him for his knowledge of the game, and he really didn't have any trouble with the older guys. But the young guys, well, we had a few free spirits and I guess they ran all over the place. The older guys wouldn't do it to him.

"The new guys who met him for the first time in spring training probably came away with the idea that he wasn't too bright. That really isn't true. Yogi is a complex person who is very compassionate for the problems of others. The one thing I remember most about him as a manager is that he never panicked. At least he never showed panic. He'd just hang in there and say we'll get 'em the next day. Just like he did with the Mets."

Whitey Ford: "I thought Yogi did a hell of a job. I was his pitching coach—both a pitcher and a coach, actually. But we lost the Series that year, it was 1964. I'd pitched only one game, the first of the seven we played. After that I was useless. My hand was getting numb. For that matter, I wasn't much help in the first game, either.

"So flying home from St. Louis, Yogi came back to me in the airplane and said, 'Will you be my coach again next year?' I said, 'Sure, Yog.' And he said, 'Thanks.' And he got fired the next day.

"When things cooled down a few days later, I called him and said, 'Thanks for assuring me of my job, Yogi.'"[2]

Tony Kubek: "The afternoon Yogi was fired my telephone rang. It was Carmen Berra. She said, 'Yogi would like to talk to you, but he can't. He feels bad. He's heard the stories about you saying he couldn't handle the players, and he wants to know if they are true.'

"I told her I never said that. I told her about the talk I had with Houk on the plane and that was the extent of it. She seemed satisfied, but I felt bad. The reason Yogi couldn't come to the phone, Carmen said, was that he was too broken up. Not about getting fired, about the idea that the players had said those things about him. She said he would feel much better when she told him what I said."[3]

Jim Bouton: "In '65 Houk finally got to pick his own man, and he picked Johnny Keane. Keane had won the pennant over at St. Louis, the players had really played for him over there, he sort of had the class-guy look about him, and he had been part of a winning organization for a long, long time with a reputation of building from the ground up, and so Ralph picked him. And he was absolutely the wrong guy. The players hadn't respected Yogi, but at least they liked him. Keane they didn't like or respect. Johnny was too old for us and too much of a traditionalist, and he never could get used to our outrageous habits and life-style."[4]

Tom Tresh: "Keane was a strong disciplinarian type and they just felt that's what the club needed at that point.

"But that kind of strategy didn't work with those kind of guys. They'd been around a long time. It's always been true in baseball. The Yankees were very, very inbred at that point. We had a big minor league system and most of your Yankees came out of this system. There were trades made but not many. About that time they started making trades that didn't have the Yankee tradition bred in them. Up to that point almost every Yankee had grown up through their minor league system. So even as a rookie they felt they'd been a Yankee for a long time.

"We played the kind of baseball, the type of baseball where we didn't run a lot, we didn't bunt a lot, we just hit and played defense. Power baseball.

"Now Keane came in and played the kind of baseball he played in St. Louis. Hit and run here, bunt here—a different type of ball. That had something to do with the crash."

* * *

Under Keane the Yanks finished a dismal sixth in 1965. The team went 77–85 for a .475 percentage, the worst record since 1925. The team batting average was .235, the lowest since 1915! But it wasn't all Keane's fault. The Yankee demise had been set in motion years before he arrived. Poor Johnny Keane had boarded a down elevator.

Eddie Lopat: "See, Topping and Webb let the club deteriorate. They were getting ready to sell the club. So they didn't want to put too much cash back in it.

"I was the GM at Kansas City then and you get a statement every year that comes out of the commissioner's office that states what club spent how much for players. So I looked at the Yankee stats and they only spent $175,000 and the other clubs were spending $600, $800, and $900,000.

"Now Cincinnatti spent $75,000 that year so we knew they were gonna be sold. And they were. You just look at the sheet. And the following year I see the list again and the Yankees only spent $75,000 and I know for sure they're going on the block, and sure enough that year, '66, they sold 'em."

Jim Bouton: "The basic downfall, of course, was one that none of us were aware of. We were able to see it later upon reflection. It was that Dan Topping and Del Webb, knowing they were going to sell the ball club, did not invest in the foundation as they had always done in the past. Why shell out a lot of money for a Rick Monday when they would be long gone by the time Rick Monday bore fruit? So there was no investment in the basic guts of the team, the raw materials. So when the twelve guys got old, there was really nobody there to replace them. CBS bought a shell—a name and goodwill. They didn't realize that our minor leagues were empty. All those years we had been giving away two young guys for Dale Long. They had to stick with us as long as they could because they didn't have anybody else. We were allowed to hang on and do badly and continue struggling because there was nobody to replace us. Why did they stick with Pepitone all those years? Because Buddy Barker wasn't any better than Pepitone was."[5]

Bob Grim: "You keep going to the well and eventually the well runs dry. When the Yankees needed somebody they'd give up three or four young players. They traded away all their young talent to acquire one or two old guys just to help them out for a year or two. So they ended up with a bunch of old players—an old team. Goodbye dynasty."

Eddie Lopat: "Another factor was that the other owners were tired of the Yankees dominating all those years so they came up with the draft. And in '65 they caught the Yankees with no players. They'd been trying to mess up the Yankees for years and they finally figured a way to do it. The Yankees went eight, nine years where they didn't get a thing.

"Prior to the draft the Yankees just outbid everybody else. Up to '64 we were picking the top ten percent, the cream of the country. That's what the Dodgers did. They went out to the Coast and their club deteriorated all at once because they all got old—Snider, Reese, Hodges. Those guys. Then they spent three million dollars the next three years outbidding everyone and in four or five years they were in the Series again.

"Now the draft eliminated that. You can't do that. You gotta wait your turn. Before if there were ten top players on the open market, the Yankees could go out and get five or six. But with the draft we got one if we were lucky."

Tom Tresh: "When the draft came about everything was kind of equalized. Before that the Yankees and the Dodgers got more than the lion's share. The draft made everybody equal. They didn't have as many good young players coming up every year. Then, pretty soon the older players started to retire. The Yanks just didn't have the replacements they had before. A lot of trades happened at that point. Pretty soon Maris went to St. Louis, Boyer went, then Blanchard was gone. There was a lot of movement. The team was really turned over. After a while the team didn't have the closeness that Yankee teams had had up to then. Before, even though we were in the minor leagues, we got to go to the Yankee camps. We got to know guys and by the time we got there, we just took our place. It was a close-knit fraternity. It was a great tradition.''

Bobby Murcer: ''What swung me to the Yankees was the idea that you would get a World Series check every year. You could just about bank on that. But when I came up in 1965 it was like I was some kind of omen. The World Series supply for the Yankees had dried up.''

Bob Cerv: ''When I left I told Houk, 'If Pepitone and Bouton and Linz are the future of the Yankees, the dynasty is over.' They weren't the type of ball players the Yankees used to have. Pepitone had a couple of good years, but Houk just dissected that team to nothing after that. They traded everybody except Mantle and Ford.

''Hell, Houk wasn't a bad manager but that wasn't a hard job to do, either. Hell, he took over a team that had 240 homers the year before. He only managed two, three years, then he was G.M. and, tell you the truth, that's when the Yanks fell apart. The G.M. usually is the one that makes the team go. With Houk they went to pot.''

When the team started the 1966 season 4–16, Keane was fired. Ralph Houk came down from the front office to save the Yankees, and the Old Major promptly led his troops to tenth place, the worst in the club's history. Houk stuck around for seven more disastrous years, until 1973.

In 1967 the team made a comeback—to ninth. After that the Yanks finished fourth or fifth every year except in 1970, when they made a whistle stop in the league lead, then faded to an out-of-sight second, fifteen games behind a strong Baltimore Oriole club.

There were few bright spots during those years. Tresh, whose career began with a bang, tailed off quickly to a weak whimper. His batting average dropped to .233 in 1966, .219 in 1967, and .195 in 1968. Joe Pepitone followed the same pattern as Tresh. Bobby Murcer, who was supposed to be the second coming of Mantle, gave the Yankees a few decent years but he certainly wasn't the Mick.

In 1968 catcher Jake Gibbs led the regulars in hitting with only a .267 average. Mel Stottlemyre was the mainstay of the pitching staff, winning twenty games three different years, but he also led the league in losses for three years.

THE MICK RETIRES

The end and total collapse of the greatest Yankee dynasty of them all was perhaps best symbolized by the retirement of Mickey Mantle at the end of the 1968 season.

Mantle had limped around on his gimpy knees the last half-dozen years, and his average reflected his pain. From 1965 to 1968 he hit .255, .288, .245, and .237, and his lifetime batting average finally dipped below .300, a fact that Mantle has rued ever since. After eighteen seasons and a team record of 2,401 games, it was time for the Mick to hang 'em up.

Mickey Mantle: "Just before I retired in 1968, Denny McLain threw me a home-run pitch that people still haven't stopped talking about. I had tied Jimmy Foxx for third highest career homers, at 534, on August 22. Getting ahead of Foxx was one of the goals I had set for myself for the season, and it was just one more factor in reaching a decision about 1969. I knew it would be a little easier to quit if I got to 535.

"I looked out at Denny and kind of motioned him to throw the ball, you know, to keep it away from me a little bit. I don't know if he was trying to let me hit it or not, but I know he wasn't working on me as hard as he usually does. The next pitch, I hit a home run, pulling the ball down the line in the upper deck. As I was rounding third, I looked out at him and he kinda grinned at me. I gave him, I kinda gave him a sign like thanks. I still don't know whether he really was trying to let me hit it or not."

Tom Tresh: "I didn't really see a decline as much as I saw a person whose legs were just getting worse and worse. He suffered other injuries so he just wasn't playing as much. It wasn't a lack of potency as much as his injuries stopped him. He wasn't getting old. He could still hit the ball as hard as ever. It was just harder and harder for those legs to work.

"A guy like Mickey doesn't want to hang around like a

token player. He felt he wasn't able to give to the team and he didn't want to be out there just because he was Mickey Mantle."

On June 9, 1969, the Yankees threw Mantle a Yankee Stadium farewell at which Mantle's number 7 was retired.

They were all there to honor Mickey—Joe DiMaggio, Whitey Ford, Yogi Berra, and the rest of the Yankee greats of the past (Casey Stengel was managing the Mets and sent a telegram). When Mickey came out of the dugout, he received the longest spontaneous ovation in Yankee Stadium history— nine full minutes.

Then Mickey Mantle stepped to the microphone before the overflow crowd.

Mickey Mantle: "When I walked into this stadium eighteen years ago I felt much the same way I do right now. I don't have words to describe how I felt then or how I feel now. But I'll tell you one thing, baseball was real good to me. And playing eighteen years in the Yankee Stadium for you folks is the best thing that could ever happen to a ball player.

"To think the Yankees are retiring my number 7 with numbers 3, 4, and 5 topped off everything that I could ever wish for. I've often wondered how a man who knew he was gonna die could stand here and say he was the luckiest man in the world. But now I think I know how Lou Gehrig felt. It's not only a great day for me, it's a great day for all the Mantles. I wish my father could have been here.

"Thank you."

Another glorious Yankee era had passed. It would take a few years, but eventually three men—a Cleveland-born millionaire, a fiery former Yankee player, and the greatest slugger of his era would bring the luster back to the Yankee tradition.

22

Steinbrenner

On June 3, 1973, CBS announced it had sold the Yankees
to a group of ten investors headed by George M. Steinbrenner III, a Cleveland shipping magnate. The purchase price
was $10 million—$3 million less than CBS had paid for the
club a decade before. Said a CBS spokesman, "CBS substan-
tially broke even on this deal, taking account of interest and
depreciation and things like that." In ten years the corporate
mind had turned a sports dynasty into a tax-loss write-off.

Steinbrenner owned 20 percent of the Yankees. He was a
man who liked to do things his way, and in no time he took
control of the club. He bought out several other partners
until he eventually owned 55 percent of the franchise, and
once he had the reins of the Yankees in hand, he went to
work.

Ambitious, outspoken, and controversial, Steinbrenner
wanted a winner in New York and he'd do anything, spend
any amount, to get what he wanted. First, he cleaned house,
dismissing Yankee president Lee MacPhail—who later became president of the American League—and then manager
Ralph Houk, a perennial loser.

Next, he hired Gabe Paul as new president and virtually renovated the entire Yankee team. Steinbrenner and Paul sold or traded Yankee regulars Matty and Felipe Alou, Hal Lanier, Gene Michael, Horace Clark, John Ellis, Mike Kekich, Lindy McDaniel, and a score of others and brought in Pat Dobson, Rudy May, Dick Tidrow, Chris Chambliss, Sandy Alomar, Graig Nettles, Lou Piniella, Alex Johnson, and Elliot Maddox. But that was only part of Steinbrenner's stable.

Free agency had just been introduced to baseball, and Steinbrenner, like no one else, knew how to use the new rules to his advantage. He spent often and a lot and built the Yanks into a winner in short order. First, he shelled out a cool $3.35 million for Jim "Catfish" Hunter, then $2.09 million for Don Gullett, $2.66 million for Reggie Jackson, and $2.75 million for Rich Gossage.

Like Colonel Jake Ruppert before him, Steinbrenner was not afraid to spend whatever money it took to build a winner. For he knew, as Ruppert had, that in New York success on the field was cash in the bank. By 1976 the Yankees had once again won the pennant, and over the next six seasons they won five division titles, four pennants, and two World Championships.

George Steinbrenner: "Owning the Yankees is like owning the 'Mona Lisa'; it's something you'd never sell. But it's a different game today. In the old days you had the players and the general manager. There was no haggling over the contracts. Roger Maris hit 61 home runs, came in the next year and they wanted to give him an eight-thousand-dollar raise. After breaking Babe Ruth's record!

"It's a different deal today. It's entertainment and it's business. Baseball is the greatest game but it's a different game. . . . Baseball is show business. How do you think we average thirty-two thousand a game here? We've got stars, that's how.

"When the Yankees came to town, it was like Barnum and Bailey coming to town. I don't mean that they were like a circus, but it was the excitement. They had these gray uniforms, but there was a blue hue to them. I'll never forget them. Watching them warm up was as exciting as watching the game. Being in Cleveland, you couldn't root for them, but you could boo them in awe. . . ."

Eddie Lopat: "In the thirties Tom Yawkey in Boston had the same idea as Steinbrenner. He went out and spent two, three million dollars, which in the Depression was a lot of money. But those guys just couldn't jell and win. That happens. There's no guarantee that when you buy the best, they'll play together.

"Steinbrenner did it and it worked. You can't call it luck."

Graig Nettles: "When George signed Catfish, we could see that George wasn't going to let any player pass by who could help us. In Cleveland or in Minnesota, they wouldn't have even made a bid on him. George could see that we needed a pitcher like Catfish, and he went out and got him. I was always impressed with the way George would go out and get the quality player, with money no object."[1]

Steinbrenner and Ruppert, however, were not totally alike. While Ruppert had spent lavishly to build his teams, he never meddled and never second-guessed his general manager or manager. When Steinbrenner took over in 1973 he vowed to follow Jake's lead. "I won't be active in the day-to-day operations of the club at all," Steinbrenner promised. "I can't spread myself so thin. I've got enough headaches with the shipping company."

But Steinbrenner just couldn't help being Steinbrenner. He meddled like no other Yankee owner ever meddled. He hired and fired personnel at all levels of the club. He made the trades. He told the manager whom to play and where to play them. He called down to the dugout on the phone or a walkie-talkie to position the fielders or tell the manager which reliever to send in. It was Steinbrenner who ran the Yankees. He called it being an involved owner. The players just thought he was sticking his nose into something about which he knew nothing.

George Steinbrenner: "I'm intense and I'm a driver. I'm a firm believer in the old adage that if you're going to lead—lead. I've been involved in everything from the ushers to the dining room to the players' equipment bags. I raise hell if the rest rooms are dirty.

"The reason baseball has its problems today is because owners weren't involved twenty years ago. They treated baseball as a hobby, as a toy, and they left all the decisions in the hands of the general managers, who were baseball men. They weren't businessmen. They didn't know how to negotiate a labor contract or how to sign a big television deal. I'm an involved owner. I want my fans to know I'm involved because they mean a lot to me.

"For example, I like to see a player look neat. Maybe I'm wrong. I have nothing against long hair per se, but I'm trying to instill a certain sense of order and discipline in the ball club because I think discipline is important in an athlete. I want to develop pride in the players as Yankees."

Tony Kubek: "He has one of the most expensive toys in the world, and what he does is manipulate people. Steinbrenner won't let anybody relax. It's what I call his corporate mentality. He throws a fear into everybody. . . . He makes the players fear for their jobs. That's his theory, and it works. But it's not a pleasant way to have to play."

Andy Messersmith: "George is no dummy, that's for sure. I think George has a little problem with team motivation. See, things are changing as far as motivation. George is from the old school. George's method is to use intimidation tactics rather than attempt to understand his players and motivate them by enjoyment. George is missing the boat in that area.

"Of course, baseball in general is about thirty years behind the rest of the world. If it's a new idea baseball men don't want to hear about it. The problem is baseball doesn't want new blood. They bring back Yogi or Martin for the umpteenth time. They don't want to hear any new tunes. You been a good boy, you can work for us later. There's nothing wrong with that except it creates a tunnel vision. Everyone's had the same vision for years. There are no new people and without new people very seldom do you get new ideas. No matter how many times you reincarnate Billy Martin, you'll always get Billy Martin."

Ray Fitzgerald: "I can think of only one man who might, just might, fit the high standards necessary to manage the New York Yankees. First, we'd have to fit him for the Yankee uniform. A 42 around the waist would be just about right, with a 15½ red neck and padded shoulders . . . shoes small enough to fit into his mouth . . . and . . . the biggest hat size available. His name would be emblazoned on the pinstripes . . . S*T*E*I*N*B*R*E*N*N*E*R . . . the only one who could possibly do the job. I see George Steinbrenner, unregistered egomaniac and all-time second-guesser, firing his team and playing all nine positions himself."

Billy Martin: "One game we were playing in Chicago, and it was the middle of the game, and the dugout phone rang. Nettles answered it. He said, 'Billy, it's George.' I said, 'You gotta be kidding me.' Graig had his hand over the receiver, and he said, 'No, it's really George.' I took the phone from Graig. I said, 'Who is this?' He said, 'George!' I said, 'Don't be calling me during the game, you asshole.' And I hung up. I said to Graig, 'Imagine that, a guy trying to imitate George.' Graig said, 'That was George.' I said, 'Maybe he'll learn not to call down here anymore.' "[2]

Sparky Lyle: "There is one other guy that makes a decision on the Yankees besides George—Cary Grant. Cary Grant used to sit up there with George in George's private box and we'd say, 'I hope we don't make an error tonight because if Cary goes, "Georgy, Georgy, Georgy," we're through.' "

Graig Nettles: "We could see George slowly taking over the ball club, buying out many of the partners. And then, after solidifying his power, he got suspended by Bowie Kuhn for two years, which led to one of the funniest things I had ever seen as a player. That spring [Bill] Virdon came into the clubhouse, and he was carrying a cassette recorder with him. George had sent a tape recording to play for us, to fire us up. He probably thought we were going to take that seriously, as though he were Knute Rockne giving his players a pep talk. He couldn't understand that we were sitting there at our lockers laughing at him. Damn, that was funny. Virdon didn't like to do it, but he was told to, so he did it, and so we were all laughing, and Virdon said, 'Okay, guys, you gotta listen to this.' It was George giving us one of his rah-rah speeches. No one could look anyone else in the face. We all turned toward our lockers to keep from breaking up laughing. We couldn't believe it. We had never heard anything like this! It was strange. Virdon stood there with his stone face, trying to keep from being disrespectful, while we all sat in our lockers howling with laughter."[3]

Bob Lemon: "I tell George what I think and then I do what he says."

Ted Dawson (interviewing Yankee manager Gene Michael): "Seeing as how none of us have ever worked for Genghis Khan, how does it feel to work for George Steinbrenner?"

Graig Nettles: "Some teams are under the gun; we're under the thumb. The sweetest words to George are 'Yes, boss.'"

Jack Buck (on Steinbrenner's new yacht): "It was a beautiful thing to behold, with all thirty-six oars working in unison."

George Steinbrenner: "You have to understand how I feel. There are five million Yankee fans just like me sitting in front of TV sets with beer and hollering the same thing. I want this team to win. I'm obsessed with winning, with discipline, with achieving. That's what this country's all about, that's what New York's all about—fighting for everything, a cab in the rain, a table in a restaurant at lunchtime—and that's what the Yankees are all about.

"I'm no angel, don't get me wrong, but the man with no dents in his armor, let him step forward. I try to do the best I can. And sometimes—as much as I don't want to—I have to inflict pain. But I also inflict some joy."

Sparky Lyle: "See, what George never understood is you can't run a baseball team like a business. You can't stand over a ball player like a pipefitter in a shipyard. It don't work that

way. You can jump all over a secretary, kick your account-
ant's ass or whatever because there's ten million secretaries
ready to take their place. But there's only one Dave Winfield
or Goose or Reggie.

"George acts like a real bastard to his help. That's why
they all end up quitting him. He goes through secretaries like
I go through beer. You do that to ballplayers, you ain't got a
team. Ya, sure he built a winner but now it's falling apart
again.

"Another thing about George—he didn't know diddly
about baseball. But he could second-guess better than anybody. One time there was a runner on third base with two
outs and I think it was Horace Clark who hit a slow roller to
second and Roy White who was at third actually crossed the
plate before they threw Clark out. So George started jumping up and down yelling, 'All right, all right we scored.'
Something like that. He thought if the guy crossed the plate
before the guy got thrown out, he scored. Two-year-old kids
ain't that dumb."

Graig Nettles: "It's a good thing Ruth isn't here. If he was,
George would have him bat seventh and say he's overweight.
There are two things Steinbrenner knows nothing about—
baseball and weight control."

THE RETURN OF BILLY MARTIN

George Steinbrenner built the Yankees into a winner
again. In 1974, under new manager Bill Virdon, the Yankees
had their best year in a decade, finishing in second, a scant
two games behind the powerful Orioles.

When the Yankees stumbled in the early going in 1975,
Steinbrenner fired Virdon and hired Billy Martin to take his
place. Martin, the old Yankee battler, the scrappy second
baseman who saved the '53 Series with his famous catch, who
slugged the Yankees to another Series victory in '54, the
original "Mr. October," immediately made the Yankees
winners again.

Billy Martin had been a success wherever he managed. At
Detroit, at Texas, and at Minnesota he had taken mediocre
teams and turned them into contenders overnight. When he

took over the Yankees he fired them with a fighting spirit they
had lacked for a decade.

Sparky Lyle: "This team could never have become what it
did without Billy Martin managing it. Billy had that fieriness.
He had that competitiveness that oozed all over him. Ralph
Houk couldn't stand how George kept interfering. Ralph got
to the point where he finally said, 'Screw it, I can't manage
like this.' It was just a matter of time before he quit. Billy,
though, fought and argued with George, which in a strange
way was good for the team because everybody saw how Billy
stuck up for himself, and they respected that. I think if Billy
hadn't come, the team would not have been capable of doing
things we now can do. Before he came we knew we were
good, but it was Billy who taught us how to come from
behind and win. It isn't an accident that no team can come
from way back and pull it out like we can, whether it's one
game or a whole season."[4]

Earl Weaver: "Martin's teams don't have any particular
style. That's why he's so good. The first thing you notice is
that no two of his teams are alike."

Billy Martin: "Managing takes a lot out of you. You can be
so high one day, and so down the next that you don't want to
eat. There's so much to explain, and it's hard to get things
across. I go over it twenty or thirty times, rehearsing it, so I'll
do it the right way when I talk to that player. You don't want
to hurt his feelings or his pride. You don't want to show him
up, so you wait until later and then tell him what went wrong.
Players are different now from when I came up. Back then,
nobody challenged authority or asked questions. Now they
all want to know why, and I like that. Every young player
wants to learn. 'Show me.' 'Teach me. . . .'

"With each club, you have to figure your personnel, and
you manage at that level. Each club you go to, you change
your style. When I managed at Detroit, there was a lot of
ability and some good older players, and I had to break up
cliques. In Minnesota, they had great talent, so it was more a
question of working finesse. Texas had a lot of young arms
and inexperience. When I went to the Yankees, I had to

throw the freeloaders out of the clubhouse and stop the country-club atmosphere."[5]

Besides Martin the winner, however, there was another side to Billy. Wherever he went, trouble followed. Martin had a temper he had never learned to control, a stubborn streak that blocked all negotiation, and he drank too much.

Jim Spencer: "I played for Billy in Texas and in New York. In Texas all he seemed to talk about were the glory days with the Yankees as a player. 'I'll be managing them someday,' he would say. A strange thing for the manager of the Texas Rangers to say. Then he came here, and all he was worried about was losing his job. He was hard to play for because he caused so much commotion on a team. Sometimes you almost lost track of the real job of hitting and catching the ball because of the turmoil."

Al Rosen: "There is no doubt that Billy is popular. The white lines are Billy's arena. Between them he becomes the king. Outside of those lines, he is out of character."

Elliott Maddox: "Everybody knows he is a liar. He just plain out lies. He lied to my face. He told me I would be a regular, not to worry. Bang, I was traded. When I said he was a liar, he got his pitchers to throw at me. I don't play baseball that way. I think you can play hard without playing dirty. I think he plays dirty. I think he is one of those men who simply lies so much that he doesn't know when he is lying and when he isn't."

Andy Messersmith: "Billy was not my type of guy. I felt Billy showed a lot of childlike tendencies. He pulled some stunts that didn't seem necessary to motivate the players. Billy's work habits weren't exactly professional and, of course, his antics are well known.

"His record speaks for itself. No one with that kind of success has been fired that often. That tells you something is going on. He'll go in there for a couple of years and something good will happen. Texas, Detroit, Oakland. But there's always a lot of negatives along with the W's and that

eventually ruins him. He got the A's going but he also took a
hell of a pitching staff and ruined them by the way he handled
them. If you're going to truly be a good manager the first
thing you've got to know is how to handle your pitching
staff."

Frank Lane: "He's the kind of guy you'd like to kill if he's
playing for the other team, but you'd like ten of him on your
side. The little bastard."

John Schulian: "A mouse studying to be a rat."

BACK ON TOP AGAIN

Gabe Paul had warned George Steinbrenner not to hire
Billy Martin because their two personalities would surely
clash. For a while, though, everything was fine between
owner and manager. The Yankees were winning again, and
Steinbrenner, happy with success, stayed out of Billy's hair.

Martin took over the Yankees for the last fifty-two games
of the 1975 campaign and the team surged to a respectable
third-place finish. Then, in 1976, in his first full year as
Yankee skipper, Martin led the club to its first pennant in
twelve years.

Graig Nettles: "Billy had set up an exciting running game
with Mickey Rivers, Roy White, and Randolph bunting,
hitting and running, and stealing bases, and Chris Chambliss,
Thurman, Oscar, and I were the big hitters. It was fun
baseball. We ran away with the division, and I had more fun
playing baseball than any time before or since, including '78.
We had a set lineup, everyone knew exactly what his role
was, Billy was clearly in charge, and everything clicked like it
was supposed to, and there were no roadblocks or distrac-
tions. The players did their jobs, the manager did his job, the
front office did its job, and everything went very smoothly.
When you're winning right from the start, that alleviates a lot
of potential problems. There didn't seem to be any problems
that year."[6]

Nettles led the league in homers with 32, the first Yankee

to capture the homer crown since Maris hit his 61 in '61. Roy White led the league in runs scored, first baseman Chris Chambliss posted 96 RBIs, and center fielder Mickey Rivers batted .302. The pitching staff won the team ERA title with a formidable crew of Catfish Hunter, Ed Figueroa, and Doc Ellis. Sparky Lyle, the league's premier reliever, recorded 23 saves.

The big man for the Yanks, however, was catcher Thurman Munson, who became the first Yankee since Elston Howard in 1963 to win the Most Valuable Player award. Munson batted .302, hit 17 home runs with 105 RBIs, and played flawlessly as the Yankee backstop.

Munson was not the typical slugging catcher who hit the long ball and not much else. He was a contact hitter, tough to strike out, who hit .300 five different times. He also hit .339 in three playoffs and .373 in three World Series, and he was the first catcher ever to drive in 100 or more runs in three straight seasons.

Munson's reputation as a human being was not as flattering, however. He disdained reporters and was curt while being interviewed. Since the press, especially the New York press, controls player images for better or worse, Thurman was never a popular Yankee.

Sparky Lyle: "Hey, Thurman was just a nice guy. Crazy, sure, but he was a good guy. The only thing is he decided the press was full of crap and the best thing to do was avoid them. That ain't too dumb. He was just a smart man who decided to protect his privacy. So the press got all over him in New York, and after that happens the fans get on you! Thurman didn't care. He figured that's the price he had to pay for his privacy. It all really started because Thurm grew a beard in defiance of George's 'dress code.' So the press made a big deal out of it and Thurm boycotted them."

Mark Belanger: "It's unbelievable to other players that Munson is thought of as silent and surly. I'd say that he is the most talkative player in baseball, and maybe the funniest, too. Munson always said, 'How's it going, kid?' to rookies, and 'How's the family?' to the veterans when we came to the plate. One day I got furious and said, 'Thurman, we all know what you're doing. You're trying to distract me and I'm hitting .190. Just leave me the hell alone. Just shut up when I'm up here or I'll hit you with the bat.'

"He got this terrible hurt expression and said, 'Jeez, Blade, I didn't know you felt that strongly. I swear I'll never say another word to you.'

"Next time at bat I step in and he says, 'How's the family, Blade?'"

The major leagues had divided into four divisions in 1969, and in 1976, for the first time in the franchise's history, the Yankees played in the Championship Series. In a best-three-out-of-five confrontation, the Yanks battled the Kansas City Royals, led by George Brett, for the American League pennant.

After splitting the first four games, the Yankees held a comfortable 6–3 lead going into the eighth inning of game number five when Brett stepped up with two outs and tied it up with a three-run homer into the right-field bleachers.

That set the stage for soft-spoken Chris Chambliss. Chambliss had improved steadily each year with the Yankees. In 1974, his first season in pinstripes, he hit a poor .243, but in 1975 he bounced back to .304. Chambliss's big year was 1976. He hit .293 with 17 homers and 96 RBIs, and his quiet confidence contributed solidly to the Yankee success. With the score knotted at 6–all in the last of the ninth of the championship game, it was appropriate, then, that Chambliss would be the one to smote the telling blow. He settled into the batter's box, pumped his stick a few times, and promptly lost the first pitch in the bottom of the ninth, to make the Yankees American League Champions for the first time since 1964.

Graig Nettles: "It was funny. We came into the dugout in the bottom of the ninth, and I told Carlos May, 'Get ready to pick up all the gloves off the dugout. When someone hits a home run this inning, all the fans are going to come streaming in.' No sooner did I say that than Chambliss hit the home run. Even before he crossed home plate, fans were flying onto the field."[7]

Billy Martin: "I wish Casey was here to see it. This was his pennant. Those guys who didn't think this team could do it, who picked against us, who said I'd never win one, where are they now? Now they can kiss my dago ass. I won it. The Yankees are back where they belong, on top."

The Yankees' joy was short-lived, however. In the World Series the powerful Cincinnati Reds clobbered the Yanks in four straight. Perhaps no one was going to stop Sparky Anderson's "Big Red Machine" of that year—Johnny Bench, Tony Perez, Joe Morgan, and Pete Rose—but the Yankees were exhausted going into the matchup and they were clearly overwhelmed.

23

Reggie! Reggie! Reggie!

Steinbrenner had his pennant, but what he was really after—what he had promised the fans of New York "within five years"—was a World Championship. In the winter of 1976 he opened his abundant bank account once more and got the last piece in the championship puzzle, the man who could lift the Yankees over that last hurdle, the man who performed in the big games, in the final days of the season, in the playoffs, and in the World Series like no other player of his generation. The man they called Mr. October because of his Series feats—Reginald Martinez Jackson. *Reggie.*

George Steinbrenner: "When I went out and got Reggie I didn't talk money, I talked tradition. I talked the Yankees. I wanted to convince Reggie this was the only place for him to play. I wanted to convince him of the possibilities of business expansion here for him. . . .

"I decided Reggie had to sign with us. I knew he would be in Chicago talking with other clubs. I called his agent, Gary Walker, and told him I wanted to see him one more time in Chicago. I wanted to be the first in and the last out.

"I sat in that lobby Thanksgiving morning, all alone, like

some little kid, waiting for my time to call. I kept thinking how I had promised my kids I would be home for Thanksgiving. This seemed more important."

Reggie Jackson: "For a day or so after the draft I didn't think I would play for the Yankees. But then Steinbrenner took it on his own to hunt me down. He's like me. He's a little crazy, and he's a hustler. It was like trying to hustle a girl in a bar. Some clubs offered several hundred thousand dollars more, possibly seven figures more, but the reason I'm a Yankee is that George Steinbrenner outhustled everybody else."

Jackson is without question the premier power hitter of his generation. He has hit over 540 career homers, putting him sixth on the all-time list, behind only Hank Aaron, Babe Ruth, Willie Mays, Harmon Killebrew, and Frank Robinson. But even more important than his hitting, Jackson is a winner. When Reggie played in Oakland (where he was MVP in 1973), the A's won three World Championships. When he played for the Yankees, they won four divisional titles, three pennants, and two World Championships. And when he moved to Anaheim, California, the Angels won their first divisional title ever. In all, he's played on eleven divisional winners on four different teams. Good teams just have a way of following Reggie around.

Eddie Lopat: "I first saw him at our camp in Arizona. I was working for Charlie Finley at the time over at Kansas City before he moved the A's to Oakland. Reggie was something back then. Right out of college. He took a few swings, and you fell in love with him. Only a handful can swing the bat like Reggie could. Maybe a guy comes along like that once every five or ten years. He also had that incredible speed. Geez, he could get to first in three-point-five. He had to be the fastest big man I ever saw. Still is. And that arm! He could really fire that ball."

Earl Weaver: "Reggie's not a difficult player to manage, 'cause he's what you call a hard player. He hustles, runs everything out, hates to embarrass himself. He'll take a guy out on the double play, or run into a wall, make a sliding catch. His whole career he's missed games because of 'hustle' injuries.

"Most important, he can reach a special level of concentration in the key situations that win games—just like Frank Robinson. And, kinda like Frank, when the score's 9–2 either way, his concentration lapses and he gives away at-bats or makes a meaningless error. That may hurt his batting average or his fielding average, but it don't hurt his team none.

"Reggie's a curious person, and he's a person who likes to be shown the respect he's earned. He'll ask you why you made a certain move that involved him, which is unusual, 'cause most players don't give a damn. You explain it. You teach him somethin' maybe he didn't know. He nods. He appreciates it."[1]

Charley Lau: "When everything is in place, in the proper sequence, he's awesome. In a season of 450 at-bats, maybe 1,200 swings, you can only count on maybe 20 perfect swings a year. When he does it, I get goose pimples."

There was never any doubt that Reggie could bang that ball, but there was another side to Reggie. Controversy swarmed around him wherever he went, like a kid running from a nest of hornets. Perhaps Reggie's biggest problem was that he didn't always realize that baseball was a team game. He played for Reggie Jackson, and what made it even worse, he didn't keep it a secret that he thought he was something special.

Reggie Jackson: "I think Reggie Jackson on your ball club is a part of a show of force. It's a show of power. I help to intimidate the opposition, just because I'm here. That's part of my role.

"You see this bat. This is the Dues Collector. This helps the Yankees intimidate every other team in baseball. That's what I do just by walking into this clubhouse.

"I've worked damn hard for everything I've made in this game. Nothing came easy, nothing. When I can't do it anymore, when I can't hit home runs and I can't put people in those seats, they'll get rid of me like a sack of flour. I've worked as hard as anybody who ever played this game. That's why I'll still be here at forty. I'll be another Pete Rose. I'll prove to them age doesn't mean a damn thing. What counts is how good you are, how you deliver the goods, not how many birthdays you have.

"I don't want to be a hero. I don't want to be a star. It just works out that way. Anything that has to do with Reggie Jackson becomes a big thing."

Eddie Lopat: "He was such a wonderful young kid, that's what I really liked about him. A gentleman. Soft-spoken, pleasant, very bright, very professional. Then Charlie Finley started to mess with him, push him, fight with him. It completely changed his personality. Reggie had to get hard, get defensive. All that bragging bullshit, I think it all started because of Finley. I think Reggie has become a great player, the best in the game when the chips are on the table. As a kid he was really likable, really soft and sweet. Now he has that hard shell, that arrogance, that heavy-handed way of doing things. Charlie did that to him. Charlie changed him. Sad. That's why when they moved the franchise to Oakland, I quit the A's. I told Charlie I didn't want to go to California. Hell, it wasn't that. I just didn't want to work for Charlie Finley anymore. The man could just take the heart out of you."[2]

Reggie Jackson: "I paid my dues. It took me seven years to get up to $100,000, and I was in four divisional championships and two World Series before I made it. One thing I learned from Charlie Finley is how to be a tough bargainer. Sure, there's a lot of feeling against me. Some club owners have said they wouldn't let me in their clubhouse. The feeling is in the air—not so much an anti-big-money thing as an anti-Reggie Jackson thing. Some of it is because I'm black and I'm articulate. The owners don't like ball players who talk a lot. Some other people don't like black people who talk a lot. That's distasteful, but it doesn't surprise me. I think most of the flak about too much money has been aimed at the black players."[3]

Reverend Jessie Jackson: "Because of his intelligence and his gifts, Reggie's domain is bigger than baseball. All the bad pitches to him do not come on the diamond. He is a fascinating man. He has a sense of history, which so many athletes don't have. I think that's why he gets up for the big games. He has a sense of moment. Greatness against the odds is the thing. Anyone can be famous. Just by jumping out of one of these buildings you can be famous. To be great is a dimension of the authentic."

Rick Monday: "Reggie Jackson is at least three different people. One of them I have always liked and admired and respected very much. The other two I can't stand. The trouble with being with Reggie is you never know which one of him you get.

"I go back to 1965 with Reggie but I guess I don't go far enough back to remember when he was shy."

Fred Stanley: "I was talking to Piniella or somebody one day about my folks back in Arizona wanting to buy a car. They were quoted a price of eleven thousand dollars, and they were debating getting it. That was steep money. Reggie overheard us. 'You wanna car for your folks?' I told him I did. He said he had a car dealership in Tempe and he could take care of it. He got them the same car for seven thousand dollars. I never forgot that favor. He never did either. He made sure eleven guys heard him ask me how my folks were doing with the car he arranged for them. I didn't resent it. That's Reggie. He has to be appreciated."[4]

Catfish Hunter: "The thing about Reggie is that you know he's going to produce. And if he doesn't, he's going to talk enough to make people think he's going to produce.

"The difference with the Yankees is guys paid attention to what he said. At Oakland nobody listened to him. We just watched him hit. Reggie's really a good guy; down deep he is. I really like him. I always did. He'd give you the shirt off his back. Of course, he'd call a press conference to announce it."

Paul Blair: "Lee May and Reggie were neck and neck in RBIs one year. So one day late in the season Reggie gets a base hit and ends up on second base and Lee comes up to the plate and he hit a shot. And Reggie don't score, see. He just kind of made a big turn at third and stops. So Lee came up to Reggie in the locker room after the game and says, 'If I end up with only 99 RBIs at the end of the year, it's your ass.' And he was serious as a heart attack. You get 100 RBIs your salary goes up by 100,000 bucks at contract time."

THE STRAW THAT STIRRED THE YANKS

Reggie's ego has always threatened to overshadow his accomplishments. When Reggie stormed into New York in 1977 and promptly proclaimed in a *Sport* magazine article by Robert Ward that he was "the straw that stirred the drink," the Yankee clubhouse erupted. The Yankees had won their division by 10½ games in '76, so they felt understandably cool toward someone who was calling himself their savior.

"You know this team, it all flows from me," Jackson was quoted as saying. "I've got to keep it all going. I'm the straw that stirs the drink. It all comes back to me. Maybe I should say me and Munson. But really he doesn't enter into it. He's being so damned insecure about the whole thing. I've overheard him talking about me.

"Munson's tough, too. He's a winner but there is just nobody who can do for a club what I can do. There is nobody who can put meat in the seats [fans in the stands] the way I can. That's just the way it is. Munson thinks he can be the straw that stirs the drink, but he can only stir it bad."

Munson, the team captain, blew up. Fran Healy, a reserve catcher and the team's peacemaker, tried to mollify the angry MVP. "Maybe he was quoted out of context," Healy said. "For three fucking pages?" Munson shot back.

Fred Stanley: "See, the thing that people forgot is that Thurman was the captain. He was Mr. Yankee. He also wanted attention; he wanted it as badly as Reggie wanted it. He just didn't know how to go about it.

"Thurman had this way of walking up and down the clubhouse when he wanted some press attention. If he didn't want it, he would hide. But when he walked, he knew one of those writers would be brave enough to stop him and ask him a question. He was waiting for them. But they never came to him [Thurman]. They all stopped at Reggie's locker, and he discussed the latest rise and fall in the stock market or something, and that just pissed Thurman off real bad.''

With Reggie on the team, things were now in place for a classic confrontation of egos. Reggie wanted to be top dog, Billy Martin didn't want anyone to tell him how to run his team, and Steinbrenner wanted to outshine both of them.

Reggie Jackson: "In Billy's eyes, I was always 'George's Boy.' That was his pet expression for Yankee free agents. George's boys. He was sitting around with some of the Yankees when it was announced I was going to sign with New York instead of Montreal, and Billy said, 'I'm going to show him who's boss round here. One of George's boys isn't going to come in and run the show.' I hadn't even met the man yet. This was January 1977.''[5]

Sparky Lyle: "See, in the first place Billy never wanted Reggie. He was trying to get George to go after Joe Rudi in the free-agent draft, because what we needed was a right-handed power hitter. Not another left-hander. We had a whole lineup of left-handed power hitters. But Rudi was just a regular guy and George knew he wouldn't pack the place like Reggie could—so he spends three million for Reggie and Billy didn't like it.''

With those three inflated egos grappling for attention and dominance of the Yankees, it didn't take long for the inevitable clash. On June 18, in Boston, a lazy fly ball hit by Jim Rice ignited the first explosion in what turned out to be five years of all-out war.

Paul Blair: "A routine fly ball went to right field and the right fielder we had out there kind of misplayed it. Not only into a single, he misplayed it into a double. And Billy went out to the mound to take Torrez out and he brought Sparky in. And as Sparky was coming from the bull pen, Billy calls back to the dugout to me and says, 'Go to right field.'

"Now really and truly I don't want to take Reggie out in the middle of the game because that's really going to show somebody up. It's on national TV on a Saturday afternoon. The whole world's watchin', so I was stalling around.

"When Billy cooled down I figured he'd forget about it. He started back out to the mound and he noticed I hadn't gone out there. So he went back to the dugout and said to me, 'I said go to right field.'

"So I picked up my glove and as soon as I came out of the dugout everybody in Fenway knows exactly why I'm going out there and *where* I'm going.

"So Reggie's laying over the bull pen fence talking and he hears the roar and he looks back and he sees me coming in and he points at himself like, 'You replacing me?' And I nod, 'Yes!'

"And he comes up to me and says, 'What the fuck are you doing here?' And I said, 'Billy's the manager. Go ask Billy.'

"Now what he said when he got to the dugout I can't repeat. But it wasn't anything nice and I can tell you Billy didn't like it.

"Good thing Elston Howard was there."

Billy Martin: "Reggie came back to the dugout, and he started making a scene. He was screaming at me, 'You showed me up. You showed me up. How could you do this to me on television?' Television, what kind of person was this who realized the game was on television? Screw television. He was yelling something about my being a racist, just ranting and raving, and he yelled at me, 'You're not a man.' I ignored him, though I was steaming inside, and then he said, 'Don't you dare ever show me up again, you motherfucker.' I won't take that from anybody, because he was talking about my mother, and no one says anything about my mother. I tried to get him. I went right after him, and Elston Howard tried to stop me, and I threw him out of the way, but I couldn't get past Yogi. Yogi has those iron hands, and he grabbed me by the crotch, and pulled me back. I swear if Yogi hadn't stopped me I would have beat the hell out of him. It's a good thing he grabbed me. It wouldn't have been any wrestling match, I guarantee you that. Reggie's big, but I wasn't afraid of him. He was lucky Yogi was there."[6]

* * *

George Steinbrenner watched this fiasco on TV in Tampa and decided on the spot to fire Martin "for embarrassing the Yankees." But Gabe Paul talked him out of it, then quit himself. Steinbrenner then flew to Cleveland and talked Paul out of retiring. Paul stayed on until the end of the season, when he decided for good that he'd had enough of the Steinbrenner circus.

The fighting and the controversy continued unabated throughout the season. The Yankees slipped out of first place in May, and on August 9 they were in third place, five games back and fading. Then Steinbrenner stepped in. He and Martin had argued all season long about Reggie's role on the Yankees. Steinbrenner wanted Jackson to bat fourth and Martin had had his slugger hitting as far back in the lineup as seventh. This time the owner insisted and Billy obeyed. Jackson batted cleanup, where he felt he belonged, and went on a rampage, driving in 50 runs in the last 49 games of the season and lifting the Yankees, who won 23 of the next 26 games, to the divisional title.

For the season Jackson batted .286, smacked 32 homers, and drove in 110 runs. Munson also had a great year, driving in 100 runs for the third year in a row—the first player in twenty years to accomplish that feat. Mickey Rivers, the quixotic, talented center fielder, hit .326, and Lou Piniella batted .330. Graig Nettles, the acrobatic third baseman, led the team in homers with 37.

On the mound Ron Guidry, in his first full season with the Yanks, won 16 games and finished fourth in the American League in ERA. Don Gullett, another of Steinbrenner's high-priced free agents, won 14 and had the best win-loss percentage in baseball. The real pitching strength for the Yanks in 1977 was in the bull pen, however. Sparky Lyle won the Cy Young Award that year. Lyle appeared in 72 games, winning 13, saving 26, and posting a stingy 2.17 ERA.

Sparky Lyle: "I never had any desire to be a starter. I always figured it was easier to pitch two innings than nine. Besides, you always give up the other guy's runs so it doesn't hurt you. You just walk up to the other guy after you ruined his ERA and say, 'Ah, shit, I'm sorry.'

"I loved relieving because you've got a chance to be in the

game every day. I don't think I could have ever been a starter mainly because I only had one pitch anyhow—my slider. Besides, all those days between starts would have drove me nuts.

"Being in the bull pen is great. When I was there we used to have hot pastrami sandwiches dropped down in the fifth. We figured, well, the short man don't have to worry before the seventh. Another thing that's great about relieving, when you go in the game, you're not too concerned about who you're gonna face because you're always gonna face the best guy that they have. So there's not a lot of thinking. You go power against power.

"When I was going in the game, the game was always on the line. It was so intense that I didn't have time to psyche out. I was so wired on the moment I forgot everything else. Everything! There was a lot of times, more often than not, that if a writer in the clubhouse asked me after the game, 'What about the pitch you threw to so and so?' I didn't even know I'd faced that guy. All I knew is I wanted to throw that ball. So I very seldom ever looked at a hitter. I never heard the fans or announcer. You've got to get in your own world out there. Sometimes I'd get on the mound, look around and call time and say, 'Hey, there's no resin bag out here.' And it was right there. I was so intense about what I wanted to do, I just never saw it."

The Yankees met the Royals for the second straight year in the playoffs, and for the second straight year the Championship Series for the American League flag went the full five games.

Reggie had been on a hitting tear for two months, but in that last game Martin benched Reggie again because Paul Splittorff, a tough left-hander, was starting for the Royals.

"Two players told me he didn't hit the ball off this guy," explained Martin. "It's not a decision I'm happy making but I have to do it. I probably wouldn't do it in the World Series but I just have to do it now."

Paul Blair: "I took Reggie's place in that game. Man, it's a good thing we beat 'em, too, 'cause otherwise Billy's gone. George would have fired him right there. He paid three

million for Reggie—that guy was gonna play, believe me. So
when Billy put me out there we all said, 'Man, that Billy's got
some guts!' He knew his tail was on the line.

"Anyway, we were trailing in that game right up until the
ninth inning. Then, I led off with a single and then Mickey
Rivers singled. That tied it. Then Randolph scored Mickey
on a fly ball for the go-ahead run. And Reggie came in there
as a pinch-hitter, got a hit and made it 5–3 and we beat them
for the second straight year."

The Yanks had done it to the Royals again. Two straight
years they had stolen the pennant in the last inning of the
final game. "We shouldn't have bothered to take our bats in
the ninth," said Royals first baseman John Mayberry. "All
everybody was thinking was, 'It happened again.' We were
dead."

REGGIE'S FINEST HOUR

The Yankees played the Dodgers in the World Series and it
turned out to be Reggie Jackson's finest hour.

Martin and Jackson continued to bicker throughout the
World Series. But in game six, with the Yankees leading
the Series three games to two, Jackson silenced Martin,
Steinbrenner, Munson, Nettles, and any other critic
who'd ever taken a potshot at Reggie. For Jackson put
on the greatest World Series hitting performance since
Ruth.

In game six, on three successive pitches, Jackson hit three
home runs against three different pitchers: the first, a two-
run shot, against Burt Hooton, the second another two-run
blow against Elias Sosa, and the third a solo job against
knuckleballer Charlie Hough. He had also hit one out in his
last appearance in game five, so that meant four homers on
four consecutive pitches.

In all, Jackson broke seven Series records, including 5
home runs in a Series, 25 total bases, and 10 runs scored. His
3 homers in one game tied Ruth's record established in 1926
and 1928 against the Cardinals. Reggie's feat powered the
Yankees to their first World Series victory since 1962 and
their twenty-first in all.

Reggie Jackson: "I never related to it as three in one game. I related to it as five in one Series. Four straight homers, five in a Series. Impossible to repeat.

"Before the second one [off Elias Sosa] I talked to Gene Michael and asked him what Elias Sosa threw. I knew I was going to hit the ball on the button after hearing from Gene, but I didn't know how quick it would come. That one iced the game, 7–3.

"I could see the mustard on it coming to the plate. It should have been by me, but I did all the mental and mechanical things correctly. I overwhelmed that baseball by the sheer force of my will.

"Before the last one I saw Charlie Hough warming up. A knuckleballer. Frank Robinson taught me how to hit that pitch in 1970 when he managed me in winter ball. I thought if I got a decent pitch I could hit another one out. Anyway, at that point I couldn't lose. All I had to do was show up at the plate. They were going to cheer me even if I struck out. So the last one was strictly dreamland. Nothing was going through my mind. Here it's a World Series game, it's going all over the country on TV, and all I'm thinking is, 'Hey, man, wow, that's three.'"

Graig Nettles: "It was probably the greatest single-game performance by a player I've ever seen. It was amazing. It was the sixth and final game, and it gave me chills when he hit that third one, which was hit even farther than the first two. It was into the back seats in center field, where only a couple other balls have been hit. There was electricity in the air, and you could just feel that it was going to be Reggie's day. It was magic. And it didn't matter in the slightest whether you liked him or detested him. You put away whatever you felt for the guy and just bathed in the magnitude of the achievement. He was my teammate, and I was pulling for him, and so was each and every guy in that Yankee dugout. We were overjoyed that he could have a day like that.

"I remember the cheers. After the third home run, I walked out to the on-deck circle as the crowd was cheering and cheering, and I took my helmet off and waved at everybody as though they were cheering me, and I enjoyed my little fantasy as the noise swirled over the whole stadium.

Then I kneeled down in the on-deck circle as Reggie continued to stand out there and wave, and I applauded too."[7]

Ed Sudol: "I'll never forget the final game. I was [the umpire] at second base, so I had a real good look at the pitches Reggie Jackson hit for those historic three home runs. Charlie Hough threw him a tremendous knuckleball; I don't know how Reggie even got his bat on it, let alone hit it about 420 feet. The other pitches were also tough ones—good corner pitches. Deep inside, I got into the excitement of the crowd. I marveled at those home runs; you have to admire the man's fantastic ability. After the final out I had to run as fast as he did to get off the field. I was bumped by several spectators pouring out on the field from the stands looking for a souvenir—a base, a piece of turf, anything. I can't describe the excitement. It was electrifying."[8]

Steve Garvey: "I must admit, when Reggie hit his third home run and I was sure nobody was looking, I applauded in my glove."

Tom Lasorda: "That is the greatest performance I have ever seen. That is the greatest performance that anyone will ever see."

24

The Comeback

THE GOOSE

Steinbrenner had received his World Championship, but he didn't rest. During the winter of 1977 he shopped on the free-agent market once more and again came away with the prize of the draft—Rich "Goose" Gossage, a relief pitcher with a 98 mph fastball. Gossage was paid $2.75 million to perform his magic, and he didn't disappoint.

Gossage is a big man with hulking shoulders and a ferocious stare, and he intimidates a batter just by showing up on the mound. He's the stopper, the guy who comes into a game in the eighth or ninth inning with a one-run lead and the bases loaded and extinguishes a hot rally like a cold rain.

Rudy May: "Look at Gossage. He's six feet four and most of it is fat. He pitches maybe an inning a week. And for that, they pay him a million dollars a year. And you know what? He's worth it."

Goose Gossage: "If my wife came out there, she'd say, 'This isn't the man I married.' It's a scary feeling, a violent feeling, and I'm not a violent person. There's not a soft spot in my heart for any hitter. I have this crazy delivery when I let everything go. I use my whole body. I'm all arms, legs, and butt. I always look like I'm overthrowing, because I throw the ball so hard, but I can be really within myself and be throwing ninety-five miles an hour. It's when I get crazy and try to throw a hundred that I get in trouble. When I'm backed into a corner, I love it. Facing a hitter is the greatest challenge in sports. It's like kicking a field goal with one second left or sinking a putt for $100,000. I wouldn't like to face myself."

Earl Weaver: "You feel guilty telling the batters to go out there and get a hit. They look at you funny, as if to say, 'You try it!'"

Andy Messersmith: "He used to make my arm hurt watching him. After seeing him hum that ball about ninety-seven, ninety-eight miles per hour, I'd start thinking, I gotta go get another job real quick here.

"Goose is a pretty good-size boy and he gets on you real quick. Plus, you look at him out there on the mound he's got that look on his face. You don't want him getting anywhere near you with that ball.

"As far as pure speed, I think Nolan Ryan might be a shade quicker. But, really, on any given day you'd have to get them right next to each other to make a choice.

"But as a hitter, I'd rather face Nolan even though Nolan has probably got slightly better stuff. But Gossage has got that *attitude*. Besides, Rich is the perfect relief pitcher. I wouldn't want Nolan coming in there with the bases drunk. It might take him a couple hours to find the plate. But Rich comes in and you're gonna see strikes, buddy. And they're gonna have heat on 'em.

"I really don't know if all the moves that Steinbrenner made really made all that big a difference for the Yanks. But I do know one thing. You get a guy like Gossage, hell, probably in that one move alone he bought himself a couple of championships.

"Goose was my best friend on the team. A fantastic human being. One of the best guys in the business. He's got a real sensitive side which you don't see as a fan. But he's one of the softest, sweetest men you'll ever meet. He's a level-headed guy too. He never let all that adulation get his head out of shape.

"He's from Colorado, a country boy. He knows what's up, let me tell you. He's in baseball to take care of the other side of the coin. Baseball's not his whole life. He's got a house up in Colorado he let me share one time. Just out there in the middle of nowhere in one of the greatest fishing spots in the history of the world. Ya, he knows what he's doing.

"I can't speak higher of anyone I met in baseball than Gossage."

Gossage notched fifteen saves and six wins for the Yanks in 1978, which should have made everyone happy. But the Yanks already had the premier relief man in the American League in Sparky Lyle, and he had just won the Cy Young Award to prove it. Lyle knew there was only room enough and work enough on the Yankees for one superstar reliever. But Steinbrenner wanted them both.

Lyle turned out to be right. He was gone by the following season. In Graig Nettles's immortal words, "Lyle went from Cy Young to *sayonara* in one year."

Sparky Lyle: "If I was George Steinbrenner and Goose Gossage came on the free-agent market, I woulda went for him myself. You're talking about a guy that has an eighty-two-mile-an-hour slider versus a guy that throws a ninety-seven-mile-an-hour fastball. I mean if you look at these two guys, which guy are you gonna take?

"My only thing was that I felt that George once he made up his mind that he was going to acquire Goose that he shoulda traded me. Let me make my own deal or whatever. I just ended up sittin' around all year.

"Goose and I were very close friends mainly because we had to be. The things that were said that year were crazy. Every time he pitched and I didn't, they came to me. Every game that I pitched and he didn't, they came to him. It was a tough year.

"Eventually Goose won out to the point where he took over that spot and then all of a sudden you were reading in the papers about that I was mad because I wasn't number one anymore. That didn't mean anything to me. All I wanted was the ball in my hands.

"I still felt George shoulda traded me as soon as he knew he wanted Goose Gossage. That would have been better for all concerned. When you are throwing in professional baseball that's the one thing you do have to understand. There is no crying when you get traded. They do things the way the IRS does.

"People would say, 'Oh, my God, you won the Cy Young Award. How could they do this to you?' Well, that wasn't the point. We're talking about a new year, a new season. We're trying to win the pennant again and that's the way it was.

"But he should have traded me."

Andy Messersmith: "One thing that Sparky never realized was that bringing in Gossage probably extended his career because there's no way they could have used him again like they did in '77. It would have killed him."

BILLY TALKS HIMSELF OUT OF A JOB

The Gossage-Lyle controversy was not the only big headline that year. The Yanks still had the George-Billy-Reggie soap opera, and it played all season long.

Reggie's heroics in the '77 Series and the great championship season did not stop the rivalry of egos and the battle for attention among Jackson, Martin, and Steinbrenner in 1978. Reggie was suspended. Billy was fired and then rehired. And the Yankees found themselves fourteen games behind the power-hitting Red Sox in mid-July.

The fireworks started in earnest in late June, when the decision was made to take the glove out of Reggie's hand. He would become the team's designated hitter, batting cleanup but sitting on the bench between innings, while Thurman Munson took his spot in right field. To Reggie this was a demotion and another slap in the face from Billy, who was once again trying to show Reggie up. Never mind that he had played his position atrociously for two seasons and that the decision was made by Steinbrenner. Reggie was tired of being made to look bad in front of the American public, and on July 17, in Kansas City, he retaliated.

Billy Martin: "I put the bunt sign on. They weren't looking for it, but Reggie fouled the ball back for a strike. The infielders moved in, so I gave Howser the sign to have Reggie swing away. Reggie looked at him, saw the sign, and when the pitch came in, he bunted anyway. Strike two. Howser called time and went down the line to tell Reggie that the bunt sign was off and that he was to hit away. Howser told him, 'You're not to bunt.' Reggie bunted anyway. He fouled the ball off for strike three, made an out. We didn't score that inning, and we ended up losing the game.

"I was so mad, it was unreal. I was sitting there on the bench saying to myself, 'Whatever you do, don't touch him, don't punch him, don't do it.' I was so hot I was talking to myself. He came back into the dugout, walked right toward me, and took his glasses off like he expected me to punch him. Maybe he even wanted me to punch him. I don't know. When he took his glasses off, I said to myself, 'I wish I wasn't the manager.' Because I wanted to haul off and punch him so badly I could taste it. I didn't make a move. Reggie sat down on the other end of the bench.

"After the game I went into the clubhouse, went into my office, and I took my clock radio and threw it against the wall. It broke into pieces. Yogi came in and tried to calm me down. 'Don't hit him. Don't do nothing to him. Don't do it,' Yogi kept saying. He said, 'I went through it, too. I went through it with Cleon Jones the same way. Don't do anything.' I told Yogi, 'I'm not going to touch him. I won't do anything,' and I got on the phone and called Al Rosen and told him that if he didn't fine and suspend Reggie, I was quitting. I said, 'He defied me, and there's no way he can get away with that. If he does, the game's crooked, and I don't want any part of it. Let him get away with that, and you might as well forget the ball club. Might as well make Reggie the manager.' "[1]

After the game Steinbrenner, Martin, and the new general manager, Al Rosen, talked by telephone and the decision was made to suspend Jackson for five days. A few minutes later Martin emerged from his office and made the following statement:

"As of this moment, Reggie Jackson is suspended without pay, effective immediately, for deliberately disregarding the manager's instructions during his time at bat in the tenth inning. There isn't going to be anybody who defies the manager or management in any way. Nobody's bigger than the team. If he comes back again, he does exactly what I say. Period. I don't get paid three million dollars. I don't disobey my boss's orders. He tells me to do something, I do it."

Reggie Jackson: (the day after his suspension): "I had not been playing regularly and I wasn't swinging the bat very well. I thought under the circumstances that bunting was the best thing I could do. Even after Howser spoke to me, I didn't realize exactly what the consequences would be. I didn't consider it an act of defiance, and I don't feel I did anything wrong. I would even do it again if I didn't know what the consequences would be. For that reason, it would have been better if I had struck out swinging and avoided the hassle.

"But the way I interpreted it, I don't think what I did was so wrong. I'm sorry I caused the guys on the club grief and uncomfort. I don't want to cause them any grief."

With Jackson gone, the Yankees won five straight games. But when Martin got word of Jackson's blasé remarks about his suspension, he exploded once again. This time he blew himself away. During a conversation at Chicago's O'Hare airport he told *New York Times* reporter Murray Chass:

"I'm saying shut up, Reggie Jackson. We don't need none of your stuff. We're winning without you. We don't need you coming in and making all these comments. If he doesn't shut his mouth, he won't play and I don't care what George says. He can replace me right now if he doesn't like it. We've got a smooth-running shop here, and I don't want him and his mouth coming along and breaking it up. If he wants to play ball, just shut up and play. I don't want to hear any more from him. It's like a guy getting out of jail and saying I'm innocent after he killed somebody. He and every one of the other players knew he defied me."

Then Billy went on, and that's when he fried himself:

"He's a born liar. The two of them deserve each other. One's a born liar, the other's convicted. That's on the record! Did you get all that?"

Billy's remark referred to Steinbrenner's conviction in a scheme whereby the principal owner of the Yankees tried to cover up his illegal campaign contributions to President Richard Nixon's ill-fated reelection.

A law was passed in 1972 severely limiting an individual's contributions to a presidential candidate. But Steinbrenner goes by his own rules. If he wanted to toss a bundle to Nixon, he'd find a way. George's scheme was simple sleight-of-hand. He made out eight so-called bonus checks to eight of his loyal employees at Amship, the ship-building firm he owned. The employees then wrote personal checks to the Nixon campaign. At the same time tricky George himself wrote out twenty-five different checks for $3,000 apiece to twenty-five different Nixon fund-raising committees. Simple enough if no one does any serious checking. With the Watergate scandal breaking just after George's little swindle, however, everything that had anything to do with Nixon was checked.

In August, 1974, just about the time Nixon resigned the presidency of the United States, Steinbrenner pleaded guilty to charges of illegal campaign contributions and an additional charge of trying to cover up his tracks with hush money for employees.

The maximum penalty for his little ruse was six years in jail and a heavy fine. But Steinbrenner got off with a $15,000 fine that he quickly, gratefully, paid.

When Steinbrenner heard Martin's ill-advised remarks about his conviction—a subject George is extremely sensitive about—Billy became a *former* Yankee manager. When reporters told him what Billy had said, George stammered, "I just don't know what to say. I've got to believe no boss in his right mind would take that."

Apparently Steinbrenner was in his right mind, because the next day in Kansas City Martin gave this tearful farewell:

"There will be no questions and answers with anyone after the statement is made. That means now and forever, because I am a Yankee, and Yankees do not talk or throw rocks.

"I don't want to hurt this team's chances for the pennant

with this undue publicity. The team has a shot at the pennant, and I hope they win it. I owe it to my health and my mental well-being to resign. At this time, I'm also sorry about those things that were written about George Steinbrenner. He does not deserve them, nor did I say them. I've had my differences with George, but we've been able to resolve them. I would like to thank the Yankee management, the press, the news media, my coaches, my players and, most of all, the fans."

By the end of his statement, Billy was in tears and had to be led away by friends. Bob Lemon, the old Cleveland Indian great who pitched his way to the Hall of Fame, was named to replace Martin. Said an ecstatic Reggie Jackson, "I felt like I'd won the lottery."

But Reggie's ecstasy was brief. Five days later, at the annual Old Timers' Game, Steinbrenner had a surprise. After the introduction of the players from past Yankee teams, announcer Bob Shepard took the mike. "The New York Yankees are happy to announce that Bob Lemon will assume the duties of general manager. . . . Managing the Yankees for the 1980 season, and hopefully for many seasons after, will be Number 1. . . ."

Before Shepard could scream "Billy Martin," 46,000 people rose and cheered their heads silly for seven full minutes. Martin ran onto the field, and every time he doffed his cap, the crowd erupted again. Billy the Kid, the local hero, was back again. Lemon would manage for the 1978 and 1979 seasons, and give way to Martin in 1980.

Reggie Jackson in the locker room sat stunned with the rest of the Yankee players. All except Sparky Lyle, that is.

Sparky Lyle: :"In the dugout the players looked at each other in amazement. The thought had never even crossed anyone's mind. Some guys just stood there shaking their heads. Other guys were staring out into space, saying, 'What do you think of that?' No one, and I mean no one, could believe it. Reggie walked around like he didn't know a thing about it. He was saying, 'What happened? What happened?' I don't believe him because you can't tell me Steinbrenner didn't tell Reggie before it was announced. As close as they're supposed to be, George isn't going to do that. The announcement was a surprise, but after all the crap that's gone on, it was anticlimactic. Everyone felt, 'Oh well, let's get the game started.'"[2]

Billy Martin: "When Bob Shepard announced it and I ran onto the field, there was so much noise I couldn't believe it was me they were cheering. I was very embarrassed standing out there, waving for what must have been ten minutes, but Mickey and Joe seemed so happy, and the fans were so great, that I lost my embarrassment. I was so elated, after being so down. Nothing like this had happened to me in my whole life. It was a tremendous salute to a .250 hitter who got fortunate, who got a chance to manage, and for the fans to show that they cared that much, it was something I'll never forget the rest of my life. Every time I think about it, it chokes me up. The New York fans are the greatest, simply the greatest."[3]

Mike Farber: "Billy Martin rose on the fifth day, the greatest return in almost two thousand years."

A LEMON OF A YEAR

Bob Lemon, an easygoing nice guy who never got too excited no matter what happened, took over the team on July 25. After three years of Martin's rantings, Lemon was a sweet change. Mickey Rivers strolled into the clubhouse two hours late one day, was fined, and that was that. No hollering, no grudges. Under his gentle hand the Yankees came alive and began the greatest comeback in baseball history.

It helped that Catfish Hunter's long-dead arm suddenly, almost miraculously, revived and he reeled off six straight wins. Ed Figueroa had his best season, winning twenty games, and Rivers and Bucky Dent recuperated from nagging injuries and played the best ball of their careers. But most of the credit had to go to Lemon for creating an atmosphere in which the Yankees thrived.

Reggie Jackson: "We never would have won it with Billy. Too much furor. We were too far behind to deal with furor.

"You can't imagine what that was like. You come to the park, and there are no reporters around your locker, waiting to get your reaction to the latest story in the papers. You can dress in peace. You can pick your game bat out, think of the opposing pitcher, clear your mind. You can breathe free. The art of hitting is combining physical skill with mental discipline, concentration, seeing that baseball in the pitcher's hand, studying it, watching it, flailing at it with your mind totally on that mission. I could breathe free again."

Bucky Dent: "My stomach stopped churning. I was under such enormous pressure playing for Billy, worried about mistakes, afraid to make a move, wanting the games to be over sometimes even before they began. Then Lemon came. All I had to do was play baseball as best I could. All of a sudden I could walk into that room and think only of the game.

"When Billy was here, the ego clash was so heavy it carried over to all of us. I hated that tension. I think everybody did. Reggie always played hard, but he knew everybody was looking at him. Now we look at him only when he does something significant in the game. He can have a bad night like anybody else, and it won't be a life-or-death matter. I think he created a lot of problems for himself, but I like the guy. He helps us win; he helps make money for me. He is a proud and confident man. I admire that in him."[4]

Lou Piniella: "It got so that I hated everything about playing for the Yankees except the games. I used to love baseball—everything, the game, the clubhouse, the fans, the fun, the talk, the friendships. Now that was all bitter to me. The squabbles, the back-and-forth back-biting disgusted me. I wished I could quit. I just wasn't rich enough. So I swallowed it."

Bob Lemon: "It's flattering that people give me all the credit for our turnaround. But the main reason we've won is that we haven't had as many injuries. I'm not Oral Roberts. I didn't touch them and make them all get well."

THE BOSTON MASSACRE

The Yankees won forty-eight of their last sixty-eight games under Lemon, quickly gaining on the fading Red Sox. By September 7, at the start of a four-game series with Boston at Fenway Park, they were only four games back. A sweep of the Sox would catapult them into a tie for first place.

But the Yankees did more than sweep. They humiliated the Red Sox, winning every game by embarrassingly lopsided scores—15–3, 13–2, 7–0, and 7–4. The Yanks outscored Boston 46–9 and outhit them 63–21. As if that weren't enough, Boston helped out the Yank's cause by donating 12 errors. It became known as the Boston Massacre.

But the Yankees' onslaught didn't stop there. The Yanks kept winning as the Sox folded. They went from being 6½ behind on September 2 to 3½ in front by September 16.

Rick Burleson: "The Yankees are together, nine guys giving their all. Us? We come to the ballpark and one guy's dizzy, another guy's hand hurts. That's bull. They've got one guy who comes out of the hospital to play. That's how much this series meant to them."

But then Boston made a comeback. They won twelve of their final fourteen, and the last eight in a row, to draw even with the Yanks on the last day of the season.

The playoff between the Yanks and Red Sox, the first in the American League since 1948, turned out to be even more exciting than the season it capped.

Ron Guidry, enjoying one of the greatest seasons any Yankee pitcher has ever had, started for the Yankees. A slight-built 160-pound left-hander, Guidry went 25–3 in 1978 for an .873 win-loss percentage, the highest in baseball history for a twenty-game winner. His ERA of 1.74 was the lowest for a left-hander in the majors since Carl Hubbell posted his 1.66 ERA in 1933. The fireballing Cajun won his first thirteen decisions without a defeat and had nine shutouts —the most for an American League left-hander since Babe Ruth in 1916! He easily won the Cy Young Award as the best pitcher in the American League in 1978.

Guidry, with only three days' rest, was not at his best that day, however. Pitching mostly on guts, he struggled into the seventh with a 4–2 lead, thanks to a three-run homer by unlikely hero Bucky Dent that barely cleared Fenway's "Green Monster."

Carlton Fisk: "After Dent hit it, I let out a sigh of relief. I thought, 'We got away with that mistake pitch.' I almost screamed at Mike [Torrez].

"Then I saw Yaz looking up and I said, 'Oh, God.'"

Reggie Jackson: "To this day, I remember how quiet Fenway Park got. Like a funeral home. Steinbrenner and a lot of his friends were seated in a box next to us, and I could hear them whooping and clapping as Bucky rounded the bases. That was all I could hear. They were the only ones moving in the whole park."[5]

Gossage relieved Guidry in the seventh and yielded a couple of runs in the eighth. But Reggie had hit a tremendous lead-off homer in the top of the inning, so the Yanks led 5–4 as the Sox came to bat in the ninth.

Rick Burleson walked with one out, and then Jerry Remy hit a line drive at Lou Piniella in right field that looked like a routine out. Except that Piniella lost the ball in the glaring Boston sun.

"I never saw it," said Piniella. "I just thought, 'Don't panic. Don't wave your damn arms and let the runner know you've lost it.'"

Feigning as if he had it all the way, Piniella stood his ground and the ball miraculously bounced a foot away from his glove. It was just going to be the Yankees' year.

"I never saw it until the ball hit about eight feet in front of me," he said. "It was just pure luck that I could get my glove on the ball and catch it before it went past me. If it had gone to the wall, those two scooters would still be running around the bases."

Fooled by Piniella's heady bluff, Burleson could only go as far as second. If he had been able to get to third, as he surely would have but for Piniella's bit of acting, then he would have scored on Jim Rice's long fly to Piniella on the next pitch. *That* would have tied the score.

Instead there were two men on and two out when the great Carl Yastrzemski walked to the plate. This was what the entire season had come down to. The best that the Yanks had against the best that Boston had. Yaz against the Goose.

Roy White: "I was just holding my breath. You wanted to close your eyes and not see him swing. The wind was blowing out and I could feel that Green Monster creeping in closer."

Graig Nettles: "All I could think of was Bobby Thompson and that '51 playoff. I figured if anybody was going to beat us, those were the guys.

"I was thinking, 'Pop him up.' Then Yaz did pop it up and I said, 'Jeez, but not to me.'

"They should have given both teams a standing ovation."

Carlton Fisk: "I was in the on-deck circle, just like I was when Yaz flew out to end the '75 Series. You know, they should have stopped the game right then and said, 'Okay, that's it. The season is over. You're both World Champions. We can't decide between you, and neither of you should have to lose.'

"I knew the season would be over as soon as Yastrzemski's pop-up came down. It seemed like the ball stayed up forever, like everything was cranked down into slow motion. I was trying to will the ball to stay up there and never come down . . . what a dumb thing to have run through your mind. Even the crowd roar sounded like a movie projector at the wrong speed when everything gets gravelly and warped.

"After the last out, I looked around and the crowd was stunned. Nobody moved. They looked at each other like, 'You mean it's over now? . . . It can't be over. . . .'

"It had only been going on for half a year, but it seemed like a crime for it to end."

Carl Yastrzemski: "No, it wasn't a good swing, but the guy made a hell of a pitch. The ball sailed in on me, and at the speed he throws, you know, there isn't much time for correction.

"I'll always think about that swing."

George Steinbrenner: "I have a tape cassette of the whole game in my office. I don't know how many times I've watched that game. It's annoyed me that our playoff game seems to have been overshadowed by us beating the Dodgers in the Series for the second year in a row. Don't people understand? Somebody wins the Series every year. There's only one game like that in a lifetime. I'd call it the greatest game in the history of American sports, because baseball is the best and oldest game, and that's sure as hell the best baseball game I ever saw."

The Yankees defeated the Royals in the 1978 Championship Series for the third straight year. It wasn't quite as dramatic as the past two years, however, as the Yanks won handily three games to one. Jackson hit .462 with 2 homers and 6 RBIs, and Munson hit the clincher in game four, a towering drive beyond the monuments in center field.

In the 1978 World Series the Dodgers came out in the first two games at Dodger Stadium and jumped all over the weary Yankees. Tired from a long pennant chase, the high-tension playoff with Boston, and the Kansas City Series, the Yankee pitching was battered and the Yankee hitting was punchless.

The Dodgers came out swinging in game three once again, but they made the mistake of hitting their shots at the best third baseman of his generation, Graig Nettles. Nettles put on what Tom Lasorda called "the greatest exhibition of fielding I've ever seen." And stopped the Dodger momentum cold with a 5–1 win.

Graig Nettles: "I feel I can play third as well as anybody. I've played it well for ten years. If I can do it for another ten years, I'll put myself in Brooksie's class.

"I am just gifted with these hands. You must be like a matador and accept the charge. It's one on one, you and the ball. You must psyche yourself up so that you want the ball hit to you. I expect every ball to be hit to me. When I do that I'm never surprised.

"It takes a little steam out of them when they hit the ball hard and they get nothing."

The Yankees swept the last four games and the Series. Reggie batted .391 with 2 homers and 8 RBIs, but it was little-known Bucky Dent who destroyed the Dodgers at the plate.

"In the Series, pitchers tend to overlook the little guys," said Fred Stanley. "They're thinking about Munson and Jackson hitting home runs. They don't want to walk the little guys with the big ones coming up, so they give them good pitches."

Dent, named the Series MVP, hit .417 with seven RBIs—four of them in the last two games—to seal it for the Yanks.

Another sentimental hero emerged in game six. The decider was pitched by Jim "Catfish" Hunter in the last days of his magnificent career.

George Steinbrenner: "Catfish was the cornerstone of the Yankees. He came to us and taught us how to win. He was a wonderful guy, and one of the all-time best competitors. Now he was coming down to the end of his career. He retired after the next season. I went to the training room where he was getting his arm rubbed down. I was thinking about this movie I once saw, called *Angels in the Outfield,* with Paul Douglas. A great old film about an old pitcher who gets a last chance and wins the big game. Great film. So I walked into the training room, and Catfish is there, and so is the trainer, Gene Monahan. I said, 'Cat, I want to tell you—you're gonna do it tonight. I know it. There's this film—' And I started telling him about it. He's got his arm back and Monahan has stopped rubbing and they're both staring at me like I'm crazy. I didn't care. I said, 'You're gonna do it.' And damn it, he beat the Dodgers and we won the championship."

Sparky Lyle: "When we got back to New York, the Dodgers really pissed us all off. In those first couple of games in L.A., the only games they won, Lopes was hitting home runs and circling the bases with his finger pointing in the air, as if to say, 'We're number one.' How bush is that? Our guys kept saying, 'We don't want to just beat them. We want to really kick their ass.' And we did. We swept the next four in a row, and people like Bucky and Doyle hit like they never hit before, and Graig made about seven of the greatest plays you ever saw, and Rivers and Roy and Thurman and Reggie hit the crap out of the ball. Then as soon as we started winning, they started crying. They were such crybabies. They have about zero class. They kept making excuses like 'If only the ball hadn't taken a bad hop.' 'If only Nettles hadn't made those great plays.' Sheeit. When Russell said, 'If you play in New York long enough, you're bound to be an asshole,' that was the last straw. Then he started bitching about how lousy our field was. He should talk about lousy. He was lousy. He couldn't have caught a ground ball with a shovel. Hell, their field was as different for us as ours was for them. You didn't see us complaining. And I'd like to see the Dodgers play that fucking Series without Garvey and Lopes like we did without Randolph and Chambliss. There would have been no contest. Except that whoever played in Garvey's place would have hit better than he did. I mean, hell, anybody can go 2 for 20, even me.

"The Dodgers weren't even the second-best team in baseball. There's no doubt whatsoever that Boston is a lot better team than they are, in every way."[6]

THE TRAGIC SEASON

Tragedy struck the Yankees in 1979. Bob Lemon's son died in an automobile crash, and the normally jovial Lemon seemed to lose his zest for managing. The team's spirits sank with him, and the Yankees struggled in the early going. Steinbrenner brought in Billy Martin once again to whip the team into shape, but it didn't work.

Then Goose Gossage got into a shower room brawl with Cliff Johnson. The two burly ball players went down hard on the slippery shower floor, and when the steam had cleared, Gossage, perhaps the most dominant relief pitcher of all time, was out for three months with a sprained thumb.

Then the team was dealt a death blow.

On August 2, 1979, team captain Thurman Munson was killed in a fiery plane crash. Munson's passing destroyed any chances the team had for a successful season. The Yankees, trying to win their fourth pennant in a row, finished fourth, 13½ games back. It was a sad time to be a Yankee.

Rick Dempsey: "After Thurman had gone, it was like baseball was finished in New York. Playing against the Yankees had lost its luster. Thurman was a battler. What every fan thinks is thrilling about the game, Thurman was part of, some way—a ninth-inning hit to win the ball game, a slide in to beat somebody up. Knock them over, knock the ball loose, block the plate, throw somebody out! Thurman was always in the middle of it."

Reggie Jackson: "From the time I heard on the radio that he was dead, the next several days were this numb sort of blur. For everyone. It was as if we were all in suspended animation, locked in time and being forced to be a part of a nightmare. We were playing Baltimore at home, and before the game George came down and spoke to us in the clubhouse. He talked about Thurman and all he'd meant to the Yankees, how it took a tragic event like this to make all of us realize what was important in life. I remember he was wearing a blue suit, and he was standing back in the corner of the clubhouse, near Thurman's locker. Finally he just broke down completely. So did Lou, off to George's left. So did Billy. . . .

"Thurman's mask was in his locker. His uniform. Everything. And no one wanted to look at any of it. . . .

"I can't remember a silence like it in my life, not before or since. We all moved around in a trance. Then we were on the field, and the game was starting. A message that George had written about Thurman appeared on the scoreboard. Then the people in the stadium began this ovation that went on and on, an eerie ovation that just would not stop. I was standing at my position in right field, and I just broke down.

"The message was about 'our captain' and how he would always be with us. The applause wouldn't stop. I couldn't stop crying. And the only thing that went through my mind was that at least I'd left him on good terms. No matter what had happened between us early on, despite all the misunderstandings, the last year had been good between us. Thurman hitting third, getting on base, doing something, me coming up after him and getting him home. . . .

"To this day, he has never been replaced on the Yankees. Had he lived, I believe we would have won two more World Series in New York, both in 1980 and in 1981. We would have gotten by Kansas City somehow in the '80 playoffs; no way could they have swept us if Thurman had been around. And we definitely would have won the '81 Series against the Dodgers. Rick Cerone came over in '80 from Toronto. He's a good kid and played like hell, but he wasn't Thurman as a catcher, as a hitter, or as a leader.

"Very few people have been."[7]

BACK ON TOP

The Yankees took the divisional title for the fourth time in five years in 1980. In the off-season Billy Martin had been fired once again (this time for slugging a marshmallow salesman), and Dick Howser was named the new Yankee manager. Howser, a former utility infielder for Kansas City, Cleveland, and the Yankees, had been a Yankee coach for the previous ten years.

Steinbrenner named Gene Michael as the new general manager, and along with Howser, he began to reshape the Yankees. They traded away Mickey Rivers, Chris Chambliss, Sparky Lyle, and Roy White. In return they received, among others, Rick Cerone, a good young catcher who would try gamely to fill Thurman Munson's unfillable shoes, and Ruppert Jones, a slick-fielding outfielder. They also signed free agents Bob Watson, a powerful slugger, and pitcher Rudy May to multiyear, multimillion-dollar contracts. In five short years Steinbrenner had spent more than $15 million on the open market, easily outsplurging any other owner.

With Billy gone once again, peace descended on the club and the Yankees won 103 games, best in the majors. The club also set a new attendance record of 2.6 million.

Reggie had his finest year, hitting over .300 for the first time ever while tagging 41 homers and driving in 111 runs. He finished second in the MVP balloting to George Brett, who flirted with the magical .400 mark all season before finishing at .390.

The Goose also had a big year on the mound in 1980, with 33 saves. Tommy John, another Steinbrenner free agent, paid off as well, going 22–9 with 6 shutouts.

For the fourth time in five years the Yankees met the Royals in the Championship Series. But this time it was the Royals' turn and they swept the Yankees in three straight.

"The Yankees are good," said Dennis Leonard of the Royals. "But they're not the same team we played in '78. They don't have Chambliss swinging the bat, they don't have Rivers slugging the ball, and they don't have Munson getting the clutch hit. They're just not the same."

BASEBALL STRIKES OUT

Major-league baseball suffered through the first prolonged strike in its history in 1981. The strike lasted seven weeks, from June 12 to August 14, knocking out one-third of the season. This necessitated a restructuring of the season, which was split into two "halves." The four teams that led their division on June 12 were declared winners of the first half. All the teams started over with a clean slate and played for the "second half" championship. The winners of the first half would play the winners of the second half.

Luckily for the Yankees, they had put on a nine-game winning streak to finish the first half in first place, two games ahead of Baltimore. In the second half the Yankees played like a team that knew they were already in the playoffs. They finished fifth with a poor 25–26 win-loss record.

Most statistics were rendered meaningless because of the truncated season. Guidry was high man on the club with 11 wins. Newcomer Dave Righetti went 8–4 with a 2.06 ERA and was named the league's Rookie of the Year. The Goose had 20 saves with an 0.77 ERA, and in postseason play he didn't allow a run while gaining 6 saves in 8 Yankee victories.

As for Steinbrenner, he was busy again in the free-agent draft, picking up the six-foot-six, 220-pound outfielder Dave Winfield for the 1981 season. George made his new star the richest man in baseball history, with a contract in excess of $20 million spread out over more than a decade.

Steinbrenner was also up to his old tricks with revolving managers. He fired Dick Howser as manager and brought in general manager Gene Michael, a man George had groomed and then hand-picked for the Yankee job to take Howser's place. He didn't last the season. In September Bob Lemon took over as Yankee skipper once again. "George has been awfully good to me," Lemon said at the time. "I'm still a company man. If he wanted me back as manager, that made me feel good. When he replaced me before, it may have been more for my own good. With the problems I had, some of the incentive was lost. It took me a while to realize that what he did was right."

In the first divisional playoff ever, the Yankees defeated the Milwaukee Brewers, the winners of the "second half," in five games. The Yanks took the first two games and it looked like a walk, but the Brewers came back to win games three and four. In game number five, however, with the Yanks trailing by two runs, Mr. October, Reggie Jackson, hit a two-run blast and the momentum had swung back to the Yankees. They won the game 5–3, and afterward the Goose put the credit where the credit was due.

"Reggie's the best. Years ago they said he was the straw that stirred the drink around here. He definitely is. When he stinks, we stink. When he's great, we're great."

"The sad part," said Bob Watson, "is that now George will come down here and take all the credit."

Then the Yanks took on the Oakland A's led by Billy Martin in the Championship Series. "I want to beat George in the worst way," said Martin. "I want to see George down. I was rooting my ass off for the Yankees to come back in that final game. I was happier than Reggie when I saw him hit that home run."

It was the ideal scenario for an explosive and dramatic series on and off the field. But the Yankees swept Oakland in three straight, and the A's and Billy went out with hardly a whimper.

The 1981 Series belonged to the Dodgers. They won the Series exactly as the Yanks had in '78, losing the first two games on the road, winning the next three at home, and finishing up with a lopsided win in their opponent's stadium.

The Yankees as a team played miserably in the Series. Dave Winfield, the $20 million left fielder, went 1 for 22, Rick Cerone batted .190, and George Frazier became the first pitcher in baseball history to lose three games in one Series.

But there were *some* Yankee "heroics." The night after the Yankees had lost game five to slip behind the Dodgers three games to two, George Steinbrenner allegedly got into a punch-out with two youthful Dodger fans in the elevator of the downtown Los Angeles hotel where the team was housed. Apparently the two had sullied the honor of the Yankees, New York, and the American way. And Sir George smote them with a single mighty blow apiece, knocking both of them cold. At least, that's the way George told it.

Edward Bennett Williams: "How could all this happen in a hotel lobby without anyone seeing it? I've heard of phantom punches, but never phantom victims. If the fight really took place the way George says it did, this is the first time a millionaire has ever hit someone and not been sued."

Graig Nettles: "And who should get all the headlines during that Series? George. He said he got in a fight in an elevator with a couple Dodger fans. The next morning we came down to leave L.A. to fly to New York, and there were a lot of cameras in the lobby. I was thinking, 'There's a lot of equipment here just to film us leaving L.A.' Then somebody said, 'Did you hear about George?' I said, 'What happened?' He said, 'He got into a fight last night in the elevator.' We got on our bus, and we saw all these cameras coming out of the hotel, and there was George walking along as they were filming him. His lip was all puffed up, and his hand was in a cast. It was hilarious to see. My wife and I were sitting on the next-to-last seat on the bus. George always sits in the front. When he got on the bus, everyone, including me, was laughing and giggling. I was down in my seat so that he wouldn't see me, and finally got back up, and George was sitting a seat in front of me. He looked at me and said, 'Where were you when I needed you?' I said, 'George, I was in bed. You told us all to get our sleep.' "[8]

Billy Martin: Upon hearing of Steinbrenner's brawl, Martin sent the Yankee owner the following telegram: "I understand exactly how you must have felt in that elevator. I only hope you don't have a good-behavior clause in your contract.

By the way, the marshmallow man I hit was saying bad things about New York and the Yankees. . . ."

After New York was soundly beaten in game six 9–2, Steinbrenner again took center stage. In a rage over his Yanks' subpar performance, George issued the following statement:

"I want to sincerely apologize to the people of New York and to the fans of the New York Yankees everywhere for the performance of the Yankee team in the World Series. I also want to assure you that we will be at work immediately to prepare for 1982.

"The fellows coming back will work harder than any Yankee team I've had. I'll tell them if they're not willing to give me that dedication they won't be back. It takes total dedication these days. For the money these guys are making, they should be totally dedicated."

Graig Nettles: "L.A. came back and beat us, and they beat us fair and square. And then George apologized to the fans of New York, which was degrading. They weren't expecting an apology. Our baseball fans are knowledgeable. They realize that there are twenty-six teams and that only two of them even get into the World Series and that only one of those two teams can win. There's no reason to apologize for being on the losing side. I could understand maybe if we had fallen down, hadn't given a good effort. But we gave a good effort, and they beat us. So why apologize?"[9]

Reggie Jackson: "I've got nothing to apologize for. You play hard, and you lose sometimes. I'm not apologizing to anyone. I've given my best since I've been here. Why not just be a pro and say the Dodgers beat us? Why make excuses? Be a man; stand up and say, 'Hey, I did my best but someone else was better. . . .'

"The Dodgers blew us out in game six—it was the one where Lem took Tommy John out for a pinch-hitter, prompting that famous scene of Tommy walking up and down in the dugout, disbelief all over his face—and we were done. I didn't do much of anything the last game. Winfield, who in George's dreams was going to replace me as Mr. October, finished up a one-for-twenty-two Series. The Dodgers, who'd lost the last four games to us in '78, finally had their revenge."[10]

Afterword:
The Yankee Future

The 1981 Series brought a lackluster end to another fabulous Yankee era. Since 1976 the Bombers had won five divisional titles, three pennants, and two World Championships. Steinbrenner continued to make bold, often ill-advised moves that somehow always seemed to work out. But then he shuffled the deck once too often. His luck ran thin when he started to gut the team of its best players. The first to go was the heart of the championship years, the straw that stirred the Yankees for five glorious seasons—Reggie Jackson.

As early as June of 1981, with Jackson wallowing in the worst slump of his career, Steinbrenner made it apparent that he felt the Jackson era was over. He began to disparage Reggie's talent to the press, to make remarks that perhaps Mr. October was washed up.

"There is no doubt in my mind that they are trying to plant seeds of doubt about my physical well-being," Jackson said at the time. "They want any team that might sign me next year to wonder about my condition. That's their game. I just don't want to play it anymore. They're trying to humiliate me, and I just don't care. Four, five years ago, I wouldn't have let them humiliate me this way. I would have told them to stuff [it], and let them suspend me. Now I just give in. I hate giving in, but I give in."

Jackson eventually overcame his temporary ennui and his

batting slump and led the Yanks to their third Series in five years. But at the Yankee victory party following their sweep of the A's for the 1981 American League crown, Graig Nettles and Reggie, who had never warmed to one another, got into a fistfight over some seating arrangements. Steinbrenner broke up the squabble, screaming, "We're disgracing the Yankees."

Then, still angry, Steinbrenner revealed his plans for Reggie. "I've had it up to here with him. He's got to be the boss of everything. He has to be the big shot and run everything. Well, he's not going to get away with it anymore. . . ."

That, in effect, was the end of Reggie as a Yankee. It was George's way of telling the world he was going to get rid of Jackson. When he sat out the first three games of the Series, Reggie might as well have packed his pinstripes. He was now a former Yankee.

Sure enough, by March, 1982, Reggie had signed a million-dollar-a-year pact with the California Angels. Jackson's potent bat brought California immediate success. They won their first divisional title ever with Reggie in right field banging out 101 RBIs and leading the league in homers with 39.

The following year, however, was the lowest point in Jackson's illustrious career. He hit only .194 with 14 homers and 49 RBIs. But Reggie hitched up his pants and came to spring training the next year in the best shape of his career. He ripped off 25 more homers and 81 RBIs in '84, and in '85 Jackson drove in 85 runs and smashed 27 home runs to bring his career total to 532, just 3 behind Jimmie Foxx and 4 behind the great Mickey Mantle. Jackson had no trouble topping those two giants of the game in 1986, passing both Foxx and Mantle by May 15 and putting him at number six on the all-time homer list, thus assuring his place in Cooperstown.

After Reggie headed West, Steinbrenner cleaned house, eventually trading away Graig Nettles, the best third baseman of his generation. Then he let the Goose get away. Nettles and Gossage eventually brought their new team, the San Diego Padres, to their first World Series ever.

Finally, George had crippled the Yankees. Gone was the

heart and soul of the championship teams. Gone was fleet but flaky Mickey Rivers. Gone was clutch-hitting Chris Chambliss. Gone were Jackson and Nettles and, of course, the Goose who laid the golden eggs on the opponent's scoreboard.

"George doesn't learn," said Sparky Lyle, "and before long he ain't gonna be winning either. Every year he gets rid of people who have helped him win the year before, and he gets somebody who's never been through a pennant race before, a guy who was never on a winner. And if he isn't careful, he's gonna have a whole club of these guys. He'll have gotten rid of all his winners, and he'll be left with a team of good ball players who have never been on winners. He'll have a hell of a second-place ball club. He'll end up having a club like Boston, a team that wins ninety-nine games but no bananas."[1]

After Steinbrenner's hasty renovation, the Yankees have suffered through mediocre seasons. Instead of waiting three or four more years, getting all he could out of his stars and bringing along his younger players slowly, Steinbrenner rushed ahead with typical impatience. The club finished fourth in 1982, third in 1983, and third in 1984. George continued to hire and fire managers at a breathtaking pace, bringing in Billy Martin in 1983 and 1985 for Martin's third and fourth tries as Yankee skipper. (In 1982 the Yankees actually had three different managers—Bob Lemon, Gene Michael, and Clyde King.) But nobody George shuffled in could spark the team.

There were bright spots in those lackluster seasons, of course. In 1982 Gossage had 29 saves, and Graig Nettles hit 18 homers, putting him first on the all-time-homer list for American League third basemen.

In 1983 big Dave Winfield had 116 RBIs and 32 homers, and newcomers Ken Griffey and Don Baylor both hit over .300. On the mound Gossage had 22 saves and 13 wins, and Ron Guidry had 21 wins and led the league with 21 complete games. And on July 4, 1983, Dave Righetti pitched a memorable no-hitter.

The Yankees were the best team in baseball after the All-Star break in 1984. But there was no catching the Detroit Tigers, who ripped off thirteen straight victories to start the season. Rookie Don Mattingly and Dave Winfield staged a thrilling race for the batting crown that year. At the All-Star break Winfield led Mattingly by 39 points, .371 to .332. Mattingly eventually won the title, however, finishing at .343, but on the last day of the season he actually trailed Winfield by .0157 points. Mattingly got four hits in that final game against Detroit to grab the hitting crown.

The 1985 season stirred the hopes of Yankee fans everywhere. The team got off to a lackadaisical start under manager Yogi Berra, and sixteen games into the season Steinbrenner sacked the popular Hall of Fame catcher and replaced him with Billy Martin. It was the thirteenth time Steinbrenner changed managers in eleven years as principal owner of the Yanks.

Despite the bitter reverberations after Yogi's firing, the Yankees rallied under Martin and were only eliminated on the next-to-last day of the season, after making several ferocious but inevitably futile runs at the tough Toronto Blue Jays, who refused to crack under the relentless Yankee pressure.

Despite the recent lack of success, the near-miss in '85 and a corps of superstars make the future look golden indeed for the Yankees. The New York offense is the most potent in baseball, and with the one-two-three punch of base-stealing king Ricky Henderson, MVP Don Mattingly, and slugger Dave Winfield, the Yanks are a good bet to keep that distinction.

In 1985 speed-burner Henderson broke Fritz Maisel's seventy-five-year-old Yankee record for stolen bases with 80 and also hit a healthy .314 and scored 146 runs. He also smashed 24 homers and drove in 72 runs, heavyweight totals for a lead-off man. Dave Winfield had another big year, driving in 114 runs, poking 26 homers, and batting .275. His 100-plus RBIs made Winfield the first Yankee to drive in 100 runs in four consecutive years since Yogi did it back in the early fifties. He also won another Gold Glove out in right field where no one in baseball is his equal.

But the big man for the Bombers is Don Mattingly. The 1985 American League MVP, Mattingly hit .324 with 35 homers and 145 RBIs. He also scored 107 runs and gathered 211 hits, including 48 doubles. Mattingly also had over 200 hits in 1984, which made him the first Yankee since Joe DiMaggio to get 200 hits in his first two full seasons in the majors.

"When I think about Mattingly, I think about those big trucks that travel the highways in New Jersey," said Reggie. "They're always loaded to the top with fruit or vegetables, so if a few fall off when the truck hits a bump nobody knows the difference. Mattingly is like that. He's got so much going for him that if he hit a bump and some of his talent fell off, he wouldn't miss it."

"When we were together in Nashville," adds Willie McGee, "I thought he was one of the best left-handed hitters I had ever seen. Even then he was something special. He put the ball in play all the time and he always hit it. I thought he would be the type of hitter who would hit .300 and drive in a lot of runs."

The Yankees, indeed, may be on the verge of another dynasty, and Steinbrenner has come up with a new man to lead the Yanks to the top. The Yank owner once again dumped Billy Martin after the '85 season, and the man he brought in to run the Yankees is a long-time personal favorite of Steinbrenner's—Lou Piniella. Piniella, who Sparky Lyle once called "the best slow outfielder in baseball," is an astute baseball man who gets along with everyone—the press, the fans, and the players. Most important of all, he gets along with George Steinbrenner. But Piniella is not just another Steinbrenner yes-man. He will fire back at George when he thinks the owner is wrong, and George seems willing to take it from Lou because he has always admired Piniella's fighting never-say-die attitude. Piniella's a winner, and Steinbrenner likes winners.

"Lou may be great as a manager," says former teammate Andy Messersmith. "He's a new type a guy. He's kind of a wild, fiery guy. That's what George seems to go for. He doesn't want that quiet Clyde King style. New York's not that kind of a town. Dick Howser, for instance, just wasn't George's cup of tea and Howser's a hell of a manager in my book."

"He's my kind of ball player," said Steinbrenner. "He's a consummate competitor. I know people who knew him as a high school athlete. He wasn't a good loser. I'm not looking for a good loser. He knows how to win. He has that desire, that intensity. I still picture the clutch play he made in the playoff game in Boston in '78. It was the greatest defensive play I've ever seen. I've watched it over and over. He didn't see the ball, but he reached out and grabbed it and made the throw. He saved the game."

But friendship will take Piniella only so far, and no one is more aware of that than Lou.

"This is a business arrangement," said Piniella. "If he hired me because of friendship alone, he made a mistake. I'm getting paid to manage this ball club; I'm getting paid to win. Other managers are fired for the same reason. I don't feel any differently and I'm sure he doesn't either. I'm going to be judged strictly on what the hell I do on the field and how the club performs for me, and that's the way it should be."

During a playing career that spanned nearly two decades, Piniella was known primarily as a clutch performer. The 1969 Rookie of the Year was a "professional hitter"—simply one of the best pure hitters the Yanks have ever had. Always a tough out, Piniella knew how to work a pitcher—pick out a good pitch and hit the ball to all fields. The book on him was he could get his bat on that ball, especially in a tight spot. In sixteen seasons Piniella notched a .291 lifetime average.

"Lou Piniella was one of the best pinch-hitters I ever saw," said Messersmith. "He had the ability to go up and do the job. He was a great hitter. Sweet Lou—that didn't describe his personality, though. It described his swing."

A volatile-tempered player, Piniella was never afraid to show his emotions on the field. His tantrums after striking out are legendary. He'd come into the dugout in a full burn and with bat in hand wipe out anything that got in his way—the bat rack, the water cooler, and one day a hundred-cup coffee maker that Mr. Coffee himself, Joe DiMaggio, had just brought in to the Yankee locker room. But Piniella is sure he's got his temper in check now.

"I think you're going to see a different side of me than what a lot of people have been accustomed to. What kept me in the major leagues was my dedication to the game and my temperament. It brought out the best in me. Hell, I can't lose that aspect. But I'm not going to be out on that field to show anybody up or make a fool of myself. There has to be a specific reason and there has to be a valid reason. I plan to be as level-headed as I possibly can. I've got that Spanish temperament, that blood, whatever it is, and I get a little excited. There's nothing wrong with that."

The hiring of Sweet Lou was met with enthusiasm by most Yankee fans. But one question stands uppermost in everyone's mind: Can Piniella, who has never managed any team at any level, handle the Yankee job?

"If you look at the managers who were able to pull it off without managing in the minors first," Steinbrenner said, "you find Lou Boudreau, who won it all with Cleveland in 1948; Gil Hodges, who did well; and Pete Rose last year. Lou is the same kind of player as Rose. The same kind of intense competitor. We'll have to see whether he's smart enough baseballwise. I don't know anyone who thinks about baseball more. We'll see if he's going to be the leader I think he can be."

"I remember very vividly when I first came to the major leagues with Kansas City," Piniella recalled. "I remember thinking to myself, I have to prove I belong and can stay in this fraternity of major league baseball players. Here I came to the winter meetings and I had a very funny feeling. I walked into the managers' luncheon and I saw all these talented people standing around, and I thought to myself, here I am again, at age forty-two, after being in the game twenty-four years, having to prove that I belong in this special fraternity of twenty-six. Here I go again—full cycle. But this is a different challenge, a greater challenge."

Piniella joined the Yankees as a player in 1973, the year after Steinbrenner took the reins of the club, and Lou has been there in one capacity or another ever since. But his days as manager could be brief if history is any indicator. The last Yankee manager to last two full seasons was Billy Martin in 1976–77. George Steinbrenner is the Dirty Harry of baseball. If the Yanks stumble in '86, Piniella is sure to make George's day.

"I didn't take this job with blinders on," said Piniella. "I'm the fourteenth manager here. It's funny—I'm the fourteenth manager and I wear 14 on my back. But I can't look at what has happened before. I've wanted an opportunity to manage in the major leagues; the opportunity presented itself and I'm thankful for it. Maybe I'm going to be the guy to break the mold and stay here for a number of years. I certainly hope so. I'm going to be prepared. I'm going to work hard at my job. I'm going to do the best I possibly can every day that I put that uniform on. If things don't work out, what the hell can I do? You can't play scared, you can't manage scared. I never played scared in my life. I've played with confidence, I've played with pride, I've played with dedication, and certainly when I manage, I'm not going to manage scared. I'm going to do the things I think will help this ball club win and the chips can fall where they may. What the hell else can you do?"

Footnotes

1 The Birth of the Yankees

1. John Mosedale, *The Greatest of All—The 1927 New York Yankees* (New York: The Dial Press, 1974), p. 69.
2. Lawrence S. Ritter, *The Glory of Their Times* (New York: Macmillan Publishing Co., 1966), p. 53.
3. Babe Ruth with Bob Considine, *The Babe Ruth Story* (New York: E. P. Dutton and Co., 1948), p. 220.
4. Donald Honig, *The Man in the Dugout* (Chicago: Follett Publishing Co., 1977), p. 222.
5. Ritter, *Glory*, p. 75.
6. Honig, *The Man in the Dugout*, p. 220.

2 The Two Colonels

1. Larry R. Gerlach, *The Men in Blue, Conversations with Umpires* (New York: Viking Press, 1980), p. 84.
2. Honig, *The Man in the Dugout*, p. 219.
3. Ibid., p. 169.

3 Babe

1. Ruth with Considine, *Babe Ruth Story*, p. 24.
2. Robert Creamer, *Babe Ruth: The Legend Comes to Life* (New York: Simon and Schuster, 1977), p. 43.

3. Claire Hodgson Ruth with Bill Slocum, *Babe and I* (Englewood Cliffs, N.J.: Prentice-Hall, 1959), p. 57.
4. Ruth with Considine, *Babe Ruth Story*, p. 24.
5. Ritter, *Glory*, p. 136.
6. Tom Meany, *The Yankee Story* (New York: E. P. Dutton and Co., 1960), p. 62.
7. Ritter, *Glory*, p. 138.

4 The Legend of Ruth

1. Honig, *The Man in the Dugout*, p. 223.
2. Ritter, *Glory*, p. 197.
3. Mel Allen and Ed Fitzgerald, *You Can't Beat the Hours* (New York: Harper and Row, 1964), p. 18.
4. Connie Mack, *My Sixty-six Years in the Big Leagues* (Philadelphia: John C. Winston and Co., 1950).
5. Anthony J. Connor, *Voices from Cooperstown* (New York: Collier Books, Macmillan Publishing Co., 1982), p. 239.
6. Ritter, *Glory*, p. 229.
7. Ruth with Bob Considine, *Babe Ruth Story*, p. 203.
8. Hodgson Ruth with Slocum, *Babe and I*, p. 102.
9. Ruth with Considine, *Babe Ruth Story*, p. 85.
10. Ritter, *Glory*, p. 82.
11. Creamer, *Babe Ruth*, p. 333.
12. Hodgson Ruth with Slocum, *Babe and I*, p. 115.
13. Ruth with Considine, *Babe Ruth Story*, p. 168.

5 The First Yankee Dynasty

1. Ruth with Considine, *Babe Ruth Story*, p. 101.
2. Ibid., p. 101.
3. Ibid., p. 103.
4. Ritter, *Glory*, p. 275.
5. Ibid., p. 232.
6. Ruth with Considine, *Babe Ruth Story*, p. 127.
7. Honig, *The Man in the Dugout*, p. 173.

6 The Iron Horse

1. Hodgson Ruth with Slocum, *Babe and I*, p. 157.
2. Joe DiMaggio, *Lucky to Be a Yankee* (New York: Grossett and Dunlap, 1947), p. 105.
3. Hodgson Ruth with Slocum, *Babe and I*, p. 156.
4. Eleanor Gehrig and Joseph Durso, *My Luke and I* (New York: Thomas Y. Crowell Co., 1976), p. 34.
5. Meany, *Yankee Story*, p. 84.
6. Honig, *The Man in the Dugout*, p. 177.
7. Gehrig and Durso, *My Luke*, p. 132.
8. Maury Allen, *Where Have You Gone, Joe DiMaggio?* (New York: E. P. Dutton and Co., 1975), p. 87.

7 Prelude to Greatness

1. Connor, *Voices from Cooperstown*, p. 179.
2. Ruth with Considine, *Babe Ruth Story*, p. 226.
3. Honig, *The October Heroes*, p. 97.
4. Ritter, *Glory*, p. 229.
5. Honig, *The October Heroes*, p. 83.
6. John P. Carmichael, *My Greatest Day in Baseball* (New York: A. S. Burnes and Co., 1945), p. 40.
7. Ritter, *Glory*, p. 236.
8. Carmichael, *My Greatest Day*, p. 140.

8 The Greatest of Them All

1. Ruth with Considine, *Babe Ruth Story*, p. 156.
2. Mosedale, *The Greatest*, p. 118.
3. Joe Reicher and Ben Olan, eds., *Baseball's Unforgettable Games* (New York: Ronald Press, 1960), p. 32.
4. Ruth with Considine, *Babe Ruth Story*, p. 157.
5. Honig, *The October Heroes*, p. 123.
6. Ruth with Considine, *Babe Ruth Story*, p. 164.

9 McCarthy

1. Allen, *Where Have You Gone, Joe DiMaggio?* p. 43.
2. Meany, *Yankee Story*, p. 101.

3. Donald Honig, *Baseball Between the Lines* (New York: Coward, McCann and Geoghegan, 1976), p. 29.
4. Ibid., p. 30.
5. Frank Graham, *The New York Yankees! An Informal History* (New York: G. P. Putnam's Sons, 1958), p. 171.
6. Gerlach, *Men in Blue*, p. 138.
7. Honig, *The Man in the Dugout*, p. 91.

10   The Called Shot

1. Honig, *Baseball Between the Lines*, p. 32.
2. Connor, *Voices from Cooperstown*, p. 245.
3. Ibid., p. 246.
4. Ibid., p. 165.
5. Honig, *The October Heroes*, p. 246.
6. Carmichael, *My Greatest Day*, p. 4.
7. Connor, *Voices from Cooperstown*, p. 196.
8. Ibid., p. 197.
9. Ibid., p. 197.
10. Ibid., p. 180.
11. Gerlach, *Men in Blue*, p. 20.

11   The Voyage of the Yankee Clipper

1. Allen, *Where Have You Gone, Joe DiMaggio?* p. 18.
2. Ibid., p. 40.
3. George De Gregorio, *Joe DiMaggio—An Informal Biography* (New York: Stein and Day, 1981), p. 249.
4. Ibid., p. 217.
5. Al Silverman, *Joe DiMaggio—The Golden Year 1941* (Englewood Cliffs, N.J.: Prentice-Hall, 1969), p. 103.
6. Silverman, *Joe DiMaggio*, p. 20.
7. Ibid., p. 113.
8. DiMaggio, *Lucky*, p. 63.
9. Allen, *Where Have You Gone, Joe DiMaggio?* p. 45.
10. Silverman, *Joe DiMaggio*, p. 66.
11. Allen, *Where Have You Gone, Joe DiMaggio?* p. 97.
12. Ibid., p. 60.
13. Silverman, *Joe DiMaggio*, p. 82.
14. Ibid., p. 82.

12 Four in a Row

1. Allen, *Where Have You Gone, Joe DiMaggio?* p. 49.
2. De Gregorio, *Joe DiMaggio*, p. 74.
3. Gehrig and Durso, *My Luke*, p. 4.
4. Honig, *The Man in the Dugout*, p. 87.
5. Honig, *Baseball Between the Lines*, p. 33.
6. Connor, *Voices from Cooperstown*, p. 85.

13 The Streak

1. Allen, *Where Have You Gone, Joe DiMaggio?* p. 108.
2. Silverman, *Joe DiMaggio*, p. 178.
3. Honig, *The Man in the Dugout*, p. 89.
4. Allen, *Where Have You Gone, Joe DiMaggio?* p. 106.
5. Honig, *Baseball Between the Lines*, p. 33.
6. Joseph L. Reichler, ed., *The World Series—A 75th Anniversary* (New York: Simon and Schuster, 1978), p. 184.

14 The War Years

1. Honig, *Baseball Between the Lines*, p. 161.
2. Silverman, *Joe DiMaggio*, p. 217.
3. Ibid.
4. Honig, *Baseball Between the Lines*, p. 164.
5. Ritter, *Glory*, p. 290.
6. Yogi Berra and Ed Fitzgerald, *Yogi* (New York: Doubleday and Co., 1961), p. 105.
7. Honig, *Baseball Between the Lines*, p. 41.
8. DiMaggio, *Lucky*, p. 139.

15 Casey

1. Casey Stengel, *Casey at the Bat* (New York: Random House, 1961), p. 1.
2. Ibid., p. 146.
3. Berra and Fitzgerald, *Yogi*, p. 205.
4. Joseph Durso, *Casey—The Life and Legend of Charles Dillon Stengel* (Englewood Cliffs, N.J.: Prentice-Hall, 1967), p. 120.

5. Honig, *Baseball Between the Lines,* p. 171.
6. Ibid., p. 44.

16   Yogi

1. Connor, *Voices from Cooperstown,* p. 70.
2. Gerlach, *Men in Blue,* p. 244.
3. Berra and Fitzgerald, *Yogi,* p. 110.
4. Allen, *You Could Look It Up* (New York: Times Books, 1979), p. 186.
5. Phil Pepe, *Wit and Wisdom of Yogi Berra* (New York: Hawthorne Books, 1974), p. 16.
6. Allen and Fitzgerald, *You Can't Beat the Hours,* p. 194.
7. Billy Martin and Peter Golenbock, *Number 1* (New York: Dell Publishing Co., 1980), p. 158.

17   The Mick

1. Honig, *The October Heroes,* p. 77.
2. Edward W. Ford, Mickey Mantle, and Joseph Durso, *Whitey and Mickey* (New York: Viking Press, 1977), p. 230.
3. Ibid., p. 69.
4. Mickey Mantle, *The Education of a Baseball Player* (New York: Simon and Schuster, 1967), p. 119.
5. Ford, Mantle, and Durso, *Whitey and Mickey,* p. 108.
6. Mantle, *Education,* p. 119.
7. Maury Allen, *Damn Yankee: The Billy Martin Story* (New York: Times Books, 1980), p. 100.
8. Martin and Golenbock, *Number 1,* p. 162.
9. Ford, Mantle, and Durso, *Whitey and Mickey,* p. 152.

18   Billy and Whitey

1. Allen, *Damn Yankee,* p. 56.
2. Ibid., p. 174.
3. Gerlach, *Men in Blue,* p. 242.
4. Ford, Mantle, and Durso, *Whitey and Mickey,* p. 169.
5. Connor, *Voices from Cooperstown,* p. 169.
6. Ford, Mantle, and Durso, *Whitey and Mickey,* p. 224.
7. Ibid., p. 150.

19 Five More Pennants for Casey

1. Gerlach, *Men in Blue*, p. 261.
2. Martin and Golenbock, *Number 1*, p. 201.
3. Allen, *Damn Yankee*, p. 175.
4. Allen, *You Could Look It Up*, p. 184.
5. Honig, *Baseball Between the Lines*, p. 152.
6. Connor, *Voices from Cooperstown*, p. 161.

20 The Great Race

1. Peter Golenbock, *Dynasty* (Englewood Cliffs, N.J.: Prentice-Hall Inc., 1975), p. 144.
2. Allen, *You Could Look It Up*, p. 173.

21 The Decline and Fall of the Yankees

1. Golenbock, *Dynasty*, p. 367.
2. Ford, Mantle, and Durso, *Whitey and Mickey*, p. 175.
3. Pepe, *Wit and Wisdom of Yogi Berra*, p. 100.
4. Golenbock, *Dynasty*, p. 377.
5. Ibid., p. 375.

22 Steinbrenner

1. Graig Nettles and Peter Golenbock, *Balls*, (New York: Pocket Books, 1984), p. 95.
2. Martin and Golenbock, *Number 1*, p. 121.
3. Nettles and Golenbock, *Balls*, p. 59.
4. Sparky Lyle and Peter Golenbock, *The Bronx Zoo* (New York: Crown Publishers, Inc., 1979), p. 177.
5. Roger Angell, *Late Innings* (New York: Ballantine Books, 1982), p. 243.
6. Nettles and Golenbock, *Balls*, p. 100.
7. Ibid., p. 101.

23 Reggie! Reggie! Reggie!

1. Thomas Boswell, *How Life Imitates the World Series* (New York: Doubleday and Co., 1982), p. 261.
2. Maury Allen, *Mr. October—Reggie Jackson Story* (New York: Times Books, 1981), p. 81.
3. Angell, *Late Innings*, p. 28.
4. Allen, *Mr. October*, p. 183.
5. Reggie Jackson with Mike Lupica, *Reggie* (New York: Villard Books, 1984), p. 167.
6. Martin and Golenbock, *Number 1*, p. 113.
7. Nettles and Golenbock, *Balls*, p. 144.
8. Gerlach, *Men in Blue*, p. 216.

24 The Comeback

1. Martin and Golenbock, *Number 1*, p. 234.
2. Lyle and Golenbock, *Bronx Zoo*, p. 183.
3. Martin and Golenbock, *Number 1*, p. 248.
4. Allen, *Mr. October*, p. 201.
5. Jackson with Lupica, *Reggie*, p. 242.
6. Lyle and Golenbock, *Bronx Zoo*, p. 248.
7. Jackson with Lupica, *Reggie*, p. 267.
8. Nettles and Golenbock, *Balls*, p. 240.
9. Ibid., p. 82.
10. Jackson with Lupica, *Reggie*, p. 307.

Afterword: The Yankee Future

1. Lyle and Golenbock, *Bronx Zoo*, p. 242.

Index